MW01235854

THE NETHERLANDS AND WORLD WAR I

HISTORY
OF WARFARE

General Editor

KELLY DEVRIES
Loyola College

Founding Editors

THERESA VANN
PAUL CHEVEDDEN

VOLUME 7

THE NETHERLANDS AND WORLD WAR I

Espionage, Diplomacy and Survival

BY

HUBERT P. VAN TUYLL VAN SEROOSKERKEN

BRILL

LEIDEN · BOSTON · KÖLN

2001

Brill Academic Publishers has done its best to establish rights to use of the materials printed herein. Should any other party feel that its rights have been infringed we would be glad to take up contact with them. This book is printed on acid-free paper.

This book is printed on acid-free paper.

Die Deutsche Bibliothek – CIP-Einheitsaufnahme

Tuyll van Serooskerken, Hubert P. van :
The Netherlands and World War I / by Hubert P. van Tuyll van
Serooskerken – Leiden ; Boston ; Köln : Brill, 2001
    (History of warfare ; Vol. 7)
    ISBN 90–04–12243–5

Library of Congress Cataloging-in-Publication Data

Library of Congress Cataloging-in-Publication Data is also available

ISSN 1385–7827
ISBN 90 04 12243 5

PRINTED IN THE NETHERLANDS

Dedicated to my father,
Prof. Dr. H.O.R. baron van Tuyll van Serooskerken

CONTENTS

LIST OF ILLUSTRATIONS AND PLATES

Illustrations:

Plates 1-12 (following the Introduction, between pages 14 and 15):

ACKNOWLEDGMENTS

Pages could be devoted to merely listing all those who have contributed to this work. The unfailing courtesy and professionalism of archivists and academics in the Netherlands must not go unmentioned. I particularly wish to thank S. Plantinga and the staff of the *Algemeen Rijksarchief;* Dr. L. Kamphuis and the staff at the *Sectie Militaire Geschiedenis;* Dr. D. Engelen of the *Binnenlandse Veiligheidsdienst;* and Dr. Wim Klinkert at the *Koninklijke Militaire Academie.* I also wish to thank Prof. Dr. J.Th.M. Bank of the University of Leiden for his valuable advice. Dr. Karel Berkhoff and – especially – Drs. Marcella Mulder at Brill Academic Publishers guided this project to its completion, and I am grateful for all their work. Augusta State University gave me time and resources for the project, and I particularly wish to thank my department chair, Dr. K. Wayne Mixon, for his unstinting support. My father, Dr. H.O.R. van Tuyll van Serooskerken, edited the project and provided many insights from his encyclopedic knowledge of Dutch history. The project could not have been completed without the patience and support of my wife, Debra, and daughter, Laura.

PROLOGUE

July 25, 1914. Young Pieter Forbes Wels of The Hague was feeling pretty good. Only days before he had heard that he had passed his *H.B.S. eindexamens,* the high school exit exams – a major rite of passage in Holland. Telegraphed congratulations had poured in from relatives and friends throughout the Netherlands. Now he could make plans to go to the southern town of Breda and attend the army's *Koninklijke Militaire Academie,* Holland's West Point, and one of the world's oldest military schools. Pieter would be following in the footsteps of his father, a career officer and major currently attached to the General Staff office in The Hague, the Netherlands' seat of government. Perhaps like many rising cadets, he dreamed of reaching the top ranks, as indeed he would (he retired as full colonel of the general staff). In the meantime, Pieter could look forward to enjoying a few more weeks of summer before he went off to the endless drills, rules, and lessons of the military school.

It was certainly a good time for daydreaming; July had been unusually warm, always a welcome thing in the Dutch royal city, nestled as it is against the North Sea. We will never know exactly what Pieter was doing or thinking on that summer evening. Whatever it was, at around 5 p.m. he was interrupted by the ring of the doorbell. Coming to the front door, he saw that it was a messenger of the national telegraph service. This did not overly surprise him, as he was expecting more congratulatory telegrams from his relatives. After the messenger left, he tore open the telegram and found himself staring at a pair of words that made no sense to him:

API API

Puzzled, he went in search of his father. Major M.D.A. Forbes Wels needed only a moment to take in the telegram's contents and the location of the sender – Cologne, Germany – before dashing out the door and making for the General Staff office. He knew exactly what the telegram meant: War was coming, and his country and army had at most a few days to get ready.

DRAMATIS PERSONAE

Only frequently mentioned individuals included. All Dutch except where specified. Only posts relevant to narrative are listed.

Aalst, C.J.K. van (1866-1939): Chair of the Controlling Commission of the Netherlands Oversea Trust Company.

Alting von Geusau, Jhr. G.A.A. (1864-1937): Minister of War, 1918-1920.

Barnardiston, N.W. (1858-1919): British military attaché in Brussels, 1902-1906.

Bethmann Hollweg, Theobald von (1856-1921): Chancellor of Germany, 1909-17. Because the head of the Foreign Office was only a State Secretary, not a Minister, the Chancellor technically controlled foreign affairs as well.

Bosboom, Nicolaas (1855-1937): Minister of War, 1913-17.

Colijn, Hendrikus (1869-1944): Minister of War 1911-13 , director of Batavian Petroleum Company 1914-20, Minister President in the postwar era.

Cort van der Linden, P.W.A. (1846-1935): Chair of the Council of Ministers (effectively Minister President), 1913-18.

Crowe, Sir Eyre A. (1864-1925): Assistant Undersecretary at the British Foreign Office, 1912-20.

Dufour, Raimond (1862-1934): Acting chief of staff under C.J. Snijders, Major-General 1917, Lieutenant General 1920, retired 1920, postwar coauthor with C.J. Snijders.

Falkenhayn, Erich von (1861-1922): Chief of Staff of the German Army, 1914-16, commander in Rumania and the Caucasus, 1916-18.

Forbes Wels, M.D.A. (1865-1930): Army officer, became chief of the general staff in 1922; contact for J. J. le Roy (see below) in The Hague.

Forbes Wels, Pieter: Son of M.D.A. Forbes Wels, recipient of coded telegram from J.J. le Roy (see below).

Gevers, W.A.F. baron (1856-1927): Envoy at Berlin, 1906-27.

Heldring, Ernst (1871-1954): Director of the Royal Dutch Steamship Company 1899-1937, member of Commission on foreign trade, member Council for Assistance with Economic Affairs, temporary member of Dutch delegation in Paris during peace conference.

Hertling, G. count von (1843-1919): German Chancellor, 1917-18.

Jagow, Gottlieb von (1863-1935): German Secretary of State for Foreign Affairs, 1912-16.

Johnstone, Sir Alan (1858-1932): British Envoy to The Hague, 1910-17.

Jonge, Jhr. B.C. de (1875-1958): Minister of War, 1917-18, Governor-General of the Indies, 1931-36.

Karnebeek, Jhr. Dr. Herman Adriaan van (1874-1942): Minister of Foreign Affairs, 1918-27.

Kriege, Dr. Johannes D.J. (1858-1937): Director of the Legal Division of the German Foreign office, 1911-18. Kriege had also been a delegate to the second Hague Peace Conference.

Kühlmann, Richard von (1873-1948): German Legation secretary at Tangier 1904-1905, The Hague 1907, Envoy at The Hague 1915-16, State Secretary for Foreign Affairs 1917-18.

Kuyper, Dr. Abraham (1837-1920): Minister President, 1901-1905, leader and founder of the Anti-Revolutionary Party.

Lancken-Wakenitz, Freiherr O. von der (b. 1867): German envoy at the occupation government in Belgium, 1914-18.

Loudon, Jhr. John (1866-1955): Minister of Foreign Affairs, 1913-1918; envoy to France, 1919-40.

Ludendorff, Erich (1865-1937): German Army Quartermaster General and its effective commander after 1916.

Marees van Swinderen, Jhr. Renneke de (1860-1955): Envoy to London, 1913-37.

Müller, Felix von: Envoy to The Hague, 1908-15.

Oppenheimer, Sir Francis (1870-1961): British commercial attaché at The Hague, 1912-18.

Renner, M.: German military attaché at The Hague.

Repington, Charles à Court (1858-1925): British military attaché at The Hague and military analyst.

Rosen, Dr. Friedrich (1856-1935): German envoy to The Hague 1916-20.

Roy, J.J. le (1868-1949): Director of the German-Telegraph Company (1905-19), formerly officer in the Royal Dutch Indies Army (1884-1904), also unofficial spy for the General Staff.

Ruys de Beerenbrouck, Jhr. Ch.J.M. (1873-1936): Minister President, 1918-25.

Schlieffen, Alfred Count von (1833-1913): Chief of Staff of the German Army, 1891-1906.

Schweinitz, Major von: German military attaché to The Hague.

Snijders, C.J. (1852-1939): Supreme Commander of land and sea forces, 1914-18.

Snijders, W.G.F.: Lieutenant General (retired 1905) and brother of C.J. Snijders.

Stuers, A.L.E. ridder de (1841-1919): Envoy to Paris, 1885-1919.

Terwisga, W.H. van (1861-1948): Commander of the field army 1915-18.

Townley, Sir Walter (1863-1945): British envoy to The Hague, 1917-19.

Treub, M.W.F. (1858-1931): Minister of Agriculture, Industry and Trade, 1913-14, Minister of Finance 1914-1916, 19-1918.

Troelstra, P.J. (1860-1930): Leader of the Social Democratic Labor Party

(SDAP) since 1894.

Tschirschky und Bögendorff, Heinrich von (1858-1916): German Ambassador to Vienna, 1907-16.

Vollenhoven, Joost van (1866-1923): Director of the Netherlands Oversee Trust Company, Director of the Dutch Bank, leader of the delegation to America in 1917, leader of a mission for reconstruction to Paris in 1919.

Vollenhoven, Dr. Maurits Willem Raedinck van (1882-1976): Legation counsel in Brussels (and senior diplomat present) 1914-19, Minister-resident at Brussels 1917-19.

Wilhelm II (1859-1941): German Emperor and King of Prussia, 1888-1918.

Wilhelmina, Queen (1880-1962): Queen of the Netherlands 1898-1948.

Wilson, Woodrow W. (1856-1924): President of the United States, 1913-21.

Zimmermann, Alfred (1864-1925): German Under-Secretary of State for Foreign Affairs 1911-16, Secretary 1916-17.

CHAPTER ONE

INTRODUCTION

A maelstrom of destruction swept through Europe in 1914-1918, a cataclysmic conflict that would change the world in countless ways. Neither large nor small nations were spared, though Spain and a handful of small countries managed to escape direct participation in the war. On the list of these fortunate few, the Netherlands' presence is the most perplexing and difficult to understand. The other neutrals were either on the geographic periphery of the conflict (such as the three Scandinavian kingdoms), or had little to offer the belligerents. Neither of these statements is true of the Netherlands. It was located at the strategic junction of western Europe's three great powers, Germany, France, and Britain, and for four years sat perched uncomfortably on the edge of the war zone. While Holland's neutrality was some protection against invasion, its independence was not guaranteed by any foreign power, its army could not hope to defeat a determined invasion, and its economy was far too oriented toward external trade to pursue an isolationist policy. In other words, the Netherlands had to maintain strict neutrality but, at the same time, remain engaged with the various belligerents, each of which felt that the Netherlands was acting to the advantage of its enemies.

The country's geography was a mixed blessing. In wartime, the army could retreat into the *Vesting Holland,* a fortified region that contained much of the country's population and could be protected by deliberate flooding. Militarily, the most sensible thing would have been to place the army in this strong position, and simply ignore the outlying areas. This was impossible, however. Neutrality required challenging each and every violation. If a foreign army entered even a remote corner of the Netherlands unchallenged, its enemies would undoubtedly invade also – not out of any hostility toward Holland, but to protect themselves. This meant that the Dutch army would have to be posted within striking distance of all likely points of violation. In addition, there were two peculiarities of Dutch geography that complicated the situation and are the keys to understanding the Netherlands' situation. First, the Dutch province of Limburg dangled between northern Belgium and Germany, right on one of the most likely invasion routes.

Second, the Schelde[i] river, which connected the Belgian port of Antwerp to the sea, ran through Dutch territory. A British relief force headed for Antwerp would have to be challenged if it tried to come via the river. These were not hypothetical problems; Germany did contemplate crossing Limburg, and Britain did consider forcing the Schelde. An additional geographic problem was that the Netherlands possessed a relatively huge colonial empire (modern Indonesia) whose continued existence depended in part on British and Japanese good will. Therefore, despite certain defensive advantages, the Netherlands was extremely vulnerable during the war, for a whole series of reasons – economic, military, and geographic.

How the Netherlands avoided the Great War has not received the attention it deserves. The subject is of interest not only to those few who care about Dutch history, or even the larger community of students of World War I. It is also a useful topic to study for anyone concerned with the whole issue of war avoidance, particularly by small powers. There is a vast literature on the subject of small states, and the Netherlands is occasionally considered.[1] Unfortunately, most works that refer to Holland's neutrality dismiss it as a result of the opinions of the great power governments, leaving the Dutch as purely passive actors on the world stage. This view, which will not survive this book, is understandable. Just as most history is made by great powers, so most history is written by scholars resident in great powers. Popular writers argue that the Netherlands was left alone because of their country's good will, even though the Netherlands was not particularly deserving of its neutrality. Such works contain no evidence of a visit to the Dutch archives, or of having consulted the massive and thorough series of published Dutch diplomatic documents. Scholarly treatments, as will be seen later, do better, but there has been no major work on the question of whether the Netherlands contributed to its own fate during the First World War.

It is my contention that it did. The Netherlands was not a passive observer of the European scene. In stages, it strengthened its military and made clear that any passage through the country would be contested. It spied on its huge German neighbor and discovered that it was included in the designs of Count Alfred von Schlieffen. During the

---

[i] The Dutch/German spelling is used throughout: In English it is called the "Scheldt," in French it is "l'Escaut."

war, it maintained a relatively large army and negotiated its way between the contradictory and often overlapping demands of the British and the Germans. Counter-espionage was used to keep track of the highly active British and German spy rings. The government engaged in unprecedented intrusions into the national economy. None of this came easily because the expenses were huge in a weakened economy; the army had to be maintained despite the almost universal contempt for military service, and the concessions that had to be made to the great powers were humiliating for a country that has never been accused of a weak sense of self-importance. Because the alternative (war) was much worse, the situation was tolerated, but only just. Tension, deprivation, and boredom among the soldiers combined to cause an attempted revolution just as the war was winding down. Finally, a major threat emerged at war's end when Belgium attempted to seize parts of the southern Netherlands. That threat was also turned back, but – again – not simply because of great power good will. The Dutch pursued an intense diplomacy to protect their sovereignty, and they succeeded (admittedly with some unintentional assistance from the Belgians).

The policies that led to this success were not developed easily. Virtually all Dutch policymakers agreed that the country should remain neutral, but some subtle disagreements existed about what neutrality really meant. These disagreements became critical in the last phase of the war (1917-1918). There were basically two schools of thought. First, there were the "idealistic" or "academic" neutralists, who believed that neutrality was best protected through strict, mechanical adherence to international law. Then there were the "pragmatic" neutralists, who believed that it was necessary to compromise with the demands of the belligerents, especially regarding economic matters.[2] In general, the wartime cabinet leaned toward academic neutrality, perhaps because of a certain tendency in Dutch thinking about foreign affairs to overestimate the importance of international law.[3]

Neutrality was also a habit.

While Holland's traditional neutrality did not develop overnight, it had a long history. The country's position was strategically complex. While small, it controlled the mouths of three of Europe's most significant rivers; the Rhine, the Meuse, and the Schelde. The treaty of Münster (1648), which recognized Holland's independence from Spain, gave the Dutch the opportunity to strangle one of their greatest competitors – and a low country competitor, at that. In the sixteenth century, four fifths of the Netherlands' exports had gone through Antwerp. Spain had to agree to the closing of the Schelde and giving the Dutch sovereignty over both sides of the river, thereby placing Antwerp's future in Dutch hands. In essence, the Dutch traded territory for commercial advantage.[4] Antwerp's trade was deliberately ruined.[5]

Holland's great trading wealth made it a great maritime power, but as great nation-states developed it ceased to be an important naval and military power. The Netherlands' role as a major player in international affairs was over with the end of the War of the Spanish Succession in 1713-1714.[6] All of Holland's major neighbors in the 18th century (France, Britain, Prussia, and Austria) were militarily stronger, and all were observed with some suspicion and even fear.[ii] Neutrality seemed the only option, and it was chosen in the Seven Years' War (1756-1763). Parallels have been drawn between the neutrality declarations of 1756 and 1914.[7] When the Congress of Vienna placed the southern Netherlands (Belgium) under Dutch control in 1815, the Netherlands momentarily looked to become a medium power, which might have led to the abandonment of neutrality; but this *mesalliance* was dissolved by the Belgian revolt of 1830. The redivision of the Netherlands would have profound consequences in World War I.

The departure of the Belgians in the 1830s roughly coincided with the beginnings of German unification. The completion of this process in 1871 left Holland with a gigantic and potentially dominant neighbor that had both economic and cultural interests in the Netherlands. Extreme Pan-Germanists sought outright annexation, although neither Bismarck nor Wilhelm II thought the Dutch could be incorporated into the German Reich.[8] No one in Holland expressed any desire for

---

[ii] This was true even then of Prussia. In 1787 G.J. van Hardenbroek heard from J. baron Taets van Amerongen van Natewisch, sheriff of Amersfoort, that the Prussian general Von Knobelsdorff (a page and favorite of the king) had claimed that Frederick the Great had visited the Netherlands to decide whether to annex Holland or Silesia, and may have been discouraged by the possibility of having to face inundations during an invasion of the Netherlands. Frederick the Great's only known voyage to Holland, however, took place in 1755, long after he had annexed Silesia. This was one of only two foreign trips he ever made, both incognito. It is true that he brought with him M. de Balbi, a colonel of engineers, so the trip may have been more than sightseeing. For the king the visit had great consequences, for it was there on an Amsterdam canal boat that he met Henri de Catt, who became his *lecteur* (and probably much more). F.J.L. Krämer, *Gedenkschriften van Gijsbert Jan van Hardenbroek* (Amsterdam: Johannes Müller, 1918), pp. 614-15.

annexation either. If Germany wished it, however, Dutch options were few. Militarily the country felt comparatively impotent. The army's mobilization during the Franco-Prussian War (1870-71) had been a model of ineptitude, showing "what a mess the Dutch army really was."[9] While the army was in better shape at the beginning of the 20th century, few quarreled with Queen Wilhelmina's assessment in 1905: "The Dutch army at this moment is not adequate to meet the demands, that it may have to face."[10] Certainly it was not ready to meet the Germans, who were indeed thinking about invading.[iii]

The potential threat from Germany led to no rapprochement with Belgium. Belgians had far more to gain than the Dutch from an alliance, and the relationship between the two countries at the turn of the century was not particularly friendly. A 1901 Belgian proposal for a joint defense of the Meuse was rejected.[11] Instead, the Dutch government opted to continue its adherence to strict neutrality.[12] Pre-war governments had also adhered to a fairly technical and strict interpretation of neutrality. For example, before the war Kaiser Wilhelm II had publicly promised that a warship would visit Krefeld, in Germany, but the Dutch pointed out that he would need permission for the ship to go through Dutch territorial waters – and the permission was denied.[13]

While the wartime cabinet leaned toward academic neutrality, officials actually working to keep the country out of the war were more flexible. The foreign minister, Jhr.[iv] John Loudon, did a remarkable job

---

[iii] In 1897 a Korvettenkapitän Schröder proposed a seaborne assault on the Schelde mouth combined with a ground attack across the southern Netherlands. He paid little attention to Dutch or Belgian resistance, assuming that the latter would withdraw into Fortress Holland, the interior defensive zone. Schröder, who commanded German marines along the Belgian coast in World War I, planned this operation as a precursor to an invasion of Britain. He made one point that should have been taken to heart by the general staff: "No violation of the neutrality of another state is more dubious in its moral and practical consequences than one that ends in a failure." Jonathan Steinberg, "A German Plan for the Invasion of Holland and Belgium, 1897," *The Historical Journal* 6 (No. 1 1963), 107-110, 112-118. Information on Ludwig von Schröder's career can be found in Hans H. Hildebrand and Ernest Henriot, *Deutsche Admirale 1849-1945: Militärische Werdegänge der See-, Ingenieur, Sanitäts-, Waffen- und Verwaltungsoffiziere im Admiralsrang,* vol. 3 (Osnabrück: Biblio Verlag, 1990).

[iv] This is the abbreviation for "Jonkheer," a predicate (not a title) indicating that someone is a member of the aristocracy, without holding one of the actual titles used in the Netherlands (in ascending order, knight, baron, and count).

of pretending to be one thing while being another – he overtly stuck to academic neutrality while quietly yielding when necessary. The army, on the other hand, could not play such a double game. In wartime, the Dutch army could not hope to survive without foreign support, yet any overt planning would be seen by other powers as a violation of neutrality. Germany, for example, would make much of the pre-war contacts between the Belgian and British general staffs (although this was a bit like a rapist justifying his act because the victim wore provocative clothing; there is not the slightest evidence that those Belgian-British talks at all influenced Germany's military planning). H.P. Staal, Dutch minister of war in 1905-1907, publicly stated that he never had military conversations with foreign powers, and hence refused to receive the British military attaché. Interestingly enough, he made this point in an interview with the German *Vossische Zeitung*.[14] The wartime supreme commander, General C.J. Snijders, was more realistic. He fully supported the neutrality policy, but could not afford to ignore either his potential need for foreign help, or the fact that he could hardly face both the Entente and the Central Powers in battle at the same time: hence, he pressured the government to give him some indication of a preference for one side or the other, arguing that to wait passively for the first border crossing would make Holland's choice of side completely accidental. He never received satisfaction on this issue.

There were at least two other traditions in Dutch foreign policy: "maritime commercialism" and "internationalist idealism."[15] These occasionally came into conflict with neutrality. Maritime commercialism came from the country's lengthy history of foreign trade and investment. The shipping companies of Amsterdam and Rotterdam simply could not afford to halt their trading with Britain, Germany, and America, and needed government channels to negotiate knotty wartime issues. On the other hand, many pacifists, diplomats, academics, and politicians wanted Holland to take a leading role in promoting internationalism. The Hague had already hosted two peace conferences and was home to Andrew Carnegie's Peace Palace. During the war Loudon received frequent suggestions that he propose peace negotiations to the warring parties. This overlooked the very real risk that such a proposal might cause one belligerent to see the Netherlands as the agent of another. Loudon did make a few very careful suggestions concerning negotiations, and the responses demonstrated that there was no chance that Holland could play a role in ending the war. It could only hope to save itself from it.

The geographic problem

Holland's geographic problem can be divided into three parts: its location, its shape, and its size. Its location placed it at the intersection of three great powers.[16] There was little optimism that a war involving even two of these powers would leave the Netherlands untouched. France was the least likely molester, unless its armies swung north to block a German advance. Unlikely as this might seem, France was a historical enemy with two major invasions of the Netherlands to its credit, the last during the Napoleonic age. France had also intervened militarily in 1830 when Belgium had declared its independence from Holland, thereby preventing the Dutch from reconquering the rebels. The British threat was considered more dangerous. Britain could easily blockade Holland's trade. The British army could also land in Holland to use it as invasion route into Germany (considered more likely by the Germans than the Dutch, interestingly), to deny Germany the use of Dutch ports or, by landing in the extreme southwest, to open routes for aid to Belgium.

Germany was by far the greatest potential threat. The possibility of Germany annexing Holland outright was considered real at the turn of the century. Pan-Germanists claimed that Holland belonged to the Reich anyway, and even Wilhelm II, generally sympathetic toward the Netherlands, would inquire as to whether the Dutch would ever voluntarily join his confederated empire. A far greater fear in Holland was that it might be dragged into the war, because Germany would enter the country for purely military purposes. These could include the seizure of Dutch ports or the use of the southern Netherlands to outflank Belgian fortresses.

In any event, the inherently hazardous nature of a small country strategically sandwiched between three large ones is readily apparent. "The status of a buffer state is perhaps the most precarious position in which a small state may find itself."[17] While a state may avoid war simply by being on the periphery of a conflict,[18] Holland's position can hardly be called "peripheral" compared, for example, to the Scandinavians. In a Franco-German war, Holland might hope that Belgium would bear the brunt alone, but with British participation the Dutch were squarely in between great warring powers.

The shape of the country also created problems. Limburg province effectively protected part of northern Belgium, while also containing useful rail links for a westward moving German army. The Schelde river was difficult to defend because fortifications on its banks were aged and the southwestern bank of the river, a region known as *Zeeuws-Vlaanderen* (henceforth Dutch Flanders) was isolated from the rest of the country. Any troops placed there were as good as lost in case of war. Holland's northeastern border faced Germany's weakest defenses and hence might be a tempting landing spot for the British, as Churchill indeed thought it. As mentioned earlier, the Dutch controlled the mouths of three of Europe's most important rivers; besides the Schelde, both the Meuse and Rhine emptied themselves through Holland.[19] Rather than strengthening the country, this merely made it a more tempting target.

Finally, even the size of the Netherlands caused difficulties. General Snijders complained that he had 900 kilometers of border to defend against potential incursions, without enough troops to do so. If he deployed his units around the periphery to protect the borders, his troops would be spread too thinly and would be defeated immediately, unable to support each other and unlikely to reach the safety of the inundated zone (which could not be flooded successfully unless the army held the invasion for at least a week, preferably two). If he concentrated his troops centrally, he could not cover all the borders. The small size of the Netherlands also meant that an invader could cross it in a few days, unless effective opposition existed.

The foreign trade problem

There were ways to reduce the risks. Most obviously, the less intercourse of any kind with foreign states, the less likely the chance of friction. This, however, was not possible. The Netherlands was exceptionally oriented toward the global economy. Investments abroad were enormous. A recent study comparing the world economy in 1914 and today found that the Netherlands had relatively greater foreign investments than any of the major industrial powers:

Outward foreign direct investment in 1914[20]

Country	% of GDP
Netherlands	85
Britain	65
France	20
Germany	20
USA	5

With foreign investments on this scale, the Netherlands government could not cut its economic ties to the rest of the world. The results would have been economically catastrophic and politically devastating; the business community would have flayed the government mercilessly. Nor would the outraged businessmen have been alone. A significant decline in foreign trade would have affected virtually every sector of the economy. International trade in and of itself was a huge industry, and had been for centuries. In the seventeenth century Holland had been a trading center without parallel, home to a trading and colonizing company (the *Verenigde Oostindische Compagnie,* United East Indies Company) that employed some 80,000 people. Rotterdam became the world's greatest port (as it still is today). Foreign trade had grown tremendously in the years between the Franco-Prussian War and World War I. Between 1872 and 1899, exports grew from 2.6 tons to 8.3 tons per capita. The harbors handled 7.4 million tons in 1867 and 37.9 million tons in 1910.[21] Inland shipping grew by a factor of 11 between 1872 and 1913. The merchant fleet was bigger than that of France.[22] Holland's wealth was commercial, not industrial, and a deliberate decision to reduce its participation in the world economy would have caused massive unemployment, bank failures, and the fall of the government. The non-commercial sectors of the economy would have fared no better. But there was never any chance that such a decision would be taken because it ran counter to the Netherlands' interests – and to its commercial heritage and instincts.

Unfortunately, much of Holland's foreign trade was with the belligerents, and the rest was vulnerable to their interference. Germany and Britain were Holland's two largest trading partners, representing more than two thirds of pre-war exports.[23] A healthy trade surplus existed with both.[24] Germany was a vital source for coal, iron, steel, salt, and chemicals. Grain and feed, on the other hand, had to come from overseas.[25] Trouble with Germany meant economic collapse, while trouble with the Entente spelled starvation. Almost half of all exports before the war went to Germany, and German demand for Dutch goods and agricultural products[26] rose during the war. Unless Germany received food from Holland, it would not export coal. If Holland exported to Germany all it could, however, Britain might retaliate by restricting grain and other shipments to the Dutch. Even before the war Britain was expected to rely on a blockade, including the application of a doctrine known as "continuous voyage." This meant that any product heading for a neutral port could be seized if its ultimate destination lay in a belligerent country. In 1907, Dutch diplomats already worried about how this might be applied in the next European war.[27] Germany, mesmerized by its plan for quick victory, had no plan for an economic blockade of Britain and therefore did not immediately make Holland's trade with Britain an issue. It did hope to use Dutch ports to defeat a British blockade, however. It was a nearly impossible situation that deteriorated rapidly in 1918, as each side made moves that with the benefit of hindsight look as if they were designed to drive the Netherlands into the enemy camp. Only the timely end of the war prevented catastrophe.

The colonial problem

The Netherlands' final strategic problem lay in its greatest visible asset: the Indies, a region whose area was forty times greater than its colonial overlord.[28] Indonesia, as this vast archipelago is called today, had been a Dutch possession for centuries, although its final conquest was recent. At the turn of the century the Royal Netherlands Indies Army (KNIL) won a short series of vicious wars against the inhabitants of Atjeh (Aceh), on northern Sumatra. Shortly before that, the Dayak headhunters of Borneo had to be subdued. It was not the loyalty of the vast native population that most worried the Netherlands, however. The colonial empire (also including possessions in the West Indies and South America) existed only by the grace of the great powers. Holland could not hope to defend the Indies from any of the great powers in the Pacific (America, Japan, Britain, and France). Of these, Britain and Japan were considered the most dangerous.[29] Tension between them might protect the Indies, because one power would hardly allow its adversary to absorb this resource-rich region. But what if tension led to war, and the colony became a battleground? Would the Dutch be forced to abandon their neutrality?

Even if all the Pacific powers were on the same side (as proved to be the case), the Indies' position would remain hazardous. If the Entente nations demanded colonial resources and these were granted, then Germany could legitimately claim that Holland was no longer truly neutral. Germany might then demand some concession in Europe, which if granted would be viewed by Britain as a violation of neutrality by Holland. An even greater danger was that war would sever connections with the Indies.

This fear had been exacerbated by the Boer War (1899-1902), during which Britain had limited and censored traffic on its vast international cable network. This brought home to the Dutch that the flow of messages, information, goods, and personnel to and from the Indies could all be interrupted by Britain – as indeed happened. This in turn led to concerns that war would also undermine the long term ties between colony and mother country. While some steps could be (and were) taken to protect wartime colonial ties, nothing could make up for the fact that Holland was a small country with a large empire, and simply lacked the force to protect it and maintain connections to it if great powers chose to interfere. Geography also played a role. No continental power had ever fared well in the empire game against Britain, whose naval superiority had ultimately meant victory over its colonial rivals, regardless of size. Hence even a great power like Germany would lose its colonies during the war, and Britain emerged as a larger global empire than it had been in 1914. If Germany could not prevent this, Holland's chances hardly merit discussion.

In other words, the Dutch colonial empire depended on British goodwill; yet Holland's own existence depended mostly on Germany. A pro-British strategy would result in Holland's absorption by the Reich, but a pro-German policy would lead to the loss of the colonies. The "bottom line" was that the strategic interests of the home country and the colonies were completely at odds. This conundrum was understood both at home and abroad. In 1905 the Queen wrote the then-Minister President,[v] Abraham Kuyper, of her fear that in wartime

---

[v] The Dutch "Minister President" has less power than a "prime minister;" he can cannot unilaterally reshuffle cabinets, for example. In the era under study the Queen still exercised substantial influence over such matters, greater than her counterparts in

the colonies and home country would have conflicting interests.[30] German Chancellor Georg von Hertling noted in 1917 that if Holland abandoned neutrality, it would have to choose between a continental and a colonial policy.[31]

A careful adherence to neutrality was the only solution. In fact, a Dutch commission proposed in 1912 that future neutrality declarations specifically include the colonies.[32] This would work only so long as the belligerents accepted that Holland was being genuinely neutral: in other words, so long as they were reasonable. Reasonableness is not the first instinct of warring peoples, especially if the conflict continues for longer than expected. Hertling's sympathy for Holland's position did not resonate everywhere in the German government. The German Colonial Secretary claimed (on the basis of a conversation with a Dutch professor resident in Berlin) that an understanding existed to the effect that if Holland lost any part of its sovereignty, that Britain would gain special rights in the Indies.[33] Germany was generally suspicious about the possible existence of Anglo-Dutch "arrangements – but Britain looked with similar disfavor on German-Dutch commercial agreements and in wartime would indeed interfere with Holland's colonial ties. It was a complex situation with no easy way out. Rising tensions made the problem all the more apparent.

---

either Britain or Germany. This may explain why Minister Presidents sometimes kept an important portfolio for themselves, or simply involved themselves directly in affairs technically with the ambit of individual ministers. Kuyper did have a foreign minister, for example, but virtually conducted Dutch foreign affairs himself (at least where matters he regarded as important were concerned).

NOTES

1   Significant works on the subject include (in order of publication): Paul Kecskemeti, *Strategic Surrender: The Politics of Victory and Defeat* (Stanford: Stanford University Press, 1958); A. B. Fox, *The Power of Small States: Diplomacy in World War II* (Chicago: University of Chicago Press, 1959); Robert O. Keohane, "Lilliputians' Dilemma: Small States in International Politics," *International Organizations* 23 (Spring 1969) pp. 291-310; August Schou and Arne Olav Brundtland, eds., *Small States in International Relations* (Stockholm: Almqvist & Wiksell, 1971); Jacques Rapaport, Ernest Muteba and Joseph Therattil, *Small States & Territories: Status and Problems* (New York: Arno Press, 1971); R. P. Barston, ed., *The Other Powers: Studies in the Foreign Relations of Small States* (New York; Harper & Row, 1973); Michael Handel, *Weak States in the International System* (London: Frank Cass, 1981); Frederic S. Pearson, *The Weak state in International Crisis: The Case of the Netherlands in the German Invasion Crisis of 1939-1940* (Washington, DC: University Press of America, 1981); Otmar Höll, ed., *Small States in Europe and Dependence* (Boulder: Westview Press (Laxenburg: Austrian Institute for International Affairs), 1983); Rista Alapuro, Matti Alestalo, Elina Haavio-Mannila, and Raimo Väyrynen, *Small States in Comparative Perspective: Essays for Erik Allardt* (Norway: Norwegian University Press, 1985); Efraim Karsh, *Neutrality and Small States* (London and New York: Routledge, 1988); Ger van Roon, *Small States in Years of Depression: The Oslo Alliance, 1930-1940* (Assen and Maastricht: Van Gorcum, 1989); and Efraim Inbar and Gabriel Sheffer, eds., *The National Security of Small States in a Changing World* (London and Portland, OR: Frank Cass, 1997).
2   James John Porter, "Dutch Neutrality in Two World Wars" (Ph.D. Dissertation: Boston University, 1980), p. vi.
3   S.I.P. van Campen, "How and Why the Netherlands joined the Atlantic Alliance – Part I," *Nato Review* (August 1982), p. 9.
4   Lamar Cecil, *Wilhelm II,* vol. 1, *Prince and Emperor 1859-1900* (Chapel Hill, NC: University of North Carolina Press, 1989), pp. 16, 35.
5   Jeremy Black, *British Foreign Policy in an Age of Revolutions* (Cambridge, UK: Cambridge University Press, 1994), p. 59.
6   Peter R. Baehr, "The Foreign Policy of the Netherlands," pp. 61-92 in Barston, *Other Powers,* passim. The Netherlands exited the war in 1713, along with England; Austria fought on until 1714.
7   C. Smit, *Tien studiën betreffende Nederland in de Eerste Wereldoorlog* (Groningen: H. D. Tjeenk Willink, 1975), pp. 1, 2.
8   Marc Frey, *Der Erste Weltkrieg und die Niederlande: Ein neutrales Land im politischen und wirtschaftlichen Kalkül der Kriegsgener* (Berlin: Akademie Verlag, 1998), 22; Horst Lademacher, *Zwei Ungleiche Nachbarn: Wegen und Wandlungen der Deutsch-Niederländischen Beziehungen im 19. Und 20. Jahrhundert* (Darmstadt: Wisschenschaftliche Buchgesellschaft, 1989), p. 89.
9   J. Grolleman and J.C. Ruiter, "Interne en externe invloeden op de legerforming in Nederland van 1870 tot 1920" (Unpublished paper. Breda: Koninklijke Militaire Academie, 1981), p. 22.

[10] Memorandum, Queen Wilhelmina, 29 April 1905, 492, C. Smit, ed., *Bescheiden betreffende de buitenlandse politiek van Nederland 1848-1919, Derde Periode 1899-1919,* Part 2, *1903-1907* ('s-Gravenhage: Martinus Nijhoff, 1958), p. 685,

[11] C. Smit, *Nederland in de Eerste Wereldoorlog (1899-1919),* vol. 1, *Het voorspel (1899-1914)* (Groningen: Wolters-Noordhoff, 1971), pp. 28-29.

[12] F. Bolkestein, "The Netherlands and the Lure of Neutralism," *NATO Review* (October 1981), p. 1.

[13] M.W.R. van Vollenhoven, *Memoires* (Amsterdam: Elsevier, 1948), p. 187.

[14] A.S. de Leeuw, *Nederland in de wereldpolitiek van 1900 tot heden* (Amsterdam: Pegasus, 1939 (1936)), pp. 118-19.

[15] J.J.C. Voorhoeve, *Peace, Profits and Principles: A Study of Dutch Foreign Policy* (The Hague: Martinus Nijhoff, 1979), pp. 42-54.

[16] Karsh, *Neutrality,* p. 83.

[17] Ibid., p. 82.

[18] Ibid., p. 81.

[19] John J. Bout, "The Dutch Army in World War I" (M.A. Thesis: University of British Columbia, 1972), p. 29.

[20] "One World," *Economist,* October 18, 1997, p. 80.

[21] Bout, "Dutch Army," pp. 3-4.

[22] Porter, "Dutch Neutrality," pp. 22-23.

[23] Hermann von der Dunk, *Die Niederlande im Kräftespiel zwischen Kaiserreich und Entente* (Wiesbaden: Franz Steiner, 1980), p. 18.

[24] Porter, "Dutch Neutrality," pp. 23-24.

[25] Ibid., p. 44.

[26] The German demand for agricultural products rose during the war because Germany, for obvious reasons, abandoned its protectionist policies. At the same time, Britain paid less for food during the war than Germany because Britain had other alternatives. H.A.R. Smidt, "De bestrijding van de smokkelhandel door het leger tijdens de Eerste Wereldoorlog," *Mededelingen van de Sectie Militaire Geschiedenis* 15 (1993),p. 44.

[27] Tets van Goudriaan to de Beaufort, 21 June 1907, 80, in C. Smit, ed. *Bescheiden betreffende de buitenlandse politiek van Nederland, 1848-1919, derde periode, 1899-1919,* part 3, *1907-1914* ('s-Gravenhage: Martinus Nijhoff, 1961), pp. 110-111.

[28] A.J. Barnouw, *Holland under Queen Wilhelmina* (New York: Scribner's, 1923), p. 97.

[29] Memorandum by Von Bethmann-Hollweg concerning conversation with Abraham Kuyper, 18 April 1916, Duitse Ministerie van Buitenlandse Zaken – Stukken in Nederland. Algemeen Rijksarchief – Tweede Afdeling, nr. toegang 2.05.16, inv. nrs. 1-6.

[30] Porter, "Dutch Neutrality," p. 54.

[31] Gevers to Loudon, 23 November 1917, 297, in C. Smit, ed. *Bescheiden betreffende de buitenlandse politiek van Nederland, 1848-1919, derde periode, 1899-1919,* part 5, *1917-1919* ('s-Gravenhage: Martinus Nijhoff, 1964), pp. 312-313.

[32] Smit, *1907-1914,* p. 852.

[33] Solf (Staatssekretär des Reichs-Kolonialamts) to Foreign Minister, 30 November 1916, Duitse Ministerie van Buitenlandse Zaken – Stukken in Nederland. ARA-II, nr. toegang 2.05.16, inv. nrs. 1-6.

1. Jonkheer mr. J. Loudon (1866-1955), Dutch Foreign
Minister 1913-1918. (Iconografisch Bureau)

2. C.J. Snijders (1852-1939): Supreme Commander of land
and sea forces, 1914-1918.

3. Mobilization announcement in the Netherlands, 31 July 1914. Troops so mobilized were to reach their call-up stations by 1 August. (From the illustrated magazine *Het Leven*)

No. 16b
14 Oct. 1914, 2e Jrg.
Verschijnt
2 maal p. week

PANORAMA
GEÏLLUSTREERD WEEKBLAD

Abonnement
per kwartaal f 1.30
DIT nummer kost
afzonderlijk 7½ Ct.
Voor BELGIË
20 Centiemen

UITGAVE VAN A.W. SIJTHOFF'S UITGEVERS MAATSCHAPPIJ LEIDEN
Redactie en Administratie DOEZASTRAAT 1 Telefoonnummer 1

DE VLUCHTELINGEN UIT BELGIË

VLUCHTELINGEN VAN ELKEN LEEFTIJD.
Moedertje is blij dat haar in Holland weer een vriendenhand wordt toegestoken.

UITGEPUT. — DOOR OPWINDING EN VERMOEIENIS UITGEPUT LIGT HET OUDE MOEDERTJE OP HAAR SCHAMELE BAGAGE NEER.

4. A Dutch magazine report of the arrival of Belgian refugees in the Netherlands in the early months of the war. (Collectie K. Kornaat)

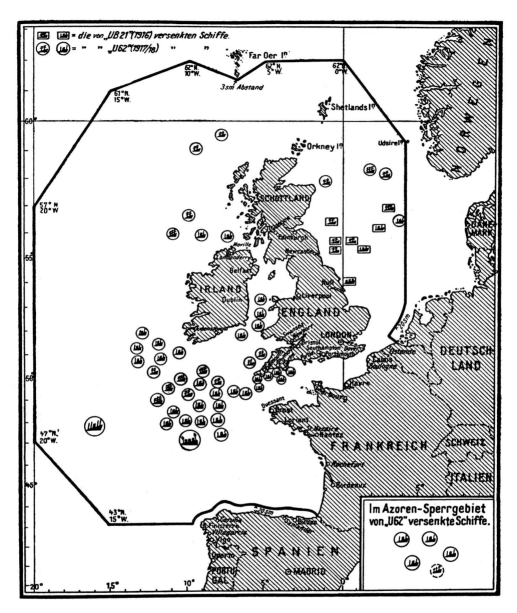

5. The German exclusion zone around the British Isles (from Ernst Hashagen, *U-Boote Westwärts*, Berlin 1931). Hashagen commanded UB-21 and U-62 which sank 62 ships from February 1916 to the end of the war.

6. Dutch soldiers on patrol on the North Sea islands.

7. Dutch soldiers mobilized in 1914-18 wonder how much more time they will have to spend on Pampus, an island fortress forming part of the defenses of Amsterdam. (Stichting Pampus)

8. On 19 June 1916, Amsterdam housewives held a Hunger March to the city hall to protest against shortages of potatoes and fuel. In this period troops were first sent to the city to guard food supplies. (From the illustrated magazine *Het Leven*)

9. In June-July 1917, supplies to Amsterdam of potatoes – the working-class staple – all but ceased (although potatoes were still being exported to England). The resulting unrest led to the arrival of more than 2000 soldiers to defend food stores against looters. Here they have parked the dogcarts drawing their machine-guns behind the Rijksmuseum. (From the illustrated magazine *Het Leven*)

10. The Dutch wartime government made serious efforts to persuade the population to eat more fish – and in particular mussels – instead of meat. The North Sea fisheries were disrupted by submarines and mines, but these mussel fishermen are working in 1917 in the northern part of the Zuiderzee. (From the illustrated magazine *Het Leven*)

11. The Dutch army drew on the lessons of the Western front and embarked upon a program of building modern reinforced-concrete bunkers and defensive positions. Here engineers are positioning antitank defenses in 1918. (Historische genie verzameling Vught)

12. British military internees from the Royal Naval Brigade wait at the station in Groningen for the train returning them home at the end of the war. (Collectie Evelyn de Roodt)

CHAPTER TWO

THE THREAT

The last decade before World War I contained a series of crises that leave the historian wondering not why the war came, but why it did not come sooner. These included the Russo-Japanese War (1904-1905), the first Moroccan crisis (1905), the increasing naval arms race symbolized by the launching of the *Dreadnought* (1906), the annexation of Bosnia-Herzegovina (1908), the second Moroccan crisis (1911), the Balkan wars (1912-1913), and the assassination of Franz Ferdinand in Sarajevo (1914). The likelihood of war grew steadily. Some great powers might convince themselves that they could gain from war, or at least that the alternative was worse. For a small state like the Netherlands the only positive result from war required noninvolvement. Accordingly, military preparations intensified and greater efforts were made to learn about German plans.

The first Moroccan crisis signaled that "Germany's ruling class was about to accept a strategy of daring coups or gambling to overcome obstacles to *'Weltpolitik'* ('global politics')."[1] This was dangerous for the Netherlands, because the country contained so many possible attractions for the Germans: Limburg province (as a march route), the ports, the mouth of the Rhine, the colonial empire, and the whole country (for annexation-minded pan-Germans). Naturally Holland stayed out of the 1905 crisis, although it did cause a minor stir when three Dutch cruisers arrived in Tangier (they were there on an ill-timed routine "show the flag" visit).[2] Of more significance was the greater interest in Dutch military strength shown by the developing Entente and, later, Germany – each wondering if Holland could defend itself against the other. The Entente was particularly suspicious because the Dutch Minister-President at this time was Kuyper (1901-1905), viewed at home and abroad as pro-German.

Kuyper had also pursued better relations with Belgium, however, something definitely not to Germany's liking. Some Belgians wanted to go even further, creating a military alliance between the two low countries. The odds against Kuyper or his successors accepting such a proposal were overwhelming, however. For the Dutch, an alliance was at best a mixed blessing. A combined Dutch-Belgian army would be numerically formidable and therefore a better deterrent, but an alliance greatly increased the chance of involvement in the next war.

Nevertheless, in 1905 an optimistic journalist by the name of Eugène Baie launched a campaign in *Le Petit Bleu* advocating a narrower relationship, to include both a military convention and a customs union.[3] German diplomats noted that the campaign received enthusiastic support in the Entente press, leading them to suspect collusion.[4] The general tone of Dutch responses was that an alliance would be more of danger than a benefit, one that would neither stop nor prevent a German invasion.[5] In the words of W.H. de Beaufort, a former foreign minister, the proposed alliance was "too big for a napkin and too small for a tablecloth."[6] Dutch general staff officers were divided.[7] The army declined Belgian General A.M. Ducarne's proposal for general staff talks, however.[8] (This turned out to be a wise precaution; when Ducarne held talks with the British military attaché, the Germans found out within a month.[9]) Frustrated, the Belgians were forced to settle for assurances that the Dutch would defend Limburg, and were told that the Meuse river bridges would be blown and that the Dutch army would concentrate on the invaders' rear.[10] This made strategic sense, but hardly mollified the Belgians. Later discussions also came to nothing.[11] Yet the Belgian proposal had a valid foundation (of which they were unaware). Schlieffen, Chief of the General Staff since 1891, had decided to invade Holland. His plan (actually more of a concept), drafted in December, 1905 and January, 1906, represented the first time that Holland was included in Germany's plan for *der Tag* (The Day).[12] Schlieffen wrote what would become the most famous military plan in world history. It called for a massive right wing to sweep through the low countries, swing toward and around Paris, and trap the bulk of the French army in eastern France. It was breathtaking in its decisiveness, daring, and simplicity – yet it was dependent on perfect execution and finding more troops than the German army actually had. The requirements of his plan exceeded Germany's military strength. Hence, he supported vigorous conscription schemes, conceding that these were not likely.[13] Schlieffen was facing war with no clear numerical superiority.[14] Striking first was his Frederician "solution" to the problem of having multiple enemies, the difficulty of attacking in the east (due to poor roads, the available space for Russia to retreat, and the poor condition of the Austrian army).[15] Gerhard Weinberg has called it

... the vast encircling movement into France that a mentally unbalanced Chief of the German General Staff had once envisioned as the best way to protect Austria-Hungary against a Russian attack, regardless of whether it also brought England into the war.[16]

Schlieffen never backed away from his concept. His post-retirement proposals were even more ambitious, calling for occupying most of the Netherlands to deny Britain a chance for using it as a base. After the war, there was great sensitivity about Schlieffen's plan to invade the Netherlands. At first it was simply denied, until documents proved otherwise. General Groener, Schlieffen's first biographer, mentions discussions concerning Belgium, but not the Netherlands.[17] Occasionally the record was deliberately falsified or misstated on this point.[18]

> In the midst of the quarrel over the famous "war guilt question" German officials, particularly in the Foreign Ministry, had grave hesitations about publishing those passages of Schlieffen's memoranda which discuss marching not just through Belgium but through Holland a well. ... [N]o one [in the Foreign Ministry] wanted to get involved in ticklish explanations to the Dutch about Schlieffen's views on Dutch policy."[19]

Another argument was that the low-countries scheme was known only to Schlieffen who had consulted "no one" about it[20] and hence left Germany's political leaders "only hazily informed about the intentions of the general staff."[21] This was not true. Wilhelm II had written Baron Holstein, the foreign office's *éminence grise,* in 1904 advocating occupation of Belgium, Holland, and Denmark in case of war.[22] Schlieffen and Holstein had a close relationship (although not, as has been suggested, going back to their younger years) and met weekly during crises. Exactly what transpired is unknown, as their correspondence was apparently deliberately destroyed and their relations are "shrouded in mystery."[23] However, when Schlieffen decided that "the neutrality of Luxembourg, Belgium and the Netherlands must be violated"[24] he did not keep this to himself: in the margin of his plan there is the handwritten note, *"mit dem Reichskanzler besprochen"* ("discussed with the Chancellor").[25] Invading Holland was also discussed publicly. In 1909, Freiherr von Falkenhausen had suggested that Germany would use Belgium *and Holland* as battlefields (although he thought that the first violation of Holland would come from Britain).Friedrich von Bernhardi wrote in 1912 that he could well imagine a German offensive with its extreme right wing passing through Belgium *and Holland* (emphasis added).[26]

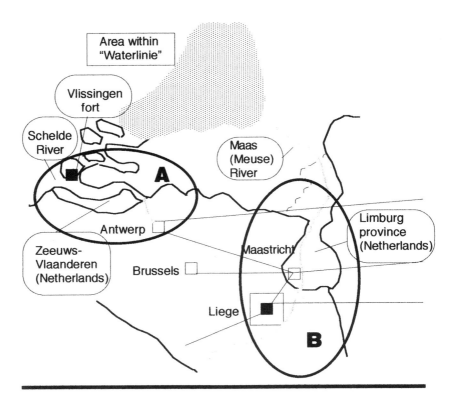

Belgium's strategic needs diverged from Holland's at two points.

Circle "A":   Ships going to and from Antwerp had to use the Schel-
               de river,both banks of which belonged to Holland. The
               beginning of the Vlissingen fort signalled that the Ne-
               therlands intended to maintain its sovereignty over the
               Schelde.

Circle "B":   Belgium, fearing a German crossing of Limburg,want-
               ed the Dutch army to deploy along the Meuse. The
               Dutch were better off deploying their army further
               north.

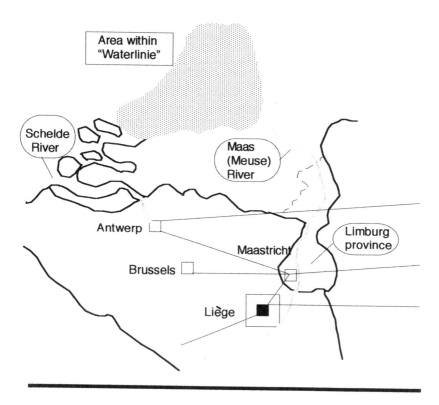

The Limburg rail net looked enticing to Schlieffen.

Schlieffen saw invasion of Holland as a military necessity. Dutch Limburg lay between northern Belgium and the northern Rhineland where Germany would deploy its main striking force, and would begin an enormous railway-station construction program to support it.[27] The mass of troops emerging from these railheads would have to make a substantial detour around Maastricht and also lose the benefit of the Dutch railway lines that connected Germany and Belgium via Limburg. Tactics and logistics undermined neutrality. Groener claims that Schlieffen hoped for an agreement with the Dutch and if it did not materialize, planned to capture Liège.[28] The latter was untrue: Schlieffen planned to avoid the Belgian forts altogether.[29] By a rapid invasion he expected to control the roads in southern Holland and northern Belgium before the British arrived at Antwerp.[30]

Yet Schlieffen did not view his Holland option in a totally optimistic light. In his first draft, he conceded that

> it is necessary to violate the neutrality not only of Belgium, but also of the Netherlands. But as long as no other expedient can be found, one has to make the best of these difficulties.[31]

The Limburg route made sense – nine corps could have used it[32] – but it would leave the German army with a relatively large exposed flank and rear. Schlieffen's right wing would be followed by 7 reserve corps and 16 brigades, more than sufficient to cover the flank.[33] Yet these troops would not be available for the great sweep south. Holland's army might be inadequate, but its four division, 100,000-man field army could not be ignored when it sat astride the communications for the right wing. Absent a very quick German victory, Britain would undoubtedly send troops to Holland, further endangering the German flank.

These problems led Schlieffen to propose a larger incursion after retirement. Apparently, this was influenced by his growing fear of a massive simultaneous attack from all Germany's neighbors, a fear to which he gave free reign in a 1909 *Deutsche Revue* article. It so impressed Wilhelm II that he read it to an assembled group of generals.[34] Since a Franco-British invasion of both low countries was now anticipated,[35] Schlieffen proposed (1912) occupying all of Holland outside of the water-protected *vesting Holland*. The Meuse would be crossed by several columns, as Schlieffen did not think that the Dutch army could defend all the crossing points. One division would push as far west as the line Naarden-Utrecht-Gorinchem, another further south would move into the Schelde Delta and to the Meuse and Waal rivers south of Rotterdam.[36] Schlieffen concluded that the Dutch were "prepared for an outflanking of the position Namur-Liège. They intend to defend the Meuse line, at least at Maastricht" but concluded that the many possible crossing points would allow the German troops to get across. He conceded that "[w]ith the further advance it will at first be necessary to have cover against the Netherlands and a landing on Dutch territory." Compressing the Netherlands into its *vesting* seemed to obviate this problem.[37]

Two different strategies were then obvious in Schlieffen's mind – to hold Holland against the British, and to seize part of it for communications. The latter was not forgotten in 1912. Schlieffen noted that the river was wide and traversed by only two rail and three road bridges; "some of these may be destroyed or occupied. . . . one must be ready to build quite a number of bridges, however."[38] Yet Schlieffen's comment concerning destruction contained a contradiction. If he really anticipated this, then the communications value of Limburg drops – destroyed bridges cannot be replaced in minutes, and his plan's success or failure could depend on operations lasting hours. A second problem is that Schlieffen obviously expects some level of Dutch anticipation, some level of preparation which could interfere with Germany's "best" approach – a *coup de main* to capture the bridges.[39] Of course, it required no clairvoyance from the Dutch to recognize the vulnerability of Limburg. The destruction of the Limburg bridges had been contemplated ever since 1882.[40] The French suggested to the Dutch during the first Moroccan crisis that German troops would go through Maastricht.[41] In addition, the German army's deployments indicated something was afoot. Shortly after the war, Lt.-General W.G.F. Snijders, brother of the supreme commander, concluded by studying dispositions that it had been Schlieffen's intention to go through Holland.[42]

But there was more. Schlieffen's plan to invade Holland had leaked. In his memoirs, wartime War Minister Nicolaas Bosboom revealed:

> That the German army leadership was seriously considering a march through Limburg in its preparations, did not have to be doubted. A few years earlier I had received reports from an individual, fairly trustworthy, German source, whose contents pointed to a definite decision to do so.[43]

He footnoted his "few years earlier" comment with the following:

In 1906 or 1907. Shortly before or shortly after the elevation of Von
Moltke to chief of the general staff.[44]

Bosboom never revealed his source. He clearly hampered investigation
by a deliberate haziness concerning the date the information was
received – not something he would have been likely to forget. Because
the plan was little over a year old in 1907, the timing of the reports
should not be attributed to inspired guesswork on the part of Bosboom's source. If the information were only interpretations, rather than
hard facts, there would have been no conceivable reason for Bosboom
to mention it in his memoirs.

How widely did Bosboom disseminate his information? Is there
evidence that the army actually reacted to his discovery, or took it
seriously? Definitive answers to these questions are not possible.[45] This
was an era when intelligence information was collected and reviewed
informally, without the paper trail we would expect to find today.
Army activity does yield a few tantalizing snippets. After 1906 there
was an upsurge in Dutch defensive activity in the Limburg.[46] The
army's annual map exercises of October, 1906 specifically covered
operations in the province.[47] The center of gravity of the army's
projected deployment shifted southward in 1906.[48] In 1907, Holland
became the first country to organize a permanent peacetime Field
Army headquarters. Reserves were improved and draft calls were
expanded between 1907 and 1910.[49] In March and August 1908, plans
were made for the destruction of the bridge at Roermond, the most
strategic crossing point in Limburg (Lieutenant General Arthur Kool,
however, had been working for this since 1905).[50] In 1908 the army
began to focus less on a direct invasion from Germany (i.e. one with
the goal of conquest and annexation) and more on neutrality violations
along the periphery.[51] The ministry of war strengthened the bridge
defenses in Limburg and also built a garrison for two battalions at
Venlo in Limburg in 1910-13.[52] These improvements cannot be
attributed to prejudice against Germany. Lieutenant General F.M.
Thiange, who became chief of staff shortly after Bosboom's discovery,
was more concerned about a British landing than a German invasion,
and Hendrikus Colijn, War Minister in 1911-1913, was, if not outright
pro-German, certainly not Hunophobic. A few of the reforms were
routine improvements, but others were not. Nor can these changes be
attributed solely to good guessing. Bosboom's intelligence coup is by
far the most likely explanation.

Yet could such defensive improvements influence German planners? In Schlieffen's case, the picture is contradictory. While he noted Holland's improving Limburg defenses, he responded by expanding, not contracting, his invasion plan for the Netherlands. For a while he appeared to hope that Holland would cooperate with Germany, something Dutch generals found difficult to believe after the war.[53] Based on anti-British comments in Dutch military circles, Schlieffen concluded that "[t]he Netherlands regard England, allied to France, no less as an enemy than does Germany. It will be possible to come to an agreement with them." Yet at virtually the same time he doubted that Germany could count on "benevolent inaction" by Holland because of its dependence on British goodwill for the survival of its colonies.[54] He concluded that the Netherlands was a natural ally of England[55] and – toward the end of his life – that its troops would form the northern wing of the French army, holding the Meuse from Liège southward.[56]

This utterly preposterous idea, for which he had not the slightest evidence, suggests that Schlieffen either ignored foreign military events or interpreted them in the light of strong preconceived notions. He claimed in 1905 that Holland had made preparations against Germany and that it would defend Maastricht, but he used this as proof of Dutch hostility, not as a reason to avoid Limburg.[57] In the 1905 war games, "[t]he Belgians and Dutch were not highly valued."[58] Of the 51 divisions assigned to his proposed invasion plan of 1912, he assigned only two divisions to be deployed against Holland.[59] Even this seemingly minuscule commitment – 4% of the total force – was troublesome. How to deal with this and many other logistical, tactical and strategic headaches would fall in 1906 to Schlieffen's successor.

Helmuth von Moltke was more pessimistic (if less paranoid) than Schlieffen, and uncertain about the likelihood of a quick victory. He did not, however, formulate a completely new plan in the eight years before World War I. He expected war but did not necessarily seek it, telling Philipp zu Eulenburg in 1906 that "if we have to fight – good; if not – better."[60] By 1913 he had decided that war "is bound to come sooner or later," and like his predecessor expected "a struggle between the Germanic and Slav races."[61] He kept Schlieffen's grand design, but was fully alive to its problems. In 1912 he sought but failed to obtain a significant expansion of the army.[62] Schlieffen's "ostrich-like refusal" to address logistics[63] left Moltke in a quandary, because the bigger the right wing – and hence the better the chance for success – the greater the likelihood that he could not supply and support the movement. A "big" right wing, as Schlieffen had famously pleaded for even on his deathbed, could not be supplied, and hence the war would be lost; a smaller right wing would have less punching power, and hence the war would be lost. Somehow, the right wing's size would have to be limited without reducing its strength.

Moltke's solution was to avoid Holland. If the Dutch army was not hostile, the right flank would be secure and hence could be smaller.[64] He would give up the railways through Limburg, but would no longer lose divisions to flank-covering missions, enable his armies to support each other better,[65] and would also secure his lines of communication, perhaps his biggest concern.[66] Even a weak Dutch attack on German lines of communication would have been disastrous. German forces could have wheeled northwards in retaliation and devastated the Dutch, but the time and troops involved would cause the invasion plan to collapse, the war to be lost, and ironically Holland would be left on the side of the victors.

Moltke would have rather had Holland as any ally. Seeing Schlieffen's suggestion of gaining Dutch approval for a passage, he wrote that "[i]f our diplomacy manages this, it will be a great advantage. We need the Dutch railways. The value of Holland as an ally would be incalculable."[67] He expected German diplomacy to fail, however.[68] Moltke did not reject assistance to Holland in case of invasion, however. Fundamentally, then, he desired an alliance with Holland but would do nothing to bring it about. But like Schlieffen, he evidently hoped that Holland would view Britain as an enemy and prevent it from crossing Dutch territory. His hope was strengthened by a lengthy 1908 report from the military attaché in The Hague, Major Martin Renner. Renner, who spent a large part of his military career in Holland, reported that coast defenses were being strengthened and that troops would be transferred westward to face Britain. Renner reported that Holland's goal was strict neutrality, maintained by force if necessary. This reassured Moltke that Holland would not become a base for Britain.[69] The German envoy, Richard von Kühlmann, thought the report was so important that he recommended that the Netherlands be given an immediate guarantee of neutrality in case of war.[70]

Most commentators on Moltke's decision of ca. 1908-1909[71] to avoid Holland have attributed it to economics. Moltke explicitly stated that Dutch "neutrality allows us to have imports and supplies. She must be the windpipe that enables us to breathe."[72] He suspected that a long war might be in the offing and correctly wanted to avoid the expected

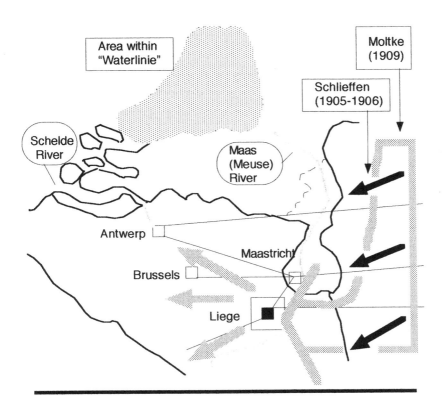

Schlieffen's plan would have sent part of his massive right wing
through Holland's Limburg province. Since Moltke's modification
(lighter arrows) required compressing two thirds of his powerful
right wing into a narrow column which would then expand again after crossing the Meuse, the Germans had to capture Liege immediately, or an epic military traffic jam would result. In other words,
Moltke took a huge military gamble by deciding to avoid Holland.

British blockade.[73] In this he would be disappointed: The British had no intention of letting Germany use Holland in this way. The British Foreign Office concluded on July 29, 1914, that Germany respected Dutch neutrality "in order to safeguard German imports via the Rhine and Rotterdam."[74] The Committee for Imperial Defense had already decided in 1912 to cut off Holland-bound German imports in case of war.[75] The Prussian finance minister foresaw this and saw no benefit in leaving Holland neutral.[76] Moltke, however, had no faith in more conventional means of breaking the blockade. He once commented that as the navy had no chance of success in a war against Britain, such a war should be avoided.[77]

Moltke, however, was more influenced by military than economic considerations. According to Moltke, Schlieffen expected Holland to content itself with a protest in case of invasion. Moltke seriously doubted this. He expected the Dutch to fight. The determined actions taken by the Dutch convinced him[78] The result would be a hostile Holland, which he felt would cost the German army so much strength (so starke Kräfte) that too little would be left for the advance west.[79] The consequences would be "disastrous."[80] He remained convinced of this to the end, writing shortly before his death that "the campaign in the west would have gone to wreck if we had not kept clear of Holland."[81] He was not alone in this assessment. The British concluded that the Dutch army could force the withdrawal of "a not unimportant portion of [Geman] troops from their direct operations against France."[82] The Dutch estimated that three army corps would have to be detached to face them,[83] a huge increase over what Schlieffen had planned. Considering the kilometrage to be covered, for once the Dutch might have been closer to the mark. Moltke commissioned a report which concluded that the *Vesting Holland* should not be underestimated and that Holland's army, although poorly disciplined, would be a "noteworthy opponent."[84]

But it was not only of the wrath of the Dutch *Weermacht* that Moltke was thinking. "A neutral Holland secures our rear" he argued, because Britain could not invade Holland to use it as base; if Britain entered the war to protect Belgian neutrality, "[s]he cannot break the very law for whose sake she goes to war."[85] The final military straw came in 1910, however, when German intelligence correctly predicted that France would go on the offensive in the next war. The 7th Army, which was to have been move northward to cover the right wing and cross Limburg under the original plan, now had to be left in Alsace to face the *furor galliae*. With the withdrawal of this substantial covering force, planning for a crossing of Dutch territory was finally abandoned.[86]

Avoiding the Netherlands was difficult, however, for two reasons: railroads and geography. Bypassing Limburg meant five fewer rail lines, and also an extremely circuitous, dense march route around the scrotum-like appendage. Moltke never denied that he had deliberately taken on great difficulties, referring to the maneuver's *"grossen technischen Schwierigkeiten"* ("great technical difficulties").[87] The 1st Army had to make the longest and most complicated march, adding three days and 60 kilometers to its route, not to mention the increased exhaustion of the troops.[88] The 2nd Army also added 3 days, although less distance, to its march.[89] Two problems resulted: congestion and compression.

The latter caused the former. The "awkward" maneuver (Moltke's own epithet) meant that the 1st and 2nd armies had to pass through a 12 mile wide space to advance onto the Belgian plain. Von Kluck's 320,000-man 1st Army would have to march south along Limburg, squeeze through a strip only 6 miles wide to the north of Liège, and then swing back to the north.[90] The 2nd Army had the same amount of space, for which its smaller size (260,000 men) provided little compensation.[91] The 1st, which had to lead the advance into France, actually would have to wait until the 2nd had passed through Aachen.[92] Deploying the 1st further south was technically impossible, yet the whole plan depended on the 1st being out in front.[93]

The importance of Moltke's decision cannot possibly be overstated, and reveals the huge – if unintentional – effect that the Netherlands had upon World War I and European history. To make up for all the technical difficulties, Moltke staked everything on a *coup de main*. If it worked, the march could proceed without delay; if it failed, the result would be the biggest military traffic jam in history and the collapse of the invasion plan. Failure to take Liège with its bridges and tunnels intact would be a disaster.[94] Without the Liège attack, the army had a fairly long time – almost two weeks – before it had to begin its march. With Liège, the wait was reduced to a couple of days. Moltke's plan leaves no time for diplomacy or politics. It is strange that Moltke, who showed such unusual broadmindedness[95] by taking economics and politics into account in his decision concerning Holland, allowed purely tactical considerations to dominate important strategic decisions. Yet he felt he had no choice. For the plan to work, he had to avoid Holland; to avoid Holland, he had to capture Liège (there being only one crossing between Liège and Holland, and it was within range of the forts' guns)[96]; to capture Liège, he had to move immediately.

Moltke was later villified in Germany for losing the war but not for attacking Liège. Few knew that Schlieffen, with his abhorrence of frontal attacks, planned to surround and bypass Liège, not storm it.[97] As Moltke could not afford to wait to reduce the forts by siege, he felt compelled to attempt a *coup de main,* conceding that it was "of paramount importance" that Liège be taken immediately and that otherwise the whole plan would have to be changed.[98] Small wonder that Ludendorff called the attack "bold" and "extremely daring."[99] But Moltke perhaps summarized the risks best when he said: "*Ich habe mit diesem Unternehmen alles auf eine Karte gesetzt . . ."*[100] And all this just to avoid invading the Netherlands!

The boldness was tactically necessary not just to capture a few forts. Belgium's military strength was great enough that Moltke had to move before it could be fully mobilized against him.[101] Moltke particularly wanted to capture railroads and railroad bridges intact, and to prevent Belgium from completing the defensive lines between the forts[102] (the Belgians had left them unfinished to avoid antagonizing the Germans). The operation was also justified later with the argument that a rapid move through Belgium might bring in the B.E.F. sooner, but this would make it all the easier to destroy quickly and make it harder for the British to organize a large force.[103]

The Liège maneuver did cost Germany time (through the length of the march, not the forts' resistance[104]), but Moltke never evinced any intention of changing the plan to invade the Netherlands after all. He was later criticized because the Dutch coast would have been a useful launching platform for attacking Britain[105] and because Germany was not able to use Holland as his much desired "windpipe."[106] One Dutch writer even concluded that Holland had survived "due to the fact that a strong and competent Chief of Staff (Schlieffen) was succeeded by a weak and incompetent one (Moltke)."[107] Yet no one has explained how Moltke could afford to further weaken his right wing. Kluck had to detach 2 corps just to mask Antwerp and occupy Belgium.[108] The Netherlands could hardly have required less, especially given the long lines of communication that would have had to be protected.

The Dutch government did not know about Moltke's change of plan, but even if it had, it is doubtful that the pressure for military improvements would have decreased. The risk of war in Europe was increasing too rapidly to permit complacency. The second Moroccan crisis provided yet another boost for this growing concern. Unlike past crises, all three regional powers were interested in Holland's actions and intentions. The British obtained assurances that Holland would defend the Meuse.[109] The French president visited the Netherlands and his attaché in Belgium discussed military matters with the Dutch envoy.[110]

The German attitude was more ominous. Holland moved forces to its eastern border during the crisis. This led the German foreign secretary, Alfred von Kiderlen-Waechter, to complain that the Dutch measures were tantamount to mobilization and showed one-sidedness.[111] Tensions were high; a warship clash took place on the disputed Eems river.[112] C.J. Snijders, then chief of staff, decided it was time to go on a fact-finding mission to Berlin, but accomplished little. His legation knew nothing about his visit or about German military affairs. His request for the appointment of military attachés was shelved.[113]

What he could do was use the crisis to push for further improvements in the army. Politically, this was not easy. War ministers were the most vulnerable cabinet members. The army was unpopular. The army's generals were divided between advocates of a strong Field Army, and a minority who those who favored a war of fortifications, with only guerilla war conducted in the lands beyond the *Vesting Holland.* The Field Army, the force that would fight initially outside the *Vesting,* was criticized for conducting maneuvers on the high, dry lands in the east, while it might have to do much of its fighting in the low-lying *polders* in the west – but getting permission to operate on the more densely populated (and valuable) western lands was virtually impossible.[114]

The army's weakness was dangerous. The more foreign powers interested themselves in Holland, the more the army would have to fulfill a deterrent role. Yet it was regarded with little respect abroad. Improvements had begun, however, in response to the first Moroccan crisis. The second Moroccan crisis added considerable urgency to the calls for reform. Under the supervision of Colijn, a war minister with genuine political experience, the army's size, training, organization, gunnery, and efficiency were al improved. A camouflage uniform was adopted.[115] Colijn's reforms made a positive impression abroad.[116] Yet training was still inadequate, fortifications were old, many machine guns were obsolete, ammunition supplies were good for only a coupe of weeks, and the air service was weak.[117] Pilots were recruited from the civilian population, not only because of their flying skills, but because they owned airplanes![118]

It was not clear whether the army's modernization was enough to enable it to carry out its changing mission. The field army was expected to oppose any incursion at any point in order to preserve neutrality. Failure to oppose a neutrality violation might be seized upon by another combatant as a reason to invade. To prevent this the field army might have to fight in places that made no military sense and from which withdrawal to the *Vesting* might prove impossible – such as Limburg. Placing the bulk of the Field Army in the province was not considered, because it would face capture, destruction, or forced retreat into Belgium – with no possibility of retreat to the *Vesting*. The regiment at Maastricht was warned in 1912 that it would have to be responsible for "maintaining neutrality" in the area during the pre-mobilization phase – an obvious reference to its vulnerability to attack.[119]

The prewar reforms were impressive but still left the army well short even of its own standards, let alone those of foreign observers. Many doubted whether the Field Army's four 22,500-man divisions could maneuver sufficiently well to give battle and then withdraw in orderly fashion to the *Vesting*. Yet this barely adequate army had to be used to convince a host of countries that the Netherlands would use force to protect its neutrality, and with some effectiveness. If the Entente powers believed that Limburg and the Meuse valley would not be defended, they might occupy Dutch territory as a defensive measure. Germany had more potential reasons to invade. Much of Germany's foreign trade flowed through Rotterdam and other Dutch ports. Holland was still viewed as a target of annexation or "attachment"by some in the Reich. Holland was seen not only as a possible pathway for an attack on Britain, but also as a route for a British army moving to assist Belgium. The mercurial Wilhelm II privately told his envoy that the occupation of Holland's harbors in wartime was inevitable.[120]

Fortunately for the Dutch, German diplomats on the whole were well-disposed toward the Netherlands. This was not necessarily the case among a more important group: Germany's soldiers. The General Staff shared Moltke's opinion that Holland would fight. "The German general staff assumed at the latest in the summer of 1911 that the Netherlands would resist a German march through Limburg."[121] Yet his generals still wondered if Holland had the capacity to block a British move up the Schelde. The Netherlands' response to these concerns was

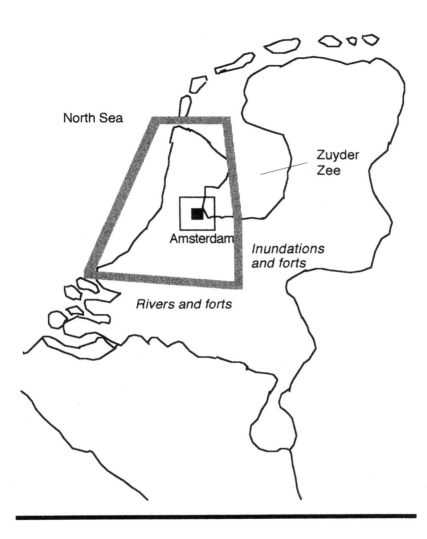

The concept behind the "Vesting Holland" was simple. The area within the
polyhedron above contained the provinces of North and South Holland and
most of the country's large cities.The eastern side was protected by inundations: the south by the Rhine and Meuse rivers; the west by the North Sea,
and the northeast by the Zuyder Zee. The east and south were protected by
fortifications as well. Amsterdam also had its own ring of forts

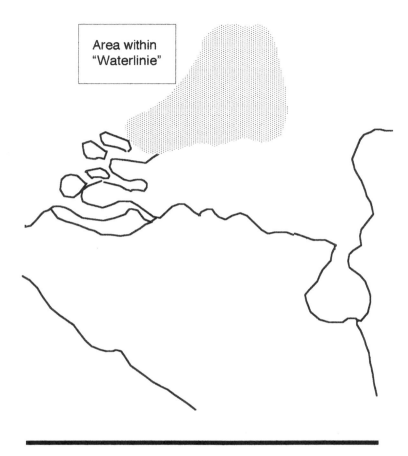

Area within
"Waterlinie"

Neutrality created a strategic dilemma for the Netherlands. Militarily, defense behind the inundations made the most sense. Politically and legally, every part of the country had to be defended.

a military plan that must rank as one of the strangest in history. The plan was to build an armored fort that would cover a river, the Schelde, that did not touch a single major Dutch port; the fort was built to convince one power that it would resist the invasion of another; and it was never built.

Normally the construction of a single fort by a minor military power would be of little interest. This project, however, became the subject of press and diplomatic interest in Britain, France, Germany, Belgium, and even the United States. The reason was that the guns of the proposed fort at Vlissingen (Flushing) would command the Schelde and could cut off aid shipments to Antwerp in wartime. Germany looked like the beneficiary. Rumors of German pressure would not die. The foreign minister, Jhr. Renneke de Marees van Swinderen, was forced to issue strenuous denials, which proved to be inadequate. He blundered with the British, allegedly telling them that the project was the result of German pressure.[122] He fared no better with the French.[123]

There were straightforward reasons for the modernization, however. In 1906 the British military attaché reported that the existing Schelde fortifications were "valueless."[124] Without some way of controlling the river neutrality might quickly disappear in a crisis. This made no impression on the newspapers and magazines that entered upon the *"Broschürenstreit über Vlissingen"* ("pamphlet struggle over Vlissing-en").[125] The French foreign minister tried to take advantage by suggesting that the Dutch plan affected all guarantors of Belgian neutrality and proposed a conference on the matter – a suggestion immediately rejected by the Dutch government as unacceptable interference in domestic affairs.[126] The German General Staff unsurprisingly endorsed the idea quietly.[127] The Belgians had the most at stake and were the most vocal, but their position was weak – partly because of Britain's lack of official interest.

The international public battle about the fort underlines a McLuhanesque aspect of its history: its only significance concerned what was said about it. The governments of the two most concerned great powers, Britain and Germany, did not think it particularly important in strictly military terms. It was planned as a form of deterrence, and it fulfilled that purpose at remarkably low cost. The fort was never built. In 1912, the budget for the fort shrank from Fl. 40 million to Fl. 12 million. By wartime, the foundations had been laid, but Krupp did not deliver the required heavy guns.[128] The fort had fulfilled its mission, however. The same can be said of the rest of the

country's modest but improving military establishment. When 1914
arrived, the Netherlands was better prepared for war than it had been
a decade before.[i] Intent to resist had been signaled. Its survival still
depended on the goodwill of its powerful neighbors, however.
Knowing what those neighbors were up to was necessary: in the case
of Germany, it was essential.

---

[i] The role of the monarch here should not be overlooked. Wilhelmina pushed
constantly for military improvements. She even regarded The Hague peace conferences
and the domestic peace movement with a jaundiced eye, fearing they would interfere
with Dutch rearmament. "Her labors were not without result." Cees Fasseur,
Wilhelmina: De jonge koningin (Meppel: Balans, 1998), pp. 392-98, 448.

NOTES

[1] Imanuel Geiss, *German Foreign Policy, 1871-1914* (London: Routledge & Kegan Paul, 1976), p. 83.

[2] Howard to Lansdowne, 23 August 1905, 146, Smit, *Bescheiden ...,* Part 6, *Buitenlandse bronnen 1899-1914* ('s-Gravenhage: Martinus Nijhoff, 1968), p. 221.

[3] J.A.A.H. de Beaufort, *Vijftig jaren uit onze geschiedenis, 1868-1918* (Amsterdam: P.N. van Kampen & Zoon, 1928), part II, p. 89.

[4] C. Smit, *Nederland in de Eerste Wereldoorlog (1899-1919),* vol. 1, *Het voorspel (1899-1914)* (Groningen: Wolters-Noordhoff, 1971), p. 114.

[5] De Beaufort, *Vijftig jaren,* part II, pp. 93-94.

[6] Barnouw, *Holland,* p. 107.

[7] Karl Hampe, *Belgien und Holland vor dem Weltkriege* (Gotha: Friedrich Andreas Perthes, 1918), pp. 33, 37-38.

[8] Chief of Staff to Minister of War (Netherlands), 25 September 1906, Generale Staf, nr. toegang 2.13.15.01, inv nrs 252, 287, 290, 288, 305, 266, 265, 200. ARA-II.

[9] Moltke to Bülow, 23 February 1906, E. T. S. Dugdale, *German Diplomatic Documents, 1871-1914,* vol. 3, *The Growing Antagonism, 1898-1910* (New York: Barnes & Noble, 1969 (1930)), pp. 239-241.

[10] Smit, *Het voorspel,* pp. 121-22.

[11] According to Bethmann Hollweg, Kuyper later claimed that he had had fellow ARP'er Colijn propose a military alliance during the latter's war ministry (1911-1913), but this was categorically rejected by Belgium. It is highly doubtful that, even if such an offer were made (and Colijn did have an impulsive streak) that his cabinet, let alone the legislature, would have ever ratified such a treaty. Memorandum, Bethmann Hollweg, 18 April 1916, Duitse Ministerie van Buitenlandse Zaken, ARA-II.

[12] Gerhard Ritter, *The Schlieffen Plan: Critique of a Myth* (New York: Praeger, 1958 (Munich: Oldenbourg Verlag, 1956), pp. 43, 48.

[13] David Stevenson, *Armaments and the Coming of War: Europe, 1904-1914* (New York: Oxford, 1996), p. 102.

[14] Wilhelm Groener, *Das Testament des Grafen Schlieffen: Operativen Studien über den Weltkrieg* (Berlin: Mittler, 1929 (1927)), pp. 209-10.

[15] T.H. Thomas, "Holland and Belgium in the German War Plan," *Foreign Affairs* 6 (January 1928), p. 316.

[16] Gerhard L. Weinberg, *A World at Arms: A Global History of World War II* (New York: Cambridge University Press, 1994), p. 109.

[17] Groener, *Testament,* p. 211, *passim.*

[18] See Paul Herre, "Die kleinen Staaten und die Entsehung des Weltkrieges," *Berliner Monatshefte* (July 1933), p. 667.

[19] Ritter, *The Schlieffen Plan,* p. 11.

[20] Holger H. Herwig, *The First World War: Germany and Austria-Hungary, 1914-1918* (London: Arnold, 1998), p. 50.

[21] Geiss, *German Foreign Policy,* p. 101.

[22] Ibid., p. 94.

[23] Norman Rich, *Friedrich von Holstein: Politics and Diplomacy in the Era of*

Bismarck and Wilhelm II (London: Cambridge University Press, 1965), pp. 101n, 305, 698.

[24] Alfred von Schlieffen, "War against France," December, 1905, in Ritter, *Schlieffen Plan*, p. 136.

[25] Smit, *Het voorspel*, pp. 20-21.

[26] Jehuda Wallach, *The Dogma of the Battle of Annihilation: The Theories of Clausewitz and Schlieffen and their Impact on the German Conduct of Two World Wars* (Westport, CT: Greenwood, 1986), p. 117n30.

[27] Captain "Ronduit," *De manoeuvre om Limburg: Eene studie over de strategische positie van Limburg* (Utrecht: Bruna, 1919), p. 8.

[28] Groener, *Testament*, p. 216.

[29] J.J.G. baron van Voorst tot Voorst, *Over Roermond! Een strategische studie* ('s-Gravenhage: H. P. de Swart & Zoon, 1923), p. 39.

[30] Schlieffen memorandum, February 1906, in Ritter, *Schlieffen Plan*, p. 161.

[31] Ritter, *Schlieffen Plan*, p. 79.

[32] Van Voorst tot Voorst, *Over Roermond*, pp. 44-45.

[33] Ibid., p. 10.

[34] E. Malcolm Carroll, *Germany and the Great Powers 1866-1914: A Study in Public Opinion and Foreign Policy* (Hamden, CT: Archon, 1966 (Prentice-Hall, 1938)), p. 609.

[35] Wallach, *Battle of Annihilation*, p. 139.

[36] Ritter, *Schlieffen Plan*, pp. 74-75.

[37] Ibid., pp. 174-75.

[38] Schlieffen memorandum, December 28, 1912, in Ritter, *Schlieffen Plan*, p. 178.

[39] Van Voorst tot Voorst, *Over Roermond*, p. 6.

[40] Memorandum, Permanente Militaire Spoorweg Commissie, 23 Feb. 1882, Generale Staf, Nr. toegang 2.13.15.01, inv. nr. 68, ARA-II.

[41] Porter, "Dutch Neutrality," pp. 95-96.

[42] J. Buijs, "De spoorbrug bij Roermond: Oorzaak van Nederlandse neutraliteit in 1914?"*Militaire Spectator* 161 (September 1992), p. 411.

[43] N. Bosboom, *In moeilijke omstandigheden: Augustus 1914 – Mei 1917* (Gorinchem: J. Noorduyn & Zoon, 1933), p. 23.

[44] Ibid., p. 23.

[45] See for example, André Beening, "Onder de vleugels van de adelaar: De Duitse buitenlandse politiek ten aanzien van Nederland in de periode 1890–1914" (Ph.D. Dissertation: University of Amsterdam, 1994), p. 279n.

[46] "Vervolg van de punten van bespreking bij de strategische oefeningen (1906)," Koninklijke Landmacht – Algemeen Hoofdkwartier, nr toegang 2.13.15.01, inv nrs 247, 251, 256, 265, 275, ARA-II; W. Klinkert, "Verdediging van de zuidgrens 1914-1918 (Part 1)," *Militaire Spectator* 156 (June 1987), pp. 213-214; "Mobilisatie" (19 December 1908), Koninklijke Landmacht – Archief van het Veldleger, ARA-II; "Aanwijzingen voor het veldleger" (n.d. but 1908 or 1909), Koninklijke Landmacht – Algemeen Hoofdkwartier, ARA-II.

[47] Inspector of cavalry to War Minister, 1 October 1906, Generale Staf, nr. toegang 2.13.15.01, inv. nr. 251, ARA-II.

[48] Deployment maps, 1906, Generale Staf, nr. toegang 2.13.15.01, inv. nr. 345, ARA-II.

[49] J. Grolleman and J. C. Ruiter, "Interne and externe invloeden op de legervorming in Nederland van 1870 tot 1920" (Breda: Koninklijke Militaire Academie, 1981.

Unpublished paper), p. 24; Smit, *Het voorspel*, 147-48; British legation, annual report for 1909, 174, Smit, *Buitenlandse bronnen 1899-1914*, pp. 282-89.

[50] Buijs, "De spoorbrug," pp. 414-15.

[51] C J. Snijders, "Nederland's militaire positie gedurende den wereldoorlog," *Militaire Spectator* 92 (September 1923), p. 539.

[52] Contracts of the Ministry of War, nr. toegang 2.13.03, ARA-II.

[53] W.G.F. Snijders, *De wereldoorlog op het Duitsche westfront* (Amsterdam: Maatschappij voor Goede en Goedkope Literatuur, 1922), p. 344.

[54] Ritter, *Schlieffen Plan*, pp. 73, 79; Schlieffen, "War against France," pp. 136-37.

[55] Bernhard von Bülow, quoted in De Leeuw, *Nederland in de wereldpolitiek*, p. 66.

[56] Memorandum of Alfred von Schlieffen, 1911 (comments on General Windheim's plan) in Ritter, *Schlieffen Plan*, p. 184; Eugen Bircher and Walter Bode, *Schlieffen: Mann und Idee*(Zurich: Albert Nauck, 1937), pp. 199-200.

[57] Ritter, *Schlieffen Plan*, p. 73.

[58] Arden Bucholz, *Moltke, Schlieffen, and Prussian War Planning* (Oxford: Berg, 1991), p. 203.

[59] Alfred von Schlieffen, Memorandum, December 28, 1912, in Ritter, *Schlieffen Plan*, p. 182.

[60] Rich, *Holstein*, p. 768n1.

[61] E.T.S. Dugdale, *German Diplomatic Documents, 1871-1914*, vol. 4, *The Descent into the Abyss, 1911-1914* (London: Harper & Brothers, 1931), p. 162.

[62] Memorandum, Bethmann-Hollweg, December 19 1912, ibid., pp. 259-61.

[63] Herwig, *First World War*, p. 101.

[64] W. Klinkert, *Het vaderland verdedigd: Plannen en opvattingen over de verdediging van Nederland 1871-1914* (Den Haag: Sectie Militaire Geschiedenis, 1992), pp. 422-23.

[65] Van Voorst tot Voorst, *Over Roermond*, p. 48.

[66] Ritter, *Schlieffen Plan*, p. 59.

[67] Von Moltke's margin notes on Schlieffen, "War against France," p. 137.

[68] De Leeuw, *Nederland in de wereldpolitiek*, p. 71.

[69] Major Martin Renner, "Die Rolle Hollands bei einem europäischen Kriege" (25 Nov. 1908), Duitse Ministerie van Buitelandse Zaken - Stukken betreffende Nederland, ARA-II.

[70] Porter, "Dutch Neutrality," pp. 81-82.

[71] It is not completely clear when Moltke made the decision. Evidence points to 1909, but he informed the foreign Office in 1908 that Holland would be left unmolested. See Beening, "Onder de vleugels," pp. 280, 280n.

[72] H. von Moltke, memorandum, 1911, in Ritter, *Schlieffen Plan*, p. 166.

[73] Fritz Fischer, *War of Illusions: German Policies from 1911 to 1914* (London: Chatto & Windus, 1975 (1969), p. 391. Snijders, *Wereldoorlog up het Duitsche westfront*, pp. 339, 341; Jules Sauerwein, "Neue Tatsachen über die Vorgeschichte des Weltkrieges," *Dreigliederung des Sozialen Organismus* 3 (12 October 1921), in Snijders, *Wereldoorlog op het Duitsche westfront*, p. 386.

[74] Eyre Crowe, minute on a telephone conversation from E. Goschen (Berlin) to E. Grey, 29 July 1914, 293, G.P. Gooch and Harold Temperley, eds., *British Documents on the Origins of the War, 1899-1914*, vol. 2 (London: His Majesty's Stationery Office, 1933 (1926), p. 186.

[75] Frey, *Der Erste Weltkrieg*, p. 363.

[76] Beening, "Onder de vleugels," pp. 378-79.

[77] Helmut Haeussler, *General William Groener and the Imperial German Army* (Madison: State Historical Society of Wisconsin, 1962), p. 41.

[78] D.H. Thomas, *The Guarantee of Belgian Independence and Neutrality in European Diplomacy, 1830's–1930's* (Kingston, RI: D. H. Thomas Publishing, 1983), p. 421.

[79] Helmuth von Moltke, *Erinnerungen Briefe Dokumente 1877-1916* (edited by Eliza von Moltke) (Stuttgart: Der Kommende Tag, 1922), p. 429.

[80] Wallach, *Battle of Annihilation*, pp. 93-94.

[81] Thomas, "Holland and Belgium," p. 318.

[82] De Marees van Swinderen to Loudon, 7 August 1914, 44, C. Smit, *Bescheiden betreffende de buitenlandse politiek van Nederland 1848-1919, Derde periode, 1899-1919*, pt. 4, *1914-1917* ('s-Gravenhage: Martinus Nijhoff, 1962), pp. 24-26.

[83] G.A.A.Alting von Geusau, *Onze weermacht te land* (Amsterdam: Ipenbuur & van Seldam, 1914 (1913), p. 7.

[84] Frey, *Der Erste Weltkrieg*, p. 38.

[85] Moltke Memorandum (1911), in Ritter, *Schlieffen Plan*, p. 166.

[86] Van Voorst tot Voorst, *Over Roermond*, pp. 14-15.

[87] Von Moltke, *Erinnerungen*, p. 16.

[88] Van Voorst tot Voorst, *Over Roermond*, pp. 6, 47-48, 50-51.

[89] Snijders, *De wereldoorlog op het Duitsche westfront*, p. 340.

[90] Bucholz, *Moltke, Schlieffen and Prussian War Planning*, p. 266.

[91] Herwig, *First World War*, p. 60.

[92] "Ronduit," *De manoeuvre om Limburg*, pp. 10-11.

[93] Van Voorst tot Voorst, pp. 12, 19.

[94] Scott D. Sagan, "1914 Revisited: Allies, Offense, and Instability," pp. 109-133 in Stephen Miller, Sean M. Lynn-Jones, and Stephen Van Evera, eds., *Military Strategy and the Origins of the First World War* (Princeton: Princeton University Press, 1991), p. 125.

[95] Basil H. Liddell Hart, foreword to Ritter, *Schlieffen Plan*, p. 8.

[96] Moltke, *Erinnerungen*, p. 431.

[97] Ritter, *Schlieffen Plan*, p. 58.

[98] Ritter, *Schlieffen Plan*, p. 69; Von Moltke, 1911 memorandum, in Ritter, *Schlieffen Plan*, pp. 166-67; Ernst Kabisch, *Lüttich: Deutschlands Schicksalsschritt in dem Weltkrieg* (Berlin: Otto Schlegel, 1936), 37; Stevenson, *Armaments*, p. 301.

[99] Erich von Ludendorff, *Ludendorff's Own Story, August 1914–November 1918*, vol. 1 (Freeport, NY: Books for Libraries Press, 1971 (1920), p. 1.

[100] Moltke, *Erinnerungen*, p. 432.

[101] See Jean Stengers, "Belgium," pp. 151-174 in Keith Wilson, ed., *Decision for War 1914* (New York: St. Martin's, 1995), pp. 158-59.

[102] Moltke, *Erinnerungen*, pp. 18, 432.

[103] Kabisch, *Lüttich*, pp. 27, 32.

[104] Van Voorst tot Voorst, *Over Roermond*, pp. 24-26.

[105] Ewald Banse, *Raum und Volk im Weltkriege* (Oldenbourg: Gerhard Stelling, 1932), pp. 163, 173, 177.

[106] Snijders, *De Wereldoorlog*, p. 91.

[107] Van Campen, "How and Why the Netherlands joined the Atlantic Alliance," p. 9.

[108] H.A.C. Fabius, "Mededelingen over de Duitsche operatiën," 8 December 1914, Hoofdkwartier Veldleger, nr. toegang 2.13.16; Inv. Nrs. 59, 128, 141. ARA-II.

[109] Porter, "Dutch Neutrality," p. 94; De Leeuw, *Nederland in de wereldpolitiek*, p. 139 (quoting from *British Documents* series).

[110] Beening, "Onder de vleugels," p. 366.

[111] Porter, "Dutch Neutrality," 96; Beening, "Onder de vleugels," p. 366.

[112] Stevenson, *Armaments*, p. 189.

[113] Snijders to Colijn, 16 November 1911, 276, and Gevers to De Marees van Swinderen, 16 January 1912, 277, Smit, *1907-1914*, pp. 719-20.

[114] W. Klinkert, "Oorlog in de Betuwe: De grote manoeuvres van September 1911," *Mededelingen van de Sectie Militaire Geschiedenis* 13 (1990), pp. 45, 46.

[115] Klinkert, "Oorlog in de Betuwe," pp. 58-60.

[116] J.P. de Valk and M. van Faassen, eds., *Dagboeken en aantekeningen van Willem Hendrik de Beaufort 1874–1918* ('s-Gravenhage: Instituut voor Nederlandse Geschiedenis, 1993), p. 589.

[117] De Leeuw, *Nederland in de wereldpolitiek*, p. 159.

[118] Klinkert, "Oorlog in de Betuwe," pp. 55-56.

[119] "Dienstinstructie" for Commander at Maastricht, No. 5, 1912, and Addendum, Archief van het Veldleger, ARA-II.

[120] Kühlmann to Bülow, 12 November 1908, in Duitse Ministerie van Buitenlandse Zaken – Stukken Betreffende Nederland, ARA-II.

[121] Beening, "Onder de vleugels," pp. 278-79n.

[122] Frey, *Der Erste Weltkrieg*, p. 34.

[123] Müller to Bethmann Hollweg, 4 February 1911, 103, Smit, *Buitenlandse bronnen 1899-1914*, pp. 149-51.

[124] Barnardiston to Grierson, 17 March 1906, Gooch and Temperley, *British Documents on the Origin of the War 1898-1914*, vol. 3, *The Testing of the Entente 1904-1906* (London: His Majesty's Stationery Office, 1928), pp. 193-95.

[125] Hampe, *Belgien und Holland*, p. 64.

[126] De Valk and van Faassen, *Dagboeken en aantekeningen*, pp. 530-31.

[127] J.A. van Hamel, *Nederland tusschen de mogendheden: De hoofdtrekken van het buitenlandsch belied en de diplomatieke geschiedenis van ons vaderland sinds deszelfs onafhankelijk volksbestaan onderzocht* (Amsterdam: Van Holkema & Warendorf, 1918), p. 444; Frey, *Der Erste Weltkrieg*, p. 363.

[128] De Leeuw, *Nederland in de wereldpolitiek*, pp. 133-34, 140-41; Müller to Bethmann Hollweg, 4 Feb. 1911, Duitse Ministerie van Buitenlandse Zaken – Stukken betreffende Nederland, ARA-II; Report by Major Renner, 6 January 1911, 98, Smit, *Buitenlandse bronnen 1899-1914*, p. 146.

CHAPTER THREE

API API[i]

Holland's need for information was not matched by any consistent effort to get it. Information gathering was informal. There was no formal military or civilian intelligence service until the eve of war. Yet, whether through accident, design, or remarkably good guessing, the Netherlands managed to be ahead of the curve, knowing about the coming war in the west before its neighbors, and was able to mobilize before any other western/central European country. Despite some involvement in the Balkans in 1914, Holland did not foresee the summer crisis any more than any other state did. But its reactions would be rapid, as was necessary if the small country was going to survive war's outbreak.

Quick mobilization was absolutely essential. First, it might deter an immediate German invasion (although, as a result of Moltke's change in the Schlieffen plan, this threat no longer existed). Second, a lack of defense might encourage Germany to move through the southern Netherlands even if that was *not* part of the original plan. Third, either Britain or Germany might view a lack of defensive effort as a reason to occupy Holland – not out of any latent hostility toward the Dutch, but to keep the country out of the hands of the enemy. Fourth, a failure to mobilize immediately would signal to the public that the crisis was not viewed as particularly serious, which would make it extremely difficult politically to mobilize later if invasion became more likely. Fifth, a later mobilization would have to occur when all belligerents had fully mobilized and could invade quickly. Holland is not Russia; trading space for time was not an option. Sixth, the whole defense of the country depended on slowing down an invader just enough to prepare the vaunted *waterlinie* – the flooded areas which would protect the western heartland. Seventh, strict neutrality demanded retaliation against neutrality violations in every corner of the country, and the regular army was much too small to accomplish this. Eighth, an undefended frontier would look like an inviting place for a defeated neighbor to cross while continuing to fight, which would inevitably

---

[i] "Fire" in Malayan.

culminate in pursuit by the victors and embroilment in the war. Ninth, a belated mobilization would be an easy and tempting target for interruption by a neighboring state. Finally, policing the border to deal with smuggling (and possibly espionage) required troops as well.

Holland had a major strategic problem: it could be destroyed easily in war against Germany, but its colonial empire was not defensible against Britain. Strict neutrality seemed to be the only hope – but this required quick and substantial mobilization *before* anyone could violate Dutch neutrality and give the non-violators an excuse to invade as well. Mobilization in turn required good intelligence. Holland would have to be in the field *before* the most likely aggressor(s) came out of the closet. Rapid mobilization depended on getting timely information. The information would have to be clear enough that the government would be willing to take the momentous step of mobilization. Parliament would have to be willing to pay the not inconsiderable bill, and civilians would have to accept disruption of their lives and the economy. Given popular hostility toward the military, this was not a given – and the government could not risk mobilization on just a rumor of war. On the other hand, responding to news reports from Reuters and Wolff would be too late.

Spies in wooden shoes

Yet information gathering was mostly informal. The army looked down on spying, and leading officials collected information in a haphazard way without writing down what they heard or who their sources were. They were every bit as secretive as their counterparts in the major powers.[1] Bosboom he at least revealed his discovery of the Schlieffen plan in his memoirs, but not his source. Most espionage, such as it was, was directed at Germany. Military information was collected at Aachen as far back as 1830. But there was very little substantial, on-going activity. Many countries began to collect information in an organized way after the Franco-Prussian War, but not Holland.[2] Minor powers are usually handicapped by their limited bureaucracy and intelligence specialization,[3] and this was especially so in Holland: intelligence was in as bad a shape in 1870 as the army.

The first Moroccan crisis had stimulated a little activity, including some cross-border trips by army officers to see what the Germans were up to. German troop movements received great attention. In general, the General Staff was pleased with these expeditions, but recognized that they were inadequate. Thiange, then still a colonel, called for improvements. A few things were done, including such administrative details as cataloging the number of carrier pigeons in towns near the border. But again, no organization was established to collect and analyze information. The General Staff had to make do with tidbits of information supplemented by educated guesses – although occasionally these were surprisingly accurate, such as the 1906 estimate of the size of the future British Expeditionary Force. Bosboom's singular discovery aside, there was no knowledge concerning neighboring states' war plans.[4] A border and coast guard was organized in 1910, and given the task of obtaining information in case of war – but its means were limited. And sources were not disclosed even in official classified communications. For example, in 1907 W.A.F. baron Gevers, Dutch envoy in Berlin 1906-1927, notified the foreign minister that German soldiers were fortifying Borkum Island, near the disputed Eems river mouth, an important piece of military-political information; but he gives absolutely no hint as to the source of his information.[5] This means that the foreign minister had no independent way of gauging the source's reliability, instead having to base his conclusions on the extent to which he trusted Gevers.

The army decided to use civilians in border areas, who could presumably slip into Belgium or Germany without attracting too much attention. Known as *kondschappers* (messengers), they were not expected to be true spies, ferreting out secret information. Instead, their job was to report public information. The idea was not new, as the first instruction for *kondschappers* dates from 1651. In the wake of the first Moroccan crisis, a *kondschapsdienst* (*dienst* = service) was organized in 1906 using civilian volunteers and trustworthy customs inspectors, who were in a good position to interview travelers. *Kondschappers* were expected to report troop strengths, regimental numbers, weapons, and even political feelings of civilians. They were to report everything, without exaggeration. Given that the *kondschapsdienst* was the only organized service for border penetration, it might be assumed that the army showed some enthusiasm for it, but this was not the case. For example, when one division commander reported in 1909 that his headquarters did not have enough badges for all his *kondschappers* (the badge was the only recognition of these usually unpaid volunteers), he was simply told not to give all of them badges.[6]

Nevertheless the *kondschapsdienst* soldiered on, in one form or another.[ii] Detailed instructions were prepared for funneling expense money to the border guards for the *kondschappers*. Both Snijders and Bosboom apparently had high hopes for their civilian "observers," but they would be disappointed. Once northern Belgium was occupied by the Germans, kondschappers trying to enter were turned back. Later, "slipping across the border" would become virtually impossible after the Germans installed a high-voltage electric fence. The head of the then brand new military intelligence service thought the *kondschapsdienst* was a failure, but one of his subordinates thought it was still better than having paid agents (there is no way to tell whether this was because volunteers were more reliable, or because they were cheaper).[7] Snijders apparently did make occasional use of visitors to gain information about the situation in Belgium. For example, he asked a Mr. Wijnmalen, a civilian, to enter Belgium on his behalf in August 1914, although not just to spy; Wijnmalen spent most of his time getting airplane parts and even a whole airplane out of Belgium for the Dutch army.[8]

Yet the soldiers also had a penchant for gathering information by traveling across the border. Typical of these trips were those undertaken during the second Moroccan crisis by a young captain and future general, Willem Röell. On July 31 and August 5, Röell traveled by rail into Germany, reporting little unusual activity but noting the presence of some reservists.

Apparently the army was still concerned. At 7:15 p.m. on August 29, the chief of staff of the 2nd Division at Arnhem relayed instructions from the minister of war for another observation trip. Röell left Arnhem two hours later for Düsseldorf, where he gathered information by the simple expedient of striking up a conversation with some German soldiers at an area army post. Except for a short nap on the morning of the 31st, Röell remained on the move, reconnoitering Cologne, Coblenz, Trier, and points in between in a 36 hour period, and sat down to write his report as soon as he returned.

At Düsseldorf Röell saw little to alarm him, but was more concerned by the number and classes of reservists who had arrived at the VIII corps (the VII and VIII at Cologne were of particular interest to

---

[ii] The paper trail of this service is confusing because reports of cross-border trips even by officers were sometimes labeled as *kondschaps* reports even though as soldiers, they were not members of the *kondschapsdienst*.

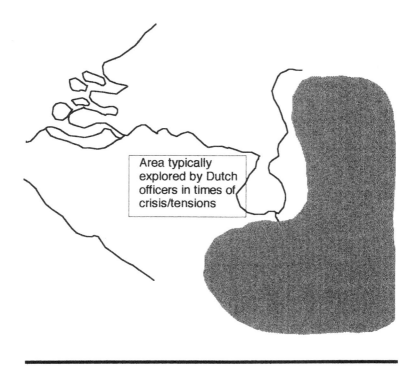

Area typically explored by Dutch officers in times of crisis/tensions

Dutch officers traveled by train to Dusseldorf, Cologne, Coblenz, and Aachen, and entered Belgium by automobile in times of crisis to check on possible German army movements.

the Dutch army because of their proximity to the route that would take them through the southern Netherlands into Belgium: at least one German plan had them doing precisely that[9]). Coblenz was quiet, but at the VIII corps garrison at Trier he again noted a large number of reservists. More significantly, he noted two regiments at Trier not normally stationed there, and part of another had been sent to reinforce another division (which he learned from a soldier who, according to Röell, spoke bad German but good French). As he traveled back to the north, he sought more information about the VII corps, located closest to the Netherlands, and found that its units were moving away, to the east, for maneuvers at Paderborn. Röell was not reassured by this, and he urged further observation of the VII corps. He also noted the presence of extra war materiel at the rail yards near Cologne, Coblenz and Moers.[10]

The army's reaction to Röell's travels is not easy to gauge. The first written response to his August 29-31 trip dealt with an unrelated bureaucratic matter before noting the divisional commander's interest. On the other hand, the war minister was very interested in Röell's observations and expressed his satisfaction with them.[11] (It should be noted that the Germans were not unaware that their troop movements would be noticed.[12]) Fortunately (for the Dutch anyway), when war arrived, the VIII corps was railroaded southward into Luxembourg, instead of westward into Holland.[13]

The 1911 Moroccan crisis and the German army's activity led to some additional intelligence-gathering activity, but many organizational and institutional problems remained. When General Snijders showed up unexpectedly at the legation in Berlin in the summer of 1911, he found that the staff knew absolutely nothing about German war preparations. Sending officers abroad, even on completely aboveboard missions, was not always easy.[iii] Time had to be wasted filtering through many rumors and tips that were little better than garbage, such

---

[iii] The Austrians, of all people, were particularly secretive, demanding to be informed *à temps* of any Dutch military missions to Austria. The appearance of a Dutch officer in Steyr in 1912 caused a diplomatic incident – even though the officer was there merely to inspect ammunition for the Royal Dutch Indies Army (KNIL). Austro-Hungarian Legation to Netherlands Foreign Ministry, 29 January 1912: Idem, 30 April 1912; Secretary-General, Ministry of Colonies, to Foreign Minister, 10 May 1912, Ministerie van Buitenlandse Zaken, nr toegang 2.05.03, inv. nrs 640, 641, 643, ARA-II.

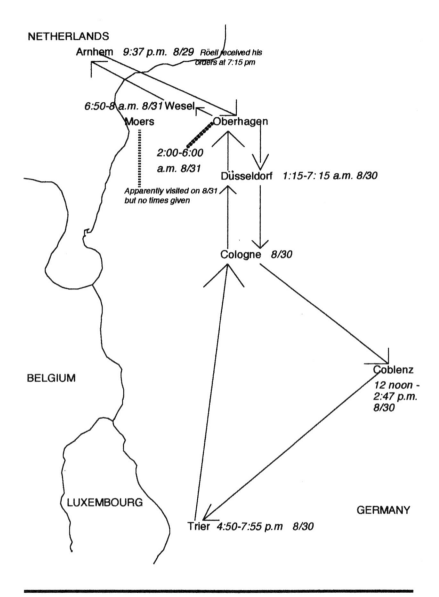

Captain Röell's 1911 visit to Germany. The Dutch army considered this observation, not espionage.

as the one received by Bosboom in 1913 from an "espionage bureau" in Switzerland that the German army was planning to march through the northeastern provinces of Groningen and Friesland. Bosboom wondered whether this was a complete swindle (money was requested for the tip) or an attempt to dislocate the army's planned deployment.[14] There was no organization to analyze the information.

Snijders' irritation about the Berlin visit led him to push for the appointment of military attachés, but this rather modest proposal initially went nowhere. Gevers worried that the appointment of an attaché in Berlin would appear as if Holland were getting closer to Germany, unless one also was sent to Paris. He also pointed out that mobilization plans in Germany were very secret and that they would begin without advance preparations, so there was nothing fur an attaché to find out – or observe. The foreign minister took Gevers' side, and the war minister (Colijn) decided that the issue was no longer of paramount importance. By early 1912 the issue of attachés was dead.[15]

This was wholly unfortunate, because – espionage aside – it left the Dutch army with too little information about progress in military science. The sending of officers to observe maneuvers and military academy classes was not enough.[iv] Germany did permit attendance at maneuvers and even visits to military academies, the latter something prohibited by the Austrians. Even if foreign visits were allowed by the host state, there were always problems of expense, personnel availability, health, etc. In addition, in times of crisis – when information was most needed – even accommodating hosts might be less so. In the tense time of the summer of 1911, a visiting Dutch officer was allowed only

---

[iv] Officers also went abroad to order and inspect weapons purchases, as Holland did not have a defense industry. These officers could also pick up information. Sometimes this practice had unintended consequences, however. In late 1913 a Captain E. Altman Jansen appeared at the doors of the Apple Electric Company claiming to represent the Dutch government and expressing an interest in the company's products. He was wined, dined and housed at company expense for a few nights, after which he disappeared. The company contacted the Dutch legation in Washington, DC, which dutifully investigated the captain's background. Not surprisingly, no ministry – War, Navy, or Colonies – had heard of him. He was a complete impostor and left no tracks. J.M. Figee to Washington legation, 21 Feb. 1914, and correspondence between Foreign Ministry and War, Navy and Colonial Ministries, and Washington legation, 25-28 February 1914, Buitenlandse Zaken, nr toegang 2.05.03, inv. nrs. 640, 641, 643, ARA-II.

one day's visit to the German artillery school – leading the Dutch to withdraw the request and send the officer to France instead.[16]

Still, the prewar period finally saw the belated establishment of a formal military intelligence service. With no attachés and no organized intelligence service, Snijders' knowledge of military affairs on the continent had some rather large holes in it. This became apparent when Colijn started to ask the general all sorts of questions which Snijders could not answer. (Snijders had already complained that he was dependent on newspapers and magazines or whatever the various ministries would send him for information.) Snijders did not reach his army's highest position by being naive about bureaucratic politics, and he made use of this seeming embarrassment by recommending the organization of a military intelligence service.[17]

At some point in 1913[v] a Captain H.K. Hardenberg was ordered to start gathering information on foreign military establishments; technically he is the first known chief of GS-III, army intelligence (he may have had a predecessor; the records are unclear). In September the size of the new organization's officer complement doubled when Lt. H.A.C. Fabius joined Hardenberg, but the latter left at mobilization. The beginning of the organization was not auspicious. Some soldiers' prejudice against espionage extended to GS-III. GS-III did not develop its own agents. It would have been difficult anyway. Many leading figures, including Snijders, had private contacts in neighboring countries to keep them informed about important events. Other branches of the army apparently also had foreign contacts. These relationships did not end, nor were these contacts/agents handed over to GS-III when it was created.[18]

There was one other activity that involved the intelligence "apparatus," and that was counter-espionage. Of course, this mostly involved dealing with foreign agents spying *in* Holland rather than *on* Holland. The major powers had only a limited interest in the Dutch military, although German diplomats occasionally filed reports on the condition and morale of the army have survived. There was also the extremely curious case in 1910 when the German envoy asked the Netherlands to overlook "accidental" frontier crossings by Prussian topographers. The request struck the Dutch war and foreign affairs ministries as "curious," especially because the topographers would be working in the

---

[v] The exact date is not known.

military sensitive area between Aachen and Roermond, and because the Dutch were being asked to let the topographers continue to work even *after* they had been notified that they were on the wrong side. The German was told that a rare involuntary crossing would cause no trouble, but that was the extent of it. The Brussels legation also reported several claims (1911-12) that Dutch military documents were being leaked to German agents. These were never verified but it is interesting that the stories came to the legation from several different sources. The military was also worried by 1913 that its most sensitive fortifications were easily accessible to the public and increasingly vulnerable to air observation.[19]

Foreign spies working in Holland against other foreign states were a greater concern, however. They were difficult to control because if (for example) a Britisher was spying on Germany from Holland, he was not a spy under Dutch law. The real danger was that if his activity went unchallenged, Germany might claim that Holland was not protecting its neutrality – especially if Dutchmen got involved. This concern preceded the war. In 1913, a retired naval officer, identified only as De Paauw, was approached by an Englishman, Demetrius C. Boulger, who wanted De Paauw to spy on Germany. They were near Nijmegen, but De Paauw had the impression that the British were also active near Venlo, in Limburg. The Englishman promised to "meet your wishes in any way." Boulger was unpleasantly surprised to discover that his contact had been a German consular agent and had been decorated by Germany.[20]

The 1914 crisis and the Netherlands

The Dutch government knew little about the machinations that converted the assassination of the heir to the Austrian throne into a world war, at least until July 25, 1914, when evidence would reach The Hague showing that continental war was imminent. The occurrence of an assassination in the Balkans, however, surprised no one. Certainly not the Serbian government, whose monarchy had gained power through assassination in 1903 and which even warned Vienna not to send Franz Ferdinand to Sarajevo.[21] Certainly not the Dutch, who – in an event with eerily modern overtones – were involved in a peacekeeping operation in Albania. That operation was not a success. An insurgency developed against Prince Wilhelm of Wied, the German ruler of the fledgling state. Just over a week before Franz Ferdinand's death, a Dutch Lt. Col. L.W.J.K. Thomson was killed during a riot, an event that drew a major reaction in Holland. Thomson was a popular officer and fairly well known political figure with a somewhat anti-German bent. A few suspected Italy of complicity in his death.[22] The situation was further complicated by the capture of two other Dutch officers by the insurgents, released only in September after extensive negotiations via Turkey.[23] Holland needed no further education about the dangers of the Balkans.

The Dutch did not expect Franz Ferdinand's death to lead to 10 million more, however. How the Balkan crisis led to World War I is well beyond the scope of this book. As much of this study examines Holland's location in the European diplomatic system of the time, however, we cannot ignore a different question: why was the diplomatic system unable to contain the crisis? Diplomacy could not deal with a situation in which some powers were unwilling to allow diplomacy to work. Until 1914, traditional diplomacy worked fairly well. According to David Vital, its drawbacks were obvious. Yet while it was little concerned with justice, and left no room for those outside the system, it was not without merit:

> The nineteenth century international system was not an attractive one
> . . . But it did have its logic; . . . What doomed it was not so much its
> faulty structure, but rather as we know the unanticipated and perverse
> refusal of one or two of its major participants and beneficiaries to abide
> by its rules and to maintain them in working order.[24]

The "failure to abide by its rules" refers primarily to the Central Powers, whose surviving member would be blamed at Versailles for the catastrophe. Whether this was justified or not, it is unquestionably true that the governments of Germany and Austria were pessimistic about their strategic futures and were willing to take advantage of the situation to alter what they regarded as a nearly hopeless situation. Militarism and the military were powerful in Germany, while the Foreign Office was correspondingly weak. The *Auswärtiges Amt* was technically not a ministry and its chief was not a minister, but a *Staatssekretar* and hence a civil servant. As a result, he did not have the *Immediatrecht,* the right to see the Kaiser directly – while numerous soldiers did. The minister responsible for foreign policy was the Chancellor, whose attention was often diverted elsewhere. While none of this directly influenced the events of July, 1914 – the Foreign Office and the military did not hold divergent views – it did influence the overall relationship between civilian and military policy-makers where foreign policy was concerned. Certainly no overtly anti-militaristic official could have held much sway in Berlin. In addition, it may explain why German policy seemed so obscure to British war minister R. B. Haldane who, on his visit to Berlin in 1912, remarked that "at the head of this highly organized people one finds confusion."[25] This confusion would be much in evidence at crucial moments in 1914 in Berlin.[vi]

Perhaps the strongly military view of world affairs explains why important figures in the Central Powers governments expected war and were not trying to avoid it. By the beginning of 1914, little of this was known, more was suspected. Gevers thought the situation precarious and did not think Germany would wait while France strengthened its army through the 3-year service law (his equanimous foreign minister, John Loudon, as usual was less pessimistic). Prince Karl Max von Lichnowsky, German ambassador in London, heard in the spring of 1914 that his counterpart in Vienna thought war imminent.[26] As the latter[vii] did not have a reputation as a militarist or warmonger, he must have been reflecting opinion in either Vienna or Berlin. The soldiers were equally pessimistic. The German and Austrian chiefs of staff, Moltke and Franz Conrad von Hötzendorff, met on 12 May and saw war as "imminent and unavoidable." Moltke shortly thereafter advised Jagow to conduct a war-provoking policy. On June 16, Quartermaster-General Alfred von Waldersee informed the German states not to send written reports to their war ministries; General Staff emissaries would soon come and explain this step. (As will be seen, this may be critical in explaining Holland's early knowledge of the coming German mobilization.) The French later accused the German army of having made abnormally large purchases on May of 1914. Recent scholarship has described Germany's actions as proof that it (and Austria) had "opted for war" while engaging "in a cover-up which to the present day

---

[vi] It probably did not help that Gottlieb von Jagow, the foreign secretary, was about to get married. Goschen to Grey, 16 June 1914, 218, Kenneth Bourne and D. Cameron Watt, eds. *British Documents on Foreign Affairs: Reports and Papers from the Foreign Office Confidential Print.* Part I: *From the Mid-Nineteenth Century to the First World War War.* Series F: *Europe, 1848-1914* (ed. David Stevenson), vol. 21, *Germany, 1909-1914* (Washington, DC: University Publications of America, 1990), pp. 411-12.

[vii] Heinrich von Tschirschky und Bögendorff.

has confused historians over German intentions." Theobald von Bethmann Hollweg, Reich Chancellor 1909-17, unintentionally reinforced this belief by stating that "we must give the impression of being forced into war," leading a senior naval officer to proclaim jubilantly when war came that "[t]he mood is brilliant. The government has succeeded very well in making us appear as the attacked."[27]

Except for a few figures like the well-connected Gevers, few Dutchmen had any inkling of the growing bellicosity and fear in the Central Powers. Some diplomats had vague realizations that the situation was unusually delicate. M.W.R. van Vollenhoven, stationed in Brussels, recalled in his memoirs that when he was posted to St. Petersburg, the German ambassador (then Count von Mirbach) told him that "if Berchtold ever becomes Minister of Foreign Affairs, I would not give a *Pfennig* for peace in Europe." No doubt Van Vollenhoven was a bit unnerved when Berchtold indeed did become Foreign Minister for the Dual Monarchy, but like his countrymen, he had no specific expectation of war at a particular time. Even in July 1914, knowledge of the danger was slow to develop. Much of what happened in the first three weeks of July was secret, and the affected governments took pains to keep it so. No one knew the extent to which Germany was encouraging Austria to take a hard line in July. As late as June 30, Tschirschky was counseling Austria to avoid "rash steps," to the German emperor's outrage. Wilhelm was able to put things right, however, by giving the infamous "blank check" to Austria on July 5, essentially assuring Austria of full support regardless of what it did to Serbia. The Emperor did this despite the absence of any military advisors, and even though the Austrian emperor, Franz Josef, assured him that the Serbian government was not involved in the assassination.[viii] In no way should Wilhelm's action be interpreted as a rash, impulsive, and unauthorized action. He granted the blank check conditioned on Bethmann Hollweg's approval, which the latter gave on July 6.[28]

None of this is proof of a grand design for a European war. Germany's apparently wanted to resolve the Balkan crisis in Austria's favor, effectively forcing Russia out of Serbia, and to do so without interference from the west (although war with France and Russia was perfectly acceptable). Hence, from the perspective of Germany's

---

[viii] Ironically, Franz Josef was wrong.

western neighbors, including the Dutch, all seemed quiet. To keep it that way and also keep the initiative, the German government adopted two important steps. First, a campaign of disinformation began. Wilhelm and Bethmann Hollweg deliberately left Berlin, to lull outside observers into believing that they were uninvolved in Austria's plans and the drafting of the ultimatum. The Emperor also canceled a visit to Vienna, allegedly because of Franz Josef's health. (An astonishing number of leaders were out of town when the Austro-Serbian war began; Wilhelm was in Norway, French President Raimond Poincaré was elsewhere in Scandinavia, Snijders was traveling in Germany and Scandinavia, and the Emperor's brother and the British prime minister were also out of town.)[29] As the crisis intensified toward the end of the month, the Foreign Office reassured the British that Germany was attempting to restrain Austria and was willing to accept mediation. In doing so Jagow deceived both his own ambassador, who would later write a furious indictment of the *Auswärtiges Amt's* behavior, and the British foreign secretary. Jagow's deception worked brilliantly for a while, but the result for Germany was, in the long run, negative. If Britain had issued a clear warning, German policy might have changed. Yet it is not fair to blame British Foreig n Secretary Edward Grey for the failure to do so, although he often has been. In fact, "the British failure to warn Germany was due as much to German secrecy as to British indecision . . . the ambiguity of British policy should be recognized as an artifact of the secret styles of the Central Powers . . ."[30] Grey did suspect the the deception but was unable to act on the basis of a mere suspicion. Britain's lack of action lulled the Netherlands further into the belief that the whole thing was another Balkan-related spat.

   This outlook would change drastically on 25 July, possibly because of early, military preparations in Germany. The military may not have been present Wilhelm and Bethmann issued the blank check, but was consulted almost immediately, probably on July 6. Representatives of the General Staff, War Ministry, Admiralty Staff and Naval Ministry consulted with the Emperor and "decided in any case to take prepara-tory measures for a war. Appropriate orders were thereupon issued."[31] On July 11 Tschirschky, who was now pressuring Berchtold to take "quick action," wrote Jagow about the demands to be made on Serbia, the 48-hour time limit, and the decision to mobilize if the Serbian reply was not satisfactory. The note would not be delivered while Poincaré was in St. Petersburg, as this would facilitate a joint Franco-Russian response. Tschirschky and Berchtold decided that the 24th might be a good date as the earlier time would facilitate mobilization.

> I may conclude by saying that the Minister and Count Forgach, who was present at this conference, begged me *not* to telegraph in regard to the preceding and mention it only in private letters, in order that absolute secrecy may be assured. I got the impression that the gentlemen feared a leak *here in Austria* if I should telegraph in cipher.[32]

Tschirschky and the Austrians may have been right about the leak, as will be seen later. But why did Tschirschky push for such a risky Austrian policy? Lichnowsky was not the only one who described Tschirschky as fairly moderate. Late in the war, the view that Germany had pressured Austria was dismissed as a ploy by "people right here in the Ball[haus]platz,[ix] also, who would be glad to load the guilt of the war on to us, and who invent fairy tales of this kind."[33]

Germany's continued to operate in secret. The emperor remained out of town, although Jagow carefully tracked the imperial yacht *Hohenzollern's* itinerary in case Wilhelm had to order mobilization. The deception of the London embassy continued. Bethmann Hollweg told Lichnowsky that war was unlikely. Jagow explained that Russia would remain quiescent if Germany supported Austria, but more candidly stated that "Austria . . can hardly be counted any longer as a fulfledged Great Power." He then less candidly added, "[w]e have an alliance with Austria (this can't be helped)," thereby creating in Lichnowsky's mind the image of a German government reluctantly and honorably supporting a weak ally. Tschirschky and his staff, of course, knew better. Jagow had informed him on July 18 that the semi-official *North-German Gazette* would not do anything to create premature alarm, and that Vienna should not interpret this as a German "withdrawal." On that same day, the Vienna embassy, again by letter, informed Jagow that the note would be presented on the 23rd, and that the hope was that the demands would not be accepted, The Austrians assured the Germans "that the demands are of such a nature that, for a state which has any self-respect and dignity left, it would be impossible to accept them."[34] Had this letter become public, mobilization everywhere, including in Holland, would have ensued immediately. For the next few days, however, most of the continent remained blissfully

---

[ix] The Austrian foreign ministry.

unaware of the storm that would break on the 23rd.

The infamous demands were handed to Serbia that day, late enough that St. Petersburg would not know before Poincaré left. European diplomacy went into overdrive, but was unable to stop a crisis which was poorly understood beyond its immediate confines. Lichnowsky, for example, saw the event exactly as Jagow wished – as a crisis precipitated by Austria with a reluctant Germany in support. Jagow explained to Wilhelm that:

> Your Majesty's Ambassador at London is to receive instructions, for the guidance of his conversation, to the effect that we did not know the Austro-Hungarian demands, but considered them to be an internal question of Austria-Hungary upon which we could exert no influence.[35]

Lichnowsky pointed out to Jagow that Russia was weak, that Germany's foreign policy was producing pro-Russian reactions in England and France, and that Austria's aggressive Balkan policy would neither solve its internal problems nor weaken Slav nationalism (the reverse was more likely). Presciently, he argued that "localization . . . belongs in the realm of pious wishes."[36]

Paradoxically, what Jagow was trying to do would have worked in Holland's favor – unknown to the Dutch, and unintended by Jagow. The Netherlands would be far better off in a European conflict if Britain remained neutral (at least in the short run. In the long run, if France entered the war and was defeated, the continent would be entirely German dominated). Nor was Jagow's balancing act a complete impossibility. Since Waterloo Britain had a limited history of continental intervention and was, according to a report he received on the 24th, focused primarily on the crisis in Ulster. That very day, however, his scheme began to unravel. Lichnowsky reported that Grey was upset about the time limit and that the note exceeded anything he had ever seen. Berchtold was having no luck trying to hold off the Russians, despite telling the Russian chargé that "every humiliation of Serbia has been carefully avoided in the note to Serbia." The Austrians also nearly blew Germany's "cover" in the situation by suggesting that Germany hand Austria's declaration of war to the Serbs. Naturally Jagow did not think much of the idea.[37]

The following day, July 25th, was a critical date for the history of the war, and also for the Netherlands' effort to avoid it. The ultimatum to Serbia would expire that evening, and Holland would get a clandestine warning (discussed below) that war was on its way. Although it was a

Saturday, no diplomats were taking the day off. The Germans continued to deny any role in the note to Serbia. Baron Schoen, ambassador
in Paris, telegraphed twice on the 25th that he had attempted to quash
rumors of a joint démarche. Lichnowsky warned Jagow that the British
government viewed Germany as "at least morally responsible in part"
for the note to Serbia. Grey was willing to mediate, but was requesting
a time extension, which Jagow rejected as too late. Lichnowsky warned
Jagow that Britain would not remain "uninterested" if France were
drawn in and the mediation offer was rejected. He dutifully repeated
this warning after yet another talk with Grey, and tried to explain to
Jagow that Britain would not accept an expedition against Serbia.
Jagow again pointed out that "an increase of the time limit will not be
possible." A frustrated Lichnowsky could only point out that Grey's
proposals were the last possibility for settlement. Of course, Jagow was
in a difficult position. He could not now tell Lichnowsky that a
settlement was precisely what Berlin and Vienna wanted to avoid, and
as for leaving France out – one of the things that would have kept
Britain neutral – that was simply impossible under Germany's war
plan.[38]

Mediation had already been rejected the previous day when a
British journalist, E.J. Dillon, a friend of Berchtold's, had offered to
act as intermediary, which Berchtold had refused "as he was absolutely
determined not to enter upon any negotiations." Berchtold simultaneously assured the Russian ambassador that he was taking purely
defensive measures, but rejected Russian requests for a delay. The
Russians apparently were more trusting than the British, or at least
pretended to be; on the 25th, the Russian chargé asked Germany to urge
Austria to delay. In fact, delays and mediation were all impossible, and
this was clear to those who mattered by the end of the day. Wilhelm II
issued fleet readiness orders at 9:30 a.m. on the 25th, clearly indicating
he thought war with Britain was possible. Bethmann Hollweg was
horrified, as he thought the British fleet was dispersing from peacetime
maneuvers (he was wrong). When the Russian foreign minister
informed Jagow that an Austrian attack on Serbia meant war, the
Emperor scribbled in the margin: "Well, go to it!" By evening, Austria
had rejected the Serbian response to the ultimatum and the Serbs had
begun to mobilize.[39]

From this point on the crisis entered a new dimension, again for the
Netherlands as well as the future combatants. War was now inevitable.
Britain's entry into that war was also inevitable, for two reasons. First,

Britain's diplomatic efforts in the preceding week had been bluntly rejected by a deceptive German foreign office, setting up an intense hostility. Second, the German war plan called for an offensive against Britain's most important ally (France), and a neutral vital to British interests (Belgium). For the Dutch, life on the edge of the proverbial gunpowder barrel was now foreordained. Russia began a preliminary mobilization either late on the 25th or early on the 26th. Austria appointed a commander in chief of the armed forces, a wartime appointment. The Dutch embassy in Vienna also reported that Russia and France were demanding postponement of any active measures against Serbia, and was assured by the *Ballhausplatz* that the *Entente* countries were unlikely to intervene. Apparently this was half-believed in Germany, where the Admiralty staff reported on the 27th that although Russia was getting ready, there was no evidence of preparations in England.[x] The hapless Lichnowsky, still being used as part of the German disinformation campaign, told Grey that Germany in principle accepted four-power mediation, although it would support Austria if the latter were attacked.[40]

Still, public opinion in Holland appeared to expect a localized war, even after Austria declared war on Serbia on the 28th. The government knew better. Loudon, as careful a foreign minister as there was in Europe in 1914, was taking no chances. On Monday 27 July, Loudon contacted the Belgians to discuss possible joint action in case of a German invasion. Paradoxically, it was the Belgians who refused to talk. On Wednesday, Loudon informed the Belgians of the intent to mobilize, and that the Meuse bridges would be mined. However, Germany would soon make clear that it had very different plans for the two low countries. Bethmann Hollweg informed the British that same day that Germany would respect Holland's neutrality but that its attitude toward Belgium depended on what actions France would take there – a lie that lost some of its impact as the British government no longer believed assurances from Berlin. In fact, no governmental statements could alter two simple facts concerning Germany's plans. First, as the whole war plan depended on the capture of Liège, the discovery by Germany on Thursday that Belgium was preparing its

---

[x] The Admiralty may have misled either itself or the readers of its report here. As Britain did not intend to mobilize a huge conscript army, it would not have to make the same level and kind of preparations that the continental countries required.

defenses increased the need to attack rapidly. Second, Germany did not have a "mobilization" plan – it had a "mobilization and attack" plan (ever since Von Schlieffen), and once it was in motion, even sincere diplomatic assurances would be meaningless.[41]

Jagow, however, tenaciously stuck to his strategy to avoid the long-feared situation in which Germany would simultaneously face all its potential adversaries. On August 3, he informed Lichnowsky that the Germans had not crossed the frontier into France, but that France had attacked across the German frontier. The following day, he told Lichnowsky that Germany would not annex Belgium, and gave as evidence that Germany had pledged respect for Dutch neutrality and could not profit from annexing Belgium without acquiring Dutch territory as well.[xi] There was some truth in this assertion, especially concerning the sensitive territory along the Schelde river, which the Dutch closed partially on August 4. This showed willingness to resist Britain, pleasing the Germans. The British government, on the other hand, indicated it expected the small neutrals to resist Germany and to expect British support, if that were necessary. Britain also indicated (on August 5) that it would use the Schelde to provision Antwerp. Fortunately the Dutch were able to come to a diplomatic arrangement that satisfied the Belgians and the British for the moment. Less success was obtained at the country's other end, where the long-running dispute with Germany over the Eems river valley still festered. When German warships began mining the entire river, Gevers had the presence of mind to inform Germany that the Dutch government regarded the border dispute as *opgeschort,* suspended, resolved. His government came to same conclusion, as otherwise the Dutch would have to have declared war on Germany.[42] Fortunately no *Entente* country regarded this as a Dutch failure to defend neutrality.

The telegram

The July crisis had seen Holland move quickly from the strategic periphery to the center. To German *Weltpolitik* practitioners, Britain was the main enemy – even though it was their sincere desire to wage

---

[xi]   Jagow considered threatening Britain with occupation of Holland, which he regarded as doomed like all other small states. Frey, *Der Erste Weltkrieg,* p. 377.

war in Europe without British interference. It was Britain that stood most obviously between Germany and dreams of world imperial stature. German officials might fear and despise Russia, or worry about French *revanchism,* but ultimately it was those nations' alliance with Britain that made them threatening. With a rising Russia and a declining Austria, it is understandable that figures as diverse as Moltke and Bethmann Hollweg feared a German decline and hence maneuvered in 1914 to either strengthen their ally or, if necessary, destroy their continental adversaries, enabling them then to compete on equal footing with Britain.

So Holland lay between Europe's two most powerful and most hostile major states, making intelligence gathering even more vital. GS-III was far too new to play any role until well after mobilization. The legations performed their tasks reasonably well, keeping the foreign ministry apprized of the Russian decision for war in case Austria attacked Serbia, the departure of the Austrian minister from Belgrade and the interpretation that war was inevitable, and that Russia would act in concert with France on Serbia's side. These critical revelations all were sent July 25th, the day that Holland began its mobilization – although a coded telegram (discussed below) was the main trigger. In addition, secret low-level talks were held with Belgium, Britain, and France to discover the other countries' war plans, although not revealing any aspect of Holland's. While some Dutch generals assumed (like their French counterparts) that German troops would stay south of the Meuse, reconnaissance into the war zone began almost immediately – too soon, in fact. When the Maastricht commandant sent a staff car to Visé, Belgium, on 3 August, everything was quiet, as the patrol had beaten the Germans there. The border guards reported German troops in a number of border villages where in fact they were not.[43] So, as was true of intelligence in all countries, some was good, some bad. But the most important item was very good indeed.

At 5:30 p.m on July 25th, a telegram arrived in the Netherlands from Cologne containing the words *API API.* The origins of the mysterious telegram lay in the relationship between a Dutch officer, Major M.D.A. Forbes-Wels, and a retired Royal Dutch Indies Army (K.N.I.L.) officer, J.J. le Roy,[xii] then a director of the Dutch-German Telegraph company,

---

[xii] It was definitely Le Roy, despite one suggestion that he was already dead by that time. F.A.C. Kluiters, *Nederlandse inlichtingen- en veiligheidsdiensten* ('s-Graven-

residing at Cologne.[44] (This explains, incidentally, the choice of Malayan, which was the principal language spoken in the Netherlands East Indies.)

J.J. le Roy was 37 when he became a director of the Dutch-German Telegraph Company, after an eventful career in the K.N.I.L. which included combat service. Discharged a captain in 1904, he was later promoted to major on the retired list. Major Forbes Wels would rise to the rank of Lieutenant General and Chief of the General Staff by 1922 (the highest peacetime military post in Holland) and retired in 1925.[45] Forbes Wels was not new to espionage, having participated in cross-border forays to check on war threats. In 1906 he traveled to Liège, Belgium, and Aachen, Germany, to check on rumors of a German invasion of Belgium.[46] Apparently a German newspaper had published information that (the Dutch believed) would only be published in case of actual mobilization.[47]

Exactly when and where Le Roy and Forbes Wels first met is not known, but they were close in age and the Dutch military establishment is not the Pentagon. We do know that the two had reached an agreement that Le Roy would send a telegram when he anticipated German mobilization, or when and if he expected war.[48] Le Roy was well placed to do this. He was in Germany; he was in Cologne, the very place where German troops would mass if they were getting ready to move into Belgium and/or Holland; and he was director of a telegraph company set up, ironically, with German help, to circumvent British imperialism.

In 1899, Le Roy had authored a newspaper article in which he noted that 20 of the world's 23 cable companies were located in London, and that Britain might be able to interrupt Holland's ties with the colonies. (He also worried about interruptions due to the pan-Islamic movement.)[49] The Dutch envoy in Berlin discussed the issue with the German foreign ministry, while the Dutch colonial minister approached a private firm in Cologne, Felten & Guilleaume Karlswerk A.G.[50] The Dutch goal was apparently to have cable access to its colonies through British, German, and French colonies, but technical difficulties of running cable through American-held islands were viewed as considerable – not to mention the political problem, namely that US anti-imperialists would oppose it.[51]

---

hage: Koninginnegracht, 1993), p. 178n2.

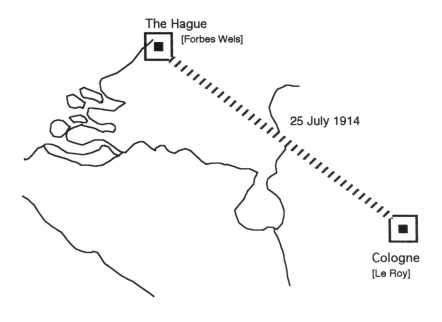

The telegram "API API" was sent by Le Roy at 10:15 a.m. and arrived at 5:30 p.m. at Major Forbes Wels' private residence.

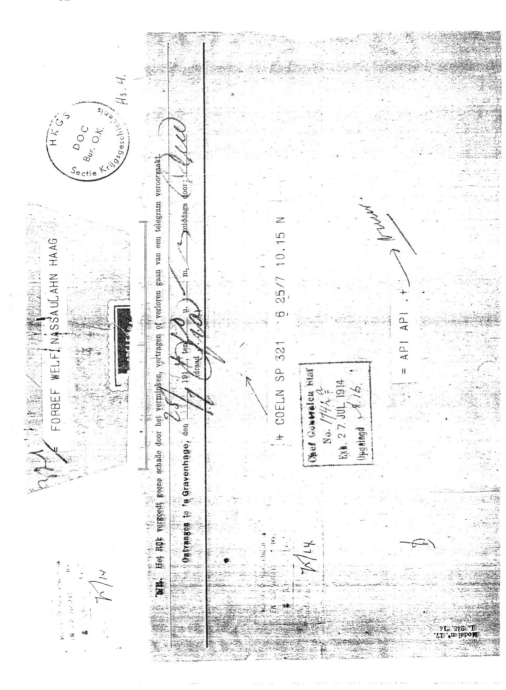

Telegram sent by Le Roy to Forbes Wels on July 25th.

During the Boer War, Britain had interfered with the telegraph traffic of other governments, especially those of Germany and Holland (led by the somewhat pro-German Kuyper). Le Roy represented some Amsterdam bankers in 1900 in an attempt to begin discussions about a bilateral telegraph arrangement. His first trip to Germany failed due to the slow response from the Dutch foreign ministry, which had reservations about a tie-in with Germany. The following spring this problem was resolved.[52] In 1901, while still a KNIL officer, Le Roy arranged the agreement between Holland and Germany to set up a joint telegraph company, with government-appointed directors (Le Roy, and O. Stoecker for Germany) and subsidies (although the company was supposed to pay 90% of its own way). Germany hoped that such an arrangement would protect its interests in wartime by linking up with a neutral.[53] Dutch officials were concerned about wartime connections with the East Indies.[54] Not everyone in Dutch official circles supported the company. Le Roy had his enemies. At least one colonial ministry official wrote to the Governor-General of the Indies in 1905 to question Le Roy's motives for setting up the company (as well as the organization's financial soundness[55]). The writer complained that he was "not reassured" about the company and "the Dutchness *(Hollanderschap)* of Mr. Le Roy is not enough for me."[56] The Governor-General was apparently unconcerned.[xiii][57]

The project went on, however, because the government shared Le Roy's basic concern; the British cable monopoly. For Holland, a small country with a big and distant colony, the fear of isolation from its empire was acute. Telegraph connections were bad and many telegrams were not arriving. The German connection was not the only Dutch attempt to circumvent Albion's web, nor were Holland and Germany the only countries trying to do so. The United States and France were also active. The Dutch in fact attempted to negotiate with the French, but this went nowhere. Other small nations were involved as well. The Danes were working hard to get information about Dutch plans while plotting the sale of their own franchise to the French. This environment

---

[xiii] In 1917, another Governor-General suspected Le Roy of being an agent for the German Telefunken firm and denied him a position as advisor. Telefunken fared better, getting approval to set up a station. Governor-General van Limburg Stirum to Minister of Colonies Pleyte (27 Sept. 1917), RGP vol. 116, nr. 241; N. Koomans, "Geschiedkundig overzicht van het radiobedrijf van den rijksdienst der posterijen en telegrafie," http://home.luna.nl/~arjan-muil/radio/ptt.htm.

had give Le Roy his opening.[58]

Le Roy and the other the other negotiators at Cologne in 1901 quickly agreed that the cable should be Britain-free and that the organization would be sited at Cologne. The agreement's contents were to remain confidential. The cable plan was a good deal for the Dutch, who could not afford to do it alone.[59] The Germans were also positive, but insisted that the discussions remain as secret as possible. Inevitably the plan was leaked to a Dutch newspaper, however. Fortunately, this did not cripple the negotiations, and the company came into being in 1904. Cable routes were planned across non-British territory. The technical and political difficulties of using American islands were overcome. The network seemed secure; to the German secretary of state for mail, Von Podbielsky, war with Britain, Russia and America at the same time seemed unimaginable.[xiv] Interestingly, despite Le Roy's intimate connections with the company's founding and his continued interest in it throughout the war, he is not mentioned in the otherwise fairly comprehensive Dutch postwar report about the company; nor is the API-API telegram.[60]

Two sources discuss the origins and arrival of the telegram, although both are based on the recollections of a single individual and it is possible that one source may have been based on the other. According to a classified internal history of the Netherlands Internal Security Service, the B.V.D, The telegram resulted from an agreement, mentioned earlier, between Forbes Wels and Le Roy, that the latter would send it if he anticipated German mobilization. On 25 July 1914 the telegram was sent from Cologne around 10:15 a.m., and it arrived in the evening at Forbes Wels' house. The major's son[xv] opened it, thinking it was a congratulatory telegram for his having passed the high school exit exam, the H.B.S. Puzzled by the telegram but realizing that it had nothing to do with his academic success, the young Forbes Wels took the document to his father, who then took it to the Chief of Staff.[61] This last item – based on the younger Forbes Wels' recollections – was incorrect, because Snijders was traveling in Germany: a government

---

[xiv]   One thing that kept the cable from being cut by the British was that the Singapore-Australia cable ran through the Dutch East Indies and could easily have been cut in retaliation. Paul Kennedy, "Imperial cable communications and strategy, 1870-1914," *English Historical Review* 86 (October 1971), pp. 743-44.

[xv]   Pieter Forbes Wels himself later reached the rank of Colonel of the General Staff. P. Forbes Wels, *De Nederlandse Cavalerie* (Bussum: C.A.J. van Dishoek, 1963).

telegram reached him at a hotel in Hamburg.[62] He did not get home from his three-week vacation until July 27.[63] (What the country's highest-ranking military officer was doing there so late in July of 1914 is a bit mysterious to me). A recent publication still places him at The Hague on the 25th, however.[64] [xvi]

The other source (recollections of an army officer who received the telegram during a 1921 cleanout of an office and wrote to the younger Forbes Wels to get an explanation) contains similar information, adding that the elder Forbes Wels considered the telegram as "of great importance" and immediately took it to General Snijders. There are some important differences. Le Roy's name was not mentioned in the letter to the army officer, and the basis for the telegram is somewhat vaguer – saying that it would be sent by "a friend . . . if he thought that war was coming."[65] There is no reference to mobilization as such.

What caused Le Roy to send the telegram? The sources cited above do not say. The first source is rather specific, referring to German *mobilization*: the second was vaguer, mentioning the *danger of war*. Even *mobilization* begs the question, because it does not clarify what Le Roy would base that expectation of mobilization on. What could Le Roy have known? More pertinently, what could Le Roy have known that the Dutch government could not have easily discovered from some other source? Le Roy was in Cologne, a critical staging area for any German invasion of Belgium, France, or the Netherlands. Could he have observed military preparations? Germany did not issue its *Kriegesgefahr* (Danger of War) declaration until July 31, 6 days later. If there were military preparations going on in Cologne on July 24th or 25th, this would run counter to our understanding of the German government's intentions and behavior in the last week of July. Either the German government was making secret war preparations even before Austria declared war on Serbia, or the German Army was making some advance preparations without waiting for further instructions from the government (not as unlikely as it sounds). The paper trail of German Army activities in 1914 is incompete, especially as some things were purposely not committed to paper. On June 16, 1914, the Quartermaster-General, Alfred von Waldersee, informed

---

[xvi] The source of the confusion may be quite simple; the acting chief of staff in Snijders' absence was probably referred to as chief of staff without the "acting" moniker by contemporary correspondents.

German states not to send written reports to the war ministries, and that General Staff emissaries would come to explain this step.[66] In any event, it is possible, if entirely unproven, that the telegram stemmed from observations he made in the Cologne area.

There are problems with the "observation" explanation of the telegram. Holland had sent army officers across the border in previous crises to observe German activities, and there is no evidence whatsoever of any policy decision to stop doing this. There is no reason why, if mobilization was suspected, another junior officer could not have been sent on the train into Germany. Of course, as a retired army officer, Le Roy was competent to have done so himself. The previous intelligence trips, however, had been made by officers directly attached to Dutch military units, to ensure immediate information for army commanders. Admittedly, Le Roy's telegram to The Hague gave the army general staff a very fast report indeed, but no details. The army had always required detailed reports based on 2-3 rail trips with actual observations at Düsseldorf, Koblenz, and Cologne, and indirect information gathering regarding German movements at towns further away, such as Aachen. Le Roy submitted no report that has survived (many contemporary Dutch and German archives were destroyed in 1945). Such a report would have served little purpose anyway: if it went ahead of or with the telegram, a coded telegram would make no sense, and if it came later, it would have come after the Dutch mobilization began. We therefore have a picture of a country beginning its mobilization based on a coded telegram from a retired officer in Cologne, six days before Germany officially began its pre-mobilization process, so that he could hardly have seen masses of reservists arriving.

Was there anything else going on in western Germany that could have caught Le Roy's attention? The French alleged during the war that Germany had begun preparations on July 23rd, such as recalling officers from vacation, putting up camouflage and machine guns at Düsseldorf, and making large purchases of supplies. Some writers have put the first preparations even earlier, although with little evidence. On the 25th intelligence chief Walter Nicolai authorized secret trips to Russia and France, but by its nature this was an activity that no one would have noticed.[67]

What then was the precise basis of the agreement between Forbes Wels and Le Roy? Once again, one source refers to 'mobilization' while the other refers to 'danger of war' and in both cases the information is second hand. It does not come either from Le Roy or Forbes

Wels senior. Even the more specific 'mobilization' does not completely clarify the situation, because it could refer either to actual observation of mobilization (as discussed above), or to information gleaned by Le Roy from some other source that led him to believe that mobilization was imminent. 'Danger of war' would have to refer to war in the west, or a general European war, not just a conflict in the Balkans. Le Roy would be an attractive source here from Forbes Wels' viewpoint for a rather obvious reason: he operated a telegraph company. Could he have intercepted – and decoded – telegrams passing through Cologne, and which ones might have gone through Cologne? As mentioned earlier, the Austrians, if not the Germans, were rather sensitive to the risk of interception.

If Le Roy's position at the telegraph service allowed him to intercept *and* decode telegrams – unlikely as this might seem – what would have triggered his telegram? Le Roy's action would have to be triggered by a telegram that he saw in time to decode and comprehend; in all likelihood this would mean one sent on July 24, possibly on the 25th, although the latter would have had to have been sent in the morning for Le Roy to have time to send his message. The telegram seen by Le Roy would have had to contain proof that the European war was inevitable, and that it would spread to the west. Among the many messages flowing across the wires in late July of 1914, there were two threads that the Dutch would have considered particularly ominous.

Germany's attitude toward the Balkan war. The Balkan crisis alone would not have triggered Dutch mobilization. Few foresaw that a crisis with Serbia meant all-out war; even the German foreign secretary claimed to believe as late as July 18 that Russia would remain quiet if faced with an Austro-German alliance (he did not believe this, and the recipient – Lichnowsky – quickly realized that Jagow was being economical with the truth).[68] Evidence of an aggressive German attitude, however, would be much more ominous. The damning telegrams between Lichnowsky and Jagow on July 25 which made clear that Germany did not support Austro-Serbian conciliation were later than Le Roy's, however.[69] Germany had of course pressed Austria to take a hard line toward Serbia, and was rewarded with a positive reply, but much of this was done by letter, not telegram .[70] On July 24, however, Ambassador Tschirschky telegraphed his government that Austrian Foreign Minister Berchtold was "absolutely determined not to enter upon any negotiations" and had rejected mediation. Tschirschky apparently anticipated no concern about this on the part of his own foreign ministry.[71] While this telegram was sent in time to be leaked or intercepted, Tschirsky's better-known telegram of the 25th, reporting Serbian mobilization and implying the imminence of war, also came after the API-API telegram.[72] This is actually rather interesting, because it reminds us that Le Roy could *not* have been responding to the Serbian mobilization itself, as even telegraphic intercepts – the fastest way of gaining that knowledge – would have come too late (the Serb mobilization began about 3 p.m. Belgrade time[73]) although Serbia's mobilization order was prepared on the 24th.

Germany's relationship with Britain. Holland worried more about an Anglo-German than a Franco-German war; after all, the country was sandwiched geographically and economically between the former pair. An internal telegram on July 23 clearly reveals that Germany was lying to Britain about the Austrian demands on Serbia, even keeping Lichnowsky in the dark.[74] This duplicity, which was pursued at the expense of France as well, failed quickly, but the telegrams of July 25 which clarify the situation came too late to benefit the Dutch spy in Cologne.[75] On the other hand, several British communications on the 24th and 25th were particularly important; Crackanthorpe's telegram from Belgrade notifying Grey that the Austro-Hungarian demands were not acceptable, Rumbold's[xvii] message from Berlin the following day that Germany expected Austria to take military action, and Grey's reply that peace required all powers to work together.[xviii]

One thing that did precede Le Roy's telegram was the Emperor's issuance of fleet readiness orders. There are several oddities about this event. As pointed out earlier, the Chancellor was against the order, believing that the British fleet was not taking any measures; Wilhelm pointed out in the margin that the British fleet was already prepared, and for once, he was right and his government wrong. The second oddity is more difficult to explain. Zimmermann records that Wilhelm issued the order at 9:30 a.m. on July 25. Wilhelm wrote in the margin of the Chancellor's telegram opposing his decision that he issued the order because his ambassador in Belgrade reported Serbian mobiliza-

---

[xvii]   Sir Horace Rumbold was British ambassador in Berlin. Mr. Dayrell Crackanthorpe was British chargé in Belgrade.

[xviii]   This last message would only have real meaning to Le Roy if he could see secret mobilization activity occurring in Cologne, indicating that Germany was *not* planning to work with other powers for peace.

tion. Mobilization in Belgrade did not begin until 3:00 p.m., July 25. The German ambassador in Belgrade did send a telegram very late on the 24th, but it made no mention of mobilization. He did use the words "military uprising," which the Emperor underlined, but it is not clear whether the Emperor would have seen it before 9:30 a.m. on July 25. The ambassador's previous telegram did suggest public pressure in Belgrade to reject the Austrian note.[76]

Regardless of what influenced Wilhelm, no Dutch observer would have had any illusions about the British reaction to the *Allerhöchste's*[xix] decision. The timing of the Emperor's order could be significant. As Le Roy sent his telegram at 10:15 a.m., there is a strong likelihood that he found out something late on the 24th or on the morning of the 25th that triggered his actions. It is unlikely that he decided to send the telegram on the 24th but waited two hours the following morning before doing so. (Some delay, of course, could have occurred between his delivering his text and the actual transmission).

To the two possible "triggers" for his act – personal observation and/or telegraphic interception – we can add two others, although both are problematical. First, Le Roy could have had a contact inside Germany who might have supplied him with information. This was not without precedent. Holland had been notified about the original Schlieffen plan by an 'inside' source. If Le Roy had been informed about the fleet mobilization, he would have understood its significance immediately. The *Kriegsmarine* did not need to mobilize for a localized Balkan war. A second and more persuasive "trigger" could easily have become known to Le Roy, although whether in time is unclear. On July 25th, , the Austrian government took control of all telegraph and wireless stations in its territory.[77] Such a move could well have been made known to a telegraph company headquarters in Germany. Yet although this would have let Le Roy know that Austria was preparing for war, was this really news, with the ultimatum to Serbia about to expire? Or could such an act be seen as a government moving from bluster and rhetoric to the first concrete step toward the battlefield? And finally, would an Austrian war with Serbia alone be regarded as a sufficient reason for Le Roy to conclude that war was threatening Holland? Again, we are in the realm of speculation.

Whichever 'trigger' sounds the most likely (and there are problems

[xix] "All Highest," one of Wilhelm's titles.

with all) it is not conceivable that Le Roy's telegram was sent purely on the basis of a hunch, or something as publicly available as a newspaper report. The Austrian mobilization began too late for his telegram[78] He would have had to make a great interpretive leap to see the Serbian mobilization order as a threat to Holland, and he had no way of discovering the Serbian order (not published until too late for the API API message[79]) It would have required the gift of prophecy for Forbes Wels and Le Roy to make such an event the basis of their pre-war agreement. The chain of contingencies is too long.

Whether the Dutch army knew of, or suspected, what facts lay behind Le Roy's telegram, is unknown. What is known is that the response was extraordinarily quick, with the first mobilization telegram (telegram "A") going out at 11:30 a.m. the morning after (July 26). Forbes Wels' proposal to add written warnings for the *landweer* reserve and the border guards was vetoed, but not because Le Roy's warning was being taken lightly.[80] Le Roy's telegram made the difference. Le Roy and Forbes Wels must have agreed on some rather specific circumstances that would trigger the telegram; otherwise the Dutch military would hardly have been willing to react as quickly as it did (although Holland did have one advantage over the larger powers; its mobilization could not possibly be interpreted as aggressive). Yet little was done after the war to clear up the story behind the telegram. Fabius apparently knew, but merely wrote that "only a few initiated people know . . . on the basis of which confidential communications the Netherlands decided to mobilize . . ." A later commentator wrote that for the country's "readiness we have to thank the resourcefulness of several military leaders" and noted that "for a long time the authorities spoke with a mixture of pride . . . and shame . . . about the telegram."[xx]

The intelligence coup could not protect the country unless sustained action resulted, however. The whole army had to mobilize. Snijders and the General Staff would now have to convince the government to take this expensive and – for the public – frightening step.

[xx] Pride because of its success; shame because it focused attention on the lack of any real military intelligence service.

The decision to mobilize

This turned out to be one of the easiest parts of his wartime service. Although there would be some resistance, most politicians were not inclined to dawdle. Fear of militarism was exceeded by fear of war, and even anti-military socialists voted for the necessary mobilization credits. There was neither enthusiasm nor opposition.

With the issuance of telegram "A" on Sunday July 26 the army began a number of "strategic preparations," including readying the most vulnerable bridges for destruction. This was something that had been worked on at least since the summer of 1906. Espionage commenced immediately with the deputy chief of the General Staff, Col. R.F. Dufour, and War Minister Bosboom agreeing to send two officers into Germany. In fact, it was Bosboom, not the vacationing Snijders, who made the critical decisions between Saturday and Monday. Dufour had the presence of mind to telegraph Snijders, in Hamburg at this moment, that his return was "desired" – probably an understatement.[81]

The steps taken on Saturday night and Sunday were apparently not known to most Dutch political leaders. On Monday, however, that would have to change. Required actions could no longer be kept secret. The second of the three pre-mobilization telegrams, "B," was sent. More noticeably, the scheduled dismissal of the *militie* and *landweer* contingents doing their regular service or summer training was cancelled, a decision that most of the country heard about on Wednesday the 29th. Bosboom gave the cabinet a detailed briefing on the army's steps to date, and he and his Marine and Foreign Ministry counterparts, J.J. Rambonnet and John Loudon, consulted the Queen. Rumors began percolating in The Hague that mobilisation was about to occur, but the British – always skeptical about Holland's intent to defend itself – were skeptical. H.G. Chilton, the British Chargé, reported that the mobilisation rumor was "a little premature" and could not be confirmed. He was wrong; The Hague was as much a crisis capital as any in Europe. By the time Snijders arrived Monday evening at 8 p.m., the pre-mobilization steps that he had carefully prepared as chief of staff were nearing the high-water mark. On Tuesday 28 July Chilton reported that leaves had been stopped, mobilization preparations were being made, and "[m]ovements of troops are being carried out all over the country and night exercises [are] taking place." On Wednesday morning he added that all main rail bridges along the

"Return desired" telegram sent to Snijders on July 26th.

German frontier were guarded, as were all harbors and piers.[82]

Anxiety about German intentions grew. To head off any possible German excuse for a *casus belli,* the cabinet, as mentioned earlier, decided Wednesday not to defend the area of the Eems valley that was under dispute. On Thursday the 30th, however, concern about Germany peaked when "reliable reports" (presumably from the officers sent across the border on Sunday) arrived indicating that the German Army was gradually changing to a war footing (full day before Germany issued its official "danger of war" declaration). The officers' reports triggered the issuance of the third pre-mobilization telegram (C), the closing of all eastern border bridges at 5:15 p.m., and the cabinet's decision to issue a statement of neutrality and a "danger of war" declaration (published on Friday, July 31). The border guards were also called up, at Snijders' urging.[83] At this point there was only one step left; full mobilization.

The crucial cabinet meeting took place at night on Thursday, July 30. The ministers decided that they had to go to full mobilization. The decision was not easy. Expense and dislocation would be great, and not everyone would react with enthusiasm. The army's work was described by one writer as, "[t]he military element began to rummage with its weapons," yet another sample of the dismissive attitude in Dutch culture toward the army. De Beaufort wondered on the 31st whether the decision was premature (he changed his mind quickly; three days later, he wondered whether parliament had held its last meeting before the Germans invaded Holland). Chilton reported that the press was "divided," with some papers "praising the caution and foresight of the Government," while others "ridiculing" the precautions as "alarmist and unnecessary."Many Dutchman thought the war could still be localized. Even the ministers hesitated to call up the troops earlier on the 30th because the 12 million guilders was "such an expense" that it could "only be justified in urgent necessity." The cost concern continued during the following meeting when the decision was made, and understandably so. Special credits of 55 million guilders had to be appropriated in August alone. Mobilization plunged the budget into deficit, and the postwar tally of special wartime expenditures would reach more than 2 billion guilders, most of it borrowed.[84] But all that lay in the future, as the Dutch government, no more clairvoyant about the length of the war than its neighbors, could of necessity only focus on the immediate crisis at hand.

Only ten minutes into a tense Friday morning, the war ministry and general staff were notified that the government had decided to proclaim mobilization on 1 August. While Snijders had always favored early mobilization to discourage marches through Holland,[xxi] he had not had to press the issue. He and is staff could now concentrate on the work at hand. Mayors, especially in border towns, were given a variety of special instructions, including preparing the citizenry for destruction of property and bridges. The minister of war was given power to requisition railways. All the reservists had to be brought to their units. This was no small undertaking. Each of the four Dutch army divisions had half its 530 officers in peacetime, but only a few hundred of its 22,000 enlisted personnel. The possibility of total chaos à la 1870 was real. Instead, the army was able to mobilize and deploy in some three days, putting some 204,000 troops into its fortifications and field units.[85]

Fabius would later suggest that the Netherlands, "as the first power in western Europe, ready to meet each threat, undoubtedly made a powerful impression on foreign countries." He exaggerated, but there can be no doubt that both Britain and Germany were relieved – for opposite reasons, of course – to see the Netherlands get ready to fight. Chilton, who like many British officials had doubted that Holland would resist, reported on August 2 that Dutch troops had been ordered to fire.[86] The German envoy took notice of the activity (he described the soldiers as *"eifrig"* ("energetic")) and explained why the Netherlands had mobilized so quickly – and unwittingly paid tribute to the success of the Dutch espionage/intelligence missions aimed at Germany:

> *Vielen möchte diese Hast der Holländer übertrieben erscheinen. Ich wusste aus der Zeit meiner diplomatischen Arbeit im Haag genau, dass der Holländische Generalstab mit der Wahrscheinlichkeit rechnete, das*

[xxi] Snijders later made an important point regarding the German march. If Germany had decided in advance to go through the Netherlands, it would have done so regardless because the maneuver around Limburg could not possibly be improvised. C.J. Snijders and R. Dufour, *De mobilisatiën bij de groote mogendheden in 1914 en de invloed van de generale staven op het uitbreken van den wereldoorlog* (Leiden: Sijthoff, 1927), pp. 255-56. Therefore, rapid mobilization was necessary just in case Germany was still dithering between several possible plans! Neither Snijders nor anyone else could know that Germany had decided to gamble its national existence on a single war plan.

deutsche Heer würde durch den Limburger Zipfel durchsstossen, um zu versuchen, die als stark angesehen Belgische Festungen zu umgehen.[87]

(Many may have considered the hurriedness of the Dutch to seem exaggerated. I knew well from the time of my diplomatic duties in The Hague, that the Dutch General Staff counted on the probability, that the German Army would attack through the Limburg appendage in order to attempt to avoid the highly regarded Belgian fortifications.)

NOTES

[1] F.A.C. Kluiters, *De Nederlandse inlichtingen- en veiligheidsdiensten* ('s-Gravenhage: Koninginnegracht, 1993), pp. 7-8.

[2] A. Wolting, "De eerste jaren van den Militaire Inlichtingendienst (GS-III, 1914-1917), *Militaire Spectator*134 (December 1965), p. 566; Bob de Graaf, "De 'Intelligence Revolution' van de 20e eeuw en haar geschiedschrijving: Een historiografisch artikel," *De nieuwste tijd* 6 (6 June 1996), p. 5.

[3] Pearson, *Weak State*, p. 19.

[4] Memorandum by Chief of Staff, June 1906: Report on carrier pigeons, n.d.: "Strategische oefening op de kaart, 1904-1905; Nederlandsche partij; Colonel Thiange," n.d.; Generale Staf, nr. toegang 2.13.15.01, ARA-II; Van Voorst tot Voorst, *Over Roermond*, p. 37; Staff meeting minues, Feb. 6, 1906, Koninklijke Landmacht – Algemeen Hoofdkwartier, ARA-II; Klinkert, *Het vaderland verdedigd*, p. 423.

[5] D. van den Berg, *Cornelis Jacobus Snijders (1852-1939): Een leven in dienst van zijn Land en zijn Volk* (Den Haag: Reverdeem, 1949), p. 72; Gevers to Van Tets van Goudriaan, 24 April 1907, 59, 62, Smit, *1907-1914*, pp. 63-64.

[6] Wolting, "De eerste jaren," p. 571; Memo, "Aanwijzingen nopens den Kondschapsdienst." 114 May 1906, Koninklijke Landmacht – Algemeen Hoofdkwartier, ARA-II; Commander 2nd Division to Field Army headquarters, 24 September 1909, and reply, 27 September 1909, Koninklijke Landmacht – Hoofdkwartier Veldleger, ARA-II.

[7] C.J. Snijders, "Aanwijzingen betreffende de kondschapsdiest, ingevolge punt 126 van de "strategische aanwijzingen 1913" (15 Nov. 1913)," Archief van de General Staf, inv nr 346, ARA-II; "Opgave van de door den Minister van Oorlog te geven bevelen," n.d. but probably early 1914, Collectie Bosboom, ARA-II; Marechaussée to Field Army, 10 Aug. 1914, Koninklijke Landmacht – Hoofdkwartier Veldleger, ARA-II; M. de Meier, "Geheime Dienst in Nederland 1912-1947." (Unpublished classified internal history: Leidschendam: Binnenlandse Veiligheids Dienst, n.d. Cited with permission), p. 19; Wolting, "De eerste jaren," p. 569.

[8] Report Wijnmalen 17 August 1914: Snijders to Capt. Walaardt Sacré, 18 Aug. 1914: Wijnmalen to Walaardt Sacré, 19 August 1914, Generale Staf, nr toegang 2.13.70, inv nrs 1, 5, 352, 997, ARA-II.

[9] Jonathan Steinberg, "A German Plan for the Invasion of Holland and Belgium, 1897," *The Historical Journal* 6 (No. 1 1963), p. 108.

[10] Report of reconnaissance of VII and VIII German Army Corps Garrisons, 31 August 1911; Report, 5 August 1911; Report, 31 July 1911, Collectie Röell, nr. toegang. 21.000, ARA-II.

[11] Memo to Röell, 2 September 1911; Note in collection, 1 August 1911, Collectie Röell, nr. toegang 21.000, ARA-II.

[12] Steinberg, "A German Plan," p. 108.

[13] Van Voorst tot Voorst, *Over Roermond*, p. 18.

[14] A.J. Vinke, "De Nederlandse militaire attaché 1907-1923" (Unpublished paper prepared at the Royal Military Academy, 1984), Library of the ARA, p. 35; Bosboom, *In moeilijke omstandigheden*, p. 23.

[15] Inventory of correspondence, General Staff, ARA-II; Gevers to De Marees van Swinderen, 16 January 1912, 626: Colijn to De Marees van Swinderen, 14 Feb. 1912, 626n, Smit, *1907-1914*, pp. 726-27, 727n.

[16] Ministry of War to Minister of Foreign Affairs, 9 Sept. 1909: Gevers to Foreign Minister, 24 Nov. 1909: Legation in Vienna to Foreign Minister, 7 March 1911: Gevers to Foreign Minister, 31 March 1911, 29 April 1911: War Minister to Foreign Minister, 19 May 1911, 24 May 1911, 10 June 1911: Gevers to Foreign Minister, 6 July 1911: Minister of War to Foreign Minister, 8 Aug 1911, Ministerie van Buitenlandse Zaken, nr toegang 2.05.03, inv nrs 640, 641, 643, ARA-II.

[17] De Meier, "Geheime dienst," p. 1; Vinke, "Nederlandse militaire attaché," p. 34.

[18] De Meier, "Geheime dienst," pp. 1, 3; Berg, *Snijders,* p. 72; Wolting, "De eerste jaren," pp. 569-71; D. Engelen, *Geschiedenis van de Binnenlandse Veiligheidsdienst* ('s-Gravenhage: Koninginnegracht, 1995), p. 34.

[19] Müller to De Marees van Swinderen, 20 January 1910: Minister of War W. Cool to De Marees van Swinderen, 4 May 1910: De Marees van Swinderen to Müller, 13 May 1910: General Staff to Minister of War, 17 June 1913: Chief of Staff to Inspector of Engineering 8 October 1913, Generale Staf, ARA-II; Brussels Legation to Foreign Ministry, 19 and 22 Sept. 1911, and 3 July 1912: Aide-Memoire, Foreign Minister, 2 Aug. 1912, Buitenlandse Zaken, ARA-II.

[20] Wolting, "De eerste jaren," p. 569; Chief of Staff to Minister of War, 18 August 1913, Generale Staf, ARA-II.

[21] Van Vollenhoven, *Memoires,* p. 401.

[22] Generale Staf, nr. toegang 2.13.15.01, inv nr 305, ARA-II; De Valk and Van Faassen, *Dagboeken en aantekeningen,* pp. 611-12; Oswald Henry Wedel, *Austro-German Diplomatic Relations 1908-1914* (Stanford: Stanford University Press, 1932), pp. 183; P. H. Ritter, *De donkere poort* ('s-Gravenhage: Daamen's, 1931), pp. 9-10; Müller to Bethmann Hollweg, 31 August 1911, Duitse Ministerie van Buitenlandse Zaken – Stukken betreffende Nederland, ARA-II.

[23] Correspondence between Loudon, Queen Wilhelmina and Envoy to the Porte Van der Does de Willebois, 14-24 July 1914, 820, 827, 828, 831, Smit, *1907-1914*, pp. 979, 989-91, 993-94.

[24] David Vital, "Minor Power/Major Power Relations and the Contemporary Nation-State," pp. 197-214 in Inbar and Sheffer, *National Security of Small States,* p. 200.

[25] American Historical Association, *Catalogue of Files and Microfilms,* pp. xiv-xvi; C.J. Snijders and R. Dufour, *De mobilisatiën bij de grote mogendheden in 1914 en de invloed van de generale staven op het uitbreken van den wereldoorlog* (Leiden: Sijthoff, 1927), p. 9.

[26] Fallon to Davignon, 29 January 1914,470, Smit, *Buitenlandse bronnen 1899-1914,* pp. 656-58; Karl Max Lichnowsky, *My Mission to London 1912-1914* (Toronto: Cassell, 1918), p. 13.

[27] Holger H. Herwig, "Clio Deceived: Patriotic Self-Censorship in Germany After the Great War," pp. 87-127 in Keith Wilson, ed., *Forging the Collective Memory: Government and International Historians Through Two World Wars* (Providence: Berghahn Books, 1996), pp. 87, 119; John C. Röhl, "Germany," pp. 27-54 in Wilson, *Decision for War,* p. 46; Herwig, *First World War,* p. 51; Van Evera, "Cult of the Offensive," p. 105; *Mensonge,* p. 9.

[28] Van Vollenhoven, *Memoires,* pp. 396-97; Emperor's margin notes on Tschirschky communiqué to Bethmann Hollweg, 30 June 1914, "German Secret War Documents," *International Conciliation* (May 1920), pp. 205-206; Vollenhoven,

Memoires, p. 402; Ulrich Trumpener, "War Premeditated? German Intelligence Operations in July 1914," *Central European History* 9 (March 1976), p. 62; Beening, "Onder de vleugels," p. 375.

29 Ritter, *Donkere poort,* pp. 5-6, 12; Beening, "Onder de vleugels," p. 376.
30 Lichnowsky, *My Mission,* passim; Van Evera, "Cult of the Offensive," p. 102.
31 Memorandum by Under-Secretary of State Baron von dem Bussche, August 30, 1917, Max Montgelas and Walther Schuecking, eds., *Outbreak of the World War: German Documents Collected by Karl Kautsky* (New York: Oxford University Press, 1924).
32 Von Tschirschky to Jagow, 11 July 1914, *Official German Documents Relating to the World War.* Tr. Carnegie Endowment for International Peace (New York: Oxford University Press, 1923), and also materials on pp. 34, 100, 120.
33 Statement of Baron von Tucher, late Minister of Bavaria at Vienna, 5 January 1920, *Official German Documents*; Botho von Wedel to Baron von dem Bussche, 5 September 1917, Montgelas and Schuecking, *Outbreak of the World War,* p. 652.
34 Bethmann Hollweg to Lichnowsky, 16 July 1914: Jagow to Chargé of the Imperial Suite, July 18, 1914: Jagow to Lichnowsky, July 18, 1914: Jagow to Tschirschky, July 18, 1914: W. zu Stolberg to Jagow, July 18, 1914, "German Secret War Documents."
35 Jagow to the Emperor, 23 July 1914, "German Secret War Documents."
36 German Ambassador St. Petersburg to Foreign Office: German Ambassador in Turkey to Foreign Office: German Ambassador to Jagow: all 23 July 1914, Montgelas and Schuecking, *Outbreak of the World War*; Bethmann Hollweg to Chargé of the Imperial Suite: Bavarian Chargé at Berlin to the President of the Ministerial Council: all 23 July 1914, "German Secret War Documents."
37 Jagow to Bethmann Hollweg: Jagow to Tschirschky: Lichnowsky to Jagow: Director General of the Hapag (Ballin) to Jagow: all 24 July 1914, Montgelas and Schuecking, *Outbreak of the World War*; Tschirschky to Jagow, 24 July 1914, "German Secret War Documents."
38 Schoen to Jagow: Lichnowsky to Jagow: Jagow to Lichnowsky: July 25, Montgelas and Schuecking, *Outbreak of the World War*; Lichnowsky to Jagow: Jagow to Lichnowsky, 25 July 1914, "German Secret War Documents;" Lichnowsky, *My Mission,* pp. 32-33.
39 Tschirsky to Jagow, 24 July and 25 July: Pourtalès to Jagow, 25 July: Russian chargé to Jagow, 25 July: Memorandum by Undersecretary Zimmermann, 25 July, Montgelas and Schuecking, *Outbreak of the World War*: Tschirschky to Jagow, 25 July: Bethmann Hollweg to Emperor, 25 July, "German Secret War Documents."
40 Van Evera, "Cult of the Offensive," p. 72; Van Weede to Loudon, 26 July 1914, Buitenlandse Zaken – Kabinet en Protocol, ARA-II; Admiralty Staff to Jagow, 27 July 1914, *Origins of the World War*; Grey to Goschen, 27 July 1914, *Engeland in oorlog voor de gewaarborgde rechten van kleine naties* ('s-Gravenhage: Martinus Nijhoff, 1914), p. 59.
41 Ritter, *Donkere poort,* p. 16; Beening, "Onder de vleugels," p. 381; Frey, *Der Erste Weltkrieg,* pp. 58-59; Goschen to Grey, 29 July 1914, United Kingdom, *Collected Diplomatic Documents Relating to the Outbreak of the European War* (London: His Majesty's Stationery Office, 1915), p. 64; Sagan, "1914 Revisited,"p. 127; Van Evera, "Cult of the Offensive," p. 94.
42 Jagow to Lichnowsky, 3 August 1914, Montgelas and Schuecking, *Outbreak of the World War*; Jagow to Lichnowsky, 4 August 1914: Fallon to Davigon, 4 August

1914: Cte. de Lalaing to Davigon, 4 August 1914: Fallon to Davignon, 5 August 1914: Van Weede to Davigon, and telegrams between Fallon and Davignon, 6 August 1914, United Kingdom, *Collected Diplomatic Documents*, pp. 326-332, 379, 381-82.

43 Sweerts de Landas Wyborgh to Loudon (2 telegrams): Van Weede to Loudon, 25 July 1914, Buitenlandse Zaken – Kabinet en Protocol, ARA-II; Porter, "Dutch Neutrality," pp. 95, 96; Klinkert, *Het vaderland verdedigd*, p. 427; Van Terwisga to HQ Field Army, 3 August 1914: Grenswacht to HQ Field Army, 11 August 1914, , Koninklijke Landmacht – Hoofdkwartier Veldleger, ARA-II.

44 De Meier, "Geheime dienst in Nederland," pp. 1-4.

45 Algemeen Rijksarchief, Stamboeken, KNIL Officieren, nrs. 634-7; Algemeen Rijksarchief, Stamboeken, Officieren, nr. 448, v. 14, Generale Staf p. 2; Centraal Bureau voor Genealogie; Indische Pensioenen, serie 6 (Officieren); Persoonskaart CBG; Encyclopedie Nederlandsch Oost-Indie. I wish to thank Drs. V. A. J. Klooster for his assistance in compiling this biographical information.

46 Klinkert, *Het vaderland verdedigd*, p. 432.

47 Report by M.D.A. Forbes Wels, 24 January 1906, in folio "Geruchten omtrent de samentrekking van Duitsche troepen nabij de oostgrens van België," Koninklijke Landmacht - Algemeen Hoofkwartier, nr. toegang 2.13.15.01, ARA-II.

48 De Meier, "Geheime Dienst in Nederland," p. 4.

49 First Lieutenant KNIL J.J. le Roy, *Algemeen Handelsblad*, 17 December 1899.

50 Van Tets van Goudriaan to Foreign Minister de Beaufort (11 May 1900 and 23 May 1900), *Bescheiden betreffende de buitenlandse politiek van Nederland* (Den Haag: Rijks Geschiedkundige Publikatien, grote serie, Derde Periode 1899-1919) [herinafter RGP], vol. 100, nrs. 219 and 223. The firm, represented by E. Guilleaume, had its offices in Muelheim, located on the eastern bank of the Rhine across from Cologne.

51 Map labelled "Nederlands-Franse Telegraafkabelovereenkomst van 6 April 1904," RGP vol. 100; Denkschrift van Van Tets van Goudriaan (5 March 1901), RGP vol. 100, n. 393; Gevers (Washington) to De Beaufort, 21 December 1900, 364, C. Smit, *Bescheiden betreffende de buitenlandse politiek van Nederland 1848-1919, Derde Periode 1899-1919*, Part 1, *1899-1903* ('s-Gravenhage: Martinus Nijhoff, 1957), pp. 363-64.

52 Van Tets van Goudriaan to De Beaufort, 11 May 1900 and 23 May 1900, 219, 223: Cremer to De Beaufort, 1 March 1901, 390: Protocol concerning conference at Cologne, 19-21 March, 1901, 402: De Beaufort to Cremer, early April 1901, 406, Smit, *1899-1903*, pp. 205-206, 213-15, 399-400, 413-418, 429-30.

53 M.W.M.M. Gruythuysen, S.U. Sabaroedin, and A.M. Tempelaars, comps., *Inventaris van de archieven van Regeringscommissarissen van het Ministerie van Kolonien 1904-1952* (Den Haag: Algemeen Rijksarchief, 1991), pp. 19, 20; "Memorie van de Regeringscommissaris bij de Deutsch-Niederlaendische Telegraphengesellschaft Viehoff inzake het belang dezer maatschappij bij de vredesvoorwaarden" (7 January 1919), RGP vol. 117, nr. 870.

54 S. L. van der Wal, ed., *Herinneringen van Jhr. Mr. B. C. de Jonge; met brieven uit zijn nalatenschap* (Utrecht: Het Historisch Genootschap, 1968 (Groningen: Wolters-Noordhoff, 1968)), pp. 48-9.

55 De Vries to Van Heutsz, 19 December 1905, and de Vries to Heutsz, 19/20 February 1906, Collectie van Heutsz, nr. toegang 2.21.08, ARA-II.

56 Smit, *1903-1907*, p. 577n.

[57] C. de Vries to Governor-General van Heutsz (19 December 1905), RGP vol. 102, nr 529.

[58] De Steurs to De Beaufort, 1 March1901, 374: Cremer to De Beaufort, 26 Feb. 1901, 387: Van Heeckeren van Kell to De Beaufort 21 Jan. 1901, 389: numerous messages regarding French cable connections, passim, Smit, *1899-1903,* pp. 373-76, 396-97, 399; Idenburg to Pleyte, 8-11 August 1914, 5, and Pleyte to Van Limburg Stirum, 2 October 1916, 638, Smit, *Bescheiden ... 1914-1917,* pp. 31-33, 644; Kennedy, "Imperial Cable Communications," pp. 748-49.

[59] "Protocol van het verhandelde in de conferentie te Keulen van 19 tot 21 Maart 1901," RGP vol. 100, nr. 402; Adm. Dept. Kol. Viehoff and Chief Engineer of Telegraphs to Min. Kol. Cremer (28 March 1901), RGP vol. 100, nr. 403; "Slot Protocol" (24 July 1901), RGP vol. 100, nr. 436.

[60] "De Duitsch-Nederlandsche Telegraafmaatschappij, hare kabelverbindingen en verdere belangen (24 Januari 1919)," ARA-II, Regeringscommissarissen van het Ministerie van Kolonien, 1904-1952, nr. toegang 2.10.46.01; Van Tets van Goudrian to De Beaufort, 20 February 1900, 181: Cremer to de Beaufort, 23 January 1901, 376, Smit, *1899-1903,* pp. 175-77, 376-79, 460n; Viehoff Memorandum, 7 January 1919, 870, Smit, *Bescheiden ... 1917-1919,* pp. 864-71.

[61] De Meier, "Geheime dienst in Nederland," p. 4; Wolting, "De eerste jaren," p. 567.

[62] Telegram to "Snyders" at Hotel Vier Jahreszeiten, Hamburg, 26 July 1914, with German text stating "return desired," Sectie Militaire Geschiedenis, The Hague, File 91/3A.

[63] Berg, *Snijders*, p. 75.

[64] Engelen, *Binnenlandse Veiligheidsdienst,* p. 34.

[65] Memorandum from Col. G.U.H. Thoden van Velzen, "Toelichting op telegram API API (n.d.)," Archives of the Sectie Militaire Geschiedenis, The Hague, SMG file 91/3A.

[66] John. C. Roehl, "Germany," pp. 27-54 in Wilson, *Decision for War,* p. 46.

[67] *Le Mensonge,* pp. 12, 14-15; Trumpener, "War Premeditated?" pp. 63n, 65. Trumpener rejects the claims of early preparation.

[68] Jagow to Lichnowsky, July 18, 1914, in "German Secret War Documents," *International Conciliation*; Lichnowsky to Jagow, July 23, 1914, Montgelas and Schuecking, *Outbreak of the World War.*

[69] Lichnowsky to Jagow, and Jagow to Lichnowsky, 25 July 1914, reprinted in Imanuel Geiss, ed., *Julikrise und Kriegsausbruch 1914* (Hannover: Verlag fur Literatur und Zeitgeschehen, 1963).

[70] Letter, Tschirschky to Jagow, 11 July 1914, *Official German Documents.*

[71] Tschirschky to Bethmann-Hollweg, 24 July 1914, in Montgelas and Schuecking, *Outbreak of the World War.*

[72] Tschirschky to Foreign Office, 25 July 1914, in "German Secret War Documents."

[73] S.L.A. Marshall, *World War I* (New York: American Heritage Press, 1985), p. 32.

[74] Jagow to the Emperor, 23 July 1914, in "German Secret War Documents."

[75] On July 25, Lichnowsky telegraphed that the British were holding Germany "morally responsible" for the excessive Austrian demands, although his telegram came too late to have influenced the Dutch. That same day, Jagow informed Lichnowsky that the British proposal for conciliation could no longer affect the situation (although he failed to reveal Germany's role in Austria's decision to press on). Lichnowsky left Jagow in no doubt that this would cause problems, and (in another telegram) that Britain would not remain "disinterested . . . in case France

should be drawn in". In a third communication, he reported that Britain was absolutely convinced that an Austro-Russian conflict meant world war, and added his own interpretation, namely that Britain would support France and Russia. At the same time, Germany told France that it had nothing to do with the Austrian note, which would have aroused suspicion in anyone with access to any of Germany's other diplomatic traffic. Four telegrams from Lichnowsky to Jagow, 25 July 1914, and two telegrams from Schoen to Jagow, 25 July 1914, in Montgelas and Schuecking, *Outbreak of the World War*; Jagow to Lichnowsky, July 25 1914, in "German Secret War Documents."

[76] Bethmann-Holweg to the Emperor, July 25, 1914, in "German Secret War Documents;" Memorandum of Under-Secretary of Foreign Affairs (Zimmerman), 25 July 1914, in Montgelas and Schuecking, *Outbreak of the World War*.

[77] Charlotte A. van Manen, *De Nederlandsche Overzee Trustmaatschappij. Middelpunt van het verkeer van onzijdig Nederland met het buitenland tijdens den wereldoorlog 1914-1919* ('s-Gravenhage: Martinus Nijhoff, 1935), vol. 1, p. 7.

[78] John H. Maurer, *Outbreak of the First World War: Strategic Planning, Crisis Decision Making, and Deterrence Failure* (Westport, CT: Praeger, 1995), p. 129.

[79] Ibid., p. 79.

[80] "Mobilisatie van de Nederlandsche land- en zeemacht in 1914" (Postwar report), Generale Staf, ARA-II.

[81] Van Voorst tot Voorst, *Over Roermond*, p. 55; Secretary of the Military Railroad Commission to Chief of Staff, 15 June 1906, Generale Staf, ARA-II; Snijders, "Nederland's militaire positie," p. 539; De Meier, "Geheime Dienst," p. 4; W. Klinkert, "Nederlandse Mobilisatie van 1914," pp. 24-33 in W. Klinkert, J.W.M. Schulten, and Luc de Vos, eds., *Mobilisatie in Nederland en België: 1870-1914-1939* (Amsterdam: De Bataafsche Leeuw, 1991), p. 25; "Mobilisatie van de Nederlandsche land- en zeemacht," p. ii; Beening, "Onder de vleugels," p. 380; Dufour to Snijders, 26 July 1914, Sectie Militaire Geschiedenis.

[82] M.W.F. Treub, *Oorlogstijd. Herinneringen en indrukken* (Haarlem: Tjeenk Willink, 1916), p. 9; "Mobilisatie van de Nederlandsche land- en zeemacht," pp. i-ii; C. Smit, *Nederland in de Eerste Wereldoorlog (1899-1919)*, vol. 2, *1914-1917* (Groningen: Wolters-Noordhoff, 1972), p. 1; Ritter, *Donkere poort*, p. 19; Cabinet minutes, 27 July 1914, 6, Smit, *Bescheiden ... 1914-1917*, p. 26; Chilton to Grey, 27, 28, and 29 July 1914, 195, 213, 257, Gooch and Temperley, *British Documents*, pp. 135, 147, 168; Beening, "Onder de vleugels," p. 380.

[83] Beening, "Onder de vleugels," p. 380; "Mobilisatie van de Nederlandsche land- en zeemacht," p. ii; Berg, *Snijders*, p. 75; Treub, *Oorlogstijd*, p. 10; Van Manen, *De Nederlandsche Overzee Trustmaatschappij*, vol. 7, pp. 9-11.

[84] Ritter, *Donkere poort*, p. 20; De Valk and Van Faassen, *Dagboeken en aantekeningen*, pp. 614, 616; Gooch and Temperley, Chilton to Grey, 29 July 1914, 323, *British Documents*, p. 208; Treub, *Oorlogstijd*, pp. 10, 11, 355; Berg, *Snijders*, p. 76; Domenico L. Roitero and Maarten C. Hoff, "Militaire misstappen van de Nederlandse leeuw" (Ph.D. dissertation: Rijksuniversiteit Groningen, 1995), p. 171; H.W.C. Bordewyk, "War Finances in the Netherlands," pp. 103-221 in G. Vissering, J. Westerman Holstijn, and H.W.C. Bordewyk, *The Netherlands and the World War: Studies in the War History of a Neutral*, vol. 4, pp. 168, 169; Vissering and Holstijn, "The Effect of the War Upon Banking and Currency," pp. 3-101 in *The Netherlands and the World War*, vol. 4, p. 53.

[85] "Mobilisatie van de Nederlandsche land- en zeemacht," p. iii; Klinkert, "De

Nederlandse mobilisatie," pp. 25-26; Berg, *Snijders,* p. 76; "Regeling van de oproeping van de landweer grens- en kustwacht, en van de land-weerbewakingsdetachementen," Generale Staf nr toegang 2.13.15.01, inv nr 206; Ritter, *Donkere poort,* p. 20; Treub, *Oorlogstijd,* p. 11; Alting von Geusau, *Onze weermacht,* p. 23; Klinkert, "Verdediging van de zuidgrens," pp. 214-15.

[86] Fabius, "De Inlichtingen dienst," p. 201; Chilton to Grey, 2 August 1914, 478, Gooch and Temperley, *British Documents,* p. 272.

[87] Richard von Kühlmann, *Erinnerungen* (Heidelberg: Lambert Schneider, 1948), p. 389.

CHAPTER FOUR

THE MOUSE THAT ROARED

The Dutch had signaled that they would fight, but had no way of knowing if they would have to fight, against whom, or when. The decision for war or peace lay abroad. If war came, the adversary would be infinitely more powerful, while, in the absence of alliances, there was no certainty of foreign military aid. The army's fighting quality lagged behind its potential adversaries, and that gap would grow as the war progressed. Any deployment that appeared to "favor" one neighbor might lead to problems with the others, so even normally tactical decisions were governed by the strategy of neutrality. This posed huge problems for the army and its hard-working supreme commander. The financial burden of mobilization was small compared to the sacrifices of the warring powers, but still not negligible; the impact of taxes and government borrowing on commerce and trade was substantial. In addition, the influence of the military could rise to a level without precedent in Dutch history. Some feared that Holland would become militaristic as a result. This might seem farfetched, but the powers of the Supreme Commander of Land and Sea Forces *(Opperbevelhebber van Land- en Zeemacht)* were immense, and he was every bit as jealous of his prerogatives, and every bit as unwilling to tolerate parliamentary involvement, as Haig, Joffre, or Ludendorff. Wartime Holland would not become a military dictatorship, but it would not remain fully democratic either.

Mobilization

The speed with which the army mobilized was in complete contrast to the fiasco of 1870. As in other western armies, the Dutch general staff had prepared a series of telegrams the receipt of which meant that certain actions had to be taken. Telegram A began the process of setting up river and harbor obstacles and could be sent during times of political tensions; B, which required a royal signature, signaled danger of war and demanded the preparation for bridge destruction, among other things; C permitted occupation of private property. Once the cabinet approved mobilization, the army first sent a warning telegram to the telegraph and telephone service, warning of imminent takeover, and then a telegram would be sent taking control of the railroads. The final step, of course, was the sending of callup telegrams all over the country. This was done some seven hours after the railroads were notified, probably to give them some time to prepare.[1]

On the whole the communication system worked well. About 92% of all the mobilization telegrams were delivered within half an hour.[2] As a result, the mobilization proceeded rapidly. The size of the country was an advantage here, for the distances to be traveled were very small, probably little more than a tenth of the 700 kilometers that an average Russian draftee had to travel. For a small power on the defensive, however, a lack of size was also a disadvantage. An invader could reach the country's heartland in a few days, and outer areas that had to be defended for the sake of maintaining neutrality (most obviously, Limburg) could be invaded within hours and overrun in little more than a day. Hence the speed of the 1914 mobilization was not an organizational victory, exceeding requirements, but a military necessity.

The emphasis on speed is everywhere in the 1913-14 plans. The most exposed units were to supplied as quickly as possible, and bridge destruction teams were to be sent immediately after the issuance of telegram B. Bridges along the German frontier were to be commandeered as well. Once mobilized, units were to take up preplanned positions without waiting for any further orders. The commandant at Maastricht, Limburg, the most endangered major city, was authorized to take whatever actions he thought necessary in case of invasion without waiting for further orders.[3] Generally this emphasis on speed was understood and led to quick response, although not everywhere. "Inconceivably, immediate action did not take place everywhere." Most problems occurred among fortification/inundation forces. The Field Army, in contrast, was in position by 3 August, although the headquarters was not completely ready[4] (an oddity, as Holland was the only country with a peacetime headquarters for the field forces).

In sheer numbers, the mobilization was impressive. In three days some 200,000 troops were brought under arms, a total that would more than double by the end of the war. About half (95,000) were in the four-division field army, with 70,000 men allocated to fortifications, 20,000 to depots, and 10,000 to border duty.[i] This meant that just over

---

[i] This number swelled greatly during the war as smuggling became a problem.

3% of the population was in uniform by the morning of August 4 – not an exceptional figure by World War I standards, but a significant organizational achievement all the same. The mobilized army contained 138 battalions, equal to 11 ½ German divisions (Germany had 115 divisions in 1914). The extent of the mobilization fooled foreign and domestic observers alike. Politicians in Parliament thought the army had 300,000 troops, and German sources also overestimated the size of the Dutch army. The Dutch war minister knew about, but did not bother to correct, these misconceptions.[5]

Organization and recruitment had come together by 1914 to produce a substantial mobilized army. The railroad plan, updated and corrected in the critical days at the end of July, worked. The small callup of soldiers to flesh out the border and coast guards was accomplished in a day (30 July). Then, on August 1, 97,000 troops were moved; the following day, another 72,000.[ii] By the evening of August 1, most units had reached 90% of their TOE strength, while over 90% of those on leave were on duty. Units requiring troops from the whole country took longer, and some specialized units had a lot of soldiers at sea.[6] But these were the exceptions. Of course none of this would have been achieved if pre-war reforms had not increased the size of annual draft classes at a much greater rate than the growth of the population. In 1880, the *landweer* class totaled about 7,000 recruits, while by 1912 the number reached 18,000 – and was supposed to grow by another 50% in the next three years. In fact, the total number called to service grew by more than 60% between 1914 and 1916, exceeding the number placed on leave.[7]

Yet this numerically impressive force had a lot of shortcomings. Some of these resulted from the peculiar ratio created by mobilization. In Germany, France, and Russia, there were about 5 or 6 soldiers mobilized for every man on active duty. In Holland, the ratio was almost 18 to 1. There were only 11,000 career soldiers. The active (read: well trained) reserve counted only 4500 men, meaning that the other 180,000 men consisted of previously trained classes – and their training, let alone their annual practices, tended to be shorter than in other countries. A few soldiers had had only four months. Bosboom

---

[ii] The first day's movements required about 500 trains. The exact number is harder to calculate than in, for example, Germany, as a number of trains in Holland combined military and civilian duty.

estimated he was short some 700 officers and 1,600 NCOs, especially because of the need to (re)train many incoming soldiers. It would have been even worse if a number of KNIL officers had not been available to take regular army commissions. Not surprisingly, Bosboom fought during the war not primarily for more troops, but for a larger permanent reserve of experienced soldiers.[8]

The army was also too small, especially as it had to face in several different directions. Divisional frontage was far too great and the field army had to be stripped of battalions for garrison duty in the most threatened provinces, Limburg and Zeeland. The government attempted to recruit volunteers from the 600,000 young men aged 17-40 not in uniform, probably thinking that volunteers would be more enthusiastic and disciplined than the draftees. This failed utterly. The *Vrijwillige Landstorm* (Volunteer Reserve) received only 2,000 volunteers. Even those who had voluntarily joined militia-like units before the war showed little enthusiasm. Of some 400 *weerbaarheidskorpsen* (preparedness corps) and *schietverenigingen* (shooting associations), only 7 produced units; only 2% of the *schutterijen* (citizen soldier associations) joined, none as organized units.[9]

Numbers were less of problem, however, than equipment. The army had too few howitzers, machine guns, grenades, gas masks, steel helmets, and mortars. Even the *Waterlinie* was questionable. Artillery could not be bought during the war because the best source – Germany – was effectively unavailable. There were only 4 airplanes (6 more were on order). Of the 115,000 rifles for new recruits, 65,000 were an older model that used different caliber ammunition. There were only about 700 shells for each of the newer field guns, less than even the Russians had (the pre-war government had concealed this shortage). Colijn had decided that there should be a minimum of 120 million rifle bullets, but there were only 85 million. Most of the 780 machine guns were an older model that could not use rifle bullets. Of the 2,000 artillery guns, 600 were of the quick-firing variety, and only 440 were mobile. Heavy field artillery was almost nonexistent.[10]

Nor was the mobilization entirely smooth. The preparation of coastal and harbor blockages and bridge destruction took longer than expected, in some cases due to confusion concerning some of the mobilization telegrams. In several towns, mayors failed to execute their duties, which included finding living quarters for the troops. In Hulst, for example, a corporal was told that he would have to take care of housing his troops himself.[iii] Traffic jams occurred because soldiers returning from leave headed for the earliest mobilization train, not the one assigned. Documents were routinely filled in incorrectly. Route marches resulted in too many stragglers – something blamed on the lack of quality footwear (there was only one pair of shoes in storage for every two soldiers on leave). In one division, there was so much concern about the low quality of shooting that some officers wanted to deprive sentries of rifles to prevent accidents. Even the army train department came in for criticism, as it would not have been possible to organize any strategic movement immediately after mobilization.[11]

Senior officers tended to give low ratings to their units' fighting qualities. The loss of trained maneuver battalions to the fortifications came in for particular criticism. This not only weakened the Field Army, but put troops in the fortifications with no experience or training for that service (perhaps explaining why they were removed within 6 months). The larger maneuver formations had too little experience and were only regarded as battle ready after months of training. The fortress troops got even lower evaluations. The picture was not entirely negative, however. Most artillery units worked smoothly, the cavalry had few problems, and the bicyclists did well. Three of the four division commanders were satisfied with their field artillery units and their engineers. Not coincidentally, the best units were the ones with the most professionals.[12]

The small size of the experienced cadre was a headache in 1914, and – due to leave policies – would remain so throughout the war. The ratio of reservists to professionals (18 to 1) actually understates the severity of the problem because a disproportionate number of professionals were tied up in the cavalry and artillery. The professionals were as good as could be expected, given that some important activities (maneuvers and gunnery practices, for example) were carried out too infrequently in peacetime. Soldiers from the active reserve were rated highly – but they were far too few in number to have a great impact. Many KNIL officers were put in functions for which they had no training or background. A number of NCOs were given officer ranks, but in in many cases they, as well as *landweer* officers with little annual training, were not up to their task. Bosboom concluded that officer education was too theoretical and not practical enough.[13]

[iii] Hulst lay in Dutch Flanders, close to Belgium; a very exposed position.

Most of these problems could be overcome by training, so long as the army had some breathing space. One Dutch battalion commander told the German attaché that it was "very fortunate" that no attack came at the beginning of the war.[14] According to the official army mobilization report, three of the four division commanders

> do not hesitate to call it good luck for our fatherland, that the army was not called upon to immediately . . . go into the field, because of which it got the opportunity to make up for the lost ground through tremendous training.[15]

On the basis of the senior officers' opinions, the army's official postwar report concluded that it would not have been ready for a campaign until three months after the wars' beginning.[16]

Training might improve with time, but discipline went in the opposite direction. Morale was high in the army in the opening days, but the soldiers soon lost interest. One officer described "obedience, self confidence, and a sense of duty" as a "missing trinity" among the soldiers. Soldiers failed to salute, sent complaints directly to the Queen, and called in sick on practice days. Experienced cadre could not deal easily with soldiers who were older, better educated, and socially superior. Soldiers on duty would leave their rifles to chat with civilians and let children play on their vehicles. Soldiers were described as "loutish." Discipline depended solely on fear of punishment. Soldiers might not be openly disobedient, but there was no evidence of any energetic commitment to carrying out the job.[17]

How much the lack of discipline affected combat readiness is hard to say. Charles à Court Repington, British military attaché in the low countries during the Boer War and a keen student of their defense, had opined that the average Dutchman was a lousy peacetime soldier but a potentially stubborn fighter, and so he would prove in a later, bigger war. But it certainly made life difficult for the more dedicated officers (the others simply ignored the problem). Usually the disciplinary problems were headaches for local commanders, but sometimes even the higher echelons had to intervene. On October 8, 1914, a group of soldiers stationed in the 4th Regiment at Leiden wrote a letter to Wilhelm II protesting the mistreatment of the Belgians and obliquely threatening war. The letter found its way into newspapers in Rotterdam and Leiden, as well as the French *Journal du Havre* (published in the city where many Belgian officials were located by this time). Not surprisingly, Snijders went ballistic and appointed an investigative commission to interrogate every soldier who might have had a hand in the letter. Handwriting analysis was used and a police detective infiltrated the unit. The investigation was vigorously pursued by the division and Field Army commanders but, despite the fact that only a limited number of soldiers could have written the letter (it was in fluent French) the culprits were never found. Snijders could only communicate his "deep indignation" to the government and (cleverly) suggested that the foreign minister point out that there was no actual evidence that the letter had come from the troops.[18] Chances are that it was written by soldiers, but Snijders as usual had to deal with a problem he could not solve and pressed on with his usual determination and, some would say, fatalism.

In that he was much like his countrymen. The mobilization was greeted with none of the enthusiasm that existed in Paris, Berlin, or St. Petersburg/Petrograd. The outward attitude of the civilian population was serious and somber.[19] This was reflected in many memoirs. A War Ministry civil servant and future war minister, Jhr. B.C. de Jonge, remembered going outside with some coworkers on August 1:

> I shall also never forget how we lay there in the quiet night listening to the unfamiliar sound of the trains, which were carrying the troops to their destinations.[20]

This somewhat eerie experience reflects no enthusiasm, and there was none. Holland had nothing to gain from mobilization except hopefully survival, and some doubted that the costly and disruptive mobilization alone would accomplish very much.[21] Yet it received near-universal support. Even the leader of the virulently anti-military Social Democrats (SDAP), P.J. Troelstra, was

> completely convinced of the necessity to defend our neutrality against an eventual German invasion, which was feared by many during the first months of the war [because I am] under the impression of the fanatical German militarism.

Troelstra did not even disapprove when his own son volunteered for military service.[22] The army took the young man – but did, given his parentage, ban him from guarding the royal palace.[23]

The Social Democrats could support the mobilization (voting for the mobilization credits despite invariably voting against the regular military budget) because there was no suspicion that there was any policy except strict neutrality. Even Snijders, viewed with hostility by

Social Democrats and more moderate parliamentarians (the feeling was mutual) was absolutely committed to neutrality, although the policy later caused him tremendous problems. He could concentrate neither against Britain (his personal preference) nor Germany (the most likely invader).

The German General Staff, however, noted his preparations. On July 29, the General Staff reported to the foreign office that Holland was preparing to mobilize, bridges were occupied by troops, forts were being garrisoned, and "provision supply is apparently ample." Jagow sent a sealed dispatch to Holland containing *Moltke's* assurance that Holland's neutrality would be safeguarded. The general's interest in Holland in this period is surprising, considering what else was on his mind.[24]

Then again, his close attention to things Dutch perhaps represented his growing awareness of the risks he took – and forced his empire to take – just to avoid the Netherlands. Moltke demanded an immediate march on Belgium (and Luxembourg) because he had to capture Liège in a few days only. The Kaiser, the Chancellor, and the rest of the government had no time to think things over and reach a calm decision. Moltke insists that the war must begin immediately – and in a purely technical sense, he is right. Had he not been so insistent, there was a chance (albeit a small one) that cooler heads might have prevailed and the war in the West headed off, or at least postponed. But the need to capture Liège and attack in the West before Russia could mobilize "caused the crisis to move beyond control."[25] This only became clear to the German government on August 1, when Moltke categorically refused to postpone his advance while Britain's intentions were being ascertained. When Wilhelm II proposed moving the army eastward, Moltke was "horrified at the prospect of changing Germany's war plan on the spur of the moment." Patrols were already on their way to the borders.[26] Moltke got his way, and he won the battle of Liège, thereby sparing the Netherlands an early entry into the war. How trivial are sometimes the events that trigger the death and maiming of millions.

His decision was influenced by his knowledge that Holland would fight – an example of successful deterrence.

As it turned out, the operation succeeded brilliantly, although chance and Belgian errors helped. The operation depended on six brigades, organized as the "Army of the Meuse," kept at combat readiness.[27] To prevent immobilization of the entire army, the Army of the Meuse had to be ready to march on 24 hours' notice.[28] The commander, Otto von Emmich, met his schedule handsomely. On August 2 his force was ready and on the road to Liège.[29] As a result, the Belgians did not have time to fortify the areas between the forts. "[T]he entire German war plan would be ruined if Germany allowed Belgium to prepare the defense of Liège."[30] Many accounts of the Liège campaign omit, however, that Moltke, Ludendorff, and Emmich were lucky. The Belgian forts fell quickly because they were badly built. Liège was built with substandard concrete, with less than half the cement per cubic meter used at Verdun.[31] One bridge was captured completely intact.[32] The Belgians did not deploy their army along the Meuse, leaving the forts unsupported.

The excessive need for speed was not the only price of Moltke's plan, however. As discussed earlier, the advancing armies had to move through relatively narrow corridors. The congestion was unbelievable. Unloading zones were 50-70 kilometers deep, so some army units had to be dropped off east of the Rhine and proceed on foot. At one point on the 40 kilometers of rail line between Herbesthal and Liège, there were 127 military trains standing still: it took 16-26 *hours* to complete the journey. The 1st Army's columns had to halt on August 16 to let various units catch up.[33] A typical corps column stretched for 56 kilometers on a single road (few corps had more) and took 11 hours to pass.[34] The Cologne railway bridge alone had to handle 2,150 military trains in the first 17 days – about a train every 11 minutes.[35] The length of the march and extra time made it difficult to prevent the Belgian army from retreating to Antwerp.[36] So dense was the mass of German soldiers circumventing Limburg that they looked like a "grey flood."[37] Any quibbles in Holland about whether mobilizing had been a good thing vanished overnight in the face of such a sight.

Neither Snijders nor Loudon could wait to see what Germany's march route was before taking actions. Of the two, Loudon had the trickier assignment. He had to maintain strict neutrality while feeling out the Belgians and the British to see how they would respond if Holland were invaded. His first action was to suggest joint defensive measures to the Belgians in the summer of 1914. He either guessed that Germany planned to cross the Meuse valley through both countries, or was privy to Bosboom's earlier discovery. The record is silent on what motivated his move, in some ways an unusual one for the cautious neutralist. He first floated the idea on Monday, July 27th, and renewed the offer on Wednesday July 29. Belgium refused to respond, some-what overoptimistically clinging to the hope that the war would pass it by. The Dutch cabinet, that same Wednesday, decided to prepare to close the Schelde to both sides, although British vessels would be allowed to help the Belgians so long as their role was limited to the 1839 treaty. In other words, if Belgium and/or Britain became *bona fide* belligerents, the river would be closed. Britain was informed of the closing preparations on Thursday the 30th. The cabinet also decided on the 29th that the Eems would not be contested.[38]

Further complicating the situation was that Britain might want to force the Schelde to aid Belgium. On Saturday August 1, the cabinet continued to discuss the Schelde situation. Cort van der Linden notified Snijders that the channel(s) would be open to anyone sending aid to Belgium. Discussions were held in cabinet about how to divide responsibility for the river with the Belgians in wartime. Loudon had his envoy in London give formal notification of the full army mobilization, more to assure the British that Germany would be resisted than to deter a British attack. He worried about the colonial empire as well. He telegraphed his legation in Washington about the balance of power in the Pacific, apparently thinking that a European war would give Japan an edge. He had nothing against Japan, but feared a Japanese interest in the Dutch colony. The legation's answer Sunday evening, indicating that Robert Lansing, the U.S. Undersecretary of State, shared Loudon's concern.[39] That did not help much, but it was still a happy day for Loudon; he now had far more important information on matters closer to home.

Sunday was a day of risk and resolution for the Netherlands. Germany finally clarified its position. It did so on that day because its invasion march began; the Germans invaded Luxembourg. This was not good news for Holland, as it was a guarantor of the tiny country's neutrality. When the Luxembourgeois Minister of State, P. Eysschen, telegraphed Loudon about the invasion, however, he noted that it violated the treaty of London (1867) but did not demand that Holland honor its commitment as guarantor of Luxembourg's neutrality. Jagow ordered his envoy in the Hague, Felix von Müller to inform the Dutch that the occupation was unavoidable due to the French advance and that Luxembourg would be compensated. In so doing, he relieved the Dutch of any obligations to assist Luxembourg, as the reference to a "French advance" made it seem unclear as to who was really responsible for the violation.[40]

More importantly, that same day (August 2) Jagow ordered Müller to hand over the note that Moltke had drafted three days earlier, with a few modifications. Jagow's instructions read:

> Your Excellency will state to the local Government that the Imperial Government is counting with security upon the assumption that the Netherlands will maintain toward Germany a benevolent neutrality and so further confirm the friendly relations between the two countries. On this assumption, the neutrality of the Netherlands will be respected to the full by Germany. The Netherlands Government must be given the impression that all of the instructions relating to this matter arrived only today. Please send an immediate telegraphic report upon the arrival of this telegram as well as the time of your announcement and the reception accorded it.[41]

Jagow had not tinkered much with Moltke's formula. He had changed Moltke's "close and friendly relations" to a more modest "friendly relations" and had dropped a flowery reference to "race- and blood-related countries."[42]

Yet even the simplified statement created problems for Loudon. For one thing, what did "benevolent neutrality" mean? Germany's "respect" for Dutch neutrality was clearly conditioned on this, yet "benevolent neutrality" had no legal meaning. Either a country is neutral, or it is not. Did "benevolence" indicate that Germany wanted some type of special treatment? How would Germany view the mobilization? Not surprisingly, Loudon limited himself to thanking Müller, later merely telling him that Holland was "counting on" correct behavior by Germany – an obvious reference to the Jagow/Müller "counting upon" language.[43] The German statement was reassuring, but it was also ominous. If Loudon had been paranoid, he might have wondered if Germany were looking for an excuse to invade Holland if Dutch neutrality ceased to be "benevolent." There is no evidence that Loudon suspected this, nor was there any reason to. Germany had not waited for any excuse before invading the other two low countries. German statement's conditionality indicated, however, that Holland's behavior would be under review. In a short war, this might not matter much, but in a lengthy conflict, Holland's security could be endangered if Berlin decided that the Dutch were not being benevolently neutral.

On that same August 2nd, however, Moltke reinforced the earlier message by inviting the Dutch envoy to his headquarters and assured him that Germany would respect the Netherlands' neutrality, asking for tolerance in case any German soldiers accidentally crossed the frontier. His feelings toward Holland were not shared by all. The mobilization sent a mixed signal to Germany. While Moltke apparently believed throughout that the Dutch were merely protecting themselves, his staff officers concluded on August 1 that Holland was mobilizing because it was "forced by England to take her stand on the side of the Triple Entente." Perhaps to check on this point, Moltke asked if the coast would be defended; Gevers informed him that the Netherlands would defend all its borders. Moltke suggested that the Dutch need only leave a few troops along the German border and asked Gevers not to share this with his colleagues.[44]

Less satisfactory to Loudon was Germany's mining of the entire Eems on Sunday. This had been anticipated by the cabinet, and had even been discussed within the foreign ministry 7 years before, but that did not make the event more welcome. Nor was he taken with the German-circulated reports of 80 French officers attempting to penetrate the German border through eastern Limburg, which could be read as an attempt to claim provocation near this vulnerable point. But he and his envoys were not tempted to swing toward the other side because of these two incidents; De Marees van Swinderen made clear to Crowe that unsolicited offers of assistance were not welcome. In addition, the closing of the Schelde estuaries proceeded, expected if not welcomed by Britain.[45]

The same day he also received official notification of Belgium's mobilization and fort preparations. The timing of this message was peculiar. The Belgian government had already sent it to its legation on Friday July 31, but the note was not handed over until Sunday. As Loudon had indicated an interest in joint operations the previous Monday and Wednesday, and Belgium now was clearly aware that it could not escape war, the delay was strange. Perhaps the note was forwarded on Sunday because Belgian foreign minister J. Davignon rethought his earlier refusal and ordered his envoy, Baron A.A.F.I.G. Fallon, to discuss military cooperation, specifically a direct communications link between Maastricht and Liège. Fallon promptly went to the Foreign Ministry, but was told that Loudon "had not arrived." Possibly he was avoiding the Belgian diplomat, expecting some sort of follow-up to Moltke's assurances. If so, he was quite correct. Müller came on Monday and gave formal assurances that Dutch neutrality would be respected. He did leave the minister and his staff in some confusion with the request for a *wohlwollende* neutrality, which, as *chef de cabinet* Doude van Troostwijk pointed out, had no legal meaning. For the moment, however, Loudon was more than satisfied with the state of events. He took the opportunity to deny categorically the story about the 80 French officers, about which the German envoy did not argue further. Fallon arrived later, was told of the German assurances, and instead of leaving with a promise of military ties, was sent away with a note informing him of the Schelde closing.[46]

Since Germany had given assurances, Loudon contemplated asking Britain for the same. The Schelde situation demanded it because of a telegram he had received late in the morning. De Marees van Swinderen had reported that the British government's position was hardening with the report of the invasion of Luxembourg and that if Germany did not give a satisfactory response to the question of Belgian neutrality, that would be considered as *equivalent to a declaration of war* (emphasis added). The implication was obvious: so long as Britain acted *as guarantor* of Belgium, then Holland could allow it to use the Schelde, because it would not be a true belligerent. But if Britain *considered herself at war* with Germany, then Britain was a belligerent and might have to be denied the Schelde by force, if necessary. Loudon hesitated. He instructed De Marees van Swinderen to ask for assurances, but told the envoy that if he disagreed with this request, to send advice instead.[47]

The situation was delicate. Either opposing or permitting the use of the Schelde might mean war. The loophole provided by the 1839 accords had now been closed. The neutrality declaration left no room for maneuver. Three years earlier, retired general and active politician Jhr. J.C.C. den Beer Poortugael had questioned whether the neutrality proclamation issued during the Italian-Turkish war covered the Schelde, as it referred only to "land." The foreign ministry had concluded that it did. The proclamation of Friday July 31 removed any ambiguity, forbidding belligerent warships in any Dutch territorial waters.[48]

This actually made Loudon's job easier and allowed him to look at the big picture, not just a few technical details. When he arrived at work on Tuesday August 4 he drafted a telegram to the Washington legation asking them to keep him informed on far Eastern developments, showing he was retaining both his composure and his global vision. He also forwarded the new neutrality declaration to his legations, issued because of the growing flood of war declarations now criss-crossing Europe. The declaration studiously avoided direct references to allowing or preventing ship access to Antwerp, despite the fact that this was now the "front burner" foreign policy issue. Cort van der Linden secretly informed Snijders that British ships entering the Schelde should not be fired upon until the barriers were in place. De Marees van Swinderen informed Grey of the neutrality declaration but, rather than demanding assurances, he merely mentioned that Germany's position was conditional on a similar guarantee from Britain. In essence, he took a middle road between the two alternatives suggested by his chief. He received the answer that Britain could not reciprocate as it did not consider itself at war yet.[49]

Grey's position regarding Holland was far more interested than the above would indicate. For whatever reasons, he preferred to handle the matter via his legation in The Hague. He initially sent two messages on Tuesday, August 4th, telling all the neutrals that they were expected to resist, and that Britain would help. Three hours later, at 2 p.m., he canceled the earlier messages.[iv] His chargé in The Hague had already discussed them with Loudon, but when he went back to the ministry to explain their cancellation, Loudon was unavailable. The *chef de cabinet,* who regretted the cancellation (which had astonished the Britisher), said that he would tell Loudon "as soon as he could find him," but did assure the British diplomat that all precautions were being taken and that Holland would resist. Loudon's absence from the ministry is not hard to explain. Based on the earlier messages, it was clear that Grey was thinking of demanding an alliance.[v] Loudon could never accept such a proposal (which the British chargé was contemplating making on his own!), especially as he thought that the army could not stop the German invasion that would inevitably follow.[50] His view hints at closer contacts with the military than the surviving record shows. He definitely managed strategic absences from his office to avoid unwelcome questions.

[iv] Grey was in considerable turmoil on August 4. He had even received a communication from Germany in which the Germans denied any interest in annexing Belgium and underscored their sincerity by noting that they were not invading Holland. If there is a stranger message in the archives, I have not found it. Jagow to Lichnowsky, August 4, 1914, 587, Gooch and Temperley, *British Documents,* vol. 11, p. 312.

[v] This was partly because of a mistake made at the British Foreign Office. Grey's 10:30 a.m. telegram to Chilton instructed him to offer *common action.* The follow-up telegram at 10:45 changed this to *alliance,* but this was a mistake. By the time the correction was made (12:30 p.m.) Chilton had already made his first visit to the foreign ministry, no doubt mentioning an alliance – something Loudon had to avoid at all costs.

Britain and Belgium now became official belligerents, and this ended any haziness concerning the Schelde. There could no longer be any discussions about opening the river with Belgium, and Snijders was told on Wednesday August 5 to use force against warships attempting to use the Schelde. Belgium was informed that the river was closed to military traffic, and that barriers were being positioned. The Belgian envoy in London reported that the British fleet would ensure free passage of supplies to Antwerp, but this was in fact not accurate. Grey told the Dutch envoy that Britain would not raise the warship issue, and – in a piece of news that greatly relieved the Dutch – De Marees van Swinderen reported that, according to his French colleague, the British army would land in France, not Belgium (although there was some skepticism about whether it would come at all). Grey, however, pressured Holland for an alliance, as Loudon had feared. Grey proposed "common action" in not entirely friendly terms – suggesting that it was a "for us or against us" situation. He told De Marees van Swinderen that a German victory would be bad for Holland, while Dutch neutrality would be beneficial mostly for Germany. He asked Holland to "consider its position" and went on to say that he would ask Japan for a joint declaration guaranteeing the safety of Holland's colonies. The Dutchman thought all this threatening.[51]

That was not Grey's intention. His note to Chilton of the same day stated that he would be glad to join in common action, but it was clearly not a demand. The situation was also influenced by false rumors of German troops entering the Netherlands. He suggested, but did not press, for common cause with Belgium, causing De Marees van Swinderen to remind Chilton of the German assurances. The two agreed that Germany might not keep its promises. Grey also had pointed out that Germany only wanted to keep the Rhine open. He did raise the Schelde issue, but the Dutchman carefully claimed only that Holland could not allow warships.[52] This was indeed Loudon's formulation. So long as British troops did not come up the Schelde, or the flow of munitions became too obvious, there would be no problem.

While Loudon was pondering that Wednesday how to interpret Britain's position, Moltke summoned Gevers again and gave his word of honor that Holland's neutrality would be respected and pointed out how many hours would have been saved if he had gone through Limburg. He also asked the Dutch not to shoot in case German troops were pushed back from Liège onto Dutch soil.[53] The two conversations with Gevers have an odd ring. Moltke could hardly have feared a Dutch offensive into Belgium; in fact, he paid little attention to Dutch military actions and decisions, with the significant exception of Holland's growing preparations for the defense of Limburg.[54] Perhaps he was just attempting to maintain goodwill; if so, he was disappointed. In a letter to his wife, he wrote that *"[d]ie wenigen neutralen Staaten sind uns gegenüber nicht freundlich gesinnt."* ("The few neutral states are not friendly toward us").[55] Whether advance knowledge of this fact would have caused him to change his plans is unknowable.

Resolution was reached the following day, Thursday August 6. The day began badly with a message from De Marees van Swinderen, in which he repeated Grey's earlier claim that neutrality only benefitted Germany and added Grey's view that Holland might be forced by circumstances to join the Entente. Chilton's meeting with Loudon that same day, however, had an entirely different character. Britain accepted Loudon's point that an alliance would only lead to a German invasion. Chilton further informed Loudon that Britain would respect the Netherlands' neutrality so long as it was not one-sided (like Germany, Britain gave a conditional assurance). No warships would go up the Schelde, however. Chilton expressed his government's pleasure that the Schelde would remain open for merchant vessels, adding that "[t]he idea that His Majesty's Government contemplated [sending warships up the Schelde] or attacking Flushing was without foundation." That was not true, but Chilton may not have known. Loudon now had assurances of neutrality from both great powers. He also came to terms with Belgium about the use of the Schelde on the 6th, deftly closing a possible loophole by pointing out that the neutrality declaration forbade warships *and naval convoys,* a point not discussed explicitly with Chilton.[56] Perhaps he felt it was not the time to be too pushy with the British.

Instead, he took the opportunity to clarify his stance, sending a dawn telegram on Friday August 7 to De Marees van Swinderen allowing his sympathy for the cause that Britain was defending, but again noting Holland's vulnerability to invasion and occupation by Germany. Holland, he conceded, might have to change its position but asked the British government to understand that the moment had not come. He also pointed out that it was in Britain's interest not to place Holland in the position of being an adverse party. This masterful telegram simultaneously sympathized with Britain and threatened to join the other side! The Dutch envoy visited Grey and sent a lengthy, somewhat mixed report on the conversation. The request for an alliance was withdrawn, but Grey then noted that the Dutch army could draw a "not unimportant" part of the German army away from northern France, and argued that staying out of alliances in peacetime and wartime represented two different issues. The Dutchman agreed with Grey that a German victory was bad, but disagreed that a Dutch entry would doom Germany. They agreed to seek guarantees for the Dutch colonies, De Marees van Swinderen reporting that a Dutch oil company apparently had successfully lobbied Grey on this issue already. The envoy apparently still felt pressured on the alliance issue.[57]

There is little evidence that Loudon, who was much less excitable than his London representative, saw this as a problem any more. In fact, he turned his attention eastward once again, asking the German government to consider the importance of avoiding conflict over the Eems River. Turning around the argument he had used with success on the British, he obliquely asked the Germans to consider the British reaction to Holland's attitude on the Eems. The British had never asked Loudon about this, so either he was being clever, or he was anticipating a British complaint. The evidence suggests the latter. On Saturday August 8, Loudon telegraphed De Marees van Swinderen that Holland had no practical reason to contest the Eems issue. At the very least this gave the envoy something to work with in case of trouble over the issue. He need not have worried. On the same day, Grey expressed his entire satisfaction with Dutch policy.[58]

The German government apparently felt the same. Despite the query concerning the Eems, which only generated irritation, even the nonpollyanish Gevers expressed some optimism on Sunday August 9th about the long-term resolution of the issue. In addition, the Dutch took on a diplomatically onerous duty on that same day by carrying Germany's second demand for the surrender of Liège, after the American ambassador had refused to do so (the demand was refused anyway). More importantly, Moltke called Gevers back in on Tuesday August 11 and gave him emphatic personal assurances that the troop concentration on the Dutch border did not mean a pending violation of Holland's neutrality.[vi] Jagow was so optimistic about the relationship

---

[vi] The concentration around Limburg was so great that contemporary observers invariably referred to it as a "grey flood."

with Holland that he actually asked the Dutch on Thursday August 13 to give him confidential information about the state of morale in Britain, a request tossed in the circular file by the Dutch foreign ministry faster than anything received during the war. Nevertheless, it does show the positive state of the two countries' relationship. The Germans went on to promise that the fall of Antwerp would not affect Dutch neutrality (27 August) and only asked that the Schelde would be defended (29 August).[59]

Whether through luck or skill, Loudon and his department weathered the summer 1914 crisis very well indeed. Germany, Britain, and Belgium had all been pacified, and conflict over nettlesome geographical conundrums (The Schelde, the Eems, and Limburg) avoided.

Even Belgium expressed its satisfaction on August 12 about the resolution of the Schelde situation. There were flies in the ointment. The situation in the Indies was dangerous, especially after Japan's August 15th ultimatum to Germany effectively demanding that Berlin hand over its colony in China by the 23rd. Japanese expansion was definitely a threat. Yet Loudon had obtained at least an expression of shared concern from the United States (August 9) and British support for the maintenance of the Dutch empire, most recently on August 17th.[60] Germany's support for the Dutch colonial empire, if not militarily meaningful in the short term, was a given.

Deployment

Neutrality had survived the war's beginning. Now the belligerents had to be convinced on an ongoing basis that Holland would remain impartial and could defend its neutrality. To achieve this, the army's deployment had to accomplish five things. Troops had to be close enough to all potentially threatened borders to oppose any violator. They had to be able to obstruct or counterattack any force using Dutch territory as a convenient through route. The Field Army had to focus on the most dangerous spots, and also on the most likely invader, while still deploying in a completely neutral way. The field forces also had to be able to retreat intact into the country's center to defend the fortified zone. The country's limited military strength made it impossible to meet all of these goals. Choices would have to be made, and these in turn would depend on the expectations that the army had.

These were mixed. The general feeling was that the German army would attach more significance to the Dutch army than of Belgium's Meuse fortifications. On the other hand, few officers believed that Dutch neutrality would be respected in a Franco-German war, let alone if Britain were involved. Britain was expected to force the Schelde, as Churchill indeed urged during the crisis. Most concern, however, focused on the southeastern frontier and Germany's intentions there, as Belgium and Dutch Limburg were such natural march routes. Snijders in particular feared that Holland would be drawn into a conflict because its territory constituted an attractive route. He was reasonably prescient, conducting map exercises during the 1913-14 winter which foresaw a Russo-Austrian war emanating from the Balkans, followed by a Franco-German war, a German crossing of Belgium, a British entry, and a halt of the German advance in northern France. One of his officers commented later that he only had to look in his exercise book in August and September to know what the next event would be.[61]

Actually, Snijders wasn't *that* prophetic, as he did not foresee the breadth of the Schlieffen plan, with its simultaneous passage through northern *and* southern Belgium. Bosboom's source in 1906-1907 apparently had not revealed the entire plan. Nor did his overall prescience solve his security dilemmas. Having to deploy the Field Army in several directions, Snijders worried that "[o]ur entire eastern frontier lay open for a German invasion. In particular the danger for crossing of Limburg seemed very great." He conceded that the Schelde would be an "attraction point" for Allied help for Belgium, but Germany was the only power/potential enemy he mentioned by name. Bosboom shared his concern for Limburg, although he was less nervous than Snijders. He felt that the army, however weak, would deter an invasion of Limburg by threatening the German flank, and that Germany would also leave Holland alone because the Netherlands formed a natural flank protector for the German army.[62]

Deployment to *protect* Limburg meant, oddly enough, that the army could not be deployed *in* Limburg. The Belgians would have dearly loved for the Dutch to put a division or two in the province, but this would have been entirely counterproductive. In case of invasion the Dutch forces would have been directly in front of the German steamroller, and would either have been pulverized or forced to withdraw westward into Belgium, losing all contact with the rest of the army. The Belgian envoy, Fallon, reported that this concern had absorbed the Dutch generals during an intensive study in the 1913-14

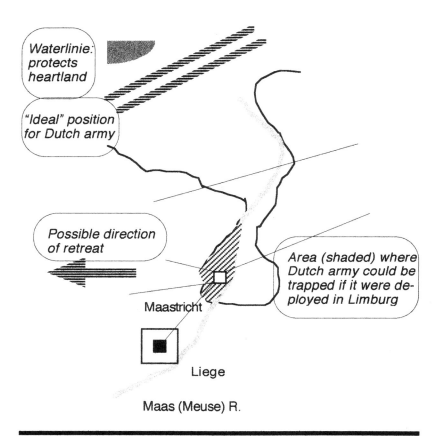

To adhre to its "rigid" neutrality, Holland had to defend Limburg. A token
defense was not enough. Large field army units in Limburg could, however, easily find themselves trapped west of Maastricht. Belgium would
undoubtedly permit withdrawal, but this would leave a large part of the
Dutch army on foreign soil, dependent on a foreign power -- effectively
the end of any kind of neutrality. The best solution was to deploy most
of the army north of Limburg, where it could simultaneously cover the
country's heartland and threaten the flank of an invader. The army would
also fortify Maastricht, prepare the Maas bridges for destruction, and place
observers on the eastern border to give the troops at Maastricht as much
warning time as possible.

winter regarding how to defend to province. The better alternative was to deploy to the north of the province, threatening the German flank, as Moltke had feared, without being exposed to destruction or isolation from the national heartland. Nevertheless, the Belgians encouraged a deployment in Limburg to the end, telling the Dutch as late as 10 August that German forces were planning to force the border to use the rail lines. General G. A. Buhlmann, the Field Army commander, did not think the Belgian claims required any additional response, and Snijders apparently concurred. Loudon merely told the Belgians that everything was ready for the defense of the Meuse line.[63] That was true, even if the forces stationed directly along the river were small. The British envoy was informed on 31 July that troops could be sent to Limburg "in a few hours" and four days later reported that "all available troops are being moved to province of Limburg." The "good authority" he cited might have been exaggerating, knowing that the British were especially interested in the defense of the Meuse, but a disproportionate amount of preparations and instructions were devoted to defending the awkward appendage. Special detachments for bridge destruction were posted in Limburg and reported directly to the Supreme Commander. Detailed instructions were prepared for the police-controlled border guards, requiring them to report all developments immediately to Maastricht. Border villages were covered by separate companies. The commander was authorized to remove anything that interfered with the defense of the area once a state of war or siege had been declared by the government.[64] Yet there were some obvious shortcomings. During the 1914 mobilization, the detachment sent to destroy the vital bridge at Roermond had to make a 24-hour automobile trip to pick up the explosives and reach its destination – and this problem had been spotted in 1912 and not corrected.[65]

If the Germans crossed the frontier, the Field Army would pressure the German flank – but then what? What if German forces then turned to advance on the Dutch field forces? Withdrawal was the only option. Germany was such a formidable opponent that the army did not even dare mention it by name when it was obviously the 'enemy' at maneuvers – unlike when Belgium was the theoretical adversary. To do otherwise would have triggered a German protest. A lengthy battle being out of the question, the country's hope lay in a withdrawal behind fortified inundations, the *Nieuwe Hollandsche Waterlinie,* which would hopefully slow down the invaders until Germany's enemies could help. At that point, plans called for resumption of

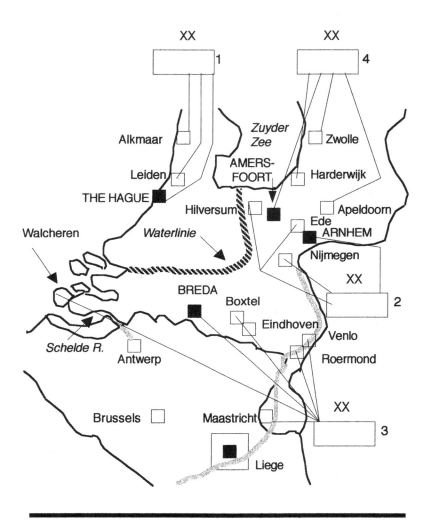

Shown above are major initial concentration points for the Field Army's four divisions. Divisional headquarters are shown in CAPS.
Fortress troop units are not shown.

fighting beyond the water lines.[66]

Theoretically, it was possible. The *Waterlinie* consisted of 65 fortified points along the planned inundation areas, running from near the Zuyder Zee toward the great Rhine tributaries. As such, it was obviously designed for an attack from the east or south. Amsterdam had its own multi-directional defense[vii] and was the army's strong point of last resort.[viii] The area required some 200,000 troops to defend it, almost exactly the mobilized strength of the army. While the inundations relied on fresh water, salt water could be added from the Zuyder Zee if necessary. Amsterdam was optimistically expected to hold out for months, especially as its guns were better quality and of the type that could withdraw into the ground. The inundations themselves relied on fairly simple guidelines; the water had to be deep enough to conceal canals, moats, etc., making it impossible to cross on foot, but not so deep that it could easily be crossed by boats, and wide enough to complicate the work of artillery spotters.[67]

The real strength of the *Waterlinie* was uncertain, however. Many of the defenses had been neglected. Money for improvements was limited, as available funds had been spent on the Field Army. The medium guns were good, but the big guns were outmoded; in many cases they were permanently mounted on top of fort walls, in which condition their survival in battle would have been unlikely. Some gaps existed, notably at Utrecht, which could only be effectively defended by the Field Army. Most of the provinces lay outside the water line, their security only indirectly assisted by the fortifications. Withdrawal into the *Waterlinie* would be difficult, as people and cattle, as well soldiers, would have to cross bridges crowded even in peacetime. Yet unless this withdrawal worked, the *Waterlinie* was useless; without the Field Army there were too few soldiers to hold the line, and without some counteroffensive capability the *Vesting Holland* would be reduced to a purely passive defense – and reduced it would be.[68]

So it all came back to the field divisions. Unless they could withdraw safely, the fortified zone would collapse. To simplify the

---

[vii] Building plans now threaten the area of the forts. Most still survive, but the countryside around them may soon fall victim to the country's enormous need for *Lebensraum* ('living space'). *The Windmill Herald,* 7 September 1998.

[viii] Conceptually similar to Belgium's reliance on Antwerp as the "National Redoubt."

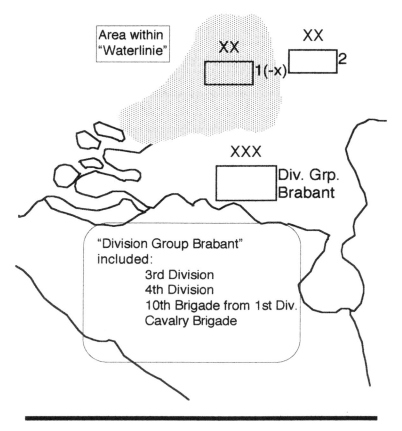

Deployment of the Field Army after October 1914.

situation, Snijders decided to deploy the Field Army so that it would be ready to concentrate anywhere to face an invader; for once, the smallness of the country was an advantage. He also secured from the Minister-President, Cort van der Linden, a commitment that he would not have to face more than one enemy or alliance.[69] Otherwise, if Germany invaded and Britain retaliated by moving into Holland to deny it to the Germans, Snijders would have to go to war against both the Entente and the Central Powers! This was not a purely theoretical possibility; in the last year of the war, Snijders would raise this issue again and receive a much more equivocal answer. But that lay far in the future.

For the present, the Field Army deployed into a box-like formation that appeared almost perfectly neutral but in fact allowed it to concentrate close to the scene of the fighting and protect threatened outlying areas, especially from Germany. On August 2-3, its four divisions moved into position. The 1st Division deployed along the coast, its headquarters at The Hague. Ostensibly it protected coastal cities from British invasion, but its location was quite handy for defending the Waterlinie and also gave Snijders some extra reserve. The 2nd Division was placed to the east and headquartered at Arnhem, there reinforced by a force of mounted artillery. The 3rd Division moved south and was headquartered at Breda, home of the Royal Military Academy, while some of its units were sent to Maastricht and Roermond in Limburg, others to Zeeland.. The 4th Division was placed centrally as a reserve, although almost immediately after the fall of Liège it was moved southward to support the tremendously over-stretched 3rd.[70]

Snijders went south for the obvious reason that the attack on Liège signaled the coming occupation of northern Belgium. Here was where the war would be. If the Entente strongly contested this German swing, Holland's Brabant province would quickly become the strategic spot. Lying between the two most threatened corners of the country, its defense was critical. He began to send troops southward, at the same time ordering the preparation of pontoon bridges in case the army had to retreat northward across the rivers into the *Vesting Holland*. When Antwerp fell he formed a large part of his Field Army into a "Division-group Brabant" which included The 4th and 3rd divisions as well as the cavalry brigade and a brigade from the 1st. This gave him a substantial concentration of troops close to the fighting.

But not without risk. Snijders worried about whether the 2nd

Division would be able to retreat into the fortified line in time. With the southward movement of the 4th and the independent cavalry brigade on 8-9 August, he had little left to cover the 2nd Division's withdrawal. The siege of Antwerp forced him to shift his Brabant forces westward, so that the 1st had to be cannibalized to protect eastern Brabant. Otherwise, Limburg (admittedly less in danger now) would be left almost unprotected. Buhlmann even suggested moving another entire division south, but Snijders had to decline; his deployment was unbalanced as it was. Public criticism of the deployment, which left the eastern defenses denuded, was not long in coming – especially from the popular *Telegraaf* (described by Snijders as a "lying gutter paper sold to the Entente"). Bosboom also had reservations, but was more critical of the tool than the workman; the army's divisions were simply too big and unwieldy, and 6-8 smaller divisions would have given Snijders much more flexibility.[71]

The creation of Divisiongroup Brabant did allow Snijders to deal with his other geographical conundrum – the Schelde and the adjoining province, Zeeland. The government temporarily simplified this problem for Snijders by instructing him to limit himself to a protest if the British sailed up the Schelde, provided that they claimed to be sailing on the grounds of the 1839 treaty with Belgium. This was a perfectly legal sidestep, as there had always been some question about Holland's right to stop assistance under a treaty which she herself had signed. Once Belgium and Britain became official belligerents, however, the rules changed, and force would have to be used. Fortunately, Britain did not demand warship access to Antwerp, instead merely demanding that German vessels not be allowed to depart, and the B.E.F. went elsewhere. Another danger arose when the Germans besieged Antwerp, and the battlefield could easily spill over into the Netherlands. The Dutch land along the Schelde was barely defensible. Troops there would inevitably be cut off, so there was little enthusiasm about building up the forces close to the river. Hence the creation of the Divisiongroup Brabant at least allowed Snijders to deploy much of his army to retaliate against an invasion of Zeeland, or defend against a subsequent attempt to use it as a base for moving deeper into the Netherlands.[72]

States of siege and war

Preparing for battles it could not hope to win was not the army's only task. It was also the supreme authority in those parts of the country that were declared to be in a state of war *(Staat van Oorlog)* or the more severe state of siege *(Staat van Beleg)*. Under "state of war," the civilian authorities still had the right to be consulted, and some property rights remained in force. Under "state of siege," however, the army exercised *militair gezag*, military authority, and could usurp the powers of all entities as high as the provincial leadership. Snijders urged the issuance of the declarations on August 2, noting that otherwise it would cost too much to seize property needed for defense.[73]

Snijders got his wish, but some problems resulted. The work created for his headquarters was vast, because his attempts to delegate the work to local junior officers was ruled unconstitutional. In addition, giving the army such immense powers ran counter to the whole Dutch way of thinking. When Cort van der Linden commented later that one disaster of the war was the increasing power of military establishments, De Beaufort groused that this was happening in Holland as well. He wrote in his diary in 1914 that the military's behavior showed that it was greedy for power. Military figures were indeed supreme in areas under state of siege.[ix] Even the war minister could little interfere with actions there, although he was urged never to admit that. The army could interfere with freedom of press and assembly, enter private residences, and censor mail. Military permission was needed for non-religious assemblies, and being a parson did not provide a blanket guarantee of freedom either. A minister who encouraged people not to take up arms in case of invasion was expelled from the 3rd Division's territory – and this action was upheld even though a state of siege had not formally been proclaimed there yet. The Supreme Commander could throw any person out of an area under "state of siege," and hundreds were unceremoniously forbidden to return to their homes by the military.[74]

The government did not hesitate long about giving the army these powers, however. Snijders got the declarations he wanted. Fortress areas and certain towns were declared under "state of war" on August

---

[ix] This practice may be compared with the French *Zone des frontières.*

5, with that extended to all the southern provinces five days later. The Waterline was placed under "state of siege" on August 5 as well. Border and river mouths were placed under "state of siege" in stages, at their peak covering most of Holland's border lands and the entire province of Limburg. The reason for this growing military power was the requirement to control smuggling, as great a threat to neutrality as the battlefront. It also allowed the military to stop the export of vital necessities – especially ships. Snijders was not altogether happy with this job, which he had through 1916, as he had to send many regulars to enforce trade laws. This further weakened his overstretched army. Nevertheless, it seems to have worked; smuggling declined.[75] And it certainly made Snijders the most powerful person in the Netherlands for much of World War I.

The supreme commander

The holder of all this power, Cornelis Jacobus Snijders, was a stern, hardworking officer of middle class origins. He was one of the 8 children of a doctor in Nieuwe Tonge whose medical ability was greater than his success in collecting bills from his farmer patients. As a result, Snijders' childhood was impecunious, if not actually poor. Acquaintances noted that father and son shared a strong will, exceptional work ethic, and somewhat didactic personalities. Unusually for a Dutch family, there was a strong attraction to the military. Father Snijders had served two years as a naval surgeon, and 4 of his 7 seven sons entered the military. Even more remarkably, three reached the rank of general. Despite the similarities in temperament, the siblings were not close. The brothers were born over a large time range – 18 years – and hence had not all grown together. Nor did Snijders get along with his older brother, W.G.F. Snijders, who retired as Lieutenant General, the highest peacetime rank in the army, in 1905. By that time C.J. and W.G.F. were estranged from each other, although no source explains why.[76]

Had this family squabble not existed, Holland's two senior military posts might have been held by brothers. Bosboom considered before the war designating W.G.F. Snijders as supreme commander in case of war, but soon discovered that this was not possible, as there was no chance the brothers could work together. Hence C.J. became supreme commander and W.G.F. played no role in the war. W.G.F. Snijders exacted some slight revenge. In 1922 he published a book on the war, including a chapter about Holland's position, without ever mentioning brother C.J.'s name. Where the friction came from is difficult to say. They did have different views on some issues, such as the gap between career and reserve officers, which C.J. Snijders wanted to reduce, but they rarely were involved in face to face debates – for one thing, W.G.F. was senior by far. There was no obvious difference in talent. The German military attaché recorded in 1902 that the elder brother was regarded as the army's best leader as well as a reformer, and one who was fully aware of the army's defects.[77]

After high school C.J. Snijders went off to the Royal Military Academy at Breda, where he chose the engineering service *(Genie)* as his branch. The choice was revealing. Engineering was a practical choice, offering the best chance for extra-army employment, but it was not a choice likely to lead to the top echelons. Engineering officers rarely went to the higher military school or to the general staff. Senior engineering officers did not even want their junior officers to attend higher military courses, and often worked in civilian clothes instead of uniform.[78] On the other hand, Holland's naturally defensive posture meant that engineering skills were exceptionally valuable, for building forts and preparing the water lines. Snijders' career went well. He participated in Holland's campaign in Atjeh (Aceh),[x] on northern Sumatra, where he nearly perished because he could not swim. He also represented the army in purchases abroad,[79] a function not given to skill-challenged officers.

Valued skill did not translate into rapid promotion, however. After almost 30 years of service, Snijders was still a captain. This was not a professional failure; there were simply very few promotion slots available. Then, in 1901, Snijders received a surprising offer; promotion to major, and appointment to the General Staff. Unfortunately, promotion and a branch shift was expensive. Snijders would have to buy new uniforms, as well as two horses with harness, and make a large deposit in a widow and orphan fund. By nature thrifty, and offended at the long delay in promotion to major (he was #1 on the promotion list in the *genie* by this time), Snijders refused the general staff appointment, becoming major of engineers instead. The offer

---

[x] Fractious as a colonial province, it now (2000) may be moving toward revolt against Indonesia.

came again in 1908, however, and this time the army brass allowed the now-Colonel Snijders to delay his appointment until his promotion to major general came through.[xi] He simultaneously succeeded F.M. Thiange as vice-chief of the General Staff, and became acting chief of staff in 1909 when Thiange was ill.[80]

Snijders' appointment seems surprising, in hindsight. Only one other officer (Bosboom) had made it to the General Staff without attending the higher military school. He knew few of the officers, excepting those he had met through his elder brother (in better times, apparently). He quickly ingratiated himself with his command, however, demonstrating that his Prussian work habits were combined with a sense of humor and a ready ability to converse with his juniors, putting them at ease. His successful execution of the job led to an offer to become Minister of War, which he promptly declined, partly because he thought he was too far to the left for the government then in office, but also because he regarded the position of war minister as unstable. About this, of course, he was absolutely right. His colleague Wouter Cool took the position instead a few months later, and did not enjoy it. Snijders was also offered a division command, but he declined that as well. Apparently being acting Chief of the General Staff agreed with him.[81]

Then there occurred a professional disappointment for Snijders which might well have prevented him from becoming Supreme Commander. Thiange died in January, 1910. Snijders expected to be appointed permanent Chief of Staff, as he had now filled the position almost since he had arrived at the General Staff. But it was not to be. Thiange's predecessor as Chief of Staff, Lt.-Gen. F.H.A. Sabron, had gone on to become war minister, but had stepped aside from that position for health reasons (precipitating the offer to Snijders to become war minister). But apparently Sabron now felt better, and was reappointed Chief of Staff, whether at his own request or someone else's is not known. Snijders returned to his position as vice chief, and so it would have remained, except that Sabron's recovery was a chimera. Only six months later, Sabron retired for health reasons. Snijders, who had become a lieutenant general on March 31, 1911, was appointed Chief of the General Staff on July 1, 1911.[82] Almost 60 years

---

[xi] There are three ranks of general officer in Holland: major general, lieutenant general, and general.

old, he had reached the highest peacetime military office his country could offer.

Snijders had already been designated potential Supreme Commander before war's outbreak, but this was a routine step that normally had no practical meaning. The events in the summer of 1914 changed all that. On 31 July 1914, C.J. Snijders was appointed Supreme Commander of Land and Sea Forces. The 62-year old general was the first non-royal in Dutch history to hold the position. He was soon rewarded with promotion to general and given a raise, but his compensation was not extravagant – 15,000 guilders, a thousand less than Bosboom – especially when his responsibilities were considered.[83]

Those responsibilities were extensive. He had to prepare to protect his country with an army that he knew had many defects. He could not and did not foresee that this waiting game would stretch to four years, an almost impossibly tense existence that seems to have sapped his strength and judgment by 1918. In the meantime, he also had to give his Field Army commander strategic instruction, run the General Headquarters *(Algemeen Hoofdkwartier)* in 's-Hertogenbosch, then in Oosterhout, and command an astonishing number of entities. These included the Field Army, whose commander reported directly to him, various independent units, a half-dozen fortification commanders, the chiefs of the Navy and the naval wharf, a few other naval officers, any ships operating separately from naval commands, and the different categories of ground forces.[84]

He made his own job harder by retaining his position as Chief of the General Staff. General Headquarters consisted of three sections. Section A dealt with strategy and leadership, Section B managed the Army, and C the Navy. The General Staff was subsumed into Section A. The Chief of the General Staff would become Chief of Staff of the General Headquarters. The Supreme Commander would run Section A, ideally thereby focusing on the "big" issues, while the Chief of Staff managed the headquarters (subject to the Supreme Commander's overall authority). Before the war, there had been some concerns expressed about the relationship between Supreme Commander and Chief of Staff, which was one of the things that had led Bosboom to see if the Snijders brothers got along well enough to smooth over any differences. Snijders solved the problem simply by keeping both jobs. This meant he was responsible for managing headquarters as well as leading the military establishment, and he became too involved in resolving secondary issues. He did appoint Col. R. Dufour as chief of staff for the headquarters, which partially solved the problem.[85]

Evaluating Snijders is difficult. He was known personally to few people, because he commanded no large units until he was placed in control of the entire army. He has been criticized as having an infatuation with numbers of soldiers over quality of weapons and tactics, although this view has not gained much support. The general was known to be well-informed and had an iron constitution. He was well-regarded by the Queen, who towered over the minuscule general, but he was not popular among The Hague's chattering classes. Parliamentarians he ignored as much as possible, and this was not appreciated. He came across to his subordinates as hard-working but stable and rarely discombobulated, finding time every morning to ride his horse for an hour, regardless of the situation. Like his French counterpart, Joffrre, he could sleep well at night no matter what the circumstances. Only the army riots in October, 1918, really caused his routine to change. He got along well with Colijn, disagreements arising only out of the minister's need to deal with political realities. Even after 4 years of work, his sense of humor did not desert him. When Hindenburg's 1918 offensive followed a prediction made earlier by Snijders' Field Army commander, the general quipped that "Hindenburg apparently sneaked a look in the CV's cards."[xii] What did apparently overstress him by 1918 was the realization that his job was impossible. He had a weak army and could form no alliances, yet had to be ready to wage war against a great power.[86]

Nor was the domestic environment promising. Snijders was working for a country that was "not a military nation." The Dutch made "good fighters, but bad soldiers" and "military service is as much detested in Holland as it is popular in Germany. It makes the task of a commanding officer very difficult and trying."[87] A Dutch officer serving with Uhlans in 1910-11 reported that he was convinced that it was a necessity for an army to be appreciated by the nation from whence it sprang; the opposite was true in Holland. The antimilitarism affected the press, which greatly worried Snijders. The despised *Telegraaf* reported in 1916 that some soldiers claimed that if Germany invaded they would throw away their guns and drink *Schnapps* with the attackers – a story Snijders undoubtedly felt should not have been printed, even if it were true. In Holland allegiance to family and

---

[xii] CV = *Commandant Veldleger*, Commander of the Field Army.

community was strong, but not beyond those parochial circles.[xiii] [88]

The most damaging allegation about Snijders was that he was pro-German. A hagiographic 1949 biography denied this, but conceded that he did have some sympathy and admiration for the German army. Nowhere, his biographer argued, did this affect his actions. In being sympathetic toward Germany, he merely mirrored the feelings of the Dutch officer corps, which could not but note the high regard in which German officers were held, or the disciplined nature of German soldiers; more than one Dutch officer wished that he could swap soldiers (no German officers ever made such a suggestion). Some 150 Dutch officers would enter Imperial service in the war. Career officers tended to remain friendly toward Germany, although reserve officers generally were anti-German. On the other hand, Renner, visited Snijders in 1915 and did come away feeling that the General was *deutschfreundlich*. Snijders spoke positively about a recent Bethmann-Hollweg speech and complimented the successful invasion of Serbia, but pointed out to him Holland's dependence on imports and the colonial connection. Snijders' adjutant later told Renner that he and the Snijders were happy things were not going well for Britain, and that the general was constantly having to fight with parliamentarians with no understanding of military necessity (referring to proposals for large-scale demobilization).[89]

What can we make of this? Snijders certainly made the German major happy, and equally certainly told him nothing that was not already in the newspapers. He probably had a specific reason in mind for inviting Renner, but there is no indication of what that purpose might have been. There is evidence that his leaning toward Germany was strictly pragmatic. If he had to go to war, he preferred to fight the Entente, simply because a British landing on the Dutch coast was much easier to oppose than a German invasion. He pushed the government

---

[xiii] The Dutch public's contempt for the army was legendary. One document that I encountered in the archives gives a good idea why being an officer in Holland was so difficult. On May 8, 1907, the mayor of Rheden sent the Chief of Staff, General Kool, a letter concerning its upcoming staff ride in his area. He pointed out that, to avoid fines, officers had to keep their horses off the bicycle paths along the main highway. Kool routinely sent this on to the staff and emphasized that horses were to be kept off the paths. Mayor of Rheden to Chief of Staff, 8 May 1907, and memorandum from General Kool, 11 May 1907, Generale Staf, nr. toegang 2.13.15.01, inv nr 261, ARA-II. Similar documents are not likely to be found in the archives of Imperial Germany.

toward Germany simply because Germany was powerful, and he wanted his small country in the safest position possible. This conclusion comes not from a friend, but from Jhr. B.C. de Jonge, war minister in 1917-18, who heartily disliked Snijders[xiv] and had no reason to relieve the general of the "pro-German" charge. Snijders' own comments back up these interpretations. In his postwar writings about the war, his view of its origins was somewhat pro-German, but not uncritically so. More pointedly, in a communication with Cort van der Linden, Snijders noted Germany's invasion of Luxembourg and its movement into the disputed Eems territory, and described Germany's stance as "unscrupulous."[90]

In one area, however, Snijders managed to emulate his later German counterparts quite well. His professional independence was enormous. This resulted from a conflict concerning the government's official instructions for him, which spawned a constitutional problem not yet solved when World War II broke out. In a nutshell, to whom was the general responsible? Was it the two military cabinet ministers, or was it the government as a whole? In the latter case, there would be no effective governmental supervision of the Supreme Commander. The issue was discussed for a number of years before the war. In 1907 the then War Minister, W.F. Ridder van Rappard, made some noises about combining the positions of minister and commander, but this was quickly rejected. Had this been done, Snijders would have been a minister and would have had to answer questions both in cabinet and in parliament. New instructions were prepared in 1909, 1911, and 1912, culminating in placing the Supreme Commander under "the Queen with the responsible minister."[91]

In 1913 the issue was reviewed by De Jonge, who concluded that the instruction was unconstitutional, as it would make the commander directly responsible to the Queen. If the reference to the Queen were dropped, however, it place the General Staff and Supreme Commander under the Minister of War, which was also unacceptable – even though almost war ministers were soldiers themselves. De Jonge argued that the instruction would have to go, however. He pointed out that colonial governors-general had sometimes tried to circumvent the colonial ministers by going straight to the Crown, and that the Supreme Commander could do the same. How could the Supreme Commander's

---

[xiv] Snijders in turn came to despise De Jonge.

need for independence be balanced with his administrative responsibilities to the war minister, and the government's need to exercise some oversight?[92]

The solution was simply to write an instruction that the Supreme Commander was responsible to the *government,* with the understanding that "government" in this case referred to the War Minister. This meant that in case of conflict between the two, the general could approach the government as whole. This was a tricky situation, in which the relationship between commander and minister "would demand much tact from both sides." Sometime in 1913-14, however, the instruction was changed. "Government" was stricken, and instead "Minister of War" was written in. De Jonge, the war ministry's chief civil servant, and Snijders, the Chief of the General Staff, were unaware of the editorial change.[xv] When Snijders was offered the appointment as Supreme Commander, he simply refused to accept the instruction. Either it went, or he did. As the government hardly wanted a brouhaha over this appointment on the eve of a possible invasion, the instruction was rewritten, and the word "government" once again replaced "Minister of War." Unfortunately for the ministers, there was more going on here than just a reversion to the original language. "Government" was now understood to refer *not* to the war minister, but to the Minister President.[xvi] [93]

Snijders had a stubborn streak, and this was just one of the occasions where it manifested itself. He had been perfectly willing to sacrifice position for principle, although he may well have judged that the government was unlikely to let him go under the circumstances. He now had no ongoing supervision during the war. Cort van der Linden was not a soldier and was occupied with countless other tasks. Bosboom, not likely to interfere anyway, and lacking Snijders' singlemindedness, now even lacked the legal power to control his general. During the siege of Antwerp, for example, he complained to De Jonge about some of Snijders' deployment decisions. De Jonge, whose ability was considerably greater than his tact, told Bosboom that

---

[xv] Who wrote in "Minister of War"? I have uncovered no document that sheds light on this question, but a possible suspect is the Minister himself (Bosboom).

[xvi] For some complicated constitutional reasons not relevant here, Cort van der Linden was referred to in the documents as "Chair of the Council of Ministers," but for all practical purposes he functioned just like any other Minister-President.

he could either leave it alone, or go to the Crown. Bosboom left it alone. A legal scholar pointed out later that the real problem was the instruction's failure to clearly distinguish between military and constitutional requirements. In the latter case, which included the "big picture" issues of national defense and overall strategy, the government through its minister of war might make decisions and issue instructions, but in strictly military matters, the general should not have to accept orders from a single minister. When the long-retired Snijders died in 1939, the matter had still not been resolved.[94]

Snijders' stubbornness would have been detrimental to the army, had he been a fossilized anti-reform soldier. Fortunately, he was not. In particular, he was an enthusiast for aviation, founding an air section during his tenure on the General Staff. Nor was this just a *pro forma* act required of him. In 1907 he had become head of the "Dutch Association for Promotion of Airship Navigation," and arranged for it to get a subsidy from the war ministry. In 1908 he submitted further reports to the ministry on airships. His appointment as deputy chief of the general staff gave him more leeway to promote aviation, although some senior officers, particularly Sabron, were unenthusiastic. Things went better, however, under Colijn. Snijders had a freer hand now for his aerial enthusiasm and sent observers or went himself to view foreign military air power in action. He ordered the establishment of the air section in 1911, although bureaucratic problems delayed the startup for two years. In 1912, the then 60-year old general stepped into an airplane at the fledgling Soesterberg air field so that he could see for himself what the airplane meant for the future.[95]

His aerial voyage only further heightened his interest. Not only did he continue to organize aerial demonstrations and competitions during the war, but he went on to become a national advocate for civil and military aviation during his two decades of retirement after his abrupt removal in 1918. Many Dutch officers of his generation, and even Colijn, thought the airplane would play a small role in the next war.[xvii]

[xvii] I have wondered whether Snijders' *lack* of higher military training had something to do with this. All other staff officers before Bosboom and himself had attended the higher war college, there inculcated no doubt with the military thinking of the age – as can be deduced from Bosboom's criticism that officer education tended to be theoretical. Is it possible that Snijders' relative lack of formal military-strategic education made him more open-minded toward the possibilities of the strange new technology of aviation?

Outside the military, however, his interest in the airplane generated a notable following. During those years he also wrote about the war, arguing trenchantly that statesmanship without morality is reprehensible and dangerous. His concern with domestic decadence led him to stand for Parliament late in life (1933) for the neo-fascist *Nationaal Herstel* (National Recovery) party. His (non-military) funeral on 31 May 1939, where Colijn gave the eulogy, took place amidst tremendous public interest.[96]

The same can not be said about Bosboom. Before World War I, Nicolaas Bosboom had hoped to become a major figure in the debate over military preparedness. After retiring as colonel[xviii] he entered politics because he saw it as the only way to strengthen defense. He spoke frequently on the issue and published two pamphlets, which brought him some attention. In 1913, Cort van der Linden organized an extra-parliamentary cabinet and sought Bosboom as war minister. It was not an entirely happy choice. Bosboom had no parliamentary experience and was a constant target for the opposition, which disliked him for ideological reasons. As war minister he was a natural magnet for assaults anyway, and even a member of the anti-military Social Democrats later expressed his irritation concerning the extent to which parliamentarians were always trying to trip up the war minister. Running one of the most expensive departments also increased his vulnerability.[97]

Bosboom had his shortcomings. His civil servants had to protect him from making legal/constitutional blunders. If Snijders had too much stubbornness, Bosboom may have had too little. De Jonge remembered that "what was annoying was that the Minister's viewpoint depended on the person, whom he had last spoken with." This was partly because he was broad-minded, for example stressing the importance of infantry despite his own artillery background. He was certainly no figurehead. He came up with a more efficient and cheaper system for expanding the army than Colijn had been able to. In the 11 months before the war, he replaced two thirds of all commanders at the regimental level and above.[98]

Outwardly his importance peaked during the war, but his influence

---

[xviii] Bosboom was promoted to general rank after his retirement; major general in 1913, lieutenant general in 1918. It is doubtful that these post-service promotions improved his standing with Snijders.

over the military declined. Contrary to one biographer, he was not solely or largely responsible for starting mobilization. When one official during those tense days asked De Jonge if the Minister was still involved, the response was: So long as he doesn't cause any delays! Once the mobilization was complete, Bosboom found himself between a parliament that was never friendly, a commander who was not a subordinate, and a cabinet that wanted him to control his general. His problems with Snijders were not personal. The nature of their positions created friction. (So it had been to during the last mobilization, in 1870.) In France during World War I, the war ministry and army administered different zones of the country, but this was not practical in a country the size of Holland. The relationship was simply one that require "mutual tact."[99]

The wartime relationship was not so much tactful as cautious. Snijders feared interference and saw the minister as a bureaucrat. He in turn irritated, rather than intimidated, his minister. They took refuge in a formal relationship, even though they spoke almost every day. Bosboom gave Snijders great freedom of action (not that he had much choice) and was generally supportive of the general, protecting him from his critics. Ultimately, that would be his undoing. In parliament and cabinet alike the feeling developed that Bosboom was not determined enough to rein in the Supreme Commander, and some even suggested that Snijders had completely pushed him aside. As a result, Bosboom would not last until the end of his cabinet. Officially, he resigned in 1917 over a dispute with parliament about the recruitment laws. This enabled him to leave office with his dignity and reputation intact. His resignation caused no stir; Snijders' biographer does not even mention it. Bosboom died a forgotten figure on 14 November 1937.[100]

With so little supervision, Snijders' power was enormous and would remain so until late in the war. Neither his ability, nor his stubbornness, nor the putative weakness of his first war minister completely explain why. Anti- and non-military politicians were somewhat reluctant to overrule or even question the general, but there was something else, or rather, somebody else: the Queen. Wilhelmina supported Snijders without reservation, letting him go only when keeping him might have threatened her throne (1918). The Queen was no figurehead or ceremonial ruler. She had far more power than the British monarch, for example. She participated several times in government affairs during the war, meeting with responsible ministers to discuss mobilization

(1914), on one occasion saving Snijders' job (1917), and on another approaching Wilhelm II and George V over ship safety issues (1917). , In 1918, she attempted to deal with the seizure of the Dutch merchant fleet by keeping the legation in Washington vacant, stopping a planned demobilization, and supporting, albeit unsuccessfully, a plan to convoy Dutch vessels to the Indies in direct defiance of the British.[101] She might not always get her way, but in the case of Snijders and his position, she did. With his army mobilized and his monarch supportive, the general was secure; his country, however, was not.

NOTES

[1] "Opgave van de door den *Minister van Oorlog* te geven bevelen en te nemen of uit te lokken maatregelen en besluiten, ingevolge de "Strategische aanwijzingen" (1913) en andere voorschriften of wettelijke bepalingen," n.d. (probably early 1914), Collectie Bosboom, ARA-II; Addendum to instructie no. 5, to commander at Maastricht (1912), Koninklijke Landmacht – Archief van het Veldleger, ARA-II; "Mobilisatie van de Nederlandsche land- en zeemacht," iii.

[2] "Mobilisatie van de Nederlandsche land- en zeemacht," 26.

[3] "Opgave van de door den *Minister van Oorlog* te geven bevelen;" Chief of the General Staff to Commander of Field Army, 10 October 1913, Addendum to instructie no. 5, Collectie Bosboom, ARA-II.

[4] "Mobilisatie van de Nederlandsche land- en zeemacht," 12-13; Buhlmann to Snijders, 3 August 1914, Generale Staf, ARA-II.

[5] De Beaufort, *Vijftig jaren,* part 2, p. 222; Klinkert, "De Nederlandse mobilisatie," p. 26; M.J. van der Flier, *The Netherlands and the World War: Studies in the War History of a Neutral,* vol. 1, *War Finances* (New Haven: Yale, 1928), p. 13; H.A.C. Fabius, "De Duitsche operatiën in België en Frankrijk tot 7 October 1914," n.d., Hoofdkwartier Veldleger, inv nr 946IV, ARA-II; Bosboom, *In moeilijke omstandigheden,* p. 29.

[6] Treub, *Oorlogstijd,* p. 12; "Mobilisatie van de Nederlandsche land- en zeemacht," pp. 14-20, 27-28, 40-42, 54, 57; Grolleman and Ruiter, "Interne en externe invloeden," p. 24.

[7] Bosboom, *In moeilijke omstandigheden,*pp. 29-30; "Overzicht van den aanwas en den afvoer van de verschillende groepen van dienstplichtigen van Aug. 1914 tot Aug. 1916," Collectie Bosboom, ARA-II.

[8] Bosboom, *In moeilijke omstandigheden,* pp. 29-30, 40, 56.

[9] Snijders, "Nederland's militaire positie," p. 542; Bout, "Dutch Army," pp. 24, 35; Bosboom, *In moeilijke omstandigheden,* pp. 50-51.

[10] C. Smit, *Nederland in de Eerste Wereldoorlog (1899-1919),* vol. 3, *1917-1919* (Groningen: Wolters-Noordhoff, 1973), pp. 16-17, 26; Bosboom, *In moeilijke omstandigheden,* pp. 31-34.

[11] "Mobilisatie van de Nederlandsche land- en zeemacht," pp. 2, 6-8, 14-20, 47, 365-67, 369-70.

[12] Ibid., pp. 364, 367-69, 371-72, 382, 384-87.

[13] Ibid., pp. 26-37, 364-5, 375, 379-80, 383; Bosboom, *In moeilijke omstandigheden,* p. 44.

[14] Porter, "Dutch Neutrality," p. 98.

[15] "Mobilisatie van de Nederlandsche land- en zeemacht," p. 370.

[16] Ibid., p. 370.

[17] Ibid., pp. 361-64, 366,372-74, 378, 379.

[18] Soldiers of the 4th Infantry Regiment at Leiden to His Majesty Wilhelm II, 2 October 1914: Journal du Havre, 4 Nov. 1914: Memoranda from division commander and Field Army commander, 8 and 19 November: Snijders to cabinet, 7 November and 20 November 1914: Snijders to investigating commission, 20 November 1914: and report of investigating commission, 7 December (erroneously dated September)

1914, Generale Staf, ARA-II.

[19] Ritter, *Donkere poort,* pp. 30-31.

[20] Van der Wal, *Herinneringen,* p. 20.

[21] See Treub, *Herinneringen en overpeinzingen,* p. 292.

[22] Jelle Troelstra, *Mijn vader Pieter Jelles* (Amsterdam: Arbeiderspers, 1955), p. 113.

[23] Fasseur, *Wilhelmina,* p. 499.

[24] Snijders to various commanders, 4 August 1914, AHK Bereden Artillerie, ARA-II; General Staff to Foreign Office, 29 July 1914: Jagow to Müller, 30 July 1914, Montgelas and Schuecking, *Outbreak of the World War,* pp. 326-27, 365; Gevers to Foreign Office, 5 August 1914, Generale Staf, ARA-II.

[25] Sagan, "1914 Revisited," p. 117.

[26] Maurer, *Outbreak of the First World War,* pp. 91-92.

[27] Herwig, *First World War,* pp. 57, 60; Maurer, *Outbreak of the First World War,* pp. 91-92.

[28] Kabisch, *Lüttich,* p. 26.

[29] Germany, Army General Staff, *Der Handstreich gegen Lüttich vom 3. Bis 7. August 1914* (Berlin: Mittler & Sohn, 1939), p. 1; Wilhelm Georg, *Unser Emmich: Ein Lebensbild* (Berlin: A. Scherl, 1915), p. 24.

[30] Van Evera, "Cult of the Offensive," p. 75.

[31] Peter Oldham, *Pill Boxes on the Western Front: A Guide to the Design, Construction and Use of Concrete Pill Boxes 1914-1918* (London: Leo Cooper, 1995), pp. 10-13.

[32] Van Voorst tot Voorst, *Over Roermond,* p. 30.

[33] Ibid., pp. 21, 32-33, 53.

[34] Ronduit, *De manoeuvre om Limburg,* pp. 14-15.

[35] Maurer, *Outbreak of the First World War,* p. 12.

[36] Van Voorst tot Voorst, *Over Roermond,* pp. 33-35.

[37] Ibid., p. 31.

[38] Porter, "Dutch Neutrality," p. 110; Smit, *1914-1917,* pp. 2, 5; De Beaufort, *Vijftig jaren,* 244; Cabinet minutes, 29 July 1914, 10, Smit, *Bescheiden ... 1914-1917,* p. 5; Gooch and Temperley, *British Documents,* vol. 11, p. 209; Goschen to Grey, 29 July 1914, with minute by Eyre Crowe, 30 July 1914, Geiss, *German Foreign Policy,* pp. 216-17.

[39] Cabinet minutes, 1 August 1914, 12: Loudon to De Beaufort, 1 August 1914, 13: Cort van der Linden to Snijders, 1 August 1914, 15: De Beaufort to Loudon, 2 August 1914, 20, Smit, *Bescheiden ... 1914-1917,* pp. 6-8, 10; De Marees van Swinderen to Grey, 1 August 1914, 408, Gooch and Temperley, *British Documents,* vol. 11, p. 245.

[40] Eysschen to Loudon, 2 August 1914, Generale Staf, ARA-II; Jagow to Müller, 2 August 1914, Montgelas and Schuecking, *Outbreak of the World War,* pp. 468, 499.

[41] Jagow to Müller, 2 August 1914, Montgelas and Schuecking, *Outbreak of the World War,* p. 501.

[42] Ibid., p. 501.

[43] Müller to Foreign Office, 3 August 1914, Montgelas and Schuecking, *Outbreak of the World War,* p. 536; Beening, "Onder de vleugels," p. 381 (citing German documents).

[44] Gevers to Loudon, 2 August 1914, Buitenlandse Zaken – Kabinet en Protocol, ARA-II; General Staff to Foreign Office, 1 August 1914, Montgelas and Schuecking, *Outbreak of the World War,* pp. 468, 469.

[45] Gevers to Loudon, 2 August 1914, 19, Smit, *Bescheiden ... 1914-1917,* p. 10; Smit, *1914-1917,* pp. 2, 3; Chilton to Grey, 2 August 1914, 462, and minute by Crowe, 2 August 1914, 470, Gooch and Temperley, *British Documents,* vol. 11, pp. 267, 269; Memorandum, 1st Section Foreign Ministry, 25 June 1907, 81, Smit, *1907-1914,* pp. 111-13.

[46] Belgian government to legation at The Hague, 31 July 1914: Note verbale, German legation, 3 August 1914: Fallon to Loudon, 3 August 1914, Buitenlandse Zaken – Kabinet en Protocol, ARA-II; Note verbale from Müller, 3 August 1914, with annotation by Doude van Troostwijk, 22: Note verbale from Fallon, 3 August 1914, with annotation by Doude van Troostwijk, 24: Loudon to Fallon, 3 August 1914, 25, Smit, *Bescheiden ... 1914-1917,* pp. 11-12; Müller to Foreign Office, 3 August 1914, Montgelas and Schuecking, *Outbreak of the World War,* pp. 563-64; *Le Mensonge,* p. 201; Smit, *1914-1917,* p. 6; C. Smit, *Diplomatieke geschiedenis van Nederland inzonderheid sedert de vesting van het koninkrijk* ('s-Gravenhage: Martinus Nijhoff, 1950), p. 308; Messages between Davignon and Fallon, 27 July – 3 August 1914, 279-85, 288-91, Smit, *Bescheiden betreffende de buitenlandse politiek van Nederland, 1848-1919, derde periode, 1899-1919,* pt. 7, *Buitenlandse bronnen 1914-1917* ('s-Gravenhage: Martinus Nijhoff, 1971), pp. 413-21, 423-25.

[47] De Marees van Swinderen to Loudon, 3 August 1914, 21, *Bescheiden ... 1914-1917,* pp. 10-11; Loudon to De Marees van Swinderen, 3 August 1914, Buitenlandse Zaken – Kabinet en Protocol, ARA-II.

[48] Den Beer Poortugael to De Marees van Swinderen, 7 November 1911, 617: 1st Section Foreign Ministry to Secretary General, n.d. (Between 7 and 24 November 1911), 618, Smit, *1907-1914,* pp. 712-15; Neutrality declaration, Article 2, *België betrokken in den oorlog,* p. 59.

[49] Loudon to De Beaufort, 4 August 1914, 27: Neutrality proclamation, 4 August 1914, 28: Cort van der Linden, 4 August 1914, 29, Smit, *Bescheiden ... 1914-1917,* pp. 13-18; De Marees van Swinderen to Loudon, 4 August 1914, Buitenlandse Zaken – Kabinet en Protocol, ARA-II; De Marees van Swinderen to British Foreign Ministry, 3 August 1914 (received 4 August), 595, Gooch and Temperley, *British Documents,* vol. 11, p. 315.

[50] Grey to Chilton (3 messages) and replies, 4 August 1914, 578, 580, 593, 604, 632, 639, Gooch and Temperley, *British Documents,* vol. 11, pp. 308, 309,314, 317, 326, 329; Porter, "Dutch Neutrality," p. 113.

[51] Cort van der Linden to Snijders, 5 August 1914, Generale Staf, ARA-II; Bout, "Dutch Army," pp. 37-38; Fallon to Davignon, 5 Aug. 1914: Lalaing to Davignon, 5 August 1914, *België betrokken in den oorlog: Verzameling van diplomatieke stukeen* ('s-Gravenhage: Martinus Nijhoff, 1914), p. 57; Smit, *1914-1917,* pp. 6-8; De Marees van Swinderen to Loudon, 5 August 1914, Buitenlandse Zaken – Kabinet en Protocol, ARA-II.

[52] Grey to Chilton, 5 August 1914, Buitenlandse Zaken – Kabinet en Protocol, ARA-II.

[53] Gevers to Loudon, 5 August 1914, Buitenlandse Zaken – Kabinet en Protocol, ARA-II..

[54] Klinkert, *Het vaderland verdedigd,* p. 423; Daniel H. Thomas, *The Guarantee of Belgian Independence and Neutrality in European Diplomacy, 1830's–1930's* (Kingston, RI: D. H. Thomas Publishing, 1983), p. 421.

[55] Letter to Eliza Moltke, 8 Sept. 1914, Moltke, *Erinnerungen,* p. 385.

[56] De Marees van Swinderen to Loudon, 6 Aug. 1914: Note verbale from Chilton to

Loudon, 6 August 1914, Buitenlandse Zaken – Kabinet en Protocol, ARA-II; Smit, *1914-1917*, pp. 7-9; Van Weede to Davignon, 6 August 1914: Fallon to Davignon and replies, 6 August 1914, *België betrokken in den oorlog*, pp. 58-65.

[57] De Marees van Swinderen to Loudon, 7 August 1914, Buitenlandse Zaken – Kabinet en Protocol, ARA-II.

[58] Loudon to Gevers, 7 August 1914: Loudon to De Marees van Swinderen, 8 August 1914, 47, Smit, *Bescheiden ... 1914-1917*, pp. 24, 29; De Marees van Swinderen to Loudon, 8 August 1914, Buitenlandse Zaken – Kabinet en Protocol, ARA-II.

[59] Gevers to Loudon, 9 August 1914 and 30 August 1914, 49, 53, 111, Smit, *Bescheiden ... 1914-1917*, pp. 30, 33-34, 78; German legation to Loudon, 29 August 1914, Buitenlandse Zaken, ARA-II; Stengers, "Belgium," pp. 163-64; Chilton to Grey, 8 August 1914, 547, Gooch and Temperley, *British Documents*, vol. 11, p. 297; Gevers to Loudon, 11 and 13 August 1914, Buitenlandse Zaken – Kabinet en Protocol, ARA-II.

[60] De Beaufort to Loudon, 9 August 1914, 30: Davignon to Fallon, 12 August 1914, 53: De Marees van Swinderen to Loudon, 17 August 1914, 72, Smit, *Bescheiden ... 1914-1917*, pp. 30, 33-34, 46-47.

[61] Smit, *1914-1917*, p. 4; Snijders, "Nederland's militaire positie," p. 536; De Leeuw, *Nederland in de wereldpolitiek*, pp. 167-68; Bout, "Dutch Army," pp. 29-30; Berg, *Snijders*, pp. 69-71.

[62] Snijders, "Nederland's militaire positie," pp. 540-41; Smit, *1914-1917*, p. 4; Porter, "Dutch Neutrality," pp. 109-10; Bosboom, *In moeilijke omstandigheden*, p. 23.

[63] Envoy in Brussels to Foreign Ministry, 10 August 1914: Buhlmann to Snijders, 11 August 1914, Koninklijke Landmacht – Hoofdkwartier Veldleger, ARA-II; De Leeuw, *Nederland in de wereldpolitiek*, pp. 143, 144.

[64] Chilton to Grey, 31 July and 4 August 1914, 375, 527, Gooch and Temperley, *British Documents*, vol. 11, pp. 232, 289; Orders concerning leaves from Snijders, 24 May 1916, Hoofdkwartier Veldleger, ARA-II; "Dienstinstructie" for Commander at Maastricht, No. 5, 1912, and Addendum, Archief van het Veldleger, ARA-II.

[65] "Mobilisatie van de Nederlandse land- en zeemacht," p. 3.

[66] Communiqué "Divisie Oostpartij," 21 September 1913: March orders, 2nd Division, 21 September 1913: March orders, cavalry brigade, 10 February 1913, Koninklijke Landmacht – Hoofdkwartier Veldleger, ARA-II; Snijders, "Nederland's militaire positie," p. 540.

[67] Smit, *Het voorspel*, pp. 24-26; Charles à Court Repington, *Essays and Criticisms* (London: Constable, 1911),p. 266; Alting von Geusau, *Onze weermacht*, pp. 10, 24-27, 31-33.

[68] Smit, *Het voorspel*, p. 23; Repington, *Essays*, p. 271; Klinkert, "Verdediging van de zuidgrens," p. 218; Alting von Geusau, *Onze weermacht te land*, pp. 10, 24-28.

[69] Chief of Staff to Field Army, 10 October 1913, Koninklijke Landmacht – Archief van het Veldleger, ARA-II; Cort van der Linden to Snijders, 1 August 1914, 12, Smit, *Bescheiden ... 1914-1917*, p. 6.

[70] Smit, *1914-1917*, p. 13; "Afwachtingsopstelling," 1-4 Divisions, 10 October 1913, and Chief of Staff to Commander Field Army, 10 October 1913, Koninklijke Landmacht – Archief van het Veldleger, ARA-II; Berg, *Snijders*, p. 107; "Mobilisatie: Concentratie van het veldleger in een bepaald geval," 1909, Hoofdkwartier Veldleger, ARA-II; Snijders, "Nederland's militaire positie," p. 541.

[71] Snijders, "Nederland's militaire positie," pp. 543-44; Snijders to Field Army, 20 August 1914: Snijders to 2nd Division, 21 August 1914, Generale Staf, ARA-II;

Klinkert, "Verdediging van de zuidgrens," pp. 215-16; Berg, *Snijders*, pp. 107, 108; Bosboom, *In moeilijke omstandigheden*, p. 40.

[72] Cort van der Linden to Snijders, 4 August 1914: De Marees van Swinderen to Loudon, 5 August 1914, Generale Staf, ARA-II; Snijders, "Nederland's militaire positie," p. 545; Treub, *Oorlogstijd*, pp. 18-20; Porter, "Dutch Neutrality," p. 117.

[73] Smidt, "De bestrijding van de smokkelhandel," pp. 53-54; Snijders to Cort van der Linden, 2 August 1914, 17, Smit, *Bescheiden...1914-1917*, pp. 8-9.

[74] Mettes, et al, *Inventaris*, p. 18; De Valk and Van Faassen, *Dagboeken en aantekeningen*, pp. 660, 794; Treub, *Oorlogstijd*, p. 15; Van der Wal, *Herinneringen*, p. 24; Van Manen, *Nederlandsche Overzee Trustmaatschappij*, vol. 7, pp. 11-15; Correspondence and reports concerning sermon by Dr. de Jong, 27 August - 14 September 1914, Generale Staf, ARA-II; Memoranda from Supreme Commander forbidding accesss to certain areas, 1917-1919, Koninklijke Bibliotheek – Afdeling Documentatie, ARA-II.

[75] Royal proclamation, 5 August 1914, Generale Staf, ARA-II; Smit, *1914-1917*, pp. 94-95; De Beaufort, *Vijftig jaren*, part 2, p. 223; Snijders memorandum, 9 August 1915, 420, Smit, *Bescheiden...1914-1917*, pp. 408-417; Van Manen, *Nederlandsche Overzee Trustmaatschappij*, vol. 1, p. 107, vol. 3, p. 428, vol. 7, pp. 16-17.

[76] J.W. Bonebakker, *Twee verdienstelijke officieren* (Nieuwkoop: Heuff, 1974), pp. 9, 11, 13; Berg, *Snijders*, pp. 10-11.

[77] Bonebakker, *Twee verdienstelijke officieren*, pp. 36-38; W.G.F. Snijders, *De wereldoorlog*, passim; Berg, *Snijders*, pp. 77-78; Report by Lt. Werthern, 28 Sept. 1902, Duitse Ministerie van Buitenlandse Zaken – Stukken betreffende Nederland, ARA-II.

[78] Bonebakker, *Twee verdienstelijke officieren*, pp. 26-28.

[79] Ibid., pp. 13, 29.

[80] Ibid., pp. 30, 32; Berg, *Snijders*, pp. 54, 61-63.

[81] Berg, *Snijders*, pp. 63-64; Bonebakker, *Twee verdienstelijke officieren*, pp. 31, 32.

[82] Berg, *Snijders*, pp. 64-66; Bonebakker, *Twee verdienstelijke officieren*, p. 32.

[83] H. K. Hardenberg, "Opperbevelhebber en Algemeen Hoofdkwartier," *Militaire Spectator* 90 (1921), p. 389; Mettes, et al, *Inventaris*, p. 19; Snijders to various commands, 1 August 1914, Hoofdkwartier Veldleger, ARA-II; Berg, *Snijders*, pp. 79-81; Bout, "Dutch Army," p. 28; Bonebakker, *Twee verdienstelijke officieren*, p. 43.

[84] Smit, *1914-1917*, p. 13; Instruction for Commander of the Field Army, July 1914 (no day given), Hoofdkwartier Veldleger, ARA-II; Mettes, et al, *Inventaris*, pp. 17-18; Alting von Geusau, *Onze weermacht*, p. 4.

[85] Mettes, et al, *Inventaris*, pp. 4, 7; Alting von Geusau, *Onze weermacht*, pp. 12-13; Hardenberg, "Opperbevelhebber en Algemeen Hoofdkwartier," pp. 392-94;Berg, *Snijders*, pp. 80-81.

[86] Bonebakker, *Twee verdienstelijke officieren*, pp. 63-64, 70; Berg, *Snijders*, pp. 82, 83, 88; J.C. Rullmann, *Dr. H. Colijn: Een levensschets* (Leiden: Seithoff, 1933), p. 102; Klinkert, "Verdediging van de zuidgrens"(Part Two), *Militaire Spectator* 156 (June 1987), pp. 255, 257; Fasseur, *Wilhelmina*, p. 496; Bout, "Dutch Army," pp. 26-27.

[87] Barnouw, *Holland under Queen Wilhelmina*, p. 58.

[88] Report by 1st Lieutenant W. J. Hoytema, 1 August 1912, Generale Staf, ARA-II; Ministerraad, inv nr 2.02.05.02, inv nr 906, ARA-II; "Public opinion in Holland concerning Germany,: 8 Dec. 1916, Duitse Ministerie van Buitenlandse Zaken –

Stukken betreffende Nederland, ARA-II; Bout, "Dutch Army," pp. 8-9.

[89] Berg, *Snijders,* pp. 98, 100-101; G.C.A. Fabius, *De verhouding tussen volk en weermacht* (Amsterdam: van Holkema & Warendorf, 1916 (date questionable)), pp. 14-15; Louis Pierard, *La Hollande et la guerre* (Paris and Nancy: Librarie Militaire Berger-Levrault, 1917), pp. 42-44; VII Corps to War Ministry, 8 April 1918: Confidential report, 21 June 1918, Rotterdam Consulate, included with message from Rosen to Hertling, 28 June 1918: Report by Major Renner, 1 December 1915, Duitse Ministerie van Buitenlandse Zaken – Stukken betreffende Nederland, ARA-II.

[90] Bonebakker, *Twee verdienstelijke officieren,* p. 53; Van der Wal, *Herinneringen,* p. 424; Snijders and Dufour, *De mobilisatiën bij de groote mogendheden,* passim; Snijders to Cort van der Linden, 2 August 1914, 17, Smit, *Bescheiden...1914-1917,* pp. 8-9.

[91] Bonebakker, *Twee verdienstelijke officieren,* p. 41; Memorandum to Minister of War concerning instructions for OLZ, 29 July 1911, Generale Staf, ARA-II.

[92] Van der Wal, *Herinneringen,* pp. 12-14.

[93] Berg, *Snijders,* pp. 78-79; Van der Wal, *Herinneringen,* pp. 14-15; Alting von Geusau, *Onze weermacht,* p. 4. For a dissenting view, see Fasseur, *Wilhelmina,* p. 496.

[94] Van der Wal, *Herinneringen,* p. 14; Mettes, et al, *Inventaris,* p. 21; Pearson, *Weak State,* passim.

[95] Mettes, *Inventaris,* p. 10; Minister of War to Chief of Staff and others, 5 May 1908, Hoofdkwartier Veldleger, ARA-II; Klinkert, "Oorlog in de Betuwe," pp. 48, 54.

[96] Snijders to various commanders, 21 February 1916: Snijders, Memorandum re "wedvlucht," probably 17 Jan. 1918, AHK Bereden Artillerie, ARA-II; De Graaf, "Colijn," pp. 38-39; Snijders and Dufour, *De mobilisatiën bij de groote mogendheden,* p. 252; Ernst Heldring, *Herinneringen en dagboeken van Ernst Heldring (1871-1954)* (Groningen: Wolters-Noordhoff, 1970; ed. Johann de Vries), p. 1051; Bonebakker, *Twee verdienstelijke officieren,* p. 71.

[97] Bonebakker, *Twee verdienstelijke officieren,* pp. 18, 33,35, 44.

[98] Ibid., pp. 19, 35-37, 44; Van der Wal, *Herinneringen,* p. 24.

[99] Van der Wal, *Herinneringen,* p. 20; Bonebakker, *Twee verdienstelijke officieren,* pp. 20, 38-39; Hardenberg, "Opperbevelhebber en Algemeen Hoofdkwartier," pp. 391, 392; Berg, *Snijders,* p. 62; Treub, *Oorlogstijd,* p. 13.

[100] Bonebakker, *Twee verdienstelijke officieren,* pp. 73, 76-77; Berg, *Snijders,* pp. 92-93; De Beaufort, *Vijftig jaren,* part 2, p. 223; De Valk and Van Faassen, *Dagboeken en aantekeningen,* pp. 696, 699.

[101] Bonebakker, *Twee verdienstelijke officieren,* p. 39; C. Smit, *Tien studiën betreffende Nederland in de Eerste Wereldoorlog* (Groningen: H. D. Tjeenk Willink, 1975), pp. 28-30; Heldring, *Herinneringen en dagboek,* p. 237.

CHAPTER FIVE

STRICT NEUTRALITY, 1914-1916

The Netherlands' experience in World War I can be divided into two phases. In the first, which lasted until the end of 1916, the maintenance of neutrality was relatively straightforward. The country clung to a legalistic vision of strict, or "academic" neutrality, which was generally accepted by the warring powers. Crises did occur but rarely appeared to threaten the country's peace. This would change radically in 1917-1918, as the opposing belligerents began to make demands which the Netherlands could not possibly meet. Each alliance believed that the Netherlands was somehow favoring the other side, and each demanded that the Dutch grant concessions that would have violated the country's responsibilities as a neutral to the other side.

Had the latter situation prevailed from the beginning, Holland's neutrality would never have survived four years of warfare. That strict neutrality worked in 1914-1916 can be attributed to several factors. First, the rapid mobilization in 1914 made a positive impression abroad. The major powers obviously did not fear the Dutch army, but they did realize that Holland would not allow another belligerent an uncontested entry. In other words, no power needed to occupy Holland to keep it out of the hands of another. Second, Dutch neutrality worked in the favor of both alliances. For the Entente, Holland was a convenient route through which to gain information, and its belligerence would only have meant that British troops would have to be diverted from the Western Front. For Germany, the Netherlands protected its army's northern flank, as Bosboom had foreseen, and provided imports, although not to the extent hoped for by Moltke. Germany was not concerned about Holland's neutrality in 1914-1916 because it expected to win the war. Belgium would become a vassal state, leaving Holland in a *Reich*-surrounded region, certainly dependent on German good will.[1]

Neutrality also worked because most Dutch officials were of one mind. Support for the policy was universal. Neither the military nor diplomatic establishments demonstrated any interest in abandoning neutrality to the slightest degree. Friction inevitably occurred between Snijders and his government about how to interpret strict neutrality and make it practical, but there was no overt opposition. Almost everyone understood what it meant to be neutral. One exception was Wilhelmina's German-born consort, Prince Hendrik, who apparently intervened on 5 or 6 August 1914 when two wounded German officers appeared in Limburg by car hoping to get through to Aachen. They were stopped, but then allowed to go on to Aachen, without parole – a serious technical violation of the law of neutrality. Hendrik may have engineered their release.[2] Hendrik was an exception, and he had no authority outside the palace, and, indeed, no authority inside it. Rumors circulated to the effect that the Queen placed him under three months' house arrest for his indiscretion.

Invasion was not the only threat. Germany made a few attempts at negotiating with Belgium in 1914-15, during which Dutch territory was definitely on the table. An alarmed Britain tried, but failed, to get Belgium to discontinue the talks. King Albert's agent, Professor Waxweiler, met with Count Törring-Jettenbach, an agent for Bavarian chancellor Georg von Hertling. Bethmann-Hollweg gave the talks his blessing. Waxweiler proposed a swap in which Belgium would give up some territory to Germany, but would gain the Dutch territory on the left bank of the Schelde, as well as some French territory. The Germans refused to consider this, but later did discuss a scheme with the Japanese under which Holland would lose Limburg and the Schelde bank but be compensated with other territory. This idea was strictly developed to extend Germany's interests and was not the product of any hostility toward Holland *per se*. The Dutch government was ignorant of these maneuvers but had no illusions about Holland's security if Germany annexed all of Belgium. German envoy Richard von Kühlmann wrote in 1916 that the Dutch would be delighted if Germany confined her annexations to the Meuse line (i.e. southeastern Belgium).[3] So just as Belgium was secretly proposing the partition of Holland, Holland was secretly hoping for the partition of Belgium.

The Netherlands in crisis

The atmosphere in Holland in the summer of 1914 was every bit as crisis-filled as in the other capitals, without the compensating enthusiasm for victorious war. Economics joined invasion and foreign machinations as a point of concern. Holland was a global mercantile center, economically dependent on trade and with much of its capital invested abroad. The finance minister was pessimistic, expecting that economics as much as politics might force Holland into the war. His response was still mild compared to the fear and "genuine panic" that occurred throughout the summer, especially in business circles.[4]

The government had to intervene with numerous measures officially aimed at stabilizing the economy, but also to reassure the public. From both perspectives, the government was regarded as having been reasonably successful. Postwar memoirs and commentaries contain little criticism of the steps that were taken, something which may be attributed the relative lack of partisanship in 1914. This made it fairly simple for the government to propose three special new taxes to support the army. Like the belligerents, Holland had to borrow to support its military spending. When the 1914 bond issue initially failed to obtain enough subscriptions, the government threatened to turn to a "forced loan" – leading to the swift purchase of the bonds, business interests obviously wanting to avoid the forced loan. The government also had to ensure that it did not appear to be allowing some to profit from the war. To this end, a special tax was imposed on dividends; a profit tax was adopted later, but soon repealed.[5] The Queen helped by ending Palace entertainment as an austerity measure, a decision popular not only with the people, but also with the Queen, who regarded entertaining as a chore.[6]

There was more to all these measures than keeping the people quiet. The threat to the country's economic health was real enough. Holland was faced with an unsolvable conundrum. It was a trading center, but it had to limit trade. Exports had to be reduced in order to ensure that the country did not starve, or that its factories ground to a halt, but this meant a reduction in trade and a worsening of the balance of payments. The conscription of two hundred thousand men adversely affected the economy as well.[7] It was not their aggregate labor that was most missed. If anything, the government feared unemployment. Rather, many individuals who occupied key company posts or important professional functions had to return to service, threatening temporary chaos in many walks of life.

Chaos was avoided, but not by much. The Amsterdam stock exchange was closed on 28 July, an event viewed at the time as an overreaction to the events in the Balkans. Heavy ownership of foreign shares seems to have triggered the decision. A demand for a complete debt moratorium was not honored, but the government did decide to stop gold exports, although theoretically it lacked the power to do so.

The need to avoid the loss of the country's gold bullion was so obvious that no party bothered to object to the extralegal decree (later underwritten by a proper statute). Even so, the legal requirement for gold backing of the currency, unchanged since 1864, had to be halved. Fearing a run on stores, the government authorized mayors to seize store merchandise. This was actually done to stifle a popular fear that merchants might withhold supplies.[i] One thing that was being hoarded, interestingly enough, was cash. The government printed huge quantities of money on the off chance that the publicly-held cash might not resurface for so long that the economy might be affected. (The finance minister, M. W. R. Treub, later wrote that he "would not reveal, what he suggested it could be used for, if it turned out that it was unnecessary for its purpose.") To deal with unemployment, the government introduced unemployment legislation on 3 August and accelerated planned public works programs. The government began buying wheat (30 July) and imposed export controls, but in some cases private firms needed no official urging. On 31 July, Rotterdam's principal coaling firm stopped loading, fearing seizure at sea.[8]

These latter measures pointed to the danger that a trading, seafaring nation would face if the war took any length of time. Here was another conundrum. If the war went quickly (i.e. the Schlieffen plan worked) then Holland would be dominated by the victorious Reich. If the war lasted a long time (i.e. the Schlieffen plan failed) then a *guerre de course* would threaten, with belligerents attacking each others' trade. Life at sea could become dangerous, especially if the British and Germans became high-handed and ignored international law (they did). How would the Dutch public react to the losses? Cort van der Linden worried that sinking of Dutch ships might trigger demands for retaliation, perhaps leading Holland into war.[9] He need not have worried. There was no chance that the public, no matter how indignant, would demand war. The fear of war remained a powerful deterrent to any bellicosity – toward either side.

The crisis atmosphere was heightened by the appearance of *1 million* Belgian refugees in the Netherlands. The behavior of the German army in Belgium produced revulsion in Holland, forcing

---

[i] This particular government intervention had an honorable history. During the Dutch revolt against Spanish tyranny, besieged towns routinely imposed laws preventing citizens or merchants from hoarding.

Gevers to explain to the Foreign Office in Berlin that this sentiment was pity for Belgium, not hostility toward Germany. Whether the German diplomats truly accepted this distinction without a difference is doubtful, but they recognized that this was a tactful way for Gevers to explain that any public relations problems of the Germans were caused by the Germans. In the meantime, the Dutch government had to cope with the appearance of a seventh of Belgium's population inside its borders. The Queen organized a royal assistance committee, while the government established a central bureau for foreigners.[ii] Not everyone was happy with the Belgian presence. The military wanted the refugees out of the southern provinces, and Snijders demanded on 13 November that the borders be closed (which was refused). The Queen's Commissioner[iii] in Limburg warned that the presence of the refugees was creating dangerously high anti-German feelings.[10]

The refugee problem mostly resolved itself. The Dutch government did begin negotiations on October 12, 1914, concerning repatriation, but as the battlefield receded, the Belgians went home on their own. After the fall of Antwerp, only a corner of Belgium remained directly affected by the fighting. About a quarter of the refugees went home in the fall of 1914, but 720,000 remained for several months. Between 50,000 and 100,000 remained for the duration of the war. The Dutch government paid passage for some who wished to go to England, but this was done quietly, and not at all if planned enlistment in an Allied army was suspected.[11]

The Germans helped, if unintentionally, by building an electronic fence along the Belgian-Dutch border. The 200-volt fence claimed some 3,000 victims, not counting those executed for trying to get through. Germany built it partly to keep people from fleeing to the Netherlands, partly to stop espionage. The fence existed to compensate for the lack of soldiers to physically guard the border. A Belgian Count d'Oultremont trained people in techniques for getting through the fence.[12] The fence was actually a blessing for the Dutch government, which also wanted to cut down on the movement of goods and people into and out of Belgium.

A trickier problem was dealing with internees; they could not be

---

[ii] Headed by one of the author's ancestors, F.W.C.H. baron van Tuyll van Serooskerken.

[iii] Roughly equivalent to a governor.

released, but their treatment had to be reasonable so as to avoid friction with the government from whence the soldiers came. Initially most were Belgian. In August-September 1914, about 10,000 Belgian and 2,000 British soldiers crossed the border and were interned. By the late fall, the number of Belgians had risen to 35,000, and a small number of Germans (about 200) and Canadians (328) had crossed the border as well. The internees included both soldiers who had been forced toward the border and deserters. Holland rigidly enforced its internment policies against all combatants. When these were soldiers, there was relatively little friction with the belligerents. As will be seen later, when warships were interned, considerable diplomatic trouble erupted.

The foreign trade problem

Diplomacy could paper over some of the difficulties relating to internment, refugees, and a host of other issues. No suave legalistic aristocrat could make Holland's economic insecurity vanish, however. The country's exposure to problems resulting from interference with trade was huge. The Dutch depended to a large degree on trade with Germany and trade overseas. Britain was committed to stopping the former, Germany the latter when it benefitted Britain. A policy of economic isolation can make a country safer,[13] but this was not an option for the Dutch. Holland imported grain from overseas and coal from Germany and Belgium, and her commercial and agricultural sectors were utterly dependent on foreign trade. An interruption of overseas shipping spelled the end of contacts with the Indies. In other words, to survive economically and imperially, Holland had to continue to trade with both sides, simultaneously convincing each side that this trade was not benefitting the other. Not surprisingly, this became harder as the war progressed, as each alliance increasingly felt that Holland's trade policies were benefitting the enemy.

Shipping was interrupted several times during the war. The first interruption came from home. When the war began, the government briefly detained vessels in port in expectation of a great naval battle in the North Sea. No immediate Armageddon materialized, but the region did become progressively more dangerous. Britain declared the North Sea a "theater of war" on November 13, 1914, and Germany followed on February 2, 1915 with a similar declaration for waters around Britain. This meant that there was a certain assumption of risk involved in sailing the North Sea and even beyond. Ships could be stopped and searched, and sunk if they were carrying "contraband." Things were quiet until March 25, 1915, however. The cargo vessel *Medea* was torpedoed, raising fears in Holland that war was imminent. Leaves were canceled and the army was brought to a war footing. Germany gave assurances that this was not the case, and the crisis was resolved. Nevertheless, the extent of the response to a single sinking shows how sensitive Holland was to any interference with its commerce.[14]

The number of sinkings rose in 1916. Losses included 36 merchant vessels, 3 sailing ships, and 26 fishing boats, leading to some 200 fatalities. A dozen vessels were stopped and destroyed by Germany for carrying contraband. In addition, Britain detained 150 fishing boats in 1916 until an agreement was reached that only 20% of their catch could go to Germany. The losses did not seriously threaten the merchant fleet's existence. Most of the lost vessels were small. Only 6 major ships were torpedoed in 1914-16, and compensation was paid for three after the war. The government feared, however, that a combination of losses and foreign demands for shipping space would make the fleet effectively unable to supply Holland's needs. This was a realistic fear, as Holland increasingly lost control of its merchant vessels. To prevent this from happening, the government forbade the sale or lease of ships to foreigners without government permission (March 18, 1916). The British, however, increasingly saw the Dutch merchant fleet as a means of solving shipping shortages, and used a variety of means to force Dutch shippers to ply the risky routes to Britain.[15] This was an ominous sign, anticipating the complete takeover of Dutch ships abroad by the Entente in 1918.

The Dutch economic relationship with Britain was difficult. Britain's economic war against Germany naturally concentrated on Holland because it was one of the few places where Germany-bound trade could still go. In addition, Britain was in a superb position to threaten Holland with cutting off trade, or cutting all ties with the Indies. The latter move, hinted at in 1916, would have cut off supplies of coffee, tea, tobacco, and cinchona bark, from which the best quinine was made – and 9/10ths of it came from Java. Britain's wartime interpretation of neutral rights was narrow. The Declaration of Paris (1856) stated that neutral ships were free so long as they were not carrying "contraband." The Declaration of London (1909) differenti-ated between "absolute" and "relative" contraband, the former referring to military goods, and gave neutrals an important right; it limited the application of the doctrine of "continuous voyage." This doctrine was particularly obnoxious to the Dutch. Under "continuous voyage," a product seized at sea was evaluated according to its ultimate destination. If it were to be consumed inside Holland, it was not contraband; if it might be on its way to Germany, it was contraband. The Declaration of London exempted "relative" contraband from the doctrine of continuous voyage. Unfortunately for Holland and other neutrals, this exemption was never ratified and the Entente nations dropped the limitation on the doctrine of continuous voyage.[16]

This was made clear quickly by the Order in Council of 20 August and proclamation of 21 September, 1914, stating that relative contraband could be seized, and that the doctrine of continuous voyage would apply. Relative contraband covered everything that could assist a country's war effort, which in practice meant everything. From London, envoy De Marees van Swinderen reported on 25 August that the British government had effectively ended the civilian/military distinction, and he was right. No longer was contraband military goods, it now included all goods. This was bad for Moltke's plans to use Holland as a "windpipe," but it was worse for the Dutch. Already in August petroleum shipments were interrupted because some were heading for Germany. In October the British mined the North Sea, although a shipping lane for Holland was left open (a practice duplicated by the Germans). On March 15, 1915, the British government practically prohibited the transport of all goods to and from Germany, eliminating the distinction between contraband and non-contraband. The results were not wholly beneficial for Britain. Agricultural exports to Britain fell by 90%. This was because Germany, deprived of many imports, needed more Dutch foodstuffs, paid much more than the British did, and used economic pressure to get them. In addition, the sometimes cavalier British behavior stimulated resentment and pushed Holland toward Germany – something Repington had feared.[17]

Two things prevented Dutch-British trade relations from collapsing. First, as a small country, there was little Holland could do about Britain's behavior. Second, the German government, outwardly more respectful in its dealings with the Dutch, was in reality no more subtle and could be equally demanding. Both great powers were involved in a sanguinary struggle for existence, and their behavior is understandable. This did not make the Dutch situation easier, however. If Britain could cut off Holland's grain, Germany could cripple her coal supplies.

In 1913, Holland had bought 18 million tons of coal from Germany, as against 2 million from Britain and a half million from the Belgians. Germany more than once threatened to cut off coal exports if Holland did not ease some of its export restrictions – which in turn had been imposed to placate the British. Germany did continue to sell coal, although in 1915 only 6 million tons crossed the border (occupied Belgium supplied 2 million more, while the British flow had fallen about a tenth). The net result was a 50% drop in coal imports, most from Germany. Germany exchanged coal for food. Its share of Dutch agricultural exports rose from 25% to 80% between 1914 and 1916. While agricultural exports overall rose 40% in 1914-1916, those to Germany rose more than 350%.[18]

Erich Ludendorff, military leader and virtual dictator by the end of the war, considered the supplies from the neutrals (Denmark was also a major supplier) to be significant, but he attempted to make sure that they were not making to much profit from the trade. Prussian *Generallandschaftsdirektor* Wolfgang Kapp was less concerned about Dutch-Danish imports, not considering them to be a life and death matter.[iv] The evidence indicates Ludendorff was closer to the truth. The money and effort that German agents poured into Holland to get more supplies was enormous, and this led to a major headache for the Dutch; smuggling. Smuggling caused shortages, rising prices, and the wrath of the Entente, where suspicions lurked from the beginning that Holland's economic policies favored Germany.[19]

The scale of the smuggling was enormous. The London *Economist* estimated on 1 April 1916 that smugglers had earned 2.4 *billion* guilders on the trade. The German authorities actively supported the smuggling, but it would have probably occurred regardless. So many products were worth much more in Germany and occupied Belgium than at home. At Bergen op Zoom, near the Belgian border, traffic was greater than before the war. "Men, women and children – especially the latter – went there on the way to Belgium, loaded with packages, and, except for money, returning empty handed." The flow was compared to the exodus from Antwerp, except for the direction. In southern Limburg, a third of all horses were reported "stolen" to cover

---

[iv] Kapp was Director of the Real Agricultural Credit Bureau. Besides an interest in foreign imports, Kapp and Ludendorff shared one other thing; they both tried to overthrow the government after the war.

up their illegal sale to Germany. In a two month period in 1915, 90 tons of rice and grains were smuggled through two border villages. Festivals were held in border villages, paid for entirely by the smuggling profits.[20]

The government worked hard to stop this economic exodus. It had to; aside from domestic problems such as inflation and shortages, the government faced increasing pressure from Britain, which was well informed about the smuggling. British agents sought their own information, but also received great help from the pro-Entente *Telegraaf*, which passed along detailed information to the British about smuggling. Albion had no grounds to complain about a lack of response, however. The "state of siege" was continually expanded to cope with smuggling. In 1914, five royal decrees were issued placing more localities under state of siege; nine followed in 1915, and towns were still being added as late as December, 1916. Even border regions in the northern Netherlands, where there was no military threat, were added. On 8 January 1916, a five-kilometer deep zone was created along the frontier in which cargo could only move on main roads and had to have documentation permitting export before entering the zone.[21]

This placed the work of smuggling control in the hands of the army, which did the job until 1 April 1916, when the Finance Ministry resumed border control responsibility. As the army retained powers over areas in state of siege, however, it was never completely out of the smuggling control business. Snijders was ambivalent about this task, writing in September 1914 of the linkage between neutrality and smuggling, but taking the reverse position in 1915. That shift earned him a critical letter from Cort van der Linden. The general was concerned, however, about the effects that smuggling enforcement was having on the combat readiness of his army. He complained about losing some of his best soldiers and NCOs when 6,000 troops were permanently transferred to border duty. Soldiers and border guards participated in the smuggling as well, or were bribed or "distracted by women" to look the other way. Some were posted in their home areas, which did not increase the likelihood of arrests. Soldiers' smuggling increased after the Finance Ministry took over, something the commander of the Field Army attributed more to boredom than greed. The army did its best. In 1915, more than 23,000 soldiers were used for anti-smuggling duty, resulting in almost 40,000 criminal complaints, some 1300 expulsions, and 62 smugglers being shot down. The rate of arrests, expulsions and shootings by the army was still rising when the Finance Ministry resumed control.[22]

Did it work? Smuggling declined in 1916, but shortages continued. The *Telegraaf* opined that these were more a function of exports than smuggling. The paper may have been correct. The export controls imposed on 2 August 1914 were not watertight. Many companies and individuals displayed a lack of concern for the situation at home. For example: In June 1915, War Minister Bosboom discovered that the Batavian Petroleum Company had equipment that would be highly useful to the army for the manufacture of artillery shells. When he tried to obtain the equipment, he found out that it had been sent in January to England.[23] Was the company really ignorant about what could be made with its own equipment, or had it sent the machinery out of the country before its use was demanded (probably with a much lower profit) by the War Ministry? Neither exports nor smuggling were the main cause of shortages, however.[v] The real problem was a lack of imports. Economic survival demanded avoidance of a complete blockade.

The Netherlands Oversea Trust Company

The first concern was the preservation of the merchant fleet. The *Maria* was sunk on 21 September 1914 by the *Karlsruhe* and became the first true wartime loss (a small vessel, the *Alcor,* was sunk in a Russian harbor at war's opening, but this was apparently due to a "misunderstanding" by the Russian navy). Dutch vessels, however, carried only a quarter of Holland's trade. This percentage was on par with that of France and America, but far behind Britain, Germany, Italy, and the Scandinavian countries, which carried half of or more of their trade under their own flags. Over half of the 10,000 ships to dock at Rotterdam in 1913 were British or German. This resulted in a quarter million tons of German shipping being laid up there when the war began. Much of this foreign presence was for Central European trade.[24] With this trade ending, Holland's shipping needs were reduced

---

[v] This did not prevent Louis Raemakers, the *Telegraaf*'s Belgian-descended cartoonist, from showing a Dutch lion drinking fuel, which then went from its tail to Germany.

– but far from eliminated. A total British blockade would be cata-strophic.

The solution turned out to be the creation of semi-private entities to control trade. By far the most important one was the *Nederlandsche Overzee Trustmaatschappij,* Netherlands Oversea Trust Company, know universally as the NOT. "It was largely due to [the NOT] that the Netherlands was kept out of the war." Its function was simple in principle; all imports were consigned to the NOT, which would ensure that goods were not for reexport to Germany. Its remit was later enlarged to include exports of domestic products. Companies violating this requirement would be reported abroad (i.e. to the British). Ships adhering to NOT requirements flew a black and white cone to reduce the chances of being stopped at sea. When it was established on 23 November 1914, its founders anticipated a short war, believing that even the great powers could not sustain such devastation. Instead, the work dragged on, and the NOT's work exploded. Its archives contain 330,425 contracts and its office received 5,000 letters per week. Tension permeated its work. Germany undermined the NOT by sending agents to purchase contraband, although on other occasions did business with the company (when legal).[25]

The NOT's governors did not worry too much about Germany; their job was to keep the British happy. To do so, the NOT had to cut off trade with Germany. Hence, the mechanism of a private company was chosen, as otherwise Germany could claim a violation of the Rhine River Treaty of 1868, which forbade trade restrictions. Germany immediately lost one of the reasons for accepting Holland's neutrality (imports), leaving it only the geographical factor that Holland protected the German army's rear. So Britain had every reason to be pleased with the NOT. Grey, expressed his happiness in early 1915. So far did the NOT go to meet British demands that Ernst Heldring, a prominent business leader, complained that too much had been conceded too fast. Heldring, no warmonger, felt that the NOT could have gained more benefits for the Netherlands by occasionally taking a more courageous position, and argued that Switzerland had done better by resisting foreign demands more than Holland had. Heldring had half a point. Greater resistance would have been futile, and Britain had effectively completed its blockade through NOT contracts.[26]

But – and this is what Heldring was referring to – British demands never stopped. The British did not trust the Dutch government, nor all of the NOT directors. On 11 March 1915 Britain had instituted strict blockade measures in the North Sea, only lifted on 11 April when Holland agreed that all non-governmental imports would go through the NOT. Only a few items from the Indies could be imported specifically for sale to Germany. A couple of other minor exemptions were negotiated, but Britain's NOT-wall was intact. The British government and its legation, however, would raise additional demands on a regular basis. The list of items that could not be imported at all grew steadily. The NOT directors found the British pressure increasingly intolerable. C.J.K. van Aalst finally reminded the British that they had allegedly gone to war in 1914 "to protect the interests of the small nations." The tone of the letters and conversations emanating from the British was frequently labeled "unacceptable" and dealings with them were considered "difficult" and "very demanding." The British legation had a habit of not answering queries from the Dutch, simply remaining silent, or issuing new demands in reply. NOT director Joost van Vollenhoven, who probably had the best relationship with the British of anyone in the NOT, sometimes returned letters with a note that he would not accept them, or delayed answering as long as possible (and sometimes not at all).[27] That was about the extent of what the NOT could do. Britain did need some things from Holland – especially butterfat – but it held the whip hand. The NOT did not control exports to Britain. The British signed an agreement with another semi-private organization, the *Nederlandsche Landbouw Export Bureau*,[vi] granting them specific percentages (that were not met) of dairy and meat exports.[28] But even if the NOT had controlled these items, it would not have had much more influence with the British.

The NOT's relationship with the British was made more difficult because the British delegation was not monolithic. The envoy in 1914-1916 was the relatively *laissez-faire* Sir Alan Johnstone.[vii] The commercial attaché, Sir Francis Oppenheimer, was far more important, and was one of the true architects of the NOT. His position was undermined, however, by diplomatic service politics. One of the consuls, Ivor Maxse, openly despised him. The British legation had an unhappy history. Johnstone was removed, partly because he was not

---

[vi] Netherlands Agricultural Export Agency. This agency was created to avoid problems with Germany.

[vii] He was replaced on 2 January 1917 by the waspish and condescending Sir Walter Townley.

considered vigorous enough in dealing with the Dutch; Townley left under a cloud related to his wife's behavior; Maxse had to apologize for launching a scurrilous and libelous attack on Oppenheimer; and Oppenheimer, whose skill outweighed his tact, suffered *inter alia* under press accusations that he was not putting enough pressure on the Dutch. The Foreign Office was not always of one mind with Sir Francis, partly because he had come from the business world and not via the normal Eton-Oxbridge route. In addition, he was Jewish, and born in Germany! He was as loyal a public servant as Britain had, but the Foreign Office did not often see it that way.

No one was better suited than Oppenheimer to run the blockade. In 1909, he had sent a study to Grey concerning the impact of a blockade on Germany and the its reliance on neutral ports. In 1912, he became commercial attaché for Germany and the Netherlands. When the war erupted in 1914, Oppenheimer was in at the founding of the NOT. He told the committee that formed the NOT, "I am here to help." Later, he claimed that the idea essentially came from him, although Van Aalst claimed it for himself. His relationship with Van Aalst was apparently brittle; the latter sent Sir Francis a copy of the NOT's official history, which skewered the British attaché in many ways. Oppenheimer got along better with Van Vollenhoven, giving him more credit for keeping Holland out of the war than any other Dutchman:[29]

> Among all the neutrals the world over, we never had throughout the years of our struggle a more honourable, a more efficient, a more resourceful friend, combining with fundamental loyalty to his own country an eager sympathy with the Allied cause.[30]

Flowery praise, which was not reciprocated by Van Vollenhoven. The latter did have more influence with the British than Van Aalst, possibly because Van Vollenhoven was the one who always went to Britain to hold discussions. (Van Aalst was afraid to cross the North Sea.) Oppenheimer successfully urged his government to award both Dutchmen the KCMG after the war[31] (the same award he received himself), but he clearly had his feelings about which one was doing the better job.

His relationship with the NOT and the Dutch was difficult from the beginning. He was not favorably impressed when De Marees van Swinderen told Oppenheimer at war's outbreak to negotiate via him, not Johnstone, calling Johnstone a "fool" – probably not the most diplomatic or tactful thing to say. Oppenheimer was unhappy and let him know it. In October, 1914, Van Aalst warned Oppenheimer not to use commercial policy to drive the Netherlands into German hands. This was actually very good advice, but the manner in which it was imparted annoyed the British diplomat.[32] Still, he had reason to be very happy during the first phase of the war.

> By the end of 1916 practically the whole of Holland's industrial life had been brought under Trust control. It was our commercial chancery at the Hague, which in turn controlled the controllers.[33]

Sir Francis left an enormous legacy for both Britain and the Netherlands. By forcing the Dutch to dance to British demands he ensured that Britain would continue to support Dutch neutrality. At the same time, Dutch surrender to British demands did not lead to as much German hostility toward Holland as might be expected. The Germans blamed Oppenheimer, who they regarded as a sort of Public Enemy # 1. He played a tremendous role in solidifying the British blockade, a vital component in the final outcome of the war. Without Oppenheimer, Britain's blockade might still have worked, but with the cruder method of simply cutting off Holland – irrevocably driving the Dutch into German aims. Among professional diplomats of his generation, Oppenheimer was a giant.

He succeeded partly because he understood the relationship between the NOT and the government, and exploited its complexities, sometimes deliberately increasing dissension between them. He hoped to use the British-tied NOT as a weapon against the more *Deutschfreundliche* elements, which, his government thought, dominated the cabinet. He recognized that Loudon's insistence that the NOT was a private organization was pure fiction. Loudon was forced to accept the British view that agreements with the NOT bound the Dutch government but, as he did not sign them, could still avoid having to officially defend those agreements. Given the Foreign Ministry's lack of focus on economic matters, it made sense for Loudon and the cabinet to acquiesce in the essential takeover of state economic affairs by a semi-private organization. The legal fiction fooled no one, but it was a useful tool.[34]

It had its drawbacks as well. The NOT, Agriculture Ministry, and Foreign Ministry went in different directions. Their activities were not coordinated, and their policies differed. The NOT was nearly autonomous in 1915-16 and was later called a "state within a state." Its independence was a double-edged sword. Its actions did not directly implicate the government but neither could it call on the government for official backing in all negotiations. When it did ask for help, the reception was not always positive. In October 1915, for example, the NOT was handed a British complaint regarding the 15-20 tons of linseed oil that crossed the border every day; it could be used to make glycerine for ammunition factories. The oil was sent across in the form of soap. The NOT went to the government, claiming that it could not handle such matters without more power over exports. Loudon was not happy, thinking that the NOT had accepted too much responsibility already. The rest of the government, however, decided that the restriction could be granted on items regarding which shortages threatened. This was pure sophistry. In essence, the government was taking the NOT under its arm to help one belligerent when the shortage had occurred because the NOT was trying to do too much.[35]

Perhaps this kind of situation explains why Loudon, a strict or "academic" neutralist despite his Entente leanings, had reservations about the institution. His government and most private interests generally approved of the NOT, the British were mostly satisfied, the Germans not overly angered by its accomodationist policy toward Britain. Loudon doubted whether its necessarily unbalanced approach could survive the war.

An enigma? Loudon, the war, and "academic" neutrality

Loudon was an ardent advocate of strict, academic neutrality, possibly the last leading official in Holland to cling to this ideal. Loudon was a pleasant and careful man, a dignified figure regarded as an excellent minister. He had enjoyed a successful diplomatic career culminating in an appointment as envoy in Washington. After the 1913 elections he was offered the ministry, leading to a situation in which neither of the ministers most concerned with national security – War and Foreign – had parliamentary experience. Fortunately, Loudon was able to hide behind the veil of secrecy and confidentiality that naturally accompanies diplomacy, and he fared better in Parliament than Bosboom did. His reputation declined toward the end of his term, as Germany came to regard him as pro-Entente and Britain considered him a liar. Neither was quite accurate. He was by nature honest.[36]

Like any competent diplomat he could be economical with how much of the truth he revealed. Yet his commitment to academic neutrality naturally put him in complicated situations as he was forced to trim his foreign policy sails toward whichever great power was blowing the hardest. British diplomats in the early part of the war described him as friendly and straightforward, but "not a forceful personality."[37] The Germans also became increasingly irritated with Loudon's failure to respond quickly to requests and demands. This had nothing to do with Loudon being lazy, but rather reflected the refined game of delaying tactics that he played, repeatedly sorrowfully informing great power envoys that he would have to circulate this or that communication of theirs to a ministry – or better yet, several ministries. Not surprisingly, the Dutch were labeled as "masters of Fabian tactics."[38] Charges of bias were more serious. Loudon was one of several cabinet ministers considered friendly toward the Entente. Bosboom, De Jonge, and naval minister Rambonnet also leaned toward the Entente, especially Rambonnet, who favored an alliance with the Entente. Loudon quashed such suggestions, backed up by Cort van der Linden, who like most other university professors, was *deutschfreund-lich*.[39]

Loudon's Entente leanings, however carefully suppressed, did exist. He was *francophile* and ended his career with a 21-year stint as envoy in Paris. Besides, no one who read about the reign of terror in Louvain and elsewhere could possibly remain unaffected. It was the Dutch chargé who had written one of the first thorough eyewitness reports of the vile atrocities committed by the invading there.[40] Loudon read these reports, and it is hard to believe that he remained unaffected.

The ministry was fairly neutral, although individual diplomats had visible preferences. The small ministry staff did not enjoy much prestige among the *corps diplomatique* and was criticized for sometimes writing impossible instructions, other times for not providing any at all. During the war, however, few accusations of inefficiency or incompetence were made against Loudon's bureaucrats. The quality of his envoys was uneven. Fortunately for Holland, Gevers was probably the best, careful and modest, but also viewed as active and able. His connections inside Germany were excellent, perhaps because he had Prussian relatives. De Marees van Swinderen, who occupied the other hot seat, did not have quite as good a reputation. He was popular but not highly regarded in London, perhaps because he was seen as too loose lipped. He had done reasonably well as Foreign Minister in 1908-13, although taking a vacation trip during the 1911 Moroccan crisis was probably not the most politic thing to do. Marcelin Pellet, the

French envoy, claimed that De Marees van Swinderen avoided serious discussions and that he had never met a foreign minister who was so uninterested in politics. His wartime service had its successes, however, leading him to lobby either for Paris or another shot at the ministry (he lost both).[41] Of the other posts, Loudon was poorly served by his Washington envoy, W.L.F.Ch. ridder van Rappard, whose open Germanmindedness endangered the delivery of munitions purchased in Washington. Rappard resigned in 1917. W.B.R. baron van Welderen Rengers in Rome, who was pro-German, reported effectively on Italy's negotiations with the Entente, and correctly predicted that Entente promises would not (and could not) be kept. The envoy in St. Petersburg, A.M.D. baron Sweerts de Landas Wyborgh, was *declared persona non grata* in 1916 for suggesting that Russia needed to end the war because of her internal weaknesses.[42] On the whole, more diplomats were friendly toward Germany. One who was not was M.W.R. van Vollenhoven, chargé in Belgium,[viii] whose impulsive actions caused Loudon more trouble than any of his envoys' leanings.

The presence of a good envoy in Berlin was not the only advantage Holland had in its dealings with Germany. Relations with Germany were aided by the sympathetic view that a number of leading Germans had of the Netherlands. The two countries did share some cultural ties, spoke similar languages, and had monarchical blood ties (although that was true of all European monarchies). Most German bureaucrats, according to Gevers, sympathized with Holland's position in 1914. Jagow, while expecting Holland to become part of the *Reich* someday, was at pains to point out that he understood the Netherlands' difficulties.[43] The German envoys to The Hague were generally well disposed toward Holland, if not always toward its government. The Hague was considered a good posting, although definitely a stepping-stone for those wanting ambassadorial rank (Holland only exchanged envoys). Still, The Hague was considered an important appointment before August 1914, and even more so after. Occupants of its legation had a good record for climbing to bigger and better things.

That was not true of the envoy at war's outbreak. Müller had been in The Hague for 7 years, a long time for a diplomat with good connections who had worked closely with Bülow and the Kaiser. That,

---

[viii] The envoy, H. van Weede, had followed the Belgian government to its exile at Le Havre.

however, explains why he was never promoted. He was already envoy
to The Hague when he was asked to review the text of the Kaiser's
infamous *Daily Telegraph* interview. Not realizing that he was
supposed to analyze it closely, he approved it. A good argument can be
made that he was more scapegoat than responsible, but it did not
matter. He was described as a very nice man, a great music lover, "not
a Prussian," but "as diplomat very insignificant." He could be feisty
when the situation demanded, as when he pushed for repressive
measures against the *Telegraaf* newspaper and its cartoonist, Louis
Raemaekers. Loudon explained Dutch press freedom laws to Müller
but did have a talk with the newspaper to quiet it down.[44] Müller was
merely echoing his government's views. Jagow had complained that
the *Telegraaf* was worse than the French *Matin,* and the legation later
got the government to do more to keep caricatures of the Kaiser out of
public views.[45] In other words, the anti-*Telegraaf* campaign did not
reflect any initiative by Müller.

His replacement showed considerably more initiative. Richard von
Kühlmann had been chargé in 1906-1908 and called that the happiest
time of his diplomatic life. He served a year as envoy to Holland in
1915-1916 before moving on to an embassy and, by 1917, to Secretary
of State for Foreign Affairs. He was highly active, setting up a
propaganda operation (the *Hilfstelle)*, building contacts, and guiding
relations through several crises. He worked hard to get Holland
compensation in the *Tubantia* affair and was a realist about the
country's vulnerability to Britain. He was intimately familiar with the
history behind Holland's neutrality policy. Generally speaking, he
opposed sharp measures and pressure from Berlin, pointing out that the
two countries would remain neighbors and that there would be many
issues to settle. He also thought Holland could be a good avenue for
negotiations. Hard feelings, he further felt, would slow Holland's
assimilation into the *Reich.* His great hope was that British tactlessness
and extortionate trade policies would drive Holland to Germany's
side.[46]

Superficially, it looked possible. If the cabinet and the diplomats
were divided in their preferences, so was the country. Both sides strove
to build support in the Netherlands with formal propaganda organizations. But about 80% of the people favored the Entente. There were
definite anti-British feelings, but these were overwhelmed by popular
distaste for militarism – and fear of Germany. A British propaganda
expert wrote that popular sentiment was composed of "dread of

becoming involved in the war, a firm resolution to defend national independence, and general sympathy on the part of the masses with the cause of the Allies." This developed from a single event; the invasion of Belgium. Even Kuyper's efforts to justify the invasion were for nought. "For millions it was no question for debate who had started the war – Germany had invaded Belgium and that was the end of the discussion."[47]

Hence, British propagandists – including the future NOT official historian, Charlotte van Manen – had a good environment in which to work. Townley and Maxse reported that people were generally well-disposed toward the Entente, mainly due to their dislike of Germany. The colonial army was pro-Allied, but the colonial office and the governor-general leaned toward Germany. The government indirectly helped Germany by whipping up anti-Entente feelings. (According to British diplomats, this was done to balance anti-German feelings and keep them from getting out of hand.) The most pro-German elements were found among army officers and aristocrats, followed by members of court society, university professors, some business people, and some Catholics who disliked the French Republic.[48]

This left Germany with an influential minority on which to build. The propaganda effort was small until Kühlmann arrived in 1915. Besides organizing the *Hilfstelle* he began to use his many contacts in The Hague from his previous posting there to find out what could be done. He was not concerned that Holland would join the Entente of its own accord, reporting in May, 1915, that only a "small minority" in the governing circles wanted military involvement for the liberation of Belgium. Kühlmann was more concerned about negative publicity that existed in pro-German publications. In August the pro-German *Nieuwe Rotterdamsche Courant* conceded that the new Europe, after the (then anticipated) German victory, would look like Hell. In October, the pro-German *Nederlander* reported on the impact of events in Belgium on public opinion and only defended Germany by contrasting German militarism and British imperialism, suggesting that the former might not be worse.[49]

Among the sources who Kühlmann turned to was Kuyper. In September 1915 they had a lengthy conversation during which they agreed that anti-German feelings among the Dutch were the result of Dutch national character but would not lead Holland into the Entente camp. Kühlmann did not think that there had been any marked shifts in public feelings, contrary to what was thought in Germany at the time. The true *deutschfreundliche* were a relatively small circle, but there were German sympathizers everywhere. On the other hand, anti-German groups were influential and active, especially among Amsterdam's merchants and workers. Demonstrating a sensitivity not always present among his coworkers, Kühlmann pointed out that Dutch concerns about the war were perfectly natural, because of the fear that what happened to Belgium could happen to Holland, and that Belgian refugees had strengthened those feelings. But he optimistically concluded that mistrust of Germany had declined, and in the long run he expected Holland to gravitate toward Germany.[50] This was music to Bethmann Hollweg's ears, as this was exactly the postwar relationship with Holland that he sought; close, but not necessarily annexed.

Kühlmann not only built pro-German contacts, but on one occasion managed to trip up an adversary. Treub was well-known as being pro-Entente: one British envoy wrote, "We must not let Treub fall." But, suddenly, he did. He resigned in February 1916, although he managed a return in 1917. His fall was explained as the outcome of a conflict with Parliament over its unwillingness to debate old-age pensions, but strangely enough, Cort van der Linden made no effort to save him. Dr. Wichert thought Treub had fallen because of conflict with pro-German financial interests. It has been alleged, however, that Kühlmann himself arranged Treub's fall. His method was simple. Treub's lifestyle has been described as "certainly not irreproachable." Put more bluntly, he had a mistress. This has toppled politicians in more tolerant places than 1916 Holland. Kühlmann managed to let the rather puritanical Queen know about the affair.[51] Wilhelmina did not make cabinet appointments, but she had many ways to let Cort van der Linden know her displeasure – and this may explain why the Minister President made no attempt to save his finance minister.[ix]

Kühlmann had no difficulty in extending his propaganda work and related efforts. This included a lengthy study of German political work in Holland by a Dr. Wichert, which Kühlmann forwarded to the Chancellor on 28 May 1916 (despite noting that it was not interesting). German officials had good relations with Kuyper, Colijn, and two other prominent politicians, Th. Heemskerk (a former Minister President)

[ix] Cees Fasseur, however, has argued that there is no evidence that the Queen intervened, and that her subsequent appointment of Treub to a national aid commission contradicts claims that she disliked him. Fasseur, *Wilhelmina,* pp. 514-15.

and Jhr. A.F. de Savornin Lohman (Kuyper's greatest rival among Dutch Protestants). There were also friends in the General Dutch Union, an organization seeking ties with Dutch Americans, the Flemish, and *Afrikaners*. Friendly contacts within the Catholic party included the Archbishop of Utrecht, Monsignor H. van de Wetering, and to a lesser degree, Monsignor W.H. Nolens (the head of the party) and Jhr. O.F.A.M. van Nispen tot Sevenaer. Wichert goes on to list a number of politicians and academics, and a few artists and mayors (including the mayor of The Hague, a future foreign minister).[52] The report does not however, tell us what any of these contacts did, nor what they were willing to do; perhaps it is nothing more than a list of people who were willing to have pleasant conversations with German diplomats. Kühlmann's limited interest in the report is understandable. He probably knew all about the listed contacts, and had more that were not listed.

Kühlmann's accomplishments apparently got Berlin's attention. He was suddenly moved from The Hague to Istanbul, a major promotion: Turkey was a German ally, and the post carried automatic promotion to ambassador. His posting there was also short before moving on to Jagow's old post.[x] Apparently he had been marked as a comer at some point. The Dutch were not happy, however, as rapid replacements without consultation made Loudon's job more difficult. In the long run, the outcome was not so bad. Kühlmann's ascension into the German government gave Holland a sympathetic ear, although this would be tempered by the declining influence of the German Foreign Office *vis-a-vis* the military. In addition, his successor in The Hague, Friedrich Rosen, was able and conciliatory, and neither brusque nor dictatorial.[53]

Kühlmann's work to influence the Dutch was obviously regarded as significant in Berlin. There were some clear-cut limitations to its significance, however. The average Dutchman was not interested in foreign affairs. Sympathies did not affect policies. Dutch politicians were, first and foremost, pro-Dutch.[54] Snijders' appeared to be pro-German, but had more to do with his realism than his sympathies. His army had a much better chance fighting alongside Germany against the Entente than the other way around. Renner's successor as attaché, Major von Schweinitz, said it best:

---

[x] Jagow had left the State Secretaryship nine months before Kühlmann's arrival.

Von grossem politischen Belang sind diese Sympathien und Antipathien
nicht. Dazu is der Holländer zu nüchtern. Im Grunde bleibt er immer
hollandophil, alles übzige is Beiwerk.[55]
(These sympathies and antipathies are not of great political importance.
For that the Dutchman is too sensible. Basically he stays ever Hollando-
phile, all the other is accessories.)

This meant that Loudon had one huge advantage in his work; everybody supported the country's basic foreign policy. The great powers
wanted Holland to stay neutral; so did the government; so did the
army; so did the anglo- and francophiles; so did the *Deutschfruend-*
liche; so did the man in the street. There would be controversy about
how to actually work it all out. Loudon preferred and held to "strict"
neutrality, whereas Germany wanted its *wohlwollende* neutrality,
Britain wanted to use Holland as a blockade outpost, and the army
wanted a foreign policy that would allow it to defend the country in
case war broke out.

Loudon won. His one powerful trump card was that the great
powers would not tolerate a small state that did not remain truly
neutral. Any advantages given to one side would lead to either counter-
demands or retaliation from the other. Only occasionally was Holland
pressured to join the Entente after August, 1914. In November the
Entente representatives in Japan pressed the Dutch envoy for an
alliance, pointing out that Germany's trade through Rotterdam was
contrary to neutrality, and, in a barely veiled threat, noting that Japan's
assurances concerning the security of the Dutch colonies came only
due to a British initiative. As this presentation was not followed by
direct Entente representations to Loudon, he could ignore it, and did.
In March of 1915, De Marees van Swinderen (acting on his own) again
asked for British assurances regarding Dutch neutrality, which the
British were willing to give if Germany did so also. Grey indicated he
would like to discuss what Britain could offer Holland if the two
countries had to make "common cause." Johnstone assured Loudon in
November that Britain would leave the Netherlands unmolested "as
long as it is not violated from any other quarter." The Entente nations
reaffirmed their support of Dutch neutrality in 1916.[56]

Loudon won because his position enjoyed strong domestic support
as well. Strict neutrality appealed to the Dutch public. Strict neutrality
was legalistic and moralistic, allowing Holland to claim the moral high
ground, and this had great political appeal. In addition, Dutch
policymakers were strong supporters of international law, to the point

of making it an article of faith. Not everyone in the government agreed. When Holland's interests were affected, such as when Germany was on the verge of taking Antwerp, some ministers wanted a less neutral position. But their argument was, in the short run, doomed. Bosboom and Rambonnet, the military ministers, did not have much political influence. Treub, the pro-Entente finance minister, did, but Loudon enjoyed Cort van der Linden's backing, so there was no chance that the cabinet would topple the policy – until late in the war.[57]

The result was a policy that required a rigid but sympathetic stance toward each belligerent. If one of the warring powers had a good legal argument for a particular Dutch course of action, it would be considered; otherwise, not. On the Entente side of the ledger, the fifty German and Austrian ships in Antwerp were denied passage down the Schelde. When two German officers left for Germany in violation of internment regulations, the Dutch demanded their return. Remarkably, they were returned. Belgium's complaint about radio interference from Dutch warships in the Schelde was taken care of. Specific steps to block the use of the Schelde were kept secret. No protest was made concerning the first British minefield (which, unfortunately, made it impossible to protest later mining by either side). The sailors from the sunken British cruisers *Aboukir, Cressy* and *Hogue* were repatriated because they had not voluntarily entered Dutch territory. Fortification of the Schelde against violators began even before Britain asked that this be done.[58] On the other side of the ledger, the Dutch forbade entry of Entente merchant vessels that were armed, including those carrying antisubmarine gear. The British complained vigorously, arguing that Holland was the only country that treated armed merchantmen as warships. Apparently Loudon and his government had no objection to being called unique, and the complaint was rejected.[59]

Yet the arguments against strict neutrality gained force as the war dragged on. In October 1914, Rambonnet raised a troubling issue; strict neutrality meant that if war came to Holland, it would be an accident which side the country might be on. Bosboom feared that the Netherlands might get dragged in on the side that had the least to offer Dutch interests. This was not a call for abandoning neutrality, but rather an argument for edging toward one side or the other, and making military preparations accordingly.[60]

The two military ministers had a vocal ally in Snijders. Snijders worried, not unnaturally, about (a) having to face in several different directions, (b) having no advance warning as to who his primary enemy would be, and (c) theoretically having to fight both sides if they both crossed the border. Snijders first questioned his instructions on February 22, 1915. He feared that he might technically have to wage war against both belligerents, because if one crossed the border, the others would do so as well. He wanted some type of guidance regarding which way the government leaned – toward the Entente or the Central Powers – because he did not want Holland's fate decided purely by "accident." Essentially, he wished to discuss assistance with one belligerent or the other before hostilities began, not after. Help that came too late would be of no use. He feared Holland would then become another Belgium. Neutrality would be history anyway once an invasion began. He pressed the government to choose a preferred side right away, give him broad powers to begin a second mobilization on his own, and recall troops on leave. The general asked the government to let him know in a timely fashion if academic neutrality was to go by the boards. He specifically wanted to know if he should keep his army spread out, or concentrated so as to coordinate effectively with potential allies. Snijders reminded the government that he needed to be kept informed about the political situation and whether conversations could begin with neighboring countries – especially as, in case of war with Germany it would be best to fight the war outside Holland, and this was unthinkable without allied assistance.[61] [xi]

Snijders' memorandum was not well received. It asked questions that the government did not want to answer, as it could not answer them if it wished to hold to "strict neutrality." The interior minister

---

[xi] This would become a repeated theme in Snijders' writings, demanding to be given a job that was militarily possible. He returned to it after the war. War with Germany was the most dangerous because Germany could mass unnoticed. Intelligence was hard to get. The danger could not be ignored by the government by saying, "it probably won't happen." Relying on the rights of small nations (i.e. international law) was misplaced, Snijders noting how many small countries were swept up into the war. He conceded that Germany saw Holland's neutrality as an advantage, but each side could benefit from possession of Dutch territory. Increasingly, demands by the belligerents reached a level where no concessions could be made. This made incursions likely – and then what? The government's argument that an alliance with the other was not automatic was unrealistic. Snijders discussed the view of the Swiss general Wille, who promoted fight-ing side by side with the invaders' enemy. Echoing Bosboom, however, Snijders argued that this made the choice of side a complete accident, as either enemy alliance might invade. Decisions had to be made in advance so that time would not be wasted once fighting began. Snijders, "Nederland's militaire positie," pp. 556, 558-62.

even prevented a copy from reaching the Queen, perhaps anticipating that she would want the questions answered. On 26 February, Cort van der Linden replied on behalf of the government. He expressed sympathy for Snijders' problems and awareness of the deployment conundrum but could not give certainty regarding direction because the situation had not changed. He could not say that the government would hold to its nonpartisan position to the bitter end, because circumstances could arise, which would force the government to take a different position. The Minister-President explained that any encroachment should be answered with violence, but that this did not automatically imply war – although it would if the entrance was premeditated. The government had no intention of doing anything that hinted of an abandonment of neutrality.[62]

Snijders found this memorandum unsatisfactory. He could hardly have reacted otherwise, as it answered none of his questions, and solved none of his problems. It was written in a hedging tone, almost as if the government were corresponding with another government. Hence in August 1915 he took up the pen again, writing a lengthy memorandum in which he pointed to the danger of a hostile force appearing without any warning, and also that it was not possible to prepare transport and movement orders for every conceivable situation. Unbeknownst to Snijders, Loudon was already running into troubles with strict neutrality. In June, 1915 Johnstone had pressed him regarding Holland's position on the possible annexation of Belgium by Germany. This was a point on which Loudon could not, and did not, claim that Holland would remain neutral. Johnstone demanded if the Netherlands would warn Germany of the Dutch opposition to annexation. Loudon said that he would, but that it was not the proper time. Johnstone reported that this was the first official admission that the Netherlands would have to go beyond strict neutrality at some point. Strict neutrality forbade Holland from taking almost any initiatives in foreign policy. When the Dutch Anti-War Council called on the government to call a conference of neutrals (October 1914), the government had to refuse. As late as 1916, Holland refused to join the neutrals in a note asking for peace. Loudon did attempt to get America to create bloc of neutrals – perhaps he was thinking back to the League of Armed Neutrality, two centuries before – but the United States refused.[xii] He also hoped that Holland could mediate peace negotiations, and obtained a reopening of diplomatic ties with the Vatican in 1915 for this purpose. Other than this, initiatives were rare.[63]

If something as innocuous as a conference of neutrals was unacceptable, choosing a military alliance in advance was beyond the pale. Changes in deployment could be noticed and questioned, and if it leaked that a side had been chosen, neutrality would be history. Loudon's commitment to "academic" or "strict" neutrality was born of practical considerations of national survival, not idealistic commitment to international law. This made the situation in Belgium particularly difficult. The situation in and future of Belgium affected and interested the Dutch like no other issue. No other point was as near-daily a topic of discussion as the future of the Belgians. Kühlmann wrote that the Belgian question would determine Dutch-German relations for a generation, and that many Dutchmen saw the two low countries' futures as tied together. Always looking to turn a bad situation into a good one, the wily German suggested offering Holland the small Belgian enclaves inside Dutch territory in return for other concessions. Jagow looked at the issue from a more negative perspective, fearing that Entente propaganda concerning Belgium harmed German interests in Holland.[64]

The German State Secretary had picked up on half of the problem. Undoubtedly many Dutchmen were affected by what had happened to Belgium, but the government worried a great deal more about what would happen to Holland, if Belgium were annexed. This was really a two-pronged problem in Holland; one part concerned discussions of annexation with Germany, the other part whether to discuss it with Germany at all. In the fall of 1914, the German approach to Antwerp made the issue acute. It was one thing for Germany to march *through* Belgium, but the *occupation* of the whole country led to suspicions that Germany might harbor annexationist designs, raising both commercial and strategic concerns. Bosboom felt that the annexation of Belgium would inevitably lead to Holland's incorporation into the *Reich* as well. Hence he, Rambonnet and Treub wanted to abandon strict neutrality,

---

[xii] This particular league (there has been more than one of this name) was formed in 1780 at the behest of Catherine the Great during the Anglo-French war arising out of the American Revolution. Holland joined in 1781, but it did no good; Britain declared war.

Rambonnet suggesting that Holland should tell Germany it would only accept a temporary occupation of Antwerp. He advocated making Dutch soil available for the guarantors of Belgian neutrality and extending a "benevolent neutrality" toward the Entente. The three ministers moderated their tone quickly, instead suggesting asking Germany how long it intended to occupy Antwerp.[65]

The rest of the cabinet firmly quashed this idea, but did not ignore the issue. Gevers told Jagow in June 1915 that Holland could not be indifferent about Belgium's future. This view was communicated to the Germans via other channels as well. Renner (now Lt.-Col.) reported at the same time that Colijn, who was regarded as *deutschfreundlich*, described the total annexation of Belgium as very undesirable. Renner added that pro-German elements generally described Belgian annexation as unlikely, not as harmless. Renner pointed out that a Dutch entry into the war would be very unwelcome, and that annexation might drive Holland to the side of the Entente. A German general told the Dutch representative in Brussels on 27 June 1915 that Germany would not annex Belgium against Holland's wishes. Gevers reported that much of the imperial government, including Hindenburg, was opposed to annexation.[66]

Loudon considered these signals and decided not to press the German government on the issue. He told Gevers on July 8 1915 that Germany would hardly be in a position to answer the question. If Germany had no plan to annex, it could not say so, because it would lose a bargaining chip. If Germany did plan to annex, it could not say so, because it would harm its position in Holland and hurt pro-peace groups in Entente nations. Instead, he advised Gevers to continue to tell Germany that Holland cared about Belgium's future. Not that the Germans needed much reminding. Kühlmann sent numerous messages on the subject, picking up on Renner's point regarding fear of total annexation. Kühlmann suggested on May 16, 1916, that annexation of Belgium east of the Meuse might be tolerated, especially as that would obviate any need for Germany to go through Limburg in a future war. The real fear, Kühlmann argued, concerned annexation of the Antwerp/Schelde region.[67] The German government's responses tended to be indirect, as Loudon had foreseen. Signals proclaiming a disinterest in annexation reached the Dutch, but usually through foreign legations,[68] not directly. Loudon was right: Germany could not do so.

Germany's activities in Belgium affected the Netherlands in several ways. One had to do with Belgium's large Flemish population, which not unnaturally resented the Walloon domination of Belgian culture. Germany hoped to exploit this. Pan-Germanists advocated a Flemish policy culminating in annexation to the *Reich,* while others contemplated a Flanders annexed to Holland. The Dutch government wanted absolutely no part of this, as it would have been a clear violation of Holland's treaty obligations, not to mention a violation of neutrality.[xiii] Bethmann Hollweg had a long conversation with Kuyper, who explained to the Chancellor that Germany's Flemish policies were failing because Germany's defeat was still viewed as possible in Belgium. Kuyper proposed that Germany create a bipolar state, in which all officials in Flanders had to graduate from a Flemish college.[xiv] [69]

The attempt to capitalize on Flemish dissension continued, to the Dutch government's displeasure. There was nothing that The Hague could really say, however. The overall treatment of the Belgian people was a different matter. This affected the Dutch more directly and could be brought up without in any way violating the requirements of neutrality. Dutch involvement in Belgian relief began in 1914. Much of the actual aid came from the United States as well as Holland, and Gevers sought free passage for ships carrying relief supplies. A thornier issue concerned Belgians who had returned home and were then deported to Germany for labor. Loudon issued a protest, pointing out that this violated the workers' asylum rights in the Netherlands, and demanded their return. The German government agreed, provided the Dutch would ensure that the returning Belgians were employed. This condition was accepted.[70] Humanitarian issues caused little conflict.

Another issue that touched on Belgium was border security. The German army was worried about an attack in the rear from the Netherlands, whether by the Dutch themselves, or an Entente power operating from Dutch soil. Germany went to some trouble to assure the Dutch that movements south and east of Holland were not hostile. The German concern about the security of the Dutch border surfaced early.

[xiii] If the Dutch government had foreseen Belgium's postwar territorial demands, it might have been more sympathetic.

[xiv] Kuyper, strongly anti-Catholic as a matter of religious principle (he was quite willing to work with Catholics politically), hoped that this would be applied to clergy as well as secular officials. The Roman Church would have to accept a government regulation concerning its clergy, and it might break the anti-Flemish tendencies of most of the higher clergy in Belgium.

It was, in fact, present in Moltke's mind at war's outbreak, when he urged Gevers to send the Dutch army westward. Assurances were given when a Zeppelin bombed Antwerp (29 August 1914), and was repeated when two cavalry divisions were deployed along the border (8 December 1914). In between, an apology was issued when German troops fired across the border on 4 September. In December 1914, Van Vollenhoven reported that Germany could not spare any troops and passed on a request from O. von der Lancken, the German Foreign Office Representative in Belgium, that the Dutch notify Germany about any Dutch troop movements. (This request provoked great hilarity in the Dutch cabinet.) Van Vollenhoven wondered if some advantage could not be taken of the German level of concern, especially regarding the interests of Dutch citizens in Belgium. Loudon thought the suggestion absurd. His confidence in his envoy was not heightened, when on a trip back to Holland, the diplomat took a German colleague along to show him that the fear of an attack in the German rear was ridiculous. This entirely unauthorized show-and-tell expedition led to a demand from the Foreign Minister himself for assurances that Baron Frays, the German diplomat, could not have seen anything that he was not supposed to see. (Fortunately, Van Vollenhoven's antics did not have much impact). In June 1915, Jagow argued that a Dutch army in the rear, plus an English landing in the Schelde was something that the German military position could not handle *(verträgt unsere militärische Lage nicht)*. In the fall of 1915, Erich von Falkenhayn, Von Moltke's successor, "wanted to avoid further complications with neutrals . . . He would have been hard pressed to find sufficient troops to meet the situation in the north had the Dutch been drawn into the war." In 1916, Germany began the building of a heavy coastal battery near the Schelde because it feared that Holland might renounce her neutrality (due to submarine warfare). In a February 1916 *aide-mémoire* and a March press release, Bethmann Hollweg worried about "the menace of war from the Kingdoms of Holland and Denmark." In September 1916, the German commander at Cleves asked for a meeting with a Dutch officer to assure him of Germany's friendly feelings and that the rumors of impending war were false.[71] It should be noted that this was at a time when Germany was particularly short of troops.

Perhaps these German worries about adding even a small opponent help explain why the relationship between Loudon and the German diplomats remained positive until 1916. Only then, for reasons beyond any diplomat's control, did friction start to increase. Loudon was careful to edit his public statements to allay German suspicions that his government was secretly pro-Entente. The Germans occasionally showed a similar sensitivity toward Dutch feelings. In 1914 and 1916, there was published a *"Lettre à un Hollandais"* authored by Professor Adolf Lasson of the University of Berlin. The document was extremely insulting toward the Dutch, essentially describing them as a miserable *petite bourgeoisie*. German sources, quick to point out that the letter was being republished by Entente propaganda sources, wrote that Lasson was an octogenerian representative of orthodox Hegelianism, and that in Germany no one paid the slightest attention to him any more.[xv] [72]

Pan-Germanism was a theoretical danger; a far more real threat was that war had become three-dimensional. Germany introduced the world to aerial bombing and large-scale submarine warfare. New technologies created unanticipated threats to the policy of neutrality. This issue acquired urgency as the year 1916 progressed and the debate over unrestricted submarine warfare began in earnest. Its impact on Holland was not ignored, German officials noting that Dutch-British trade was already stagnating. Even the *Kriegsmarine* conceded in late August that Holland and Denmark were likely to join the Entente and admit British troops. Romania's belligerency drained Germany's reserves of manpower even further, so much so that the submarine campaign was temporarily slowed. There were literally no troops available, even to stop the Dutch army. The planning for the submarine campaign continued, and Germany began to fortify the Dutch border at Hindenburg's urgings. Jagow explained to Gevers that this was a precaution against a British invasion. When Gevers questioned Jagow about the timing, he was told that the Allies' problems in 1916 made the British "capable of anything." Gevers decided that he believed Jagow, but that "great vigilance" was "urgently needed."[73]

On this point he was surely preaching to the choir. There had been plenty of incidents that demonstrated the need for vigilance. The first bombing of Holland occured on 22 September 1914, when a plane (believed to be Belgian or British) dropped a bomb on Maastricht. Then on November 4, 1915, a German submarine ran aground at Terschelling and was interned. The German protest against the internment were so vigorous that, according to Treub, a disarmed

---

[xv] Probably not true; Lasson remained prominent.

Netherlands would have had to concede. On 8 December 1915 parliament held a secret session (soon leaked to Kühlmann) to hear the protest and decided that the time for demobilization had obviously not come. The sub stayed, later to be joined by a British and two more German submarines. Then to add to German anger, on February 2, 1916, an airship was shot down by Dutch troops. According to messages tossed into the sea by the doomed crew, the ship had encountered troubles, drifted over Holland, and encountered heavy rifle fire. The ship later disintegrated, probably as a result of the gunfire. The remains of the L-19 disappeared over the North Sea along with the crew. Germany protested on the grounds that the shooting was unprovoked; a damaged warship forced to come ashore should not be fired upon. The Dutch response was that if the L-19 had to land because of trouble, that meant it was already in violation of Dutch territory. In addition, the Dutch claimed the airship had been warned.[74]

These incidents paled beside the sinking of the *Tubantia*. The unfortunate liner was not the first Dutch ship to go down, nor was it the first time that a sinking had created friction between Holland and Germany. The expanded submarine campaign of 1915 was "not a great deal less than a declaration of war." Protests over the sinking of the *Katwijk* without warning in April 1915 led to a German decision not to sink any more neutral ships.[75] This provided a temporary, if incomplete, respite. Then, on the night of March 15-16 1916, the *Tubantia* went down.

The *Tubantia* was brand new, the largest ship in the Dutch merchant fleet, and at 14,000 tons displacement was the biggest neutral vessel lost during the war. The costly if not particularly profitable ship was the pride of the Royal Dutch Lloyd line. Its loss was a national shock. The ship had been on its way to South America when, at 2 a.m on 16 March 1916, it had stopped to anchor near the Dutch coast – precisely to avoid being misidentified and attacked. The liner was completely lighted. Suddenly, two crewmen spotted a stream of bubbles coming toward the ship, followed by an explosion. Fortunately, only 80 passengers were on board, and they and all crewmen were brought to safety. The ship and its cargo were a complete loss, however. German denials made absolutely no impression, especially because a smaller Dutch liner, the *Palembang,* was sunk two days later – possibly while still in Dutch waters. Pieces of a German *Schwarzkopf* torpedo were discovered later in the wreckage. The German navy never conceded deliberately sinking the *Tubantia,* claiming that it had been struck by a torpedo fired ten days earlier that had somehow stayed afloat.[76]

What could German diplomacy do amidst national fury? Kühlmann proved equal to the task. He launched an effort to spread rumors about a pending British invasion. Johnstone had written earlier that the wily German had proven adept at starting rumors in the past; Kühlmann lived up to his reputation. Careful orchestration was evident. Claims of a pending British landing came from Berlin and from Bucharest, while the legation in The Hague spread the rumor wherever possible. Jagow told Gevers of the "threat" on March 30th. The German envoy in Romania, claiming he had heard it from the French and Russians, sent it forward as well. British newspapers were soon reporting that the story was coming out of the German consulate in Amsterdam. Jagow repeated the rumors on March 31, pointing out that Germany would have to intervene if the British did.[77]

Kühlmann has received most of the credit for the propaganda coup, a tremendously successful effort to divert public anger from the sinking of the *Tubantia*. He was well prepared, having suggested in 1915 that Holland's fear of British landings should be exploited. The Dutch leadership, however, was not misled. While there were panicky reactions in the street, the government declared an alert more to impress foreigners than to deter a British invasion. The 4-day alert (March 30-April 2) did not include the "second mobilization" required if invasion were truly imminent. The only concern was that the German army might act on its own and preempt a British occupation of the southwest. Beyond that, Loudon thought that Dutch intelligence would have picked up some evidence of British concentrations, and hinted as much to the German envoy. Loudon also pointed out that the area where the British were supposedly going to land was within range of Germany's own massive Flanders batteries. Jagow merely expressed his appreciation for Holland's defensive measures.[78] Loudon did continue to monitor the situation, but he agreed with De Marees van Swinderen's conclusion; the fact that Britain had troopships available was not the same thing as troops actually filling those ships.[79]

The military chiefs shared Loudon's relative lack of concern. Bosboom, who had followed the Gallipoli operation with professional interest, doubted that Britain would want to attempt another amphibious landing. The war minister told Kuyper the possibility still worried him, but he was confident that the landing would fail. The two military ministers decided leaves would be canceled effective March 31, thereby recalling thousands to the colors and increasing effective strength by about 10-20%. Snijders concurred, even though he was even less concerned, and was opposed to anything as drastic as a redeployment. The leave recall was more to impress the Germans – as it did – than because perfidious Albion was truly expected. The government benefitted, in that there were fewer demands now for demobilization. Perhaps the level of concern in The Hague is best measured by Loudon's chat with Johnstone during the crisis; he asked him if the British were up to something. Naturally Johnstone said no, and his government followed with a public denial on April 5th.[80]

That exchange typifies the Dutch relationship with the British in the early part of the war, when the NOT and other semi-private organizations bore the brunt of the Anglo-Dutch relationship's frictions.[xvi] It was perhaps just as well. When Loudon questioned Britain's contraband list (2 November 1914) Johnstone[xvii] pointed out that the Rhine River treaty between Holland and Germany made Rotterdam a partly German port. Loudon refused to sign a trade agreement on this basis, worrying about strict neutrality. Without the NOT, his relationship with the British might have declined precipitously. De Marees van Swinderen did have to fend off one last attempt by Grey (March 1915) to establish an alliance. The Englishman did not push the issue, fearing that a pro-Entente Holland would become German-occupied Holland. Grey's emphasis on the British commitment to neutrals' rights, however, was a bit much for the Dutch diplomat. With more accuracy than tact, De Marees van Swinderen expressed his skepticism that Britain had really gone to war over Belgium's neutrality. He asked Grey if Britain would have gone to war for Denmark, to which the response was: "That is too hypothetical."[81]

True crises in the Anglo-Dutch relationship developed late, but it could have been otherwise. As mentioned earlier, there was a school

---

[xvi] Neither Loudon nor Snijders could have been pleased, however, when Snijders' older brother, the retired Lt-Gen. W. G. F. Snijders, entered upon a public argument with Alan Johnstone in which the elder Snijders compared the execution of German spy Felicie Pfaadt in France with the execution of Edith Cavell. Kühlmann to Bethmann Hollweg, 7 September 1916, 63, Smit, *Buitenlandse bronnen 1914-1917,* pp. 93-95.

[xvii] Perhaps some inkling of Johnstone's attitude toward Loudon can be gauged from the last two sentences of a telegram to Grey after meeting Loudon in 1916: "His Excellency begged above remarks may be treated as absolutely confidential." "Above repeated to Paris." Johnstone to Grey, 28 March 1916, 178, Smit, *Buit-enlandse bronnen 1914-1917,* pp. 251-52.

of thought in Britain that wanted to send the BEF up the Schelde to Antwerp. In addition, Churchill proposed on 31 July 1914 to land forces on the barrier islands near the Eems, considering both Dutch and German islands. The Dutch islands were rejected out of hand, as a Dutch declaration of war was considered "inevitable" and the Dutch had enough small warships to cause trouble. On 7 January 1915, Churchill got approval from Asquith, Kitchener, and the War Council to proceed with an attack on German Borkum, but the Royal Navy sank the plan. Had it not, this would have created a war zone in the Eems river valley. More seriously, four times in 1915-16 the British stopped and searched vessels carrying mail to the Indies. (The Germans got into the act as well, intercepting the mailboat *Koningin Regentes* on 20 December 1916. Dutch destroyers attempted to intervene and fighting might have broken out then and there, had they not yielded. Former foreign minister W. H. de Beaufort regarded this as close to a *casus belli*.[82])

These interceptions remind us of the tenuous link that existed between Holland and her enormous colony. There was real concern that the colony would start to develop independently if it lost its connection to the motherland. There were numerous disagreements with Britain and Germany about the rights to enter coastal waters in the Indies. Captain Karl von Müller, for example, had planned to operate through the Indies with his raider, the *Emden*. He was surprised to discover that the ten-ship Dutch naval squadron intended to enforce neutrality, especially to avoid giving Japan a pretext for moving in. When Müller arrived on 27 August 1914, he discovered that his collier had been chased away. The prewar plan to send supply ships to neutral ports was no longer practical.[83] Apparently the Colonial Ministry and the Governor General shared Loudon's commitment to "strict" neutrality. Not because of its legalistic purity, but because it offered the best – and perhaps only – chance to hang on to the colony. Yet Britain's denial of a right to convoy by neutrals (small neutrals, anyway) placed the connection with the colony purely at Albion's discretion.

The British were also actively involved in espionage in Holland. Grey called Holland "the keyhole into Germany." The Germans were no less active. To stop this, GS-III chief H.A.C. Fabius formed links with a number of police chiefs to track agents, whether engaged in relatively harmless propaganda work, or doing things of a more sinister nature. House searches of suspected spies were common, and numerous mentions of attempted border crossings and shootings can be found in the records. Telephone calls between the German legation and its consulates were routinely intercepted to identify German agents. The activities of attachés were monitored. Newspapers were forbidden to publish information about enemy forces, including airships, for six hours after observation. When a wireless telegraphy station began operation in the Belgian enclave of Baarle-Hertog on 22 October 1915, the goverment sealed off the whole settlement with barbed wire fences. Police chiefs in the major cities were cooperative, helping Fabius turn spy networks into Dutch information sources – the alternative being immediate expulsion. Loudon's ministry cooperated, routinely forwarding diplomatic complaints about espionage to GS-III. The most spectacular public case concerned the government's attack on the *Telegraaf*. Ostensibly this was because the paper was endangering neutrality with its vitriolic articles and cartoons. True, the paper was a magnet for German complaints. There is evidence, however, that the government suspected the *Telegraaf*'s editor and publisher of being in British pay, which would technically make them spies.[84]

Military intelligence had certainly improved by the middle of the war. The army fought espionage while continuing its own, although officers in the information-gathering business continued to deny that they were really spies; they still maintained that they only sought information that was visible to all Military attachés, finally appointed in 1916 for Berlin, Paris and Bern, soon proved their worth. Fabius, who had argued for their appointment in 1914, considered them his best sources, even though their instructions were somewhat vague – basically, to study the current war. The attaché in Berlin, Col. Muller Massis, sent numerous reports, and his French counterpart not only got to the front line, but even fought there![85] Fabius, an energetic officer who would reach the rank of general and whose career spanned both world wars, gathered a growing staff that issued pamphlets on the structure of the German army, trench warfare, and infantry tactics, quickly grasping that infantry alone could no longer win battles. The organization grew quickly, with a secret budget of 25,000 guilders by 1916, almost doubling by the end of the war. The officers in GS-III were a close-knit group, symbolized perhaps by Fabius' marriage to one of his subalterns' sisters.[86]

The intelligence services expanded into many areas. A separate branch, GS-IV, was established a few months after GS-III in order to deal with censorship, cryptography, and smuggling. KNIL Captain H.

Koot and his staff deciphered several British and German codes during the war, and were able to read all the messages sent by the German military attaché in The Hague – a considerable advantage, as it would turn out. (A later German code was deciphered immediately after the war, although this may have been done through the simple expedient of buying it from a German officer hard up for cash.) Koot may have acquired his taste for cryptography during his service in the Indies, as the navy there was considerably interested in code breaking (and separately broke part of a German code during the war). Ten officers and 35 enlisted men worked on radio interception, in part to cut down on the number of foreign spies operating out of Holland. Apparently GS-III was involved with this work, because its staff obtained information about the British army by deciphering the messages of the German attaché. The intercept service was abolished in the inevitable postwar downsizing, but not when the shooting stopped; the government thought it wiser to wait until the Versailles treaty was signed.[87]

The attempt to cut down on foreign espionage was prosecuted vigorously. Extreme measures were taken. From 1914 on Dutch citizens were forbidden to listen to radiotelegraphic signals and broadcasts from foreign belligerents. No antenna could be set up without permission. Holland's most prominent radio pioneer, Jan Corver, had his apparatus sealed in 1915 because his broadcasts were interfering with a GS-IV intercept station. His 1916 request to experiment for two weeks with directional antennas was denied because the army advised that it would not further any public interest. Only a year later did Corver get the minister of war to lift the ban on listening. When a request was filed for radio equipment for the British prison camp in Holland, the army promptly seized the machinery.[88]

Snijders issued new instructions for the *Kondschapsdienst* on 24 March 1916, once again encouraging its use for finding information about foreign armies in bordering territories – which could only refer to one army, but, neutral even in print, the General Staff memorandum does not mention Germany by name. The practice of sending officers into Germany continued. For example, one young army officer traveled to Germany in 1916 and reported that Germany's manpower situation was stretched to the breaking point – a very important piece of information for the government, since this meant Germany did not have much to spare for Holland. The officer reported that morale was declining among people and soldiers. The British were most hated, the French were respected, the Russians were pitied, and little positive was heard about Austria. His contacts felt that Holland's friendship must be kept at all costs. Paranoia was high; industrialists were demanding protection for the Rhineland, and a rumor even swept Cologne that the Dutch army had occupied Wesel (!). Surprisingly, a number of Germans in Düsseldorf were aware that the "invasion crisis" of March 1916 had been engineered by German diplomats. Most of the report would have been to Snijders' liking, with one exception; the prominent German industrial Fritz Thyssen believed that if Germany even thought Britain was going to invade Holland, Germany would have to be there first.[89]

The foreign trips were not without their problems. Cross-border information gathering became more difficult as the war progressed. Entry into Belgium was difficult and events there could not be observed on a regular basis. Getting into Germany was actually easier, but not much. Intelligence officer Captain Van Woelderen managed it only because of connections with some officers in Berlin. Information dribbled in, sometimes from foreign legations (Bern was a particularly good source), more often from officers who "happened" to be traveling Germany. Unfortunately, this practice led to one of the biggest diplomatic blow-ups between Holland and Germany in the first three years of the war.

On December 27, 1916, German envoy Friedrich Rosen contacted Loudon and accused the Dutch army of methodically spying inside Germany. Rosen threatened "undesirable" effects on the two countries' relations if the matter was not cleared up. The charge was that numerous Dutchmen were traveling around Germany asking for information that might be useful for the Dutch army, or, what was a far more serious charge, useful for Germany's enemies. Under-Secretary of Foreign Affairs Alfred Zimmermann even suggested to Gevers on 1 January 1917 that it looked like Holland was planning military intervention, which he could not understand as the war had given so many terrifying examples of what might happen.[90]

The charges came not from German counterintelligence, but from the German consulate in Amsterdam. A consular employee had befriended a Dutch reserve officer, who had received permission to go to Germany but had to report back about what he saw. When it was discovered that his brothers were volunteers in German field hospitals, the Dutchman was told they would also have to provide information.

He was then given a list of questions by the Dutch army.[xviii] The consul noted that the list of questions was lithographed, indicating it was not an isolated incident. The consul recommended that extra care be taken in talking with Dutch officers, although he did note that those he knew were friendly toward Germany. The consul reported that the consulate had promised to keep the officer's name confidential, and then gave it in the report; Cornelis Maria van Oyen. He had entered Germany to visit his sick mother, who was living in Berlin.

The consul reproduced the entire questionnaire, most of it calling for an enormous quantity of military information. Questions covered location and direction of divisions, numerical strengths, levels of mobilization, strength and organization of troops in garrison, and whether there were new formations and depot troops near the Dutch border. Specific questions were asked about the districts of the I, VII, and VIII army corps, located close to the Dutch border. Regarding Belgium, the questionnaire asked about defense lines, rail line construction, garrison strengths, troop concentrations at numerous specified points, and bridges and forts in the Schelde estuary. The questionnaire also contained a number of general questions covering, among other things, technical information about artillery, grenades, Zeppelins, command and control of weapons, and air defenses. The final part of the questionnaire asked about the "polder war" along the Yser, and how artillery was deployed behind inundations.[91]

That last item was of very practical use to the Dutch army's defenses, but there were many other questions that only made sense in the context of an offensive into Belgium or even into Germany. Zimmermann was very concerned – both about the information that could harm Germany, and the risk of exposing the Dutchmen who had furnished the German consulate the information (he did not reveal that there was only one). The German Army insisted on a reduction of travel by Dutch officers and was also interested in the source of the information. Rosen transmitted the complaints and pointed out the unacceptability of Dutch officers obtaining information useful only for an enemy or a hostile Holland. Loudon showed, as he would on more than one occasion, that he was made of sterner stuff than usually thought. He argued that every general staff asked such questions and that he could not see anything abnormal. Rosen left with an assurance

---

[xviii]   A more detailed source is not specified.

from Loudon that the matter would be investigated – something which reassured him very little, knowing Loudon's penchant for delaying "investigations" forever. He therefore also spoke to Cort van der Linden, perhaps fearing not so much Holland's military investigations, but what Berlin's impatience would mean for Dutch-German relations.

The answers came back from several channels, but all said basically the same thing: we're not spying. Officers did note what they saw, but did not delve into secret information. If the questionnaire was real, then this answer was obviously not true; much of the information requested in it was not publicly available at all. The Germans did not, however, show the Dutch the questionnaire.[xix] As a result the Dutch foreign ministry concluded that the Germans had no evidence, that their accusations were odd, and that the integrity of the Netherlands General Staff was beyond question. Gevers, who was not shown the questionnaire either, noted that there was no evidence of General Staff involvement, and that the expansion of German defensive works near the border might have generated mistrust. Zimmermann did not argue the point, merely saying that the matter had been brought to the attention of the German envoy in The Hague.

In The Hague, the Dutch response involved several levels. First, Loudon twice assured the Germans that Holland was not handing any information over to the Entente, correctly divining that that was the real source of the friction. Second, Cort van der Linden assured Rosen that the questions did not emanate from the General Staff. Rosen accepted this, and suggested to his government that the questionnaire was the individual effort of some single general staff officer. Finally, Snijders assured Cort van der Linden on 3 January 1917 that the General Staff only gathered information necessary for Dutch security, and questioned deserters. He added that the sending of Dutch subjects abroad with lists of questions did not take place. He offered to discipline any individuals exceeding their authority, if the German legation could supply evidence. Loudon and Cort van der Linden both passed this on to Rosen, Loudon adding that he was pained by the suggestion that information was being sought that would benefit Germany's enemies.[92] Loudon may have been serious, but his comment can hardly have reassured Rosen, who thought Loudon was completely

---

[xix] The Germans did not actually have a copy of the Dutch questionnaire. Their source, allegedly Van Oyen, had *read* his questionnaire to the consular employee.

in the Entente camp. A close look at the government's denials of the German charges is revealing. Espionage is not really denied, although the sending of a specific list of questions was.[93]

Does this prove that the Amsterdam consulate's scoop was accurate? The questionnaire contains Dutch idioms and terms not likely to come from the inventive pen of a German. Furthermore, the sheer detail of the list of questions at least lends it an aura of believability. At the same time, the Dutch general staff was certainly not sharing information with the Entente. If the questionnaire came from the Dutch army, then the questions that proved so offensive to Germany were perhaps inserted by an officer simply trying to make the list comprehensive. The other possibility, however remote, is that Van Oyen was being "run" by a superior officer who was spying for the Entente. Admittedly this sounds a bit like a Frederick Forsyth plot, but that does not mean that it could not have happened. In addition, there are several surviving reports from Dutch officers in the files, on such diverse subjects as the quality of defensive works and the morale of the population. A Lt. R.J. Schimmelpenninck, who was also going to visit his mother in Germany (Frankfurt, not Berlin), was definitely given a list of questions. His name was also entered into a book listing officers with foreign connections.[94] The latter information comes from the diary of a GS-III officer. Perhaps GS-III, in the best modern approach to "deniability," was running its mission in the shadows – showing how quickly it evolved from a clipping service to a true clandestine agency.

Snijders needed the information but not the increased friction with Germany. His problems multiplied as the war dragged on. When the war began, his army had enjoyed great public support; after a few months, that support began to waver. In fact, the first demands for demobilization came in December 1914. Suggestions were made that if there was an increased danger, the government would have time to recall troops. Demobilization demands continued for the entire 1914-1916 phase of the war. Bosboom did not cope well with the shift of attitudes in parliament, but he dutifully stayed on. Even former national leaders like De Beaufort complained that demobilization was possible but that the government and the military leadership refused to contemplate it. Snijders repeatedly explained to the government that remobilizing the army would be an enormous undertaking; just shifting from mobilized to ready for battle would require recalling 200,000 troops, requisitioning vehicles, horses, and supplies, moving exposed bases, headquarters, and government offices, and some places would have to be evacuated immediately. He railed against the "political amateur strategists" in parliament, who failed to consider the time needed for mobilization, and the likelihood that the invader might interrupt the timetable. The Western Front was only three days' march from Holland.[95]

Demobilization was abandoned, but the compromise solution was not satisfactory. Leaves were granted in ever large numbers. This hurt unit cohesion, and made it more difficult to stop granting leaves. During the 1916 *Tubantia*/British invasion crisis, Bosboom was politically unable to end the leave cancellation before Easter. As a result, thousands of soldiers went AWOL and had to be punished. Leave requests poured into headquarters at a rate reaching 2,000 *per day,* forcing Snijders to take himself completely out of the leave decision process (June 1915). Otherwise, he could not have done anything else. "Regular" leaves took about a tenth of the troops away. The government, however, pressured Snijders to allow all sorts of "special" leaves, for businessmen, fishermen, taylors, water engineers, miners, tax inspectors, mayors, doctors, metalworkers, etc. By July 31, 1915, the army's paper strength totalled 350,000, but the actual breakdown was:

On duty	130,000	In training	20,000
On leave	20,000	Reserves	150,000

By the end of 1916, the situation was worse. At any given time, one out of every three mobilized soldiers were away. Snijders saw his strength and quality deteriorating, compensated only by paper strength. The large reserve was available on six days' notice, but that was far too long in case of a sudden invasion.[96]

Perhaps Snijders exaggerated – even the German army thought Holland's defenses improved after the war began. In 1915 Snijders prepared a "recall leaves" order and a "grant no more leaves" order which would shorten the period needed to bring the army to battle readiness. The latter order would automatically bring back all those on "special leave."[xx] He also planned to concentrate the Field Army well

---

[xx] On 24 May 1916, however, he pointed out that commanders should *not* take steps that would make the public think war was imminent. Some officers had apparently gone further, seizing vehicles, ships, and horses, etc., from civilians. Hoofd-

north of the border to gain a little time. He prepared a lengthy memorandum (9 August 1915) in which he complained about anonymous criticisms emanating from inside the government (and perhaps the army: Snijders did not specify). He then detailed his proposal for dealing with leaves and then discussed a proposed reorganization of the army that would make it more flexible. He conceded that his deployment left divisions weakened by detachments and spread out too far, without any strong reserve, but explained why these problems were the inevitable result of his mission and geography. Concerns about Flanders/Zeeland had forced a southwestern shift of the army and robbing of the coastal 1st division to compensate. Snijders also devoted a great deal of attention to how to defend Zeeland, a collection of peninsulas and islands that, in a conventional sense, was undefendable.[97]

And that, of course, lay at the crux of Snijders' problem, and his outlook as well. In a sense the country was not defendable, because neither of the likely invaders – but particularly Germany – could be stopped with the forces he had. He could slow them down, and perhaps hold the *Vesting Holland,* but he needed complete cooperation from every sector to achieve that. To give battle and then withdraw safely required a coordination which an army disorganized by leaves might not be able to achieve. His firepower and equipment deficiencies were no help. Bosboom did his best, trying to buy guns in America, but only older models were available. The warring powers, even Japan, were not able to supply. Germany sold some, but used the shipments to gain more goods from the Netherlands;[98] clearly trade and military policy could collide at any time. While the army was probably strong enough to put up a respectable fight, it was fortunate that there had been no invasion or direct threat in 1914-16; or perhaps unfortunate, because it had lulled Snijders' countrymen into a false sense of security.

The events of 1917 would change that.

kwartier Veldleger, ARA-II.

NOTES

[1] Frey, *Der Erste Weltkrieg,* p. 365.

[2] Report on detention of two German officers, Lt. Bijl de Vroe, Adjutant to His Royal Highness Prince Hendrik, 8 August 1914, Sectie Militaire Geschiedenis.

[3] David French, *British Strategy and War Aims, 1914-1916* (London: Allen & Unwin, 1986),pp. 62, 165-66; Fritz Fischer, *Germany's Aims in the First World War* (New York: W.W. Norton, 1967 (Originally published as *Griff nach der Weltmacht* (Dusseldorff: Droste Verlag, 1961))), pp. 218, 221, 232, 266.

[4] Heldring, *Herinneringen,* pp. 190, 194; M. W. R. Treub, *Herinneringen en overpeinzingen* (Haarlem: Tjeenk Willink, 1931), p. 289.

[5] Ritter, *Donkere poort,* pp. 27-28; Treub, *Herinneringen,* pp. 329-30, 338-39, 342.

[6] Susan Townley, *'Indiscretions' of Lady Susan* (London: Thornton Butterworth, 1922), p. 304.

[7] C.J.P. Zaalberg, "The Manufacturing Industry," pp. 3-111 in Zaalberg, E.P de Monchy, A.J. Romeyn, F.E. Posthuma, and H.W. Methorst, *The Netherlands and the World War: Studies in the War History of a Neutral,* vol. 2 (New Haven: Yale University Press, 1928), p. 8.

[8] Ritter, *Donkere poort,* pp. 21-23, 25; Treub, *Herinneringen,* pp. 289-90, 292, 301-303, 306-308, 311-312; E.G. Maxse, UK Consul, Rotterdam, to Grey, 31 July 1914, 356, Gooch and Temperley, *British Documents,* vol. 11, p. 221.

[9] De Valk and Van Faassen, *Dagboeken en aantekeningen,* p. 705.

[10] Kühlmann to Bethmann Hollweg, 16 May 1916, Duitse Ministerie van Buitenlandse Zaken – Stukken betreffende Nederland, ARA-II; Gevers to Loudon, 30 August 1914, ARA-II; De Beaufort, *Vijftig jaren,* II, p. 239; E.A. van den Heuvel-Strasser, "Vluchtelingenzorg of vreemdelingenbeleid: De Nederlandse overheid en de Belgische vluchtelingen, 1914-1915," *Tijdschrift voor geschiedenis* 99 (No 2 1986), pp. 186-87, 188-89, 194, 195; Treub, *Herinneringen,* p. 309-11.

[11] Van den Heuvel-Strasser, "Vluchtelingenzorg," pp. 192, 194-95; De Beaufort, *Vijftig jaren,* II, pp. 240, 241; Van der Flier, "War Finances in the Netherlands," p. 57.

[12] *The Windmill Herald,* 7 May 1998 and 8 June 1998; *De Volkskrant,* 16 April 1998.

[13] Bengt Sundelius, "Coping with Structural Security Threats," pp. 281-305 in Höll, *Small States,* p. 303.

[14] Heldring, *Herinneringen,* p. 191; De Monchy, "Commerce and Navigation," p. 123; Porter, "Dutch Neutrality," p. 172; Smit, *1914-1917,* p. 66.

[15] Smit, *1914-1917,* pp. 103-106; Porter, "Dutch Neutrality," pp. 135, 174; De Monchy, "Commerce and Navigation," p. 126; Barnouw, *Holland under Queen Wilhelmina,* p. 126.

[16] Daniel R. Headrick, *The Tools of Empire: Technology and European Imperialism in the Nineteenth Century* (New York: Oxford University Press, 1981), p. 72; F.E. Fox Adams, "Memorandum respecting Means of Pressure which can be brought to bear on the Dutch Government through the Control of Jute," 25 October 1916, 210, Bourne and Watt, *British Documents,* Series H, *The First World War* (ed. David Stevenson), vol. 7 (Washington, DC: University Publications of America, 1989), p.

383; Smit, *Tien studiën,* pp. 80-81.

[17] De Monchy, "Commerce and Navigation," pp. 118-19, 125; Loudon to De Marees van Swinderen, 13 August 1914, 59: De Marees van Swinderen to Loudon, 25 August 1914, 95, Smit, *Bescheiden ... 1914-1917,* pp. 38-39, 66-67; Smit, *1914-1917,* pp. 58-59; Porter, "Dutch Neutrality," p. 170; Charles à Court Repington, *Vestigia: Reminiscences of Peace and War* (Boston: Houghton Mifflin, 1919), p. 177; Smit, *1917-1919,* pp. 4-5.

[18] De Monchy, "Commerce and Navigation," p. 139; Porter, "Dutch Neutrality," pp. 137-38, 140, 169.

[19] Ludendorff, *Ludendorff's Own Story,* vol. 1, p. 420; Ralph Haswell Lutz, ed., ed., *Fall of the German Empire, 1914-1918,* 2 vols. (Stanford: Stanford University Press, 1932), vol. 1, p.88; De Steurs to Loudon, 21 August 1914, 85, Smit, *Bescheiden ... 1914-1917,* p. 57.

[20] Smidt, "De bestrijding van de smokkelhandel," pp. 46-50; Smit, *Tien studiën,* p. 9, 92; Pierard, *La Hollande,* p. 45.

[21] Bout, "Dutch Neutrality," p. 80; Smidt, "Bestrijding van de smokkelhandel," p. 52; Van Manen, *Nederlandsche Overzee Trustmaatschapij,* vol. 7, pp. 17-21, 220-22, 224-28, 424; Smit, *Tien studiën,* p. 94.

[22] Smidt, "Bestrijding van de smokkelhandel," pp. 48-50, 52-54, 64-66, 68-70.

[23] British legation to Grey, 2 August 1914, 462, Gooch and Temperley, *British Documents,* vol. 11, p. 267; Pieraard, *La Hollande,* p. 50; De Leeuw, *Nederland in de wereldpolitiek,* pp. 190-92.

[24] Van Manen, *Nederlandsche Overzee Trustmaatschappij,* vol. 1, pp. 22-23, 26, 32-33, 95, 102.

[25] De Monchy, "Commerce and Navigation," pp. 120-21; Van Manen, *Nederlandsche Overzee Trustmaatschappij,* vol. 1, pp. vii, 74, 85, 110-11, vol. 2, pp. 12-13, 63-64; Smit, *1914-1917,* p. 87.

[26] Smit, *1914-1917,* pp. 26-27; De Marees van Swinderen to Loudon, 19 January 1915, Buitenlandse Zaken – Kabinet en Protocol, ARA-II; Heldring, *Herinneringen,* 197-98, pp. 202-203; Smit, *Tien studiën,* p. 87.

[27] Smit, *Tien Studiën,* pp. 88-89, 90-91; Van Manen, *Nederlandsche Overzee Trustmaatschappij,* vol. 3, pp. 228-29, 240-41, 448.

[28] Memorandum by Secretary of State Helfferich, 6 Oct. 1916: Holtzendorff to Hindenburg (22 Dec. 1916) and Zimmermann (6 Jan. 1917), *Official German Documents,* pp. 1174, 1217; Porter, Dutch Neutrality," pp. 135-36, 138.

[29] Oppenheimer to Grey, 28 September 1909, 2, Bourne and Watt, *Germany 1909-1914,* pp. 1-17; Francis Oppenheimer, *Stranger Within* (London: Faber and Faber, 1960), pp. 244, 246, 338.

[30] Oppenheimer, *Stranger Within,* p. 269.

[31] Ibid., p. 358.

[32] Ibid., p. 243; Smit, *Tien studiën,* p. 85.

[33] Smit, *Tien studiën,* p. 91.

[34] Ibid., pp. 86-87; Van Manen, *Nederlandsche Overzee Trustmaatschappij,*vol. 3, pp. 231-33.

[35] Van Manen, *Nederlandsche Overzee Trustmaatschappij,* vol. 2, p. 214; Smit, *Tien studiën,* pp. 40, 93-94.

[36] Porter, "Dutch Neutrality," p. 185; De Valk and Van Faassen, *Dagboeken en aantekeningen,* pp. 599, 816; Bout, "Dutch Army," pp. 11-12; Smit, *Tien studiën,* p. 32.

[37] Smit, *Tien studiën.* p. 32.

[38] Ibid., p. 11.

[39] Ibid., pp. 30-32, 37-38; Smit, *1914-1917,* p. 137.

[40] Legation to Loudon, 31 August 1914, Buitenlandse Zaken – Belgisch gezantschap, ARA-II.

[41] De Valk and Van Faassen, *Dagboeken en aantekeningen,* p. 285; Smit, *Tien studiën,* pp. 42-44.

[42] Smit, *Tien studiën,* pp. 46-53.

[43] Gevers to Loudon, 14 Sept. 1914, 141, Smit, *Bescheiden ... 1914-1917,* p. 107; Gevers to Loudon, 8 December 1914, Buitenlandse Zaken – Kabinet en Protocol, ARA-II; Snijders and Dufour, *De mobilisatiën bij de groote mogendheden,* pp. 257-258.

[44] De Valk and Van Faassen, *Dagboeken en aantekeningen,* p. 713; Müller to Loudon, 21 Jan. 1915, 314: Loudon to Müller, 1 March 1915, 324: Gevers to Loudon, 10 March 1915, 342, Smit, *Bescheiden ... 1914-1917,* pp. 298-99, 321-14, 325-26.

[45] Gevers to Loudon, 21 April 1915, 371: Kühlmann to Doude van Troostwijk, 7 August 1915, 419, Smit, *Bescheiden ... 1914-1917,* pp. 352-53, 407.

[46] Smit, *Tien studiën,* pp. 59-66; Kühlmann to Bethmann Hollweg, 8 May and 8 December 1915, Duitse Ministerie van Buitenlandse Zaken – Stukken betreffende Nederland, ARA-II.

[47] Smit, *Tien studiën,* p. 28; Frey, *Der Erste Weltkrieg*, p. 283; Bout, "Dutch Army," p. 91.

[48] Maxse to Townley, 17 July 1917, 98, and Townley to Balfour, 18 July 1917, 99, Bourne and Watts, *British Documents,* Part II, Series H (ed. David Stevenson), vol. 8 (Washington, DC: University Publications of America, 1989), pp. 240-43.

[49] Kühlmann to Bethmann Hollweg, 8 May and 4 October 1915, Duitse Ministerie van Buitenlandse Zaken – Stukken betreffende Nederland, ARA-II.

[50] Kühlmann to Bethmann Hollweg, 26 September 1915, Duitse Ministerie van Buitenlandse Zaken – Stukken betreffende Nederland, ARA-II.

[51] Treub, *Herinneringen,* pp. 342-43; Barnouw, *Holland under Queen Wilhelmina,* pp. 144-45; De Valk and Van Faassen, *Dagboeken en aantekeningen,* pp. 776-77; Smit, *Tien studiën,* pp. 32-37, 66-68; Kühlmann to Bethmann Hollweg, 28 May 1916, with report by Dr. Wichert, Duitse Ministerie van Buitenlandse Zaken – Stukken betreffende Nederland, ARA-II; Smit, *1914-1917,* p. 136.

[52] Kühlmann to Bethmann Hollweg, 28 May 1916, with report by Dr. Wichert, Duitse Ministerie van Buitenlandse Zaken – Stukken betreffende Nederland, ARA-II.

[53] Gevers to Loudon, 1 October 1916, 637, Smit, *Bescheiden ... 1914-1917,* pp. 643-44.

[54] Barnouw, *Holland under Queen Wilhelmina,* p. 97; Smit, *Tien studiën,* pp. 7, 28.

[55] Frey, *Der Erste Weltkrieg,* p. 292.

[56] Alting von Geusau, *Onze weermacht,* p. 6; Asbeck to Loudon, 8 November 1914: Asbeck to Loudon, 9 November 1914: De Marees van Swinderen to Loudon, 26 March 1915: Memorandum, British Legation, 27 March 1915: Johnstone to Loudon, 26 November 1915: Weede to Loudon, 14 April 1916, Buitenlandse Zaken – Kabinet en Protocol, ARA-II; Grey to Johnstone, 26 March 1915, 522, Bourne and Watt, *British Documents,* Part II, Series H (ed. David Stevenson), vol. 1 (Washington, DC: University Publications of America, 1989), p. 286.

[57] Smit, *1914-1917*, pp. 12, 17; Barston, *Other Powers,*pp. 65-66.

[58] Treub, *Oorlogstijd,* pp. 26-27; Bout, "Dutch Army," p. 50; Belgian Legation and Navy Minister to Loudon, 21 September 1914: Cort van der Linden to Snijders, 12 October 1914, General Staf, ARA-II; Barnouw, *Holland under Queen Wilhelmina,* pp. 119-20; Bosscher, "Oorlogsvaart," pp. 315-55 in R. Baetens, Ph. M. Bosscher, and H. Reuchlin, eds., *Maritieme Geschiedenis der Nederlanden,* vol. 4, *Tweede helft negentiende eeuwen twintigste eeuw, van 1850-1870 tot ca. 1970* (Bussum: De Boer Maritiem, 1978), pp. 336-337; Snijders to Cort van der Linden, 12 October 1914, 195: Loudon to Wilhelmina, 13 October 1914, 196, Smit, *Bescheiden ... 1914-1917,* pp. 182-84.

[59] Treub, *Oorlogstijd,* p. 22; Barnouw, *Holland under Queen Wilhelmina,* pp. 117-19; De Beaufort, *Vijftig jaren,* II, p. 243.

[60] Smit, *1914-1917,* pp. 14, 15.

[61] Bonebakker, *Twee verdienstelijke officieren,* p. 51; Klinkert, "Verdediging van de zuidgrens" (Part Two), pp. 251-52; Bout, "Dutch Army," pp. 123-25; Porter, "Dutch Neutrality," pp. 204, 205; Berg, *Snijders,* p. 102; Snijders to Cort van der Linden, 15 February 1915, 321, Smit, *Bescheiden ... 1914-1917,* pp. 306-309.

[62] Cort van der Linden to Snijders, 26 February 1915, 322, Smit, *Bescheiden ... 1914-1917,* p. 310.

[63] Snijders memorandum, 9 August 1915, 420, ibid., pp. 408-17; Johnstone to Loudon, 19 June 1915, 668, Bourne and Watt, *British Documents,* Series H, vol. 1, pp. 381-82; Pierard, *La Hollande,* pp. 52-53; De Valk and Van Faassen, *Dagboeken en aantekeningen,* p. 856; Frey, *Der Erste Weltkrieg,* p. 365; Fasseur, *Wilhelmina,* p. 511.

[64] Kühlmann to Bethmann Hollweg, 8 May and 29 May 1915, and 16 May 1916: Jagow OHL and others, 10 June 1915, Duitse Ministerie van Buitenlandse Zaken – Stukken betreffende Nederland, ARA-II.

[65] Porter, "Dutch Neutrality," pp. 120, 121.

[66] Renner, "Holland und die Frage der Zukunft Belgiens," 10 June 1915, Duitse Ministerie van Buitenlandse Zaken – Stukken betreffende Nederland, ARA-II; Gevers to Loudon, 10 June 1915, 397: Van Vollenhoven to Loudon, 27 June 1915, 403: Gevers to Loudon, 2 August 1915, 414, Smit, *Bescheiden ... 1914-1917,* pp. 376, 383, 400-402.

[67] Loudon to Gevers, 8 July 1915, 406, Smit, *Bescheiden ... 1914-1917,* pp. 389-391; Kühlmann to Bethmann Hollweg, 16 May 1916, Duitse Ministerie van Buitenlandse Zaken – Stukken betreffende Nederland, ARA-II.

[68] Panhuys (Bern) to Loudon, 5 April 1916, Buitenlandse Zaken – Kabinet en Protocol, ARA-II.

[69] Memorandum by Bethmann Hollweg regarding conversation with Kuyper, 18 April 1916, Duitse Ministerie van Buitenlandse Zaken – Stukken betreffende Nederland, ARA-II; Marilyn Shevin Coetzee, *The German Army League: Popular Nationalism in Wilhelmine Germany* (New York: Oxford Univesity Press, 1990), p. 110.

[70] Lutz, *Fall of the German Empire,* vol. 1, pp. 688-89, 718-19; De Beaufort, *Vijftig jaren,* II, p. 241; Smit, *1914-1917,* p. 181.

[71] German Legation to Loudon, 29 August 1914, 106: Gevers to Loudon (2 messages), 8 December 1914, 181, 274: Van Vollenhoven to Loudon, 9/10 and 10 December 1914, 275, 276: Gevers to Loudon, 6 October 1914, 277: Van Vollenhoven to Loudon, 9/10 December 1914, 13 December 1914 and 23 December 1914, 277, 278, 291, Smit, *Bescheiden ... 1914-1917,* pp. 74-75, 165-

66, 259-62, 270;   Aleks A.M. Deseyne, "The German Coastal Defenses in Flanders, 1914-1918," pp. 40-59 in Steve Weingartner, ed., *A Weekend with the Great War: Proceedings of the Fourth Annual Great War Interconference Seminar* (Shippensburg, PA: White Mane, 1994), p. 43; J. A. Snijders Jr. to C.J. Snijders, 22 September 1916, Hoofdkwartier Veldleger, ARA-II; Jagow to OHL and others, 10 June 1915, Duitse Ministerie van Buitenlandse Zaken – Stukken betreffende Nederland, ARA-II; Paul G. Halpern, *A Naval History of World War I* (Annapolis: Naval Institute Press, 1994), p. 302; *Official German Documents,* pp. 1135, 1148.

72 Johnstone to Grey, 14 December 1914, 14, Bourne and Watt, *British Documents,* Part II, Series, H, vol. 4 (Washington, DC: University Publications of America, 1989), pp. 9-10; Pierard, *La Hollande,* pp. 27-30; "JPWS," *Nederland en Duitschland: Een keur van documenten bijeenverzameld door een Nederlander* (Den Haag: N. V. Expl. Mij. Van Dagbladen, n.d.), p. 2.

73 Undersecretary of State of the Imperial Chancellery Wahnschaffe to Bethmann Hollweg: Holtzendorff conference notes of meeting with Bethmann Hollweg, Hindenburg, and Ludendorff, 29-30 August 1916, *Official German Documents,* pp. 1153, 1206; Bonebakker, *Twee verdienstelijke officieren,* p. 52; Gevers to Loudon, 24 October 1916, Buitenlandse Zaken – Kabinet en protocol, ARA-II.

74 Report on bombing of Maastricht, 23 Sept. 1914, Generale Staf, ARA-II; Van Manen, *Nederlandsche Overzee Trustmaatschappij,* vol. 2, p. 220; Treub, *Herinneringen,* p. 297; Treub, *Oorlogstijd,* pp. 21, 32-33; Kühlmann to Bethmann Hollweg, 8 December 1915, Duitse Ministerie van Buitenlandse Zaken – Stukken betreffende Nederland, ARA-II; De Beaufort, *Vijftig jaren,* II, p. 244; Stephen Longstreet, *The Canvas Falcons: The Men and the Planes of World War I* (New York: Barnes & Noble, 1970), pp. 112, 113; Smit, *1914-1917,* pp. 39-40.

75 Van Manen, *Nederlandsche Overzee Trustmaatschappij,* vol. 2, pp. 33-34; Halpern, *Naval History,* p. 298.

76 Heldring, *Herinneringen,* pp. 165-67, 352; GS-III report, n.d. but between 23 March and 1 April 1918, ARA-II; Van Manen, *Nederlandsche Overzee Trustmaatschappij,* vol. 3, pp. 345-46; Fallon to Beyens, 17 March 1916, 370 Smit, *Buitenlandse bronnen 1914-1917,* pp. 503-505; Barnouw, *Holland under Queen Wilhelmina,* p. 124; *Daily News Leader,* 3 April 1916; De Valk and Van Faassen, *Dagboeken en aantekeningen,* pp. 788-89; Halpern, *A Naval History,* p. 307.

77 Kühlmann to Bethmann Hollweg, 17 March 1916, 36, Smit, *Buiten-landsebronnen 1914-1917,* pp. 51-52; Frey, *Der Erste Weltkrieg,* pp. 76-78; Johnstone to Loudon, 26 November 1915: Gevers to Loudon, 30 March 1916 and 13 April 1916: De Marees van Swinderen to Loudon, 15 April 1916, Buitenlandse Zaken – Kabinet en Protocol, ARA-II; Porter, "Dutch Neutrality," pp. 187-88.

78 Kühlmann to Bethmann Hollweg, 8 December 1915, 8 April 1916, DuitseMinisterie van Buitenlandse Zaken – Stukken betreffende Nederland, ARA-II; Bonebakker, *Twee verdienstelijke officieren,* p. 52; Smit, *Diplomatieke geschiedenis van Nederland,* p. 313; Loudon to De Marees van Swinderen, 11 April 1916, 535, Smit, *Bescheiden ... 1914-1917,* pp. 543-44; Porter, "Dutch Neutrality," p. 188; Smit, *1914-1917,* 112; Loudon to Gevers, 31 March 1916: Gevers to Loudon, 2 April 1916, Buitenlandse Zaken – Kabinet en protocol, ARA-II.

79 De Marees van Swinderen to Loudon, 15 April 1916, 543 *Bescheiden ... 1914-1917,* pp. 547-49.

80 Memorandum by Bethmann Hollweg of conversation with Kuyper, 18 April 1916,

Duitse Ministerie van Buitenlandse Zaken – Stukken betreffende Nederland, ARA-II; Smit, *1914-1917,* pp. 110-11, 114, 117; Porter, "Dutch Neutrality," pp. 188-89; Berg, *Snijders,*p. 89; De Beaufort, *Vijftig jaren,* II, pp. 271-72.

[81] Smit, *Tien studiën,* pp. 17-18; De Marees van Swinderen to Loudon, 26 March 1915, Buitenlandse Zaken – Kabinet en protocol, ARA-II; Van Manen, *Nederlandsche Overzee Trustmaatschappij,* vol. 7, pp.97-99.

[82] Halpern, *A Naval History,* pp. 101-104; Van Manen, *Nederlandsche Overzee Trustmaatschappij,* vol. 2, pp. 223-24; De Valk and Van Faassen, *Dagboeken en aantekeningen,* p. 852; Memorandum, Von Holtzendorff, 22 December 1916, *Official German Documents,* p. 1254.

[83] See Buitenlandse Zaken, 2.05.23, # 825, ARA-II; Halpern, *A Naval History,* pp. 74-75.

[84] "De mobilisatie van de Nederlandsche land- en zeemacht," *passim;* Ministerraad, 2.02.05.02, # 906; Reports of intercepted conversations, Generale Staf, ARA-II; Engelen, *Binnenlandse Veiligheidsdienst,* pp. 11, 12, 34-35; Treub, *Oorlogstijd,* pp. 34-35; Van Manen, *Nederlandsche Overzee Trustmaatschappij,* vol. 2, pp. 232-33; Kühlmann to Bethmann Hollweg, Duitse Ministerie van Buitenlandse Zaken – Stukken betreffende Nederland, ARA-II; De Valk and Van Faassen, *Dagboeken en aantekeningen,* pp. 761, 765.

[85] Inventory of correspondence, General Staff, ARA-II; Vinke, "Nederlandse militaire attaché," p. 33; Wolting, "De eerste jaren," p. 569; Wolting, "Uit het dagboek van Kapitein van Woelderen," *Militaire Spectator* 135 (January 1966), p. 32; Berlin attaché reports filed in Algemeen Hoofdkwartier – Afdeling Bereden Artillerie, nr toegang 2.13.62.01, ARA-II.

[86] De Meier, "Geheime dienst," pp. 1, 2; P.J. van Diesen, "Nederlandse inlichtingendiensten tussen 1914 en 1940" (Unpublished paper. The Hague: Sectie Militaire Geschiedenis, n.d. ARA library), p. 1; Kluiters, *De Nederlandse inlichtingen- en veiligheidsdiensten,* p. 178; GS-III, "Gegevens betreffende het Duitsche leger," n.d., 448/9: GS-III, "Het gevecht in de loopgraven," n.d., 128/2: "Tactische eigenschappen der infanterie," n.d., 5411/223A, Collection of the Sectie Militaire Geschiedenis, The Hague; Wolting, "Uit het dagboek," p. 32.

[87] Kluiters, *De Nederlandse inlichtingen- en veiligheidsdiensten,* pp. 192-93; De Meier, "Geheime dienst, p. 25; Bosscher, "Oorlogsvaart," p. 335; F.A.C. Kluiters, *De Nederlandse inlichtingen- en veiligheidsdiensten. Supplement: Crypto en trafficanalyse* ('s-Gravenhage: Koninginnegracht, 1995), pp. 54-55, 58; Wolting, "Uit het dagboek," pp. 32, 34.

[88] Kluiters, *Supplement,* pp. 55-56.

[89] Snijders to various commands, 24 March 1916: Lt. J. W. Peppelman van Kampen, "Rapport omtrent veschillende aangelegenheden van militair-technischen, alsmede van meer algemeenen aard betreffende Duitschland," received 26 September 1916, Generale Staf, ARA-II.

[90] De Valk and Van Faassen, *Dagboeken en aantekeningen,*pp. 799-700; Klinkert, "Verdediging van de zuidgrens," p. 216; Legation Bern to Loudon, 31 March 1916: Rosen to Loudon, 27 December 1916: Gevers to Loudon, 1 January 1917, Buitenlandse Zaken – Kabinet en Protocol, ARA-II; Rosen to Loudon, 27 December 1916: Gevers to Loudon, 1 January 1917, 714, 719, Smit, *Bescheiden ... 1914-1917,* pp. 732, 735-36.

[91] Consulate-Amsterdam to Bethmann Hollweg, 7 December 1916, Duitse Ministerie van Buitenlandse Zaken – Stukken betreffende Nederland, ARA-II.

[92] Loudon to Gevers, 5 January 1917, 722, Smit, *Bescheiden ... 1914-1917*, p. 739; Rosen to Hertling, 30 December 1916: Zimmermann to Rosen and General Staff, 21 Dec. 1916: General Staff to Foreign Office, 29 December 1916: Rosen to Bethmann Hollweg, 12 January 1917: Loudon to Rosen, 10 January 1917, Duitse Ministerie van Buitenlandse Zaken – Stukken betreffende Nederland ARA-II; Gevers to Loudon, 1 January 1917: Snijders to Cort van der Linden, 3 January 1917, Buitenlandse Zaken – Kabinet en Protocol, ARA-II; Wolting, "Uit het dagboek," p. 33.

[93] Wolting, "Uit het dagboek," p. 32; "Uittreksel uit een rapport van een Nederlandsch officier over Duitschland," 11 Dec. 1916, AHK Bereden Artillerie, nr. toegang 2.13.16.01, inv nrs 5, 7, ARA-II; Loudon to legation, 3 January 1915, Buitenlandse Zaken – Belgisch Gezantschap, ARA-II.

[94] Wolting, "Uit het dagboek," p. 32.

[95] Smit, *19114-1917*, pp. 27-31; Van der Wal, *Herinneringen*, p. 23; De Valk and Van Faassen, *Dagboeken en aantekeningen*, p. 746; Snijders, "Nederland's militaire positie," pp. 553-558.

[96] Smit, *1914-1917*, pp. 115, 116; Bonebakker, *Twee verdienstelijke officieren*, pp. 45-46, 74-76; Snijders, "Nederland's militaire positie," pp. 548-49.

[97] Frey, *Der Erste Weltkrieg*, p. 75; Klinkert, "Verdediging van de zuidgrens," p. 216; Snijders, "Nederland's militaire positie," pp. 545, 546, 551-52; Snijders memorandum, 9 August 1915, 420, Smit, *Bescheiden ... 1914-1917, pp. 408-17*.

[98] Bosboom, *In moeilijke omstandigheden*, pp. 106-107; Bosboom to Snijders, 28 August 1915, AHK Bereden Artillerie, ARA-II; Snijders, "Nederland's militaire positie," pp. 564-65.

CHAPTER SIX

NARROW ESCAPES, 1917-1918

In the last two years of World War I, the Netherlands slid from crisis to crisis. Submarine warfare disrupted trade. Food shortages became common, triggering discontent and riots. Relations with both warring camps worsened, and Germany made barely veiled threats of war. Trade agreements collapsed. The Entente seized a large part of the merchant fleet. Each alliance made increasing demands whose acceptance was viewed as a violation of neutrality by the other. Academic neutrality became impossible to maintain. Under the strain, cracks developed in military and foreign policy leadership circles. Finally, the country faced the threat of revolution at war's end.

Why such a dramatic difference between 1917-18 and 1914-16? The nature of the war had changed. By 1917, the warring powers were in desperate straits. Russia was collapsing, and Austria's condition was not much better. Germany was reaching the end of its manpower tether and could not foresee a land victory. The German government therefore decided to opt for unrestricted submarine warfare, total war at sea. The two western Entente powers were not in much better shape. France had surrendered its primacy on the Western Front to Britain, especially as the result of the ten-month bloodbath at Verdun. Britain's economy was increasingly strained by the war as it maintained its giant navy while supporting a land commitment on a scale unforeseen in 1914. In such conditions, it is not surprising that the belligerents became less patient with Holland, which each saw as effectively aligned with the other. The American entry into the war (6 April 1917) was a disaster for Holland. For the last nineteenth months of the war, there was no neutral major power. Until then, the United States and the Netherlands had shared similar views on the rights of neutrals. When Woodrow Wilson led America into war, however, his cherished commitment to the rights of neutrals evaporated. Holland was on its own.

As a result, the war began to affect the average Dutchman more. In the first phase of the war, the people had had to endure a few privations, higher taxes, and the tension of being surrounded by war, as well as the inconvenience and dislocation imposed by conscription. Yet for more than two years Holland had generated enough sympathy among the belligerents for its precarious position that it had managed to negotiate its way out of difficulty and obtain the supplies it needed. By 1917, the warring states could not afford to be sympathetic, and their huge losses made their governments emotionally unable to consider Holland's position anyway. "The screw was turned ruthlessly by both sides." Political room to maneuver was lost. The consequences for the man in the street were not long in coming. In July 1917, riots took place in Amsterdam in response to the potato shortage. Ships were stormed, and bloodshed resulted. The reason for the riots was that Holland was actually exporting potatoes to Britain and Germany, to meet treaty requirements. Without potato shipments to Germany, for example, Holland would receive no coal — with catastrophic results.[1]

Exporting amidst shortages shows the compromises that the government was obliged to make. The people had no patience for foreign policy when they saw the desired potatoes shipped abroad; foreign powers had no patience with the Dutch government's domestic problems. Part of the food problem was caused by a decline in shipping. In 1917, 87 ships (359,082 tons) were withdrawn from service for about six months due to the threat of submarine warfare. Another 31 (81,667 tons) were sunk; two were confiscated. Some 82 new ships were added in 1917 — ship-building was a growth industry in World War I — but imports declined continuously. The problem was not the decline in overall tonnage, but the constant interruptions, and hence unpredictability, of supply. Foreign policy problems were an even greater cause of shortages, however. In 1918, the German government stated that it would sell no more coal to Holland unless the Dutch provided more farm products in return. The Entente governments refused to supply fodder or fertilizer, unless the Dutch government promised not to buy coal from Germany with farm products. Clearly, this was an impossible situation. While German intelligence claimed in April 1918 that the Dutch still had "plenty of everything," the reality was that food rations fell below normal minimums by March. Coal was so scarce that the use of electric light was strictly rationed. Bread rations fell to 300 grams per day. Tea, coffee, whiskey, meat, and many grocery items were unobtainable in mid-1918. Prices were "exorbitant," indicating that the food subsidy program was breaking down.[2]

The economic crisis also worsened because of events in Russia. The Netherlands' high level of foreign investment made its economy vulnerable to disruptions abroad. Holland was Russia's fourth largest creditor. The competent envoy in St Petersburg/Petrograd, W.J. Oudendijk, did his best to protect private and public Dutch interests in Russia, although he had few illusions about what he could accomplish. He joined the whole diplomatic corps to protest the stoppage of payments on bonds with, to Loudon's discomfiture (who wanted him to go only with the other neutrals). Oudendijk did get the government to recognize two Russian banks[i] as Dutch, allowing them to wrap up their own affairs. Oudendijk's activities went beyond the field of money. He went to see Boris Chicherin, the Bolshevik Commissar for Foreign Affairs, on 1 September 1918 to ask for the release of the Tsarina and her children, and was told to convey to his government that they could not leave, but were safe (they had been shot July 16th). He had more success at the *Cheka*[ii] where he obtained the release of British and French citizens held prisoner – for which he later received the KCMG. This achievements was small comfort to Dutch financial interests. The Bolshevik state's debt repudiation cost Holland a billion and half guilders in capital and 70 million guilders per year in interest on government bonds.[3] For the average Dutchman, such fiscal catastrophes lacked the immediacy of the potato shortage. Somewhere along the line, however, the costs had to be reckoned, and the national economy was unquestionably weakened.

The government began to show signs of strain under the pressure. Cort van der Linden's aloof style no longer impressed everyone. Heldring complained that there was no consistency in his decisions and suggested that the Minister President merely blundered from one crisis to the next. The cabinet chief in turn became less enamored of Loudon's strict neutrality, twice intervening personally when relations with Germany reached the edge of war. Relations between the government and the supreme commander deteriorated as well. The war minister and the general feuded, while the general was increasingly irritated with the government's lack of clarity on strategic matters. When the Field Army commander (Van Terwisga) asked if the government thought he was

---

[i]   Banque Russo-Hollandaise and Nederlandsche Bank voor Russischen Handel.

[ii] Acronym for "Special Commission," the first Bolshevik secret police organization.

wrong to ask for reinforcements, Snijders wrote in the margin: "About this I cannot inform the CV. The Government is silent." The Minister for Agriculture, Industry and Trade, F.E. Posthuma, was so hesitant to make any decision that even the delay-oriented Loudon complained.[4]

Problems with Posthuma were rather important, because he was at the center of the government's continuing fight to keep trade policy and food imports on an even keel. A skilled politician, he stifled parliamentary criticism on food issues by making parliamentary committees co-responsible on food issues. This was a clever move, but it further slowed the decision-making process. Posthuma did organize the NUM, *Nederlandsche Uitvoer-Maatschappij* or Netherlands Export Corporation, to handle exports in areas not controlled by the NOT. Started on 1 September 1917, this new organization was designed to liberate the government of some of its direct responsibility to the belligerents, just as the NOT had done. The NUM was not strong and Posthuma was not happy with the organization (apparently he had formed it under some pressure). The Entente viewed it as pro-German anyway. The organizational structure was complicated. While the NUM reported to Posthuma, its activities had to be financed by Treub, back at the Treasury now that his third marriage had ended discussions and speculation about his personal life. Agreements were signed with the opposing belligerents in 1918 on agricultural matters, however, so some success was achieved. An "Agricultural Agreement" was reached with the British Trading Association, and a "Provisorium" was reached with the *Deutsche Handelstelle.*[5] Governmental trade policy in 1918 was successful, preventing a complete collapse, but the situation remained complicated.

One thing that made it so was the rapid decline of the NOT. As German pressure increased, Holland's ability to keep the British happy deteriorated. A phase of the war appeared in which the demands from each great power on Holland exceeded what the opposing great power would accept as within Holland's neutrality obligations. But another reason, allegedly, was the press campaign. Oppenheimer's rhetoric and actions became more confrontational, including a 1917 move to have Dutch grain ships held by the British. Loudon was able, via De Marees van Swinderen, to get the ships released. But the minister had had enough. A pacific man, he formally complained about the strong language emanating from the legation and commercial chancery, but was told by Eyre Crowe that the diplomats were acting under instruction.[6] This did not seem much of an explanation to Loudon, and the

NOT was also dissatisfied. Referring to Oppenheimer's demands, the NOT's official historian commented:

> Slowly there appeared a certain nervous exaggeration, caused by the fear, originating from, people thought, that the mistrust *(of Sir Francis in London)* would become stronger. It seemed as if he wished to provide contrary evidence, a defense against this mistrust. Exaggerated letters, exaggerated tone and remarks in the negotiations, exaggerated inflated demands . . .[7]

Some of this might be disregarded as the words of a historian who was a firm supporter of Van Aalst, and apparently wrote much of the work under his supervision. Yet even the British government did not always support his methods.[8] Sir Francis did not adequately realize that the NOT's position became untenable once the USA entered the war, and continued to demand concessions that the NOT could not meet because its largest source of imports was now in *Entente* hands – leaving no major neutral to support the Dutch political position either. Oppenheimer was also prone to blame the government for interfering with the NOT, or to blame the NOT for government actions.[9]

The twin death-blows to the institution were unrestricted submarine warfare and the American declaration of war. Many imports were cut off. The USA moved from supporter to critic of the NOT, and the Allies no longer accepted NOT certificates, demanding additional documentation that cargo was not bound for Germany. The NOT was becoming a target for humorists in the port cities because its ships were not even coming in. Van Aalst was forced to cut off relations with the British legation in July, 1917. The ties were restored, but the NOT was never the same. The Foreign Ministry took control in September 1917, holding regular meetings of all commercial institutions, including the NOT, but the NOT was not even involved in the shipping space negotiations with the USA that fall and winter. By July, 1918, the NOT had been told that only the Dutch government would negotiate with other foreign governments. Despite its steady and ignominious decline, the NOT has been considered a "crowning achievement" of the pragmatic neutralists, because it managed to accommodate Britain.[10]

The decline of the NOT made relations with other countries' diplomats all the more important. Here too, there were unfortunate developments. Kühlmann left in October 1916, while America and Britain replaced their envoys the following January and February, respectively.[11] In each case, the result was an envoy somewhat less sympathetic toward Holland than his predecessor. From Loudon's perspective, Johnstone was the biggest loss. While Johnstone was not considered particularly able by all observers, he had worked for smooth relations. Loudondid not expect similar sympathetic treatment at the hands of Sir Walter Townley, Johnstone's successor.[12] His fears proved to be well founded. Townley came to the Hague in a combative frame of mind. His wife called it "that difficult post." His government expected him to take a harder line, and also to pursue espionage more intensively. The British Prime Minister told Townley that Holland was "the locked door" between Britain and Germany, and that he "wanted some one reliable at the keyhole of that door." This was an allusion to the event that precipitated the change – Johnstone's failure to telegraph instantly Bethmann Hollweg's speech outlining possible peace terms.

Townley took a harder line, so much so that when his departure was announced, it was simply recorded without a single word of regret in any of the diaries or papers of Dutch diplomats. Loudon, by then out of office, considered it very good news indeed. The Britisher had described him as "Loudon, who is genuinely on our side, is a spineless person, who is so entangled in his 'strict neutrality,' that he has become a political liar." Townley got no reward for having carried out his instructions. He had to retire early, mainly as a result of the behavior of his spouse, described as his "silly wife" by the German envoy. This characterization was not entirely fair, because Lady Susan Townley did sterling work for interned British soldiers, and had a useful friendly relationship with Dutch officers (she was able to get a pass from Snijders to go into Belgium at Sluys in October 1918).[13] Nevertheless, it is clear that no one in the Townley-Netherlands relationship benefitted from the experience.

Friedrich Rosen, the new German envoy, was more personable. He was more like his predecessor than Townley was. Both supported Dutch neutrality, and both would rise to the top of the German diplomatic professions, Kühlmann as State Secretary for Foreign Affairs, Rosen as Foreign Minister under the Weimar Republic (Kühlmann was forced out in July 1918, however, an event considered a blow to Dutch interests; Rosen served only 5 months in 1921). He was no fan of Loudon's, however. He considered Loudon's commitment to neutrality as self-deception and described him as the *"keineswegs deutschfreundliche Aussenminister Loudon"* ("by no means german-friendly foreign minister Loudon"). More than once, feeling that Loudon's delaying tactics (which Rosen attributed to a lack of energy) risked war, he went directly to individual political parties or the Minister President to settle issues. His frustration with Loudon's delays overcame tact when, seeking for weeks to get an export permit for some horses, he told Loudon the following story:

> A tortoise used a hundred years to climb a stair. When he got up there, he slipped and fell down. He said: God has punished me for my hurrying too much.

Rosen got the permit the next day.[14] [iii]

Rosen arrived in The Hague with unusual instructions: none at all. He thought this strange, considering the acknowledged importance of the post. His memoirs are revealing; he noted that Germany had respected Dutch neutrality, even though the Limburg route would have made things easier, but then wrote that he had not expected Dutch gratitude for this – suggesting, however obliquely, that Holland should be grateful for Germany doing what it was legally supposed to do in the first place, but had not done in Belgium – leave neutral states alone. Rosen thought Loudon was pro-Entente, and blamed this on the minister having a wife[iv] raised in Paris, who hated Germany. Cort van der Linden he saw as less partisan and more *deutschfreundlich*. Rosen was less sanguine about Dutch attitudes than Kühlmann had been. He thought anti-German attitudes had increased, because of anti-military attitudes and the burden of military service, economic harm of the war, and the country's republican attitudes, its monarchy notwithstanding. But he saw light at the end of the proverbial tunnel. The Dutch wanted the war to end, which a German military victory could bring about; the quick victory over Romania had made a great impression; and, most importantly, sympathy for the Belgians was rapidly declining.[15]

[iii] Loudon was looking for pretexts, as the Entente was trying to block the export. At one point he had the audacity to suggest to Rosen that legally the horses might have to be slaughtered and the skins remain in Holland. It is not known if Rosen telegraphed his suggestion to Berlin. See Rosen, *Aus einem diplomatischen Wanderleben*, vol. 3/4, pp. 90-91.

[iv] The number of careers affected by suspicions of spouses in this period is remarkable. Rosen here suspected Loudon because of his Paris-raised, American-born wife. The pro-German Dutch foreign minister after September 1918, H. A. van Karnebeek, did not entirely trust Rosen because of the latter's wife, who was English. Eyre Crowe, the famous British undersecretary, lost influence because his wife was German. Townley lost his job because of his wife's behavior.

This may have stemmed from one of two things: friction with the 50-100,000 Belgian refugees still in the country, and the publicly fractious relationship with the British, Belgium's self-proclaimed protector. Feelings at the Foreign Ministry and elsewhere toward Britain became less positive, and not only because of Townley's personality. During the potato crisis, for example, the British government threatened "serious consequences" (short of war) if its demands were not met. Britain threatened to close the shipping lane through the minefields, leading the Queen to write George V and point out that Belgian relief shipments would perforce have to end. The British also bombed Zierikzee on April 30, 1917 (an accident for which compensation was paid), and entered Dutch waters on three occasions. The most serious occurred on 16 July 1917, when British warships attacked German vessels off the Dutch coast. Numerous protests followed, with only one positive effect – the German government expressed its approval for its handling of the matter.[16]

A bigger problem, from Loudon's perspective, was the connection with the Indies. Britain asserted broad rights regarding its powers to inspect ships and seize goods and people traveling between Holland and the Indies, interrupted cable traffic when it wished to pressure Holland on other matters, and restricted the right of Holland to convoy vessels there. This last issue caused much friction. Townley, for example, complained that private parcels were being transported on Dutch warships which would be a way for Germany to send seditious propaganda around the world. He gave specific examples of the "parcels," showing that he had good sources. The Dutch delayed the sending of a 1918 convoy to meet an endless series of British demands, leading the navy minister to resign.[17]

The British, on the other hand, continued to be irritated with the Dutch for two reasons. First, the government was perceived as pro-German, and even Loudon came in for much scorn because he was thought too willing to give in to German demands. Second, Holland's smuggling barrier continued to leak. Railroad employees were notorious smugglers. Strips along the border were forcibly vacated to stop the practice, and in other places no horses were allowed. Regular shootings and even gunfights took place along the Limburg border. Whole families were expelled from their homes if children were repeatedly caught smuggling. Passages and tunnels in the border-straddling *Pietersberg* were blown up in January of 1917 because smugglers were using them to avoid the infamous electric fence.[18] Despite all these efforts, from the British perspective there were too many legal and illegal ways in which supplies continued to flow into Germany in violation of earlier understandings.

No one seriously expected that the Entente would invade or attempt to annex Dutch territory, despite rumors to that effect. But Britain's pressure was viewed as problematical, because it eventually could cause the collapse of neutrality. Cort van der Linden thought in July 1917 that Britain's policies "are driving us in the arms of Germany." The British were not concerned. Across the channel, Eyre Crowe considered the "want of generous appreciation of our attitude . . . disagreeable," unknowingly echoing Rosen's attitude. Not everyone agreed. The foreign editor of the London *Times* saw Holland as a "1st class neutral," especially compared to Sweden. Oppenheimer took an intermediate position, rejecting suspicions that Loudon was pro-German, complaining however that Loudon was "improperly . . . but . . . prudently . . . prone . . . to favour the German side" simply to maintain Holland's neutrality, but he pointed out that this "policy, persistently pursued, was not likely to diminish German demands." He did not know that Loudon was actually notorious for delaying or opposing German demands almost to the brink of war. Oppenheimer recorded, however, that Germany's military successes in 1918 had produced a feeling of "resigned despondency" in The Hague and that Loudon thought that Britain was "finished." Even so, Oppenheimer found the envoy "quite unexpectedly cordial,"[19] perhaps reflecting some genuine sympathy; if he truly thought Britain was finished, there was no need to be extra nice.

Loudon was "unexpectedly cordial" because of his experience with aggressive German demands. Rosen was not responsible for these. A bigger factor was the rise of Hindenburg and Ludendorff to a quasi-dictatorial position in Germany. The Foreign Office was repeatedly forced to concede to Gevers that resolution of issues depended on the views of the military authorities. For example, in March 1917 Loudon alleged that Germany committed a treaty violation when the military commander at Münster ordered the dismissal of Dutch employees at a petroleum company. When Gevers brought this complaint to the Foreign Office, the official he spoke to conceded the point but "noted that it was practically better not to raise the issue," raising a few German countercomplaints. Gevers argued that the Netherlands was within its rights to pursue the issue. The German agreed and promised to help, saying the Foreign Office "would use its influence with the military authorities." Gevers concluded (correctly) that "once again we have to do here with one of those conflicts between the civilian administration and the military authorities, where the former are pretty much powerless."[20]

The attitude from Germany became more threatening in 1917 for two other reasons. First, the conclusion of the Romanian campaign left Germany with more troops to cover the Dutch border. Second, the submarine campaign created a chance, as mentioned earlier, of Dutch belligerency. Hence some of Germany's actions of early 1917 were intended as a deterrent. As late as October 1916, troop movements near Holland were explained in terms of possible British threats and of Hindenburg's policy to cover all borders. Then in January 1917, 40,000 German troops were concentrated on the border, partly as deterrence, partly to get military talks started – although Rosen wrote the chancellor that such an idea was a "fantasy," and the Dutch army declined to respond to the suggestion. The deployment stimulated rumors in the first week of January that Germany was about to invade to seize ports and supplies, but as these stories came from Entente capitals, they were disregarded. More seriously, the German Foreign Office expressed reservations about Holland's ability to defend the Schelde. Gevers was irritated that this old issue had been revived, and noted that it was becoming a "chronic problem" for the Germans. The German functionary, *ministerialdirektor* Dr. J.D.J. Kriege, then explained that Ludendorff was concerned – ominous, that! – about the safety of German installations along the coast. When Gevers rejected Kriege's suggestion of staff talks, Kriege unhappily commented that this would leave Holland's future to be decided by accident – exactly the position taken by Snijders earlier.[21]

Advice from various corners discouraged pressure. Renner advised Ludendorff that an ultimatum would only cause a worse attitude, less foreign trade with Holland, and perhaps belligerency, with the whole country becoming a British base. The Emperor concluded that *"Holland ist in Ruhe zu lassen"* ("Holland should be left alone"). He would maintain that attitude throughout most of the war, congratulating Wilhelmina on her firmness toward the British and Americans (23 March 1918) and telling Rosen that he saw Holland as having adhered to neutrality in a very correct way (5 November 1918), asking that his view should be passed on to Wilhelmina. As this was very close to his abdication and flight, it might be viewed as self-serving, but it probably did represent an honest sentiment. Chancellor Georg von Hertling saw Holland as trapped between two impossible choices – a purely continental or purely colonial policy – and applauded strict neutrality (23 November 1917). Gevers assured Hertling that Holland would defend itself by force of arms, which Hertling also applauded. (Hertling also stated that Germany had not always taken Dutch interests into account as much as he had wished. It is interesting to speculate whether this was due the by then obvious failure of the submarine campaign, or whether, like Wilhelm a year later, he was thinking of the postwar era already.)[22]

These sentiments did not eliminate pressure from Germany. There were too many friction points, and the German military command had a distinctly different attitude. No protestations regarding Holland's virtuousness emanated from OHL or the navy. Ludendorff favored the annexation of Belgium because, *inter alia,* "Holland will be attracted to us" provided an alliance with Japan could guarantee the Dutch colonies. The navy, was far more militant, because of Holland's internment of warships. The first German warship to enter Dutch waters, the destroyer V-69, was released because she had not done so to avoid pursuit. The British armed merchantman *Princess Melita* was also released, leading to bitter complaints – which the German Foreign Office carefully noted came from the navy. Then on 22 February 1917, a German submarine stranded; another did so 11 March, in the latter case due to a navigation error. Loudon absolutely refused to release them, and Renner warned that no amount of pressure would cause Holland to abandon either its position or the U-boats. A compromise was later reached on one of the subs,[v] although bitterly opposed by Loudon.[23] The German navy was angry for a simple reason: It needed the boats. In the midst of its unrestricted submarine campaign, it could hardly afford to lose any; a single submarine in the right place at the right time could wreak havoc. To lose boats *to the Dutch* seemed unthinkable, and hence the pressure was put on the Foreign Office to get the boats back by any means necessary.

---

[v] The problem was submitted to an international commission, which ruled that one boat (UB30) should be released, while the UB6 should stay. The same commission ruled in a similar Solomonic way on compensation for certain sunken Dutch merchantmen.

There were several things working in the navy's favor. Holland needed a shipping channel in the North Sea as much as Germany needed its boats. The German army supported the navy's demands. Ludendorff had no particular sympathy for Holland and had created a military command, the *Hollandstellung,* under a General von Moser, which was a convenient pressure tool. Dutchmen caught in Belgium spying for the Entente were imprisoned or executed. Pro-German elements in Holland encouraged settlements favorable to Germany. The German government was also becoming more supportive of the navy because it was irritated by the virulently pro-Entente *Telegraaf,* and they were not mollified by the paper's prosecution in 1917. The editor was convicted, angering the Entente governments, for an article referring to "the crooks in the center of Europe." He was freed on appeal, however, which in turn caused Rosen much anguish. He complained about the outcome, forcing Loudon to assure him that the verdict did not mean that agitators were free of the possibility of punishment (although the phraseology suggests that the chances of conviction were not too good). There was not much that the Dutch could do to face down the rising tide of German criticism. True, exports to Germany were still important; Kühlmann received a round of applause when he announced to the Reichstag that a coal and credit agreement had been reached with Holland.[vi] But the Dutch could hardly threaten to cut off trade.

German ire was further roused by the feeling that the British were already "using" Holland as a base in one sense: its air space. Germany's submarine installations along the Belgian coast were a tempting target for air attacks. Local German officers complained that British aircraft were swooping in from Dutch airspace and returning that way before German aircraft could scramble. The complaints reached Ludendorff, whose experience during the sand and gravel crisis (see below) disposed him to demand action on the issue. Rosen dutifully took up the matter with his military attaché, Von Schweinitz, who investigated and concluded that the charges did not demand action. The German diplomats pointed out to their government on May 28, 1918, that, since 15 March, the Dutch had observed 27 airspace violations, of which 5 were by Entente planes. All 5 Entente (presum-

---

[vi] It has been suggested that this was mainly because it was the only good piece of news he had.

ably British) planes had been shot at, as had 19 of the Germans. Rosen argued that Holland was not being passive, but lacked the equipment to stop the forays. He also noted that they had been protested. Schweinitz took the issue further. Like his chief, he thought the Dutch were sincerely trying to stop the intrusions, but he also addressed whether this was a proper *casus belli* for Germany. Stating that this was a matter for "grand politics," and not a military matter, he argued that it was not in Germany's interest to push the matter. The German army could defeat the Netherlands quickly, because despite its Vesting and 1 million men,[vii] it lacked heavy guns, air power, and antiaircraft guns. He pointed out, however, that this would still draw German strength away from other fronts, 6 million people would have to be governed, and Germany, he concluded, could not politically afford a second Belgium. He also mentioned the role as arbitrator in the postwar period. While Schweinitz viewed Holland as something of a geopolitical beauty mark *(Schönheitsfehler)*, he concluded once again that *"das uns mit einem neutralen Holland am besten gedient ist."* Politically, he wrote on June 9th, an invasion would cost diplomatic ties, prisoner exchanges, neutral relations, and face Germany with another Belgium-type situation. Militarily, Germany would have to face a million soldiers, manage six million civilians, and lose protection for its right flank and industrial areas.[24]

The attaché had done a good job of reminding his government of the exact cost of an invasion. The Chancellor would be sensitive to the political downside, while Ludendorff was probably still sane enough at this point to know that he was about to run out of troops. Schweinitz's report was read approvingly by the Emperor, who wondered on June 3, 1918, if German antiaircraft equipment should be sent to help. Gevers suggested the following day that the Germans use their guns at Brugge and Zeebrugge against the airplanes, and – keeping his army's interests in mind – proposed allowing Dutch officers to come and observe. Schweinitz, meanwhile, wrote Snijders twice, on 6 June and 20 June 1918, summarizing the German complaints. Snijders explained that everything possible was being done, but criticized the German observers, who were either seeing nonexistent airplanes or mistaking

[vii] I am at a loss to explain how Schweinitz arrived at that figure. I suspect that he deliberately exaggerated. If so, was he doing so to further discourage his more aggressive colleagues at OHL?

their own for the enemy's. He suggested some contacts between German and Dutch border officials might be useful, but added that Dutch guns would have to fire on pursuing German as well as British aircraft (so much for the chance of Germany sending equipment).[25]

The attaché concluded from his contact with Snijders that the general was "meticulously neutral" although *"deutschfreundlich"* inside. On 9 June 1918, Schweinitz once again explained that war with Holland would not serve German interests, although its occupation would benefit the navy. He did urge strong Dutch protests, because he felt that these might have some influence in Britain. If the overflights ever became systematic, then Holland would be obliged to break relations with Britain. He also noted the unsettled state of *"Luftrecht"* ("aviation law"). Rosen added that Snijders was honestly trying to resolve the problem and warned against actions that would alienate Dutch officers. Snijders, in fact, told Loudon on 12 July that the German complaints might be justified.[26]

Ludendorff, however, was not satisfied with Dutch efforts, claimed that he could not supply much assistance, demanded a strong Dutch protest to the British, and then stated he desired *"dass Holland Farbe bekennt, ob es mit uns oder gegen uns gehen will"* ("that Holland shows its colors, whether it will go with us or against us"). Had he stuck to this point, Dutch neutrality would have been over. The following day (11 July 1918), however, Ludendorff returned to the matter at hand, arguing that German violations were mere carelessness while Britain's were on purpose, and praising Schweinitz's report. On the 12th, he argued that he could pursue attacks coming from neutral airspace, and demanded that Holland tell Britain it regarded the overflights as a hostile act (something which the Dutch government would never do, because once such a statement is made, the only possible resolutions are satisfaction or war). Ludendorff evidently had strong feelings on this issue, as he concluded by stating it was best *"wenn Holland endlich über unser denken und fühlen klar sieht"* ("when Holland finally clearly sees our thinking and feelings"). The Kaiser shared Ludendorff's feelings about what Holland should demand. Some officials at the Foreign Office agreed on both of Ludendorff's salient points – the need for a stronger Dutch protest, and the right to pursue.[27]

Rosen dutifully took the issue up with Loudon, pointing out the difference between German and British overflights, and pointed to a map found with an English pilot as proof of intentional violation. He told Loudon of the impression that this was creating in Germany, namely that Holland's neutrality was favoring the Entente. He then suggested, reasonably enough, that this impression could be removed if Holland showed Germany how it was protesting. Loudon verbally discussed protests (which were, in fact, issued in every case of a known violation) but explained, also reasonably, that it was contrary to his government's principles (his principles, actually) to disclose protests to the opposing warring party. Rosen and Loudon did discuss possible actions against the British aircraft, but Snijders rejected direct telephone links between the opposing border posts. Loudon did not, incidentally, send the German envoy away empty handed; he had more sense than that. He provided a written response regarding when protests were made, and told Hertling that Britain had occasionally apologized and promised to give instructions to its air force. The Dutch concluded concluded that the British violations were not systematic, but informed the British government that continued violations would to lead to doubts about the orders given British fliers. Rosen concluded that there was no reason to doubt the strength of Dutch protests. Although the issue continued to fester, and one captured British lieutenant confessed that he overflew deliberately, Rosen was generally satisfied. The Kaiser was as well, once again ordering that *"gegen Holland nichts unternommen wird"* ("no action is to be taken against Holland"), at least not without his personal approval.[28] The crisis receded. Perhaps it did because OHL had so many problems by the height of summer that the British planes ceased to be a major issue.

Still, it had been a close thing, as Ludendorff's messages show. Any day could bring similar dangers, and only peace could bring security. The Netherlands could only bring this about through mediation, but this was an even less realistic course in 1917-18 than in the first part of the war. Any proposal would be viewed with great suspicion in London and Paris, where it would be assumed that the proposal came from Germany. In May 1917, the envoy in Paris reported that Dutch overtures would be viewed as being made on behalf of Germany, and that the Entente powers were convinced that if Germany were not totally defeated, it would start its campaign again later. In September 1917, Loudon did discuss mediation with the British, but Balfour did not think that Germany would accept any terms.[viii] Loudon tried again

---

[viii] He may have been right; the British army was in the midst of its disastrous Passchendaele offensive, and Germany was planning its spring offensives.

in March 1918, but again the British rejected the approach, because Germany refused to meet its precondition – a guarantee of an independent Belgium.[29]

This must have sounded reminded Loudon of his 1914 explanation to the cabinet why Germany could not in advance agree not to annex Belgium. Yet by late 1917, at the very time that Loudon approached Balfour, cracks were appearing in Germany. Admiral Holtzendorff commented that "[t]he frightful loss of life is already such as to justify a feeling of anxiety for our future development." Kühlmann was willing to let Belgium go provided Germany's position in the east could be secured. In the spring and summer of 1918, he worked to open lines of communication to America, hoping to split the enemy alliance. When the Germany army made it clear to the government in the late summer and early fall of 1918 that the war would have to end, Ludendorff and the Kaiser considered seeking mediation through Wilhelmina.[30]

Still, Loudon's sense of how peace initiatives would look were well founded, judging from the reception of private Dutch proposals made by Jhr. Dr. B. de Jong van Beek en Donk, an officer of the Netherlands Anti-War League and founder of the Central Organization for a Durable Peace. His approaches to the British went nowhere. Sir William Tyrell, Assistant Unsecretary at the Foreign Office, called him a mischievous busybody, while Balfour said that "his proceedings are as tiresome as his name." Rosen, who called the pacifists *"gute Menschen"* but *"schlechte Politiker,"* described De Jong van Beek en Donk as a "devoid of understanding *[verständnisloser]"* idealist. The Dutchman also traveled to Switzerland with a German professor Quidde to see Dr. George David Herron, regarded as a spokesman for Wilson. Herron was not impressed with either, and told Quidde, "[Germany's] psychology presents to me, I must say, the most inscrutable problem of human history." The German Foreign Office reprimanded Quidde for taking someone as "indiscreet and irresponsible" as De Jong van Beek en Donk along.[31] None of this suggests that Loudon would have fared well trying to mediate – and he might have endangered his position.

Instead, war would continue. The longer it continued, the more dangerous it was for the Netherlands; public mediation was not possible; private mediation was not effective; the NOT was losing its effectiveness, and other organizations could not take up the slack; and relationships with both neighboring great powers were somewhere

between decline and collapse. With the Foreign Ministry and the NOT
increasingly circumscribed and uncertain, military affairs became much
more important. The relationship with Germany was "increasingly
military,"[32] and to a lesser extent this was true with Britain as well.

Was the Dutch military in this period in a position to fulfill this
role? Foreign observers thought it was. Townley described the soldiers
he saw as "very fit" and "present[ing] a very soldierly aspect."
Schweinitz, while having no illusions about how long his host country's army could battle against his own, thought that Fortress Holland
could defend itself against a British intervention: *"In dieser Eventualit-
ät würde die holländische Armee keine unwichtige Rolle spielen"* ("In
this eventuality the Dutch army will play a not insignificant role"). By
1917 an additional 66 infantry battalions had been organized. The army
grew to a total strength of 450,000 by October, 1918, and machine
guns, communications, and fortifications were improved throughout the
war. Brabant's fortifications were extended throughout the war.[33]

The weaknesses of the army and its position still outweighed its
improvements. Zeeuws-Vlaanderen, the territory most vulnerable to
invasion, was undefendable and the troops stationed there would have
be to withdrawn. Once the Brabant fortifications were breached, a
quick withdrawal into the *Vesting Holland* was the only feasible
strategy, hence the army devoted considerable resources to building
more bridges for that retreat. The 450,000-man army existed only on
paper. Half its soldiers were on leave or part of the reserve. The new
battalions had never worked together and might do so for the first time
under fire. The divisional organization was clumsy; a plan was drawn
up to create twelve smaller divisions that would be organized during a
pre-invasion (hopefully) "second mobilization." Snijders was not keen
on having a second mobilization if not absolutely necessary, and talked
the government out of doing it in both 1916 and 1918. Even leave
cancellation, a less drastic step, caused enough problems, including a
riot in 1918 that ultimately triggered Snijders' removal. The general
conceded that the "second mobilization" might not be the ideal time to
reorganize the divisions, but otherwise he would have to go to war with
the old army plus a large number of unattached reserve battalions.
Neither situation looked good. The continuing shortage of qualified
junior officers and NCOs further strained the army, and many were
constantly away from their units to train and educate new personnel,
and to deal with smuggling and internment.[34]

Gunnery was inadequate. Little heavy artillery had been bought before the war, due to political opposition and doctrinal disputes. Coastal gunnery was improved, partly by installing equipment allowing existing guns to fire on aircraft, partly by stripping guns from less crucial coastal fortifications and moving them to the critical southwestern coast. The navy, which had a vital role to play in that area, had no dreadnoughts. A pre-war proposal had been floated to obtain 9 battleships, but nothing had been done. According to German intelligence, civilians did not think their military could resist either side, and were surprised that Germany had not invaded.[35]

With the military situation tenuous and the diplomatic situation worse, the army inevitably started thinking about contacts with potential allies. Snijders' position on this was complex. Like Loudon, he thought actual talks inconsistent with the neutrality policy. He pointed out to the foreign minister that in asking for such talks, Germany was trying to get from Holland what it blamed Belgium for doing with Britain (he was referring to the 1906 Belgian-British staff talks, used as a justification by Germany for the 1914 invasion). He did want the government to identify who the most likely ally would be, so that he could plan accordingly. The threatening tone from Berlin and OHL led to a modification of policy on talks with foreign armies. Captain J.C.C. Tonnet, military attaché in London, was asked to have preliminary conversations with British military sources. Judging from Snijders' margin comments on Tonnet's May 26, 1918 report, the general was pessimistic. He expected that even with an alliance, Holland would go the way of Belgium and Romania. When Tonnet suggested that, in case of war, his mission would gather information about the coming of troops and supplies, Snijders penned: "I would rather have the troops and supplies themselves." Next to Tonnet's proposal that artillerymen be trained in Britain, Snijders wrote: "Before the Central Powers invade our country, this can not be done. Afterward, it is too late."[36]

Nevertheless, the conversations went on in May and June 1918, amidst strict secrecy. Snijders issued guidelines for cooperation with allies in case of invasion, which minimized operations beyond the *Vesting*. War Minister De Jonge, who had pressured Snijders to make the contacts in the first place, discovered that Tonnet had no instructions for getting heavy artillery from Britain, and found the Foreign Ministry unhelpful. Tonnet sent a Major Insinger to Oppenheimer to point out that the transfer was in Britain's interests, and the guns came. Some contacts with the Germans occurred as well. The German naval attaché reported on 17 October 1918 that he had conferred with the Chief of the Dutch Naval Staff. He wrote cryptically that: "English preparations for a landing are known to the Dutch Navy . . . "[37]

Rising tensions called for greater restrictions on the great powers' propaganda and espionage efforts, either of which could be used as an excuse for an invasion. There was not much that could be done regarding propaganda, especially since the *Telegraaf* debacle. Britain had a propaganda bureau organized by Lord Northcliffe that used British internees to distribute propaganda in Holland and used border restaurants between Nijmegen and Maastricht to get propaganda into Germany. In addition, Entente propaganda was also fed into Holland via Dutch papers' foreign correspondents who happened to be on Entente payrolls. The British Minister of Information (Beaverbrook) kept close tabs on the propaganda bureau's work. German propaganda entered the country easily, as the Dutch press preferred the German Wolff press service over Reuters, finding the latter long on theory and short on details. German propaganda was also aimed at Flemish nationalists, an activity that was beyond Dutch control even though it would have had profound long-term implications for Holland if it succeeded. The Bolsheviks decided to establish a propaganda bureau in Holland as well, but the delegation, none of whom had Russian names, were stopped by the Germans. The Bolsheviks asked the Dutch government to intervene, but naturally no help came.[38]

Espionage was a different matter, and investigations and arrests accelerated. German spies regularly came to the area around Baerle-Hertog/Baerle-Nassau, the Belgian enclaves combined into one territory during the war. The agents were not seeking information, but rather trying to interfere with its radio station.[39] The Rotterdam police actively worked with GS-III to catch spies. In January 1917, they invaded the house of a suspected German spy name Nussholz. A woman in the house tried to destroy papers, but she was stopped. It turned out to be a long list of questions about subjects like:

> Arrangements with the United States for defending the colonies,
> how Schouwen-Duiveland and Zeeland islands would be defended,
> type of fortress cannons,
> the strength of Dutch naval gunnery,
> troops available to block a British invasion,
> the Schelde blockade,
> quantity/quality of airplanes,

why Holland is building airbases and whether they were for Britain, and whether Britain is involved in training pilots in the Netherlands.

This list (Snijders claimed to have others) clearly shows that German was very concerned about Holland's ability to defend its coast against Britain, and did not take Dutch assurances at face value. Nor did the Germans completely trust in Holland's neutrality, judging from the last two questions.[40] The general was no less concerned about foreign espionage, proposing that, as espionage charges were exceedingly difficult to prosecute,[ix] port cities where spying was occurring be placed under state of siege.[41] This would have allowed the government broad regulatory powers not otherwise available.

Occasionally the Dutch profited from German espionage. In May 1917 a GS-III officer succeeded in "doubling" a German agent involved in planning the destruction of the strategic Moerdijk bridge in case of a British landing in the Netherlands.[42] This shows that the Germans were more concerned about Holland's ability to stop Britain than to stop Germany. But this was a natural viewpoint for Germany, given the point at which this spy mission occurred: on the eve of Germany's unrestricted submarine warfare campaign.

The submarine campaign

The submarine campaign was the great turning point of the war for the Netherlands. Both neighboring great powers were fighting, not for battlefield victory, but for survival. The entry of the United States was now only a matter of time. Trade would become even more constricted. The danger of a *casus belli* rose. A "strictly" neutral state can only remain so if it is prepared to go to war if its neutrality is violated, even if the circumstances are unsuitable. Otherwise, other belligerents may claim that the neutral state is giving an advantage to the violator, hence abandoning its neutrality. The submarine campaign increased the chance of such an incident.

The Germans knew all this, but decided to risk war with the remaining neutrals because there were no military alternatives left.

[ix] While anyone could be prosecuted for stealing Dutch military secrets, German and British spies were spying on each others' countries, and it was not clear that this was a violation of Dutch espionage laws.

202

Erich von Falkenhayn, Chief of Staff 1914-1916, did not think the war could be decided on land. Bethmann Hollweg, who hedged on how successful the campaign might be, saw it as the "last card."[43] The decision had not been taken lightly. On August 30, 1916, after a conference at OHL, the army leadership had reluctantly counseled against the campaign, as recalled by Ludendorff:

> Only with extreme regret could we refuse to pronounce in favor of unrestricted submarine warfare, on the ground that, in the opinion of the Imperial Chancellor, it might possibly lead to war with Denmark and Holland. We had not a man to spare to protect ourselves against these states, and even if their armies were unaccustomed to war, they were in a position to invade Germany and give us our death-blow. We should have been defeated before the effects, promised by the navy, on an unrestricted U-Boat campaign could have made themselves felt.[44]

At the conference itself, Ludendorff was indeed worried: "If it is possible that Holland and Denmark may go against us, we have nothing wherewith to oppose them." Other senior officers agreed. Hindenburg, the most senior, loved the idea of a submarine campaign but feared "the possibility of new declarations of war and of landings in Holland and Denmark. A number of divisions would become tied up there which we are not now in a position to spare." Admiral Holtzendorff felt that "Holland would take up arms against the first Power to attack her." Some of this can be attributed to Kühlmann, who worried about Holland's attitude and pointed out that the Dutch could attack Germany in the rear. He did not persuade everyone. The war minister, Wild von Hohenborn, did not "consider an attack by neutrals at all probable." He was in the minority, and two things resulted from the conference. First, Ludendorff ordered the construction of border defenses. Second, and more importantly, the submarine campaign was postponed – because of the Dutch/Danish threat, not because of a possible US entry.[45]

In September and October 1916, the collective viewpoint of the German government began to change. The admiralty did not wish to postpone the campaign forever and argued that the Netherlands would not join the war over the submarine issue. Renner and Kühlmann disagreed, and their arguments made an impression. As late as October 16th, Hindenburg still worried about hostilities from Holland and Denmark. Under-secretary Hellferich worried about "the inevitable menace of our neutral neighboring states." But the situation was changing rapidly. Romania's defeat and subsequent westward transfer of troops neutralized the Dano-Dutch menace. By November, Ludendorff had troops in place and no longer expected the two northern neutrals to enter the war. Holtzendorff pointed out on December 22nd that neither could gain from the war – Copenhagen could be shelled, and Holland would be forced to flood itself. This became the prevailing attitude. "The government had by now lost its early anxiety as to the attitude of Holland and Denmark, and none was felt as to Switzerland, Spain, Sweden, or Norway."[46]

The American reader may wonder at this point whether the discussion of Dutch/Danish potential behavior is not brought out disproportionately; surely Germany was more concerned about the American entry? Strangely enough, no. Under-Secretary Albert, for example, did express concern (6 November 1916) about an American entry, but only insofar as this would affect the attitude of the neutral states. One officer was appalled to discover that Field-Marshal Hindenburg discussed the reactions of Holland and Denmark at length, but said nothing at all about the United States. It was not that war with America came as a surprise: it was expected, and had been discussed with the embassy in Washington. The reason for the cavalier attitude toward an American entry can be found easily enough. The German army general staff counted the US Army as roughly equivalent to that of Denmark, Switzerland, or the Netherlands. Falkenhayn once commented that "it was a matter of complete indifference to us whether America would declare war." The argument by Major Wetzel of Ludendorff's staff that the US had shown the capacity to mobilize in the Civil War, was ignored.[47]

On January 9, 1917, the decision was taken at a conference at Pless to begin the campaign. Thinking about Dutch reactions had changed markedly. Bethmann Hollweg did not think that either Holland or Denmark would enter the war, at least not so long as the submarine war looked like it was working. Hindenburg went further: "We are ready to meet all eventualities and to meet America, Denmark, Holland, and Switzerland too." Ludendorff discussed the "measures of security taken against the neutrals," which included fortifications, establishing divisional commands along the border, shifting troops from Romania to Belgium, and increasing the number of soldiers by January 1917 along the Dutch border to about 40,000 (the number rose further during the year). The reinforcements along the Dutch-Belgian border were not totally aimed at Snijders. The Germans still feared a British attack through the Netherlands, "with or without the help of the Dutch."[48]

The German leadership did not want to alarm the neutrals, however. At Pless, Ludendorff gave assurances that his security measures "will have nothing about them in the nature of a challenge; they will be purely defensive measures." More remarkably, *Ministerialdirektor* Dr. Kriege traveled incognito to The Hague on 30 January and again on 1 April, to talk with Cort van der Linden, who he knew personally and who was considered *deutschfreundlich* – hence his nickname in the British legation, "Caught under den Linden."[x] On January 30th, the two had a very pleasant, secret conversation. Cort van den Linden declared that he understood Germany's position and that Holland would not go to war over the U-Boat issue. A British invasion would be resisted. Discussing anti-German feelings in Amsterdam, Kriege suggested to Cort van der Linden that he tell Amsterdam's leaders that as the city was fortified, it could be *"in Schutt und Asche gelegt zu werden"* ("razed to the ground"). The two gentlemen had a hearty laugh about this. Kriege accepted the Dutchman's declarations on policy, he wrote, because of the peaceful resolution of other issues (including the *Tubantia* sinking). Cort van der Linden further explained that exports to Germany might have to halt, to which Kriege pointed out that this would endanger coal supplies, and suggested a more "balanced" approach. Cort van der Linden drew a promise from Kriege to raise the coal shipments. Cort van der Linden closed the meeting with flowery pro-German language about German heroism, which Kriege amazingly took at face value (there is every indication that the Dutch minister president was being a clever opportunist, something he was rather good at).[49]

Attention to Dutch attitudes and intentions among the Germans reappears sporadically through the early months of 1917. Kriege asked Gevers (again!) On 17 February about what exactly Holland had to opposed British landings (perhaps this question was necessitated by the arrest of Mr. Nussholz). Kriege also pointed out that the German Army would not stand by if Holland could not defend itself against a British invasion. This was not a real "threat," as if there really was an invasion by one side, the Dutch expected the other side to intervene anyway. Renner assured Bethmann Hollweg on 29 March that Holland would never accept the "Greek role," with part of the country taken over by the Entente. The Chancellor told the Reichstag in May that concessions

[x] The *Unter den Linden* was one of Berlin's main boulevards.

had been made to the neutrals. This could have referred to Kriege's promise about coal deliveries, but in addition the neutrals were confidentially briefed by naval attachés about a safe route around northern Britain.[50]

What were Holland's attitudes and expectations when the unrestricted submarine warfare campaign began? There was little that could be done about it; at least, given the British behavior, the Dutch were not new to blockades. Rumors swept the country. One (which was caused by Germany's troop movements, not the submarine attacks) was that 700,000 German troops were massed along the border. De Beaufort, who recorded the story, concedes that Germany could occupy the Netherlands in ten days, as the army's supplies would be exhausted after the first battle. The only hope, he thought, were the inundations. While Snijders did not believe such exaggerations, he asked for instructions on 30 January, and this time he received them. He was to issue a leave withdrawal in case either great power neighbor asked to cross Dutch waters or territory, and could treat an actual attempt *or an ultimatum* as an act of war, which would allow him to discuss an alliance with the non-invading power.[51] This shows that the cabinet was greatly worried, no longer answering the general with coy speeches about strict neutrality.

Once the fear of war receded, national sympathies began to shift more toward the Entente. Holland was, after all, a seafaring nation, and this may explain why more and more Dutchmen now began to hope for the defeat of Germany. Until 1917, the Entente's trade war had caused the most anger. Losses to U-Boats affected popular emotions. The Dutch Foreign Ministry tried to squelch popular outbursts, fearing they might force the government's hand. Realizing the problem, the German Foreign Office accepted a deal to transfer some unused German freighters in the Indies to Dutch control to assuage popular anger. Loudon went further, even trying to stop a press campaign over the losses. Popular anger over the issue undoubtedly reflected impotence. Few steps were available to the Dutch government to counteract the situation. On February 10, 1917, a law became effective which allowed the government to requisition shipping space, whether for naval reasons, shipping shortages, or to bring in basic foods. Dutch waters were constantly swept for mines by the navy's smaller vessels (one was sunk in the process).[52]

The losses themselves were not crippling. The interruptions, however, were more serious. Ships might stay in port for days or weeks when danger threatened. At the beginning of the campaign, the Dutch and British governments independently ordered Dutch vessels to stay put. This produced an economic downturn from which the country did not recover until 1919, and then slowly. The most notorious incident occurred on February 22, 1917, when 7 Dutch ships left Falmouth for the Netherlands, and a German submarine torpedoed all 7. Six sank; one was towed back to Falmouth. At the time official German sources claimed that the sinkings were "accidental" because Holland had been promised that it was safe for its commercial vessels to sail the route. This was not true; the sinking were no accident. Dutch military intelligence had intercepted a message from attaché Renner, who felt that the Dutch ships should not be allowed to leave Falmouth "unpunished." Wilhelmina corresponded with the Kaiser about the losses (27 February) and did gain some assurances. In April 1917, however, another 7 merchantmen were sunk, this time truly because of a misunderstanding. It made no difference to the Dutch. At one point, every ship plying the Holland-Britain service had been sunk.[53]

Renner's action concerning the Falmouth ships was aimed at Holland as a whole. The owners of the 7 ships were under British pressure to sail, even though the Dutch government preferred them to stay. Interestingly enough, even though the government knew 2 days before the sailings about Renner's message, it made no effort to stop them – whether because of displeasure with the shipping companies, or fear of giving away the ability to intercept Renner's telegrams, is impossible to say. Rosen would discuss compensation only after the war and on the basis of humanitarian sentiments. Loudon considered this completely unacceptable, and had Gevers tell Bethmann Hollweg so.[54] The Foreign Office expresssed consternation and offered reparations; Gevers believed that the German government was *"étranger à la catastrophe."*[xi] Yet when a message reached Loudon on 27 February, no compensation was mentioned. The colonial ministry reminded Loudon that 40 German steamers were sitting in Indies ports at that moment. On the 28th, Germany offered a complicated plan including compensation for crewmen and the use of German ships, which could be purchased after the war.[55]

Gevers enlightened Loudon on March 1 and again two weeks later

---

[xi] It is interesting that Loudon, who had a copy of Snijders' message revealing Renner's proposal to sink the ships, did not share this information with Gevers.

about Germany's difficulties in formulating compensation proposals. The problem, shipping space being concerned, was the Naval Office *(Marine Amt)*. Undersecretary Zimmermann confidentially showed Gevers an accusing letter he had written to the navy, which had responded by telling Zimmermann "in a definitely crude fashion that he should not interfere in matters, which were not within his competence." Gevers described Zimmermann as *"brieschend"* (foaming). He also reported that the Kaiser and Chancellor were those most interested in compensation for the sunken ships, although the Chancellor rejected Loudon's reproach. Two weeks later, Zimmermann was forced to report that the Navy had caused Wilhelm to change his mind, and Kriege even blamed the Dutch shippers for going to sea. Kriege only wanted to discuss postwar compensation, but Gevers held his ground and demanded compensation out of the German ships held by Holland. Kriege responded with a convoluted objection; the ships might be used to benefit Britain, and the Germans might have to torpedo their own ships. The conversation took an interesting turn; Gevers said that he did not believe that Kriege could mean that objection seriously, and Kriege more or less conceded the point.[56]

While there is an element of humor here, it should be noted that Holland's position hung by a thread. It could not even negotiate effectively with the Foreign Office, because of the latter's obviously limited influence on the military establishment. In relation to Germany, Holland's rights and existence depended on a German military only reined in, if it all, by Wilhelm II. But that was not all. The rights of neutrals were disappearing, and so would the most important neutral.

The loss of the USA

The American declaration of war was foreseen. In virtually every capital, planners and diplomats assumed that a resumption of unrestricted submarine warfare would bring the United States into the war. Woodrow Wilson's vigorous response to the sinking of the *Lusitania* in 1915 indicated that he would protect the passage of American people and goods across the Atlantic. The Dutch assumed that Wilson did so in order to protect the rights of neutrals, especially since the President was viewed as in idealist. Wilson particularly appealed to Loudon, who had Washington experience. As it turned out, the President shared many of Loudon's views about a proper international order. None of this mattered, however, in the short run. Once the United States entered World War I, Wilson ceased to champion the rights of neutrals. After April 6, 1917, not a single major state remained neutral.[xii] The resulting reductions in trade, ship seizures, and loss of ties to the Indies, led to the US entry being labeled as a worse event than unrestricted submarine warfare. Many Dutchmen initially welcomed the USA's belligerency, but were soon disillusioned. The USA broke relations with Germany on 4 February, only five days after the German campaign was proclaimed. Snijders immediately wrote Cort van der Linden, expressing his concern that this would deprive the neutral nations of their most influential leader. The Minister President agreed, but he could do nothing except wait for the consequences. By August, the USA essentially placed a blockade on the neutral powers, and coaling became difficult. The Dutch were angry, attacking the "injustice" of Wilson's new policy. Holland's most prolific author on World War I. C. Smit, has downplayed this, noting that the American actions were simply a function of military necessity.[57] Wilson could not claim military necessity, of course, as this was exactly the justification used by Bethmann Hollweg for the invasion of Belgium.

The gap between justification and reality was particularly evident in the most spectacular event in US-Netherlands relations in this period: the seizure of the Dutch merchant fleet. Holland's commercial shipping was in dire straits already, suffering from submarine attacks and coal shortages, but the Entente now began to demand the use of the Dutch ships as well. This did not concern shipping owners that much, but it did the country, because of its absolute dependence on grain imports. The threat built slowly. On February 17, 1917, Balfour informed De Marees van Swinderen that he would only release Dutch ships if shipments from Holland met agreed targets, and when regular sailings from Holland to Britain resumed. The USA also began to restrict Dutch ship sailings. In May 1917, Britain requisitioned 11 Dutch-owned ships sailing under the British flag. The following month, the British government seized Dutch-flag vessels with British owners![58]

In the wake of these ship seizures, it is not surprising that speculation began about what the Entente's long-term demands might be. The seizure of Dutch ships outright (along with those of other neutrals) had

---

[xii] I am not counting China as a "major state" in this period because of the turmoil resulting from the revolution of 1911-12.

been contemplated in Britain since March. Townley had been asked what the reaction might be, leading him to anticipate an "immediate outburst of indignation." By October, newspapers were speculating that Holland's vessels were about to be seized. Instead, negotiations began which culminated in an arrangement under which a ship could leave America only when another left for an American port. When Germany protested, Loudon pointed out that the alternative would be an outright seizure. In the spring things changed. The pressure increased, judging by the frantic telegrams from De Marees van Swinderen. Holland needed extra grain, and was told it could only come if Dutch ships would go through the so-called danger zones. Holland capitulated, insisting only that its ships not carry troops or munitions.[59]

It was too late. Negotiations, counteroffers and delaying tactics ceased to work with the Entente, just as they were failing with the Germans. Balfour labeled the Dutch response as "quite unacceptable" and sent a message via Townley on 20 March 1918:

> We are not favorably impressed by such a reply and, unless we receive an unqualified acceptance of our proposals by tomorrow evening, we can only regard it as a refusal.[60]

At least this message left no ambiguity about the next step. The Dutch considered caving in to the British demands, but they couldn't. Voluntarily allowing the Entente to use Dutch ships for military purposes would be the end of neutrality. There was no chance the Germans would accept it. All the Dutch could do was await the inevitable. On March 20 and 21, the British and Americans seized the Dutch vessels in their ports. Some 135 ships totalling 450,000 tons of Dutch shipping passed into Entente hands. A third of the fleet was gone, and other ships entering Entente ports would doubtless experience the same.[61]

Such an action had to be justified, especially as the Entente nations claimed to be protectors of international law and at war for the rights of small states. The President argued that the 'free will" requisite for an agreement was lacking, as Germany had promised to attack Dutch ships whose use was granted to the Entente.[62] Wilson also claimed that the ships were lying around uselessly, an argument frequently repeated but also disputed.[63] Such a fact alone could not be used as a legal justification for the seizure. U.S. The State Department, however, was equal to the task. It dug out an ancient legal concept called *jus angariae* – the right of angary. It had existed for centuries. "Angary" generally referred to compulsory service exacted by a government for a public purpose. The "right of angary" referred to a belligerent's right to use or destroy neutral property of any kind. In maritime law, it referred to the forced service imposed on a vessel for public purpose, or to put it more simply, seizing a merchant vessel in port to compel it, with compensation, to carry troops and supplies.[64]

This was what Wilson alluded to on March 21, 1918, when he seized the ships under the "indisputable rights as a sovereign." This was a peculiar document coming from a President whose view of international relations has been identified, however naively, as based on the equality of nations.[65] It claimed, after all, a sovereign power that in practice could only be exercised by great states. The British, not surprisingly, were impressed. As a powerful naval state, the doctrine had great appeal. Francis Oppenheimer wrote:

> Owing to the interminable delays on the part of the Dutch government to come to terms . . . the Allies found themselves in the end compelled greatly as a result of impatience on the part of the United States Government, to resort to sterner measures. They took the law into their own hands by requisitioning Dutch ships detained in Allied ports. The right to requisition neutral ships under certain circumstances is a belligerent right – the right of Angary – recognized by international law.[66]

This statement reveals many things, not the least the exceptional quality of Sir F.O. himself, who both praises and blames the US government, and glosses over two important facts. First, the right of angary was not quite as "recognized" as Oppenheimer claims. The United States had abolished it before the war, viewing it as obsolete. Second, the reference to "interminable delays" and "impatience" beg the question – in genuine negotiations, is the smaller state *forced* to concede and sign? The realistic answer, of course, is yes. But this would hardly accord with the more noble pronouncements emanating from Wilson. The reality was that the Entente nations had their backs against the wall. The collapse of the Western Front seemed imminent, and everything had to be rushed to Britain and France to save the situation.[67]

The impatience of the Entente with Dutch dithering is understandable, and its action might have been more acceptable to the Dutch if it had not been dressed up with hypocritical cant. This may explain why Dutch anger was mostly directed at Wilson, not the British. The anger was substantial. There had already been murmurs of discontent about the concessions made before, and now there was the sheer feeling of impotence in the face of the Anglo-American action. Troelstra "warned the government that it was too soft and gave in too easily to foreign pressure," which some felt had helped trigger the seizure. The right of angary was called "[something] dug out of old archives" and "obvious violation of rights," and "the indignation was great." German successes produced a certain amount of *Schadenfreude*. The mixed feelings which already existed about American culture became stronger.[68]

The cabinet met immediately after the announcement to decide how to react. The issue was not simply one of giving in. An insufficient reaction might trigger German accusations of not maintaining neutrality. The other extreme, of course, would involve going to war. According to the secretary-general of the foreign ministry, there was some overt support for a declaration of war, although this has been disputed. No notes of the meeting survive. Treub wrote after the fact that some felt that a violation of Dutch sovereignty had taken place, but the group soon realized that such a finding would require the issuance of an ultimatum: "With the issuance of an ultimatum our country would have burned its bridges behind it." If the ultimatum were ignored, there would have been only one step left – joining the Central Powers. Instead, the cabinet decided to issue a protest claiming *rechtsverkrachting*, literally "rape of the law." The protest, which received little attention but was viewed as too strong (and even "too violent") in the seizing countries, also accused the USA's action of being "in conflict with the traditional friendship between the two countries."[69]

The cabinet issued the protest, and later authorized Snijders to cancel leaves once again. This was all that could be done. Despite the indignation about the *jus angariae* claim, and "though its application naturally caused much commotion, acquiescence was inevitable."[70] Cort van der Linden put the best spin on the situation in his speech to parliament:

> There are moments, also in the life of a statesman, where he has to let out what lives in him. The Government, Parliament, and people are now one. Never during the whole war have we been so unified, without distinction of party, without distinction of class, without distinction of religion. I hope that my words will be heard far across the borders, if from this place I pronounce a flaming protest against the injustice, the coercion, and the humiliation which has been done to us. More than our fleet and

more than our bread we love our independence and our rights. And to
that we shall hold, and be loyal, even if we are beggared.[71]

It was a magnificent speech – it reads far better in the original Dutch
than in translation – and obscured the lack of action that the government could take. It did not obscure it from the Germans. The Dutch
government had hoped that letting the Entente steal the fleet would be
more acceptable than giving it away, but the German government was
in no mood for fine distinctions. Ludendorff complained that Holland
had *"eingewilligt"* ("permitted") the demands. Schweinitz tried to
explain that Holland was in no position to stop the ship thefts, and that
Holland was withholding ship sailings pending some sort of resolution.
OHL was not mollified, because the seizures strengthened the Entente
at a critical time; Germany's situation was just as desperate as the
Entente's. Germany declared the seized neutral fleets[xiii] as sailing in
enemy service, and that any of those neutrals' ships were subject to
German seizure now. Intense negotiations occurred. Germany offered
terms for safe-voyage grants, which Sweden, for example, accepted,
but Holland did not. Gevers expressed regrets about German threats
and compared Germany's halt of exports to Holland (to get its way:
Rosen had suggested this, if only as an alernative to ultimatums or
invasion) to the Entente blockade. Kühlmann pleaded "military
necessity," "with which," Gevers recorded, "people here try to justify
so much."[72]

The Germans were displeased with the Dutch response to the theft.
The German government issued a statement that it would sink any
merchantmen of a fleet of which a large proportion had been seized and
was sailing in Entente service. Holland responded that this was
unlawful. The Germans rejected the Dutch protest, leading to a further
(but impotent) Dutch protest. The Germans did offer a safe-conduct
guarantee for ships whose contents they could inspect, which eventually led the United States to declare that any ships sailing under a
German safe-conduct pass could be seized. This was too much even for
the British, who accepted Wilson's position with great reservations.
This was small comfort to the Dutch, who could not regain their fleet
(until November 25, 1918) nor satisfy the German government, which
thought the Dutch were doing far too little.[73]

[xiii] Scandinavian countries' fleets were also seized.

In this the Germans had an ally in the Queen. Wilhelmina was furious, taking the whole episode as a personal insult (which, in a technical sense, it was). She wanted badly to respond in some way, and hit upon a straightforward method: a convoy. Convoying had been discussed two years earlier, when De Marees van Swinderen had suggested that the USA and Holland might start convoying their own merchant vessels. Further joint efforts with the USA in this area went nowhere, however. Then on 12 April 1918 a plan was proposed in cabinet to send a small convoy to the Indies escorted by the cruiser *Hertog Hendrik*.[xiv] This challenged Britain's self-proclaimed right of *droit de visite,* as the ships could not be searched. When Britain was notified by the Dutch government of this plan, Britain immediately answered that the right to convoy through a blockade was not recognized. The Dutch government offered to let Britain inspect ships' papers. Britain consented to let this one convoy go, but raised objections to particular items and persons being transported. The cabinet, which as a group did not think the convoy that important, agreed to delay, to the disgust of ministers Rambonnet and Posthuma. Rambonnet, as mentioned earlier, resigned. His colleagues thought the exercise a dangerous publicity stunt; the Queen was deeply distressed by the outcome, and named Rambonnet as one of her adjutants. The Queen was no figurehead, and with a little more support might have gotten her way on the convoy.[74] The results, had Britain then chosen to stop it anyway, would have been incalculable.[xv]

What were the results of the shipping crisis? At first glance, the ship seizure did not seem to cause immediate problems. Shipping companies' shares rose, as vessels in American ports could sail again, and good compensation was paid for destroyed ships. The people might feel "maltreated" and "humiliated," in American envoy John Garrett's words, but the shipping companies were pleased. Even senior Foreign Ministry official Doude van Troostwijk called it "the best solution of

---

[xiv] Until this point it had been policy that Dutch warships should not interfere with inspection and seizure of Dutch merchantmen, but could should if a merchant vessel were fired on. The issue had not arisen as the fleet stayed within its own waters. Fasseur, *Wilhelmina, p.* 514. The cruiser *Hertog Hendrik*, a sister of the *Koningin Regentes,* normally remained in the Indies with the other large fleet units.

[xv] Had the navy had battleships, would the government have been hesitant about convoying supplies to and from the colonies? If it had, without British approval, would that have increased the likelihood of war with Britain?

the problem." In one sense he was right, because diplomatically America and Britain were sympathetic toward the Dutch situation and this would be extremely valuable during the Versailles conference. The State Department, in fact, was working by fall to improve relations. But the domestic economic problems were significant. Shipping might be moving, but it was not moving to Holland. Ships also had to be held in Dutch ports until assurances were received that they would not be seized. Belgian relief was threatened, as Holland hinted at a cutoff. Starvation in Belgium would have meant the movement of more Belgians to German factories, freeing up more Germans for military service. Townley headed off that particular threat with one of his cleverest moves, when he pointed out that this would harm the Queen's position as patron of relief work.

The real danger of the ship seizures was that it brought the Netherlands to the edge of war, and not because of a few militants like the Queen and Rambonnet. The ship seizure was, in the words of American diplomatic historian Thomas Bailey, "the most spectacular single act of force employed by the United States against the neutrals." Strict neutrality was no longer possible. The Anglo-American action was one which Germany could not accept, and hence there was literally no middle ground for Loudon to stand on. Only a sudden shift in German attitude, in the summer of 1918, made his task possible once again. The critical event, of course, was the swing in the Western Front, followed by Germany's collapse. Neither Holland's neutrality, nor her economy, could have survived much longer. If the economy had collapsed, one of the major motives for neutrality, or what was left of it, would have collapsed. In the words of German scholar Marc Frey,

> *Politisch immobilisiert von der OHL und wirtschaftlich abhängig von deutscher Kohle, von Grossbritannien und den Vereinigte Staaten mit einem Embargo belegt und in den westlichen Hauptstädten als politischer Vasall der Reichsleitung betrachtet, befreite erst der grosse Umschwung an der Westfront seit Ende Juli 1918 die Niederlande aus einer Position völliger Handlungsunfähigkeit.*[75]
>
> (Politically immobilized by OHL and economically dependent on German coal, covered by an embargo by Britain and the United States and viewed in western capitals as a political vassal of the Reich, only the great turn of the Western Front at the end of July 1918 freed the Netherlands from a position of complete trade incapacity.)

This kind of dependence could never have supported a policy of neutrality for any length of time. One can construct many scenarios of what might have happened had the war continued, but none of those scenarios would likely culminate in continued neutrality. The German response to the ship-seizure crisis illustrates precisely how close to the precipice Holland was.

The sand and gravel crisis

The ship seizure itself annoyed German authorities who saw it as a benefit for the Entente. The perceived lack of vigor in the Dutch response was considered much more serious. Just as various Entente figures regarded Holland as leaning toward Germany, some German leaders – among them Ludendorff – viewed the Dutch as pro-British. In other words, Holland's attempted neutrality was increasingly viewed by each side as a benefit for the enemy. Ludendorff, of course, was further angered by the alleged British overflights of Dutch territory. His irritation turned to fury when Holland issued new demands that Germany allow inspections regarding the ultimate destination of the large quantities of sand and gravel shipped via the Netherlands to Belgium.[76]

Ludendorff instead demanded compensation, in the form of resumed sand and gravel shipments but, far more importantly, the free use of the rail line that crossed Limburg from Dalheim to Roermond. A host of other items were tacked on to the demands; the use of more Dutch shipping, release of 36 German ships in Antwerp, more agricultural products, and other economic benefits. As this list contained items that Holland could not possibly accept without burning its bridges to the Entente, it appears constructed to force Holland to abandon its neutrality. It was. Ludendorff was tinkering with the idea of war with the Netherlands. He had already suggested this at the time of the overflights. To add credibility to the threats, he moved two divisions to Ghent – at a time when every soldiers was needed for the great spring offensives – and further threatened to cut off all coal shipments.[77]

Loudon, Snijders, and military intelligence all saw the Ludendorff threats as largely a bluff. Snijders saw no need for special precautions. There is evidence that the Dutch were wrong. Ludendorff's willingness to push the issue as far as necessary was real, and his power in Germany was growing. The spring offensives were going well; victory seemed possible now; it seemed like a good time to pressure the Dutch. The ultranationalist *Vaterland* party, founded by Tirpitz, wanted a tougher foreign policy towards the Netherlands. Kühlmann was opposed, leading Ludendorff to force him out. Other elements in the General Staff at least wanted to take the lands on the southern bank of the Schelde. The navy's hostility toward the Netherlands ensured solid support for Ludendorff's "get tough" approach. Smit has suggested that, if Ludendorff's control in Germany had been complete, Holland's neutrality might have collapsed.[78]

Rosen certainly thought so; he took Ludendorff's threats very seriously, and feared that the threats might force Holland into the Entente camp. From his perspective, the danger was even greater because of Loudon's perceived pro-Entente attitudes.[xvi] Rosen would labor mightily to convince Loudon to take a flexible position, and when that failed, tried the same approach more successfully elsewhere in the Dutch political establishment. The substantial concessions eventually given by the Dutch parliament satisfied Wilhelm (who had initially supported Ludendorff) and much of his government, and headed off a German ultimatum, which Rosen thought only days away. As a result, Rosen has been credited with stopping Ludendorff's invasion plans. He certainly avoided the issuance of an ultimatum, which, had it been issued, would have terminated Holland's neutrality. As by definition the only two "acceptable" answers to an ultimatum are Yes and No, the former would have placed Holland in the Central Powers, the latter among the Entente. The only other possible interpretation of the crisis is that Rosen was manipulated by a German government which had no intention of invading Holland, but was merely seeking concessions. This is a doubtful scenario. It does not accord with Ludendorff's personality, nor was he familiar with Rosen or the Dutch leadership. The Dutch war minister during the crisis, not an alarmist by nature, felt that the Netherlands "had been brought to the edge of war."[79]

The transshipments of sand and gravel to Belgium was not a new issue. Relying on existing trade treaties, Germany had been sending the stuff to Belgium since 1915. In December 1915, British secret services

---

[xvi] According to Rosen, Loudon visited Verdun after the war, and "confessed" that while he was the representative of a neutral state during the war, he was not neutral at heart. This statement should be interpreted in light of the fact that Loudon was envoy to France at the time. He was, however, unquestionably *francophile.*

noticed the transports (probably because the *Telegraaf* was reporting them), leading Grey and later Balfour to complain that Holland was becoming a military highway for Germany and that this violated the Hague Convention of 1907 which prohibited the passage of military supplies through a neutral country. The Dutch were already concerned. In November of 1915, Snijders had written Loudon expressing his concerns that the shipments might violate neutrality as the materials could be used for building fortifications as well as military roads. Loudon filed a protest on December 23, 1915, with only moderate results. The following year, in the wake of Balfour's complaint, another protest was made which led to limited permission for Dutch officials to inspect[xvii] the ultimate destination of the building materials. The inspections resulted in a report that the materials were being used for civilian purposes, including the rebuilding of roads destroyed by the retreating Belgians. "The British were not amused." The shipments increased from 75,000 tons in 1915 to 420,000 in 1916.[80]

Any hopes that Loudon may have had that the issue would fade away were dashed in 1917. Despite gaining a giant ally, the Entente's situation was not good. The submarine campaign was doing grievous damage, the French assault on the German lines culminated in a mutiny among the rank and file, and the British offensive (Passchendaele, or 3rd Ypres: July-November 1917) had fared no better. Entente complaints grew. Loudon briefly cut off German transshipments in August, but this was viewed as entirely inadequate in London. On October 1 or 2, 1917,[xviii] the British government cut off telegraph service to the Netherlands. This meant two things; businesses temporarily lost contact with their overseas agents, and the links to the empire were sliced.[81]

The issue was an emotional one among the British, reflecting the enormous tension and fantastic casualties of the time. Townley and Oppenheimer both were furious about Holland's failure to resolve the issue satisfactorily, either through a permanent cutoff or insisting on the right to make thorough inspections. Townley indicated that war

---

[xvii] The German reluctance to allow inspections is usually attributed to the fact that the sand and gravel was being used for military purposes. A better explanation might be that the Germans did not want any foreigners snooping around their fortifications, as the information might be leaked to the British.

[xviii] Sources differ on the exact date.

between Britain and Holland was possible over the sand and gravel question.[82] In his memoirs Oppenheimer described Holland's attitude over the issue as "rigidly hostile" and described the matter as Britain's "worst grievance" with the Dutch. He lambasted his hosts for failing to interfere with the traffic "although the Netherlands was one of the powers which had guaranteed the neutrality of Belgium"[xix] and implicated Holland in the shedding of British blood:

> It was said at the time that the attitude so persistently maintained by Mr. Loudon, as Dutch Minister of Foreign Affairs, in this transit made him (though presumably of British descent) responsible for the loss of more British lives than the activities of any other Dutchman in history.[83]

Strong stuff, but a fair reflection of a British view that went beyond Oppenheimer and even finds its way into recent British publications. An Admiralty report in July 1917 concluded that "had we forced Holland to discontinue this traffic . . . the Hindenburg defences could have never been built, except at enormous sacrifice of other necessary operations." The British studied the composition of captured German bunkers around Ypres and found that the materials did indeed come from Germany and took this as proof that it was part of the huge shipments coming through Holland. Echoing Oppenheimer and Townley, a recent work reflects the British feelings of the time, viewing the passage of the sand and gravel as part of a deliberate Dutch plan to profit from the situation. "The Dutch were *more than pleased* to report that the materials were indeed for civilian use" (emphasis added). "[T]he Dutch expounded denials and excuses." Concerning the findings about materials used at Ypres: "These findings were reported to the Dutch, but by then it was too late – they had earned more than enough Deutschmarks."[84]

None of the British officials concerned with the question in 1917 seemed to give much thought as to why Loudon did not do more to cut off the trade. Here Britain claimed to be at war for the protection of small neutral states, yet not a word came from Townley or Oppenheimer about whether pressure was coming from the other direction. This outward obliviousness may, of course, have been nothing more than diplomatic necessity. You cannot simultaneously be reasonable toward

---

[xix] As a diplomat, Sir Francis either should have known that this was incorrect, or did know, but preferred not to bring in the truth at this point.

a foreign government while demanding that it do something. On the other hand, Oppenheimer's vigorous comments were published long after the event. Why no thought about the threat of German action? Ludendorff gave much more more attention to the Netherlands in 1917. His concern was mainly about a British landing in the Schelde, and was thinking about whether Germany should invade the area preemptively. This possibility had been hinted at numerous times by German diplomats to the Dutch. *Ministerialdirektor* Kriege bluntly suggested that Germany might have to take action despite its desire to respect Dutch neutrality. Snijders, not an alarmist when it came to German intentions, was quite worried in the fall of 1917. The very casualties that probably influenced the British outlook complicated the situation further. Holland could only place itself squarely at odds with Germany if Britain were prepared to send help. In the fall of 1917, the British army had indeed considered such plan, but by January 1918 its situation was so parlous that *the single brigade* designated to help Holland was not even available; it had been sent to France.[85]

So Loudon was already dealing from a very poor position in late 1917. Between submarine warfare, American belligerency, British anger, and German threats, his room to maneuver was virtually nonexistent. In this situation knowledge about the use of the sand and gravel was practically irrelevant, no matter what it meant legally. Besides the British 1917 claims and Snijders' letter much earlier, Loudon received a private letter on 19 October 1917 alleging that the materials could not possibly all be going for road repairs. Van Vollenhoven reported from Brussels that the stuff was going straight to the front. The ministry was not entirely convinced. Van Vollenhoven mentioned a confidential source, leading the ministry's secretary general to comment, that "we really ought to know" who the source was. All that mattered was that Loudon's one neighbor could strangle Holland, while the other could smash it. He attempted to get Britain to accept arbitration on the issue, just as he had done with the Germans regarding the submarines; no luck.[86]

Instead, his ministry signaled Rosen through very indirect channels about the British pressure, and not a moment to soon. Loudon would soon need all the help Rosen could give him. Bowing to British pressure, he asked Germany on 26 November 1917 to allow Dutch experts to investigate the British charges. When this was refused, Loudon had no alternative but to cut off the sand and gravel shipments (although he managed to delay this step until the following February).

In the meantime, on January 7, 1918, the first German request came for the reopening of the railway over Roermond, closed since the beginning of the war. Snijders felt that the reopening would clearly only benefit Germany, and hence would violate neutrality. The foreign ministry and the government agreed completely, and the line remained closed. This meant that Holland was now at loggerheads with Germany on two important issues, but the railroad simply could not be opened to German use while the diplomatic crisis with Britain continued. Loudon tried to temporize, informing the British that reduction in sand and gravel shipments was difficult, as it would look like a concession to pressure. De Marees van Swinderen received a surprisingly sympathetic reception, but reported that he needed to sign an agreement on the matter with the British, which Loudon promptly rejected.[87]

So by late February 1918 Holland's relations with both great powers were in a state of decline, with each making demands that the other would not allow Holland to accept. There was a momentary respite concerning sand and gravel, as Germany was not insisting on its transit at the moment (perhaps because its armies were moving forward and fortification was not a priority) but Loudon had no illusions anymore that the issue would disappear of its own accord. He did take the opportunity (March 1) to explain to his London envoy that a formal agreement could not be signed with only one belligerent. The British proposal would require continuous monitoring of the use of sand and gravel. Loudon pointed out that all sorts of judgments would have to be made regarding shelters and roads which could be used by soldiers or civilians. Britain demanded monitoring, without specifying how this monitoring was to occur, and he noted that Britain could hardly influence whether Germany would grant permission. Loudon did assure De Marees van Swinderen that shipments would be limited somewhat in quantity, but noted that the British proposals were incomplete, and in some ways unacceptable. This was an obvious hint to negotiating further, and it was taken. De Marees van Swinderen wrote Balfour on March 7, 1918, and was able to report a week later that Britain accepted a Loudon idea of forwarding to both governments the conclusion of a Dutch commission. The pressure stayed on, however. On March 20th Townley presented a *note verbale* complaining that the exports of sand and gravel were still continuing.[88]

The timing of Townley's visit was wholly unfortunate, although neither he nor the minister knew it. That very day, Ludendorff wrote his foreign ministry demanding the use of three railways as well as

Dutch waterways, to be used for *military* materiel. Anger as well as need lay behind his message; he also wanted the admiralty to increase attacks on Dutch shipping. Another message followed on the 21st restating the previous demands and adding the release of ships in Antwerp and the resumption of sand and gravel shipments. Rosen thought the last was the most realistic request. Ludendorff explained on 2 April that as Holland had allowed Germany's enemies to move extra supplies for their front (by "accepting" the ship seizures), the Dutch could not refuse his "modest" demands. He again insisted on the use of the Limburg railways for military transport. The navy supported Ludendorff's aggressive posture, pointing out that Rhine river barges could be detained inside Germany to put additional pressure on the Dutch. German intelligence also reported that it was a good time to pressure Holland.[89]

On April 4, Rosen was formally notified of the demand for the use of the railways. The legation studied the matter – how to clothe such a move in respectable diplomatic garb? – and sent a notice to the Dutch foreign ministry 5 days later, arguing that the failure to reopen the railroads was contrary to an 1874 treaty.[90] While Loudon was pondering this claim (or, more probably, how to dispose of it), Balfour informed the Dutch on the 11th that the shipment of metals, sand and gravel violated neutrality, and further argued that the behavior of Germany in Belgium

> impose[s] a special moral obligation on all other governments not to stretch by a hair's breadth their obligations as neutrals, so as to assist directly or indirectly in the gross breaches of law and humanity committed by Germany in Belgium.

Worse, in a sense, Balfour informed Holland that the United Kingdom refused to discuss the matter further.[91] If Balfour was so exercised over sand and gravel moving through Holland, how would he react to the movement of German guns and ammunition across Limburg? Not surprisingly, Rosen found the foreign minister obdurate when he visited him on April 16. Rosen received an absolute refusal, attributing this to the government's desire to go to the utmost before allowing its neutrality principles to be constricted. Rosen did not know the details of the British pressure and never (as far as we know) learned of Townley's visit the following day, demanding an answer to the *note verbale* of March 20th concerning sand and gravel shipments.[92] What Rosen did know was what lay behind the pressure from Germany, and how dangerous it was. It was no longer a question of diplomatic maneuvers but rather of military threat. He made his first tentative end run around the foreign ministry, complaining to Colijn and others on the 17th that German pressure would be bound to increase because Loudon did not seem to be aware of the facts, had a habit of promising to bring matters to the attention of other departments, but in the end never responding to the legation (Rosen apparently not knowing that Loudon, who had little left to him except delaying tactics, was doing the same to Townley). Colijn believed the complaint, adding that the foreign ministry "is badly equipped."[93]

Rosen correctly anticipated more pressure from his government. Ludendorff was confident that Germany's strong military situation would compel Holland to accept whatever was demanded. In a sense, of course, this was true. Loudon's pessimism about the Entente military situation ought to have made him more vulnerable to German demands. Nevertheless, the foreign minister stubbornly stuck to his strict neutrality guns. This provoked Rosen to circumvent the minister. His legation was also sending hints that German patience with Loudon was at an end. On the 18th, the same day that yet another Ludendorff missive arrive at the Foreign Office, *legationsrat* Baron A. von Maltzan spoke with Dr. C.F. Gerretson, an associate of Colijn's, complaining about Holland's "legalistic" treatment of German matters, while giving in to all the Entente's demands. Gerretson stoutly argued that the remedy was a reinvigorated Entente policy, not a weaker policy toward the Central Powers, and proceeded to reject every one of Maltzan's contentions. Maltzan became irritated, especially when Gerretson pointed to German writers who had specifically defended the legality of the right of angary. Maltzan reminded Gerretson that Germany had been very considerate toward Holland and that the failure to respond was doing weakening Holland's friends in Germany. He then demanded that the rail use, sand and gravel issues be resolved by Monday 22 April, adding that:

> Too late, I fear, the Dutch government will become aware at a certain moment, that it is no longer dealing with the German government, but with the general staff.

Gerretson forwarded the information to Colijn, who promptly informed Loudon, suggesting that giving an answer by Monday was more important than the answer's content.[94]

Apparently the foreign ministry took the hint – partly. On Saturday

April 20, Rosen was already able to report that Loudon had no objection to resuming cargo traffic over Roermond, provided that Holland's neutrality regulations were taken into account. This was not a total capitulation. Loudon informed the envoy that Holland would be willing to consider German complaints about Rhine river traffic, but refused to moderate his stand on the sand and gravel, regarding any German pressure on the issue as a violation of Holland's neutrality. Rosen's frustration was so great that he informed his superiors that all arguments with Loudon about the seriousness of the matter were *"nutzlos"* ("useless").[xx] This unwelcome information came to the Foreign Office just as as 3 more Ludendorff missives arrived. Ludendorff reported that he had moved two divisions toward the Netherlands and was prepared to send more, recommended the withholding of coal as a pressure tactic, and opined that Loudon was taking a hard line mainly to cover himself with the Entente. The German government apparently agreed, because it decided that military force was not yet necessary. Over the weekend, however, Ludendorff's position hardened, perhaps because of Rosen's report. By Tuesday 23 April, he had taken the position that if Holland did not accept his demands in 14 days, military pressure would have to be used, "including a march into Holland."[95]

Since the German Foreign Office was clearly being overshadowed by the military, the Dutch government tried to go over the heads of both by having the Queen contact the Emperor on April 23 and appeal to his feelings of friendship. Instead, Wilhelm became highly agitated, penning in the margin that Holland had favored the other side, having become a *"Schildträger der Entente"* ("shield-bearer of the Entente") and hence responsible for lengthening the war. Holland would have to fulfill the German demands. His official reply was more sober, but still argued that Germany had effectively protected Holland for four years. This was all reported immediately to the German Foreign Office, which also received a statement from the German navy on the 23rd claiming that German demands were still not being taken as seriously as necessary in Holland, and foreseeing the need for military action. There was something in this. The Dutch government was only

---

[xx] Loudon did have one advantage over the Germans, small as it was. All the German legation's telephone conversations to Germany were being intercepted and decoded by military intelligence. Kluiters, *Supplement,* p. 57.

moderately concerned. Snijders reported no new troop concentrations adjacent to Holland and speculated that Germany wanted Britain to hold back some of its reserves from the front, in case of an invasion of Holland.[xxi] In any case, he wanted to take no exceptional measures. Loudon discovered that German officers were trying to start low-level peace negotiations with the British, hardly the action of a Germany on the edge of victory. The German navy suggested that the Dutch were getting conflicting signals from Rosen and the Berlin government and argued for unity in dealing with the Dutch.[96]

Actually, Rosen had already taken action to force the recalcitrant Dutch to budge. He had approached Cort van der Linden and other cabinet members on the 23rd, and felt that a *modus vivendi* could be achieved. Loudon was still resisting, and Rosen telegraphed that success or failure might depend on the fall or survival of the foreign minister. To circumvent Loudon, he visited not only Protestant leaders such as Kuyper and Savornin Lohman, but also the Social Democrats' Troelstra, and he sent Dr. Gneist to speak to the Liberals' Marchant and the Catholic leader Monsignor W.H. Nolens (Rosen later visited the latter himself). During his conversation with Cort van der Linden on the 23rd he had complained that negotiations with Loudon were no longer possible. Cort van der Linden pointed out that the Dutch were not convinced that Germany was on the verge of victory and that Rosen needed to take that into account.[97] On Wednesday April 24, therefore, he went to the ministry and, following instructions from Berlin, handed over a list of demands which included free transshipment of everything except weapons, airplanes, and munitions. The sand and gravel would move freely; Germany would declare that it was for peaceful means, and Holland would not be allowed to inspect. The Foreign Office, responding to the Admiralty's call for united action, called Gevers in on the 24th to inform him of the seriousness of the situation and the attitude of the military staffs, and then promptly telegraphed the results of the meeting to Rosen. The following day, Thursday April 25, Rosen handed over a more detailed list, although omitting the absolute deadline that the Foreign Office had chosen (May 1).[98]

The Thursday memorandum looked to the Dutch like an ultimatum. Snijders, who had been notified three days earlier by Cort van der

---

[xxi] This was not just the general's personal position. Fabius had received information on 27 April 1918 that some in the Entente thought exactly the same thing.

Linden that Holland might have to reach a decision unacceptable to Germany, was now instructed to stop granting leaves the next day, Friday 26 April. The Germans were not of one mind as to how to proceed as the 25th came to an end, however. Rosen himself held complicated views. On the one hand, he protested to Berlin that the use of threats of violence was a mistake. He also reported, however, that he had returned to the foreign ministry on the 25th and found Loudon less flexible than the day before about meeting his demands. Rosen continued to negotiate through other avenues, including the Minister President, and busily planted press stories about Entente outrages and the reasonableness[xxii] of the German demands. Ludendorff continued to push for the use of force, and – taking the exact opposite viewpoint from Rosen – was disappointed that no direct military threat was included. Accepting that only an invasion would lead to the meeting of the demands, and conceding that war with Holland was undesirable, Ludendorff nevertheless pressed for a May 5 cutoff of the demands. In the meantime, however, the *Allerhöchste*[xxiii] had apparently had a change of heart and ordered that a break with the Netherlands was to be avoided, no troops should be massed, and no ultimatum would be issued.[99]

Even if this last message had been known to the Dutch leadership, it would have provided scant comfort. In an environment where Ludendorff knew exactly what he wanted and the Emperor changed his mind with some frequency, Wilhelm's pro-Dutch view could prove momentary. Rosen's warnings had had their effect. When parliament met on the 26th, all major factions were aware that the Dutch-German relationship was on the edge of collapse. It was one of the few times during the war that parliament was consulted during a crisis. This revealed Cort van der Linden's uncertainty about whether peace could be maintained. Risking war without full political support was unthinkable. It was not an easy moment for Loudon. Quite properly, he was on the hot seat. Loudon reported that an agreement allowing for the transshipment of German army supplies was simply not possible in the context of neutrality. He reported that Gevers thought the situation serious and that the German army was in charge. Under the circumstances, Loudon thought that the sand and gravel issue could be

---

[xxii] His view.
[xxiii] "All-Highest," one of Wilhelm's titles.

conceded. The debate was vigorous, with a few individuals (like former war minister K. Eland) arguing for holding out, as Holland would only have to face a small part of the German army. The vast majority, however, favored negotiations. Supporters ranged from De Savornin Lohman on the right to the social democrat Troelstra, the latter arguing that the army's condition made war at this moment suicidal.[100]

Rosen received immediate information about the top secret parliamentary meeting. He was accurately informed about the tenor of the debate, but erroneously reported that 98 of 100 members present had voted to accept the German demands. No such vote was ever taken. Whether he was misled by his source, or whether he misled his superiors, is impossible to say. However, he had succeeded in getting some of his demands met without an actual ultimatum. The ministers decided on the 26th to allow transit of road materials, but still dragged their feet on army supplies. On the 27th details on the concessions were handed over by Gevers, Loudon having decided that all future transit issues would be handled in Berlin. This was both because of the *échec* he had suffered at home, and his poor relationship with Rosen – who he reproached, albeit in a friendly fashion, about contacting the individual political parties. Rosen did not apologize. He regarded Loudon as not well informed and unenergetic, although he no longer wished to see him forced out. More than anything, Rosen was relieved that war had been avoided.[xxiv] Even the threat, he felt, might drive Holland toward the Entente, and he felt that war would be a detriment for Germany.[101]

The matter had not completely gone Germany's way. Ludendorff therefore again pushed for a threat of force and other measures on the 26th, stating that he could not afford to leave troops near Holland forever (one source reported the movement of an entire army corps to the border). He also suggested more active preparations for war with the Netherlands. On the 27th Wilhelm expressed satisfaction with the actions of his army during the crisis, thereby hinting that he was moving back toward Ludendorff's position. Rosen reminded Loudon of the "serious consequences" if the minimum demands were not met,

---

[xxiv] He was pleased with his work, but not entirely happy with the result. He wrote in his memoirs that what amazed him the most was that the army never did use the sand and gravel. Rosen, *Aus einem diplomatischen wanderleben,* vol. 3/4, p. 162. This has been disputed, most notably by Oldham in *Pill Boxes.*

perhaps anticipating more of the minister's famous delaying tactics. In addition, Rosen was a bit concerned about some of Loudon's comments to parliament, but was assured by Cort van der Linden that the foreign minister was speaking mainly to show the Entente that the problem was inherent in Holland's position.[xxv] [102]

That difficulty was that the Entente nations could legitimately object to the concessions. Gevers tried to avoid this by negotiating (29 April) for exclusions from shipments. The Germans agreed, for example, not to ship food for soldiers through Limburg, so long as fodder for horses could go through. He could not get a blanket promise to omit military supplies, but he found the Germans to be somewhat more flexible than in previous days. Fewer messages were coming from Ludendorff, and Rosen had warned the Foreign Office that Holland was more likely to behave like Serbia or Belgium than Luxembourg if threatened with war. Rosen also was troubled by a point raised by Cort van der Linden; the pressure had not been good for pro-German feelings, although the Minister President still claimed Holland was more likely to get dragged in on Germany's side than against it. Rosen doubted that the demand for military transit was legal and repeatedly condemned the use of military threats and ultimatums. He felt the demands had been made too suddenly – especially as they came two months after Germany had renounced the use of transit routes through Holland. Despite his frequent criticisms of Loudon, he did not blame the minister for pro-Entente feelings in the country.[103] Whether Rosen's advice caused his Foreign Office to become more flexible is difficult to state with certainty, but the record suggests that his advice was valued. On the other hand, it was not the Foreign Office but the military from whence the pressure had come. Fortunately, Ludendorff's interest in Holland waned. His great offensives were impressive but not decisive, and his frontage had grown significantly. On June 3 he did ask that Holland keep Entente personnel away from the Roermond rail line to prevent sabotage, but it was no longer as great an issue to him as it had been in April.[104]

The Entente's actual response to the transit agreement (28 and 29

[xxv] This was of course a peculiar thing for Cort van der Linden to say. The parliamentary meeting was secret. Rosen should not have known what Loudon said, but the Dutchman seemed unperturbed – was he the source of Rosen's information about the meeting? Also, why did Rosen not see anything unusual about the argument that a statement in a *secret* meeting was designed to influence the attitude of foreign states?

April 1918) was tepid. While Townley complained on the 28th about the ending of inspections of transiting materials, he expressed more concern over securing the Schelde from a German invasion. The next day he and the French envoy, H. Allizé, more or less accepted the German declaration that the sand and gravel were not being used for military purposes. Both envoys assured Loudon that they completely understood the Netherlands' difficulty and wanted to avoid a Dutch-German war. They raised no difficulty about the Dutch decision and, in Loudon's opinion, made only *pro forma* objections. Loudon later met Allizé alone and discussed the possibility that Germany might wish to export military materiel. The French envoy assured him he need not worry.[105]

Townley's reasonableness was due to military reality, not a change of heart. If the Entente had taken the hard line that it was entitled to, Holland's neutrality would have been history. Britain could not have sent a single unit to the Netherlands in case of invasion, and hence counseled moderation in responding to German demands. The British thought Ludendorff might try to capture the Schelde basin anyway, and was only looking for an excuse. Loudon also consulted the Americans, asking if it was in US interests for Holland to refuse the demands; Wilson deliberately did not reply, thereby leaving the impression that the USA regarded the sand and gravel transit as a domestic Dutch matter. The Entente governments all decided to accept Holland's decision[xxvi] and merely issue formal objections, in no way encouraging Dutch belligerency.[106] So long as the Germans were gaining ground, the transit of sand and gravel for fortifications was not militarily important.

As the British cause prospered, however, British attitudes changed. Complaints about Germany's use of the Roermond rail line multiplied (and were used by Rosen as an additional argument *not* to pressure Holland further).[107] On or about 17 July, Townley expressed his government's fury on the matter, writing that

My government are of the opinion that further discussion of the

---

[xxvi] The settlement with Germany was based on the 1907 Rhine River treaty. Frey, *Der Erste Weltkrieg,* pp. 274-78. This was, interestingly, the very agreement which Britain had used to justify its blockade of Holland, arguing that that treaty made Rotterdam in part a German port. The NOT and its agreements with Britain were largely justified in terms of this treaty as well.

misinterpretation of the conciliatory and benevolent attitude, which they adopted towards Holland at the critical period of the negotiations with Germany, would have no useful effect. [*In the margin, Loudon wrote:* Indeed!][108]

Loudon's response was conciliatory, a week later conceding that there might have been a "misunderstanding." His envoy in London was blunter. De Marees van Swinderen took Lord Robert Cecil to task about Townley's note. This had no effect, because the message's tone was not Townley's doing. His legation was unhappy about its wording, but instructions were instructions. The issue continued to fester. The British chargé filed complaints about military supplies crossing Limburg as late as October, 1918.[109]

By then westward transit was no longer an issue,[xxvii] as the outcome of the war was no longer in doubt. Holland had escaped with its neutrality more or less intact, although it could hardly be called "strict" after April. Germany had succeeded in getting many of its demands (not all) accepted, for three reasons. Britain accepted the need for Holland to be flexible because the alternative was German capture of a large part of the North Sea coast. Militarily, Holland was not in good shape to resist Germany without foreign assistance. Among many other problems, the army was seriously short of ammunition in April. There was a third factor, however, that explained Holland's flexibility that was not known to Rosen, to Ludendorff, or to Townley. On April 26, the very day that the crisis reached its peak, there had been a major blowup between the war minister and the Supreme Commander, raising serious questions about the latter's fitness to lead.[110] It was the worst possible time to even think about war with the most dangerous neighbor.

The De Jonge – Snijders controversy

The conflict between Snijders and his minister, and ultimately his government, had personal and political origins. Snijders was a difficult to work with, but he had a basis for his views. The general was increasingly pessimistic about Holland's defenses as the war devel-

---

[xxvii] Eastward transit would become an entirely separate issue in November 1918 and during postwar negotiations.

oped, not only because of his own army's problems but the tactical and technological breakthroughs being made elsewhere, with which his force could not keep up. His pessimism in 1918 was seen as outright defeatism by his critics, realism by his defenders. The scale and intensity of the war overwhelmed him:

> What has struck me the most in this war, is the magnitude of its appearance. I do not mean its expanse and the extent of the globe, on which it takes place, but the mass and the stupendous violence . . . the technical perfection of the means of war; the nothing-respecting, ruthless ways of war; the use of everyone and everything, that indirectly or directly can further reaching the military goal; the complete denial of any separate or individual concern in order to gain victory.[111]

He concluded that in a war such as this, "against hundreds of thousands, our field army generates too little respect . . ." The GS III reports crossing his desk gave him every reason to have a darker and darker view of the war. One of these, for example, reported how a 1,300-man unit near Ypres had been trapped between friendly and enemy fire; only twenty escaped. Firepower slaughters could not but dampen the outlook of the general on his ammunition- and artillery short army. He calculated that it would take 5 days just to get his soldiers back from leave, and another two weeks to set up the inundations, and increasingly doubted whether he would get the time.[112]

His pessimism became increasingly obvious as the 1918 spring crises loomed. Some of his concerns were shared by the war minister, Jhr. B.C. de Jonge, despite their later tussle. They agreed that the army's equipment was inadequate – only 10 days' artillery shells on hand, two grenades per soldier, 11,000 steel helmets, and only 5,000 of the newest model gas masks, resistant to the latest poisons. Where they parted company, however, was on the impact of the German spring offensive. De Jonge "did not seem impressed" by the German offensives. Snijders, on the other hand, was impressed – and depressed – by a German offensive which broke through the front and advanced 40 miles, 15 in a single day. A similarly rapid attack in Holland could completely disrupt the defense. The advantage of the defense in World War I was one of the few things that seemed to give Holland an advantage, however small; the Germans now seemed to have overcome this. Snijders knew via the military attaché in London that the British could not possibly help and wanted to pull the army back into the *Vesting* right away (something that was politically impossible). He also knew that the history of Anglo-Dutch military cooperation was anything but smooth and had ended more than once in mutual recriminations. He simply felt that a German invasion was unstoppable (which he publicly revealed ten years after the war) and needless to say, made short work of a field army proposal to take the offensive in case of war. His pessimism led him to exaggerate the number of German soldiers he might have to face.[113] Even so, he can hardly be blamed for doubting the feasibility of his posture – and the government's. He accepted its policy of neutrality; he believed, however, that its government's instructions were unclear and unrealistic, and made his job impossible.

The government and the general had been drifting apart conceptually for most of the war. The cabinet felt that Snijders suffered from "a certain confusion of thought" regarding neutrality. "The government nevertheless did not help the general out of his dream, probably because it had nothing to gain by doing so." This was also one of the few issues regarding which the Queen agreed with the cabinet instead of the general. A few ministers were not keen on letting the allegedly *deutschfreundlich* Snijders negotiate. The conflict developed because the government saw the army as a tool to keep the country neutral, while Snijders was also responsible for defending the country if neutrality failed. How could he be expected to wage war, when he could not prepare to wage war? On 30 January 1917 he pointed out that the existing neutrality policy could deprive the Netherlands of freedom of choice regarding which side it would be on. Snijders focused Cort van der Linden's attention on views of the Swiss supreme commander, Wille, who had stated that Switzerland would fight alongside the enemies of whomever invaded Switzerland. While Snijders felt such comments should have come from the government, not the general, he approved of the sentiment. On the other hand, he went on, if one side plans an invasion and the other, discovering that, invades preemptively, the choice of sides remains an accident, a function of whose army travels to the border the fastest. To stress the urgency of the situation, he wrote the Minister President again on February 5, 1917, reporting increased numbers of German infantrymen, artillerymen, and – perhaps most ominously – bridge builders.[114]

Cort van der Linden's response was interesting; it was not a response at all. Instead, he asked the general to review a number of scenarios developed by Bosboom, perhaps a hint that, notwithstanding the instructions fiasco of 1914, the government preferred for Snijders to work with his minister. (It was also a means of avoiding Snijders' questions.) Bosboom believed that Britain was unlikely to invade because it could just as easily pressure Holland via its colonies and was not likely to attack across the North Sea given the insecurity from submarines. Germany, he thought, had little motive to invade, because Holland constituted an avenue for trade and a protector of the German right flank. He conceded that Germany would attack if it thought that Holland was about to join the Entente, if the "naval" party gained the upper hand, if Dutch ports became vital for submarine warfare, or Germany starved and needed every bit of food it could get. Presciently, the minister also worried about a possible German withdrawal across Dutch territory. He did endorse Snijders' request for the power to mobilize in case of a sudden invasion.[xxviii] [115]

Snijders considered Bosboom's approach "a too great nonsense" and saw no way to attach strategic ideas to the various cases. He expressed his disappointment and, while conceding that it was not possible for the government to deal with every case in advance, stated his desire for general instructions if war broke out. He pointed out that "protecting neutrality" talk overlooked the fact that once one fights to protect neutrality, one is at war. Resisting both sides was simply not an option, an argument he underwrote by summarizing his material and geographic problems. He did not get what he wanted. Instead he received a memorandum from Bosboom on February 17th assuring Snijders that the government was carefully following political developments but did not consider the current danger great. Oddly enough, some of Snijders' arguments were repeated the following day by Kühlmann to Gevers. The German argued that it might be better to discuss military arrangements in advance. When Gevers declined, Kühlmann argued that it was irresponsible to let everything depend on "chance."[116]

The whole affair had left the government discombobulated. Snijders was angry at the cabinet, the cabinet was unhappy with Snijders, and no one was pleased with Bosboom. The war minister's three years of wartime survival was remarkable, given his tenuous relationship with the army on one side and parliament on the other. He was helped by parliamentary support for the army which, to the great disgust of pacifists, was surprisingly solid. Now, however, his position was rapidly becoming unstable. Feeling a need to reassert himself and

---

[xxviii] A power the general had actually held since 29 May 1915.

clarify the situation, he wrote a memorandum for his colleagues detailing Snijders' view and its obvious weakness – choosing sides and having secret conversations was, in essence, an abandonment of neutrality. Bosboom pointed out that the Netherlands did not have political and economic interests similar to either warring party to the degree necessary to justify choosing a side. Bosboom described choosing the most likely winner as unworthy and unlikely to produce a diplomatic advantage; besides, Holland might make the wrong choice.[xxix] Unlike his general, Bosboom did think neutrality could be maintained even after an invasion. Perhaps an ally would have to be chosen then – but only then. Snijders' proposals for a more central deployment he criticized on more technical grounds. His conclusion was that the instructions desired by Snijders simply could not be given.[117]

Snijders did not totally give up on his quest for clarification, but he knew it was an uphill battle. He even wrote Loudon, the apostle of strict neutrality, pointing to the danger of a German invasion in response to, or in anticipation of, a British invasion. He argued that this raised the risk of simultaneous invasion and that academic neutrality would have to be dropped at that point. He wrote elsewhere that the government now understood that he would not fight both belligerents. Actually, this was incorrect; the government had no such understanding.[118]

The general's problems were compounded by a change at the war ministry. A majority of Bosboom's cabinet colleagues had long felt that he was simply not up to controlling Snijders. The minister was not seen as a strong figure, inside or outside his department. In addition, he fell afoul of parliament over the timing of certain draft callups. There were also questions raised about the weakness of the army, especially now that the threat of war was so much greater than in 1914-1916. Younger officers complained, in the words of a German agent, about *"die fossilen Generäle im Haag"* (the fossilized generals in The Hague). Material shortages continued to be an issue. All these things came together to sink Bosboom, who would probably have gone down sooner if a major crisis had occurred earlier. His fall on May 15, 1917,

---

[xxix] Bosboom argued that Belgium could have retreated to Antwerp to maintain its neutrality even after the invasion; more realistically, he predicted that Belgium would get next to nothing at the peace table.

created absolutely no excitement; even De Beaufort did not mention it in his diary.[xxx] [119] Bosboom was gone.

After a brief acting ministry under Rambonnet, the department was taken over June 15, 1917 by Jhr. B.C. de Jonge. He was an unusual choice. He was a civil servant in the war department, and would be the first true civilian war minister – he had never served. De Jonge began his career at the colonial ministry and moved in 1910 into a top job at the war department when another candidate declined. He had no particular wish to make the move, finding his new department "stuffy, narrow-minded, bureaucratic." He attributed this primarily to the desire of civil servants "to be on good terms with the military gentlemen." He was not too happy with Bosboom's appointment, since at first the new minister only consulted soldiers.[xxxi] De Jonge accepted the ministry with some hesitation, only after a Major E.F. Insinger, whom he regarded highly, agreed to assist him. His obligatory meeting with the Queen was a harbinger of things to come, as the redoubtable monarch warned him not to interfere with military matters (!). Evaluations of De Jonge vary. Heldring reported that Treub thought highly of De Jonge, but Heldring – never one to let a compliment go unchallenged – noted that Treub was known to have terrible judgment of people. A friend of Heldring's described De Jonge as narrow-minded and lazy. Judging from his stellar career, De Jonge was neither. Despite a difficult ministry, he did enjoy it occasionally. At one point, the agriculture minister wanted access to military food supplies in Amsterdam, and when De Jonge refused, threatened to send his inspectors to break open he stores. De Jonge answered, "[d]o you think that this [threat] makes a great impression on a Minister who has more than 400,000 men under

---

[xxx] Snijders was not much concerned either. I have found no references by Snijders to Bosboom's fall.

[xxxi] Obviously, De Jonge had a jaundiced view of the professional soldiers as a group. But even he seems to have become somewhat "militarized" during the war. At one point early in the war, he sought NCO rank for a subordinate who, mobilized as a private soldier, inconveniently always had to be last entering or leaving a room. The army refused, declaring that "you don't become a sergeant just like that." De Jonge then successfully pursued a commission for the young man. Yet he concludes the tale as follows: "De Brauw himself nevertheless caused me a great disappointment. A few days after his promotion I left the department in his company. When our paths diverged, he took *horribile dictu* – his *képi* off as if it were a hat! The Department was right after all: you don't just become a sergeant, let alone an officer." Van der Wal, *Herinneringen*, pp. 22-23.

arms?"[120]

No such wit and repartee characterized his relationship with Snijders. Their first meeting was tense and formal. De Jonge approached his meeting with the "dour soldier" nervously, but felt it went well. Things began to deteriorate soon after, however. Snijders felt some of De Jonge's actions were an indication of mistrust, and a bitter argument developed in July 1917 over the stationing of troops in Amsterdam. De Jonge opened contacts with the British military attaché, Col. Oppenheim, to get heavy weaponry, and was also involved in Captain J.C. Tonnet's contacts with the British general staff in 1918. Snijders found all this out when Tonnet reported to him. He was not used to an independently-acting war minister and their relationship declined accordingly.[121] When Holland moved toward crisis in March and April of 1918, De Jonge's – and the government's – faith in the general began to wobble, especially because of his extreme pessimism. On March 18th, Snijders told the cabinet that the country was practically defenseless against a British invasion, as well as against any German operations aimed at preventing it. He recommended stopping leaves and contemplated recommending a second mobilization. On Monday, April 22, his report to the cabinet was "little reassuring" – something the politicians attributed to the general's "sad family circumstances."[xxxii] [122]

On Friday the 26th, De Jonge met with Snijders, Major Insinger, and Capt. Röell, to find out what Holland could do if Germany attacked. Snijders was beyond his ordinary pessimism. He talked about how help would come too late, how his equipment was "old junk," and detailed his specific lackings in materiel. None of that was new, but Snijders then told De Jonge and the two officers that "all resistance from our side would be *doelloos* (pointless, purposeless)." Later in the conversation he described resistance as "fruitless" and concluded that the country would be destroyed. The second mobilization would only slow down the inevitable a few days.[123]

De Jonge and the two officers listened in disbelief. What then had the four costly years of mobilization and preparations been for? Snijders' explanation that it was for the "moral effect [which] to this point has spared us the war" did not satisfy them. Snijders did give

---

[xxxii] Mrs. Snijders had died April 14. Bonebakker, *Twee verdienstelijke officieren*, pp. 57-58.

specific reasons why he had so little hope. He was particularly concerned with the devastating effects of enemy artillery. He expected the Germans to attack Zwolle, cutting off the north. The forces along the Yssel and the whole Divisiongroup Brabant would have to withdraw. Units in Zeeland would be open to attack from three directions. The forces to defend the *waterlinie* were too few, the rivers were low, and Amsterdam could be shelled from beyond the *waterlinie*. The general recommended, finally, that the country would do better to join Germany, as he was in a better position to stop a British invasion.[124]

This was exactly what De Jonge feared; that his commander's pessimism, communicated to the government, would lead to the abandonment of neutrality. He and the two officers conferred after Snijders left and decided that the general would have to go. De Jonge was not yet ready to suggest that to the rest of the cabinet, however. He reported the conversation to Cort van der Linden late in the evening, but made no recommendations and left out the *"doelloos"* comment.[125] He decided that he needed to confer immediately with other senior officers, partly to see if they all shared Snijders' vision, partly to select a replacement for Snijders. He also had the two other officers present at the meeting with Snijders study the situation. What they learned was revealing, if not conclusive.

The four officers who he consulted were Lt.-Gen. W.F. Pop, the chief of staff at headquarters, Maj.-Generals J. Burger, the deputy chief, and W.H. van Terwisga, commander of the Field Army, and Col. D.G. van der Voort Maarschalk, commandant of Fortress Holland. Of the four, only Pop fully shared Snijders' views, while Burger was the most optimistic. Terwisga's declared willingness to die for Queen and country struck De Jonge as more diverting than impressive: "In difficult circumstances we have little use for dead generals." The succession question was complicated. Van Terwisga and Pop he he decided he could not recommend. Van Terwisga was expected to leave if Burger were promoted to the top job. Pop would have to be shuffled off to the Field Army, which he might not accept, although Dufour was a possible alternative. A Maj.-Gen. Van de Hoog was considered for the job but this would bypass several other officers. So replacing the chief would be difficult.[126]

Pop was not the likely choice because his thinking paralleled Snijders.' He thought resistance would be brief if the Allies could not help. He estimated that Germany would send an attacking force of 16 divisions, numerically twice the size of the defense. In contrast, Burger thought the army could hold out a reasonable time, provided some organizational improvements were made. The differences in opinion resulted from different assessments regarding the size of the opposition. Burger did not see how Germany could send very much to invade Holland, given commitments in France. He did worry that Germany might want to snatch Vlissingen. Col. Van der Voort Maarschalk conceded that the forts could not resist a Liège-style bombardment, but felt that if the inundations worked, it would take Germany 6 weeks to prepare for such an attack. He did ask for more money to improve fortifications and, like Snijders, felt the troops too few to defend the inundations if the Germans sent a very large invasion force. Significantly, he reported that it would take 14 days to fill the inundations and garrison them completely. De Jonge also spoke with one of Van der Voort Maarschalk's subordinates, the commandant at Naarden, whose only major concern was that a withdrawal to Amsterdam would be difficult.[127]

De Jonge's most useful conversation was with Van Terwisga on May 8. The Field Army would have to slow down an invasion until the fortifications were ready. Its commander thought a German attack unlikely unless it assisted Germany's main effort. His main concern was to protect areas that the Entente would need to come in and oppose the Germans. Most personnel on leave would be back on duty in a single day. The numerous new reserve battalions had relieved the Field Army of many of its duties. The Field Army would be driven back into the *Vesting Holland* if Germany invaded with 400,000 men, but Van Terwisga, like Burger, just did not believe Germany could spare that many troops. Van Terwisga was mainly worried that it was difficult to launch counterattacks out of the fortified area. He concluded by recommending to De Jonge that the 1st Division be shipped southward, and that if Germany massed anywhere near a half million soldiers, the army be withdrawn immediately.[128]

By then De Jonge had reports from Röell and Insinger, both of which disputed some of Snijders' assertions. Röell pointed out that all combatants were using older artillery, not just the Dutch, and that much could be achieved by concentrating artillery at the weakest points in the fortifications. He did share the Pop/Snijders vision of a 15/20 division attack, noting Hindenburg's refusal to attack until he had the number of troops he wanted. The Field Army should be able, Röell thought, to cover the "second mobilization." Insinger agreed with Burger that

Germany could not afford to send a large force right now. He did not think an effective invasion could be mounted with less than 250-300,000 soldiers, including support troops. Insinger did worry about surprise attack, but concluded that defense for a reasonable time was possible if the troops were concentrated in the *Vesting*. He recommended abandoning Zeeland, pointing out that denying the Schelde to the Germans was primarily a British concern. More optimistic than the other officers, Insinger thought a resistance of months was possible.[129]

De Jonge was now ready to approach his fellow ministers. Having secured Burger's agreement to become Supreme Commander, De Jonge wrote the cabinet on 8 May 1918 that the general would have to go. He conceded that Snijders had great personal qualities, prestige in the army, and ability, but that he had lost faith in his assignment. De Jonge no longer trusted Snijders, the minister wrote, because the general had worked for 4 years for readiness, which he now claimed was irrelevant. De Jonge added that the real goal was to hold out long enough to get equipment from the Entente, more likely now that no more guns were going to Russia. The army was in better shape than in 1914, and the combatant states were nearing exhaustion. He agreed with Snijders' contention on problems of equipment, organization, etc. He reviewed the views of the other senior officers, including agreements as well as disagreements with Snijders, but concluded that either he or Snijders had to resign. De Jonge saw his position in parliament as impossible and added that he could not serve with a Supreme Commander who saw things as "pointless" and suggested that Snijders either "had lost his faith in his assignment or never had it." In a final shot at the general, he wrote a month later that "[n]ever should he have spoken as he did in the well-known April week," and if Snijders were right,

> Then it is the self-interest of the belligerents, diplomacy or dumb luck, that has kept us out of the war, and our exertions have indeed been *doelloos* (pointless).[130]

De Jonge's arguments impressed a cabinet long wearied of the general. The entire cabinet supported the minister, deciding on May 13 that either Snijders went, or the whole cabinet would resign. With one large exception: Cort van der Linden did not take a position. This allowed him to inform the Queen, known to be friendly toward the general, on the 14th, while functioning as an intermediary. The response was telling about the position of the monarchy in Holland. The Queen wanted to keep Snijders, and when informed about the cabinet's threat to resign *en masse,* answered that "one should not delay traveling gentlemen" and sent back no message for De Jonge. On the 16th he went to Wilhelmina, at the Minister President's suggestion. When Wilhelmina tried to explain the meaning of Snijders' *doelloos* comment, the minister answered "that there was one language that he understood particularly well, and that that was Dutch, as a result of which he did not require any explanation of the word *doelloos,* not even from Her Majesty." The meeting ended on a somewhat frosty note.[131]

The short-term resolution of the crisis, which De Jonge attributed to Cort van der Linden's "wisdom and tact," had a comical aspect. Snijders offered his resignation to Cort van der Linden. The latter took the resignation to the Queen, who refused it. The Queen then asked Cort van der Linden to countersign the refusal. The Minister President pointed out that De Jonge would have to cosign the document, but the Queen refused. Instead, she decided to write Snijders herself and tell him that he had Crown support. Cort van der Linden went along with this essentially unconstitutional resolution. The cabinet might have been tempted to press the issue, but elections were just around the corner (3 July) and could only ask the Queen to inform the new cabinet leader of the situation.[132] De Jonge, as will be seen momentarily, decided to do a little more.

Snijders did not remain mute. On May 29th, he submitted a lengthy memorandum to the ministers, justifying his position and explaining his use of the word *doelloos.*

> If the government desires from the Supreme Commander a rosy conception and optimistic projections, that misrepresent the actual situation, then it will have to look around for a successor. And then I can only passionately hope, that the bitter truth will never enter to do justice to my warning voice.[133]

Snijders repeated some of his earlier arguments. The army could not offer "lasting resistance" or "resistance for a long time." The country would be occupied quickly, and regions where resistance occurred would be devastated. He admitted use of the word "doelloos," but explained he meant it in the sense of "fruitless" (i.e. not intending to say that resistance had no purpose whatsoever). He denied that he intended to warn to government against war with Germany under any circumstances. Instead, "doelloos" referred to the fact that sooner or later Holland would lose: "In no case can I have intended to call the institution of our national defense *'doelloos'*."

> I must reject the supposition that I, as a serious and honest man, would
> give my name and the full devotion of my person to a cause, of which I
> myself would declare that it is *"doelloos."*[134]

He had told De Jonge that mobilization had kept Holland out of the war
for nearly 4 years, reminding his readers that "[t]he goal of the military
of a small nation is in contemporary times primarily preventive." But
he felt that the government could not ignore the "highly unfavorable
outlook" in case of war with Germany, as opposed to the "less
unfavorable ratio" in case of war with the Entente. He reiterated his
fear that the Entente could not help, reminding the government of the
fates of Serbia, Montenegro, Belgium, and Romania. The army could
not stop a German invasion force that Snijders estimated at 20-25
divisions, let alone long enough to allow the inundations to fill. Nor did
he hold out much hope for resistance in the fortified zone. A German
attack would be a strategic error, but would nevertheless "end in our
destruction." An Entente invasion would be equally unfortunate, but
less serious, because it would involve a sea landing, could be threatened by submarines, and Germany could easily send assistance.[135]

Turning to the opinions of the other officers, he complained that he
had not seen Röell's and Insinger's reports, and that only he and Pop
had the whole picture. Van Terwisga's plans he called "lighthearted,"
reckless and unjustifiable. He cited the opinion of the Dutch attaché in
Berlin, Col. Muller Massis, who predicted devastation because
Germany's strategy would be to annihilate the new opponent in the
shortest time possible, even if this meant withdrawing troops from the
Western Front. Muller Massis thought that Holland would be "pulverized" and reported that although the German troops were no longer of
the same quality as in 1914, "according to what I hear about Dutch
troops from time to time" the same was true in the Dutch army.
Snijders conceded that he had taken the job in 1914 knowing that the
country would be "crushed" and had spent four years trying to make
improvements." There had been some, but "[t]here is not the least
foundation for overestimating our strength and our resistance ability
against the attack of a great power."[136]

Snijders' arguments were logical, but contained some strange
features. He proposed immediate withdrawal to the fortified lines, even
though they could not be held. This contradicted Dutch military
thought since 1881, and more interestingly, contradicted his own

previous writings. He gave no indication of how Germany would mass the numerical superiority he anticipated.[137] His estimate of 20-25 divisions had no particular foundation, and ran counter to his previous views, when he repeatedly minimized the German military threat, carefully noting the relatively small German presence on the Dutch borders. Finally, he was asking the government to abandon its neutrality on the basis of a purely military calculation, i.e. joining the stronger opponent. Bosboom had always strenuously opposed such a strategy, which he thought would look like opportunism to the belligerents, and would lead to no gains at the peace table (but no doubt resentment from the other side).

The cabinet was concerned, as shown by its support of De Jonge during this crisis. It is remarkable that the minister and the general survived in office. De Jonge's support in cabinet was very strong, however. At least seven ministers would have left with him, precipitating a political crisis and bringing the whole matter out into the open. As far as Snijders' future went, the cabinet ministers agreed that they had lost confidence in him to varying degrees, but would not ask for his resignation because the elections were around the corner. They did decide to let the incoming government know how they felt.[138]

De Jonge, who had the most at stake, went into the most detail. He prepared a detailed memorandum for his successor, alleging Snijders' shortcomings. Noting that the Minister of War had to depend on the Supreme Commander, he accused Snijders of failing to have informed him before the April crisis of his views. Hence, De Jonge continued, his own position had become untenable. He also did not accept many of Snijders' views. He raised seven specific concerns, all directly or by implication critical of Snijders' conduct:

> Insufficient attention to improving the quality of defenses,
> failing to prepare a second line of defenses for the eastern fortifications,
> failure to establish a central bureau to coordinate the inundations,
> a need for more cooperation for road improvements,
> failure to bring battalions outside field army into higher formations,
> a lack of instructions for the attaché in London in case of war with Germany,[xxxiii] and

---

[xxxiii] He conceded that those contacts had now been made, but only because he had insisted to Snijders that this now be done. Snijders, of course, quite properly refused to have any meaningful conversations with foreign armies unless it was authorized by

refusal to consider changing army deployment to bring it more in tune with defense needs and worry less about deployments purely relating to the international position (i. e. Zeeland and Brabant).

This last problem, De Jonge argued, meant that the government could not reduce mobilization costs (as strength could not be cut until deployment was changed) so long as Snijders was the Supreme Commander. This was a clever argument, because many politicians in The Hague were irritated by the army's insistence on huge numbers and the general staff's refusal to consider demobilization. De Jonge once again argued that Snijders would have to go:

> My conclusion is, that no matter how highly we may esteem the person of general Snijders, how many good, yes even exceptional characteristic he may possess, how unquestionably it may be that he will do his duty and more when once it finally comes to fighting, his leadership under the exceptional circumstances of these 4 years has not been the most desired for our country, at least is not any more at this moment.[139]

When the new government came into office, the general took the opportunity to wax eloquent about the proper relationship between commander and minister. He had refused a position subordinate to a single minister in 1914 because national defense was too important to be left to a single minister, and the Supreme Commander had to have independence. This was necessary for him to discharge his legal responsibilities to the government, but also his moral responsibility to the whole nation. The unexpectedly long peace, he admitted, required some limitation on his powers and activities, but did not justify reducing him to a bureaucrat of a particular department. He had to have full ability to correspond with other ministries.[xxxiv] His basic position; if you trust me, give me freedom of action; if you do not, I must resign.[140]

If this memorandum seems peculiarly unresponsive to De Jonge's complaints, there was a simple reason; Snijders did not know about them. De Jonge had not bothered to send the general a copy. The new minister promptly forwarded it, however. Snijders went ballistic,

---

the government. He also could have questioned the minister's authority to instruct him in this area, but did not do so – an unusual omission for him which I find revealing concerning his state of mind and health at the time.

[xxxiv] Snijders was undoubtedly right about this. For one thing, he controlled the navy, which had its own cabinet department.

drafting a twenty-page memorandum to the cabinet, complete with documentary references. The general expressed his "deep indignation" about what De Jonge had done, that going behind his back was unacceptable behavior "among gentlemen," and called it "a stab in the back" and an "ignoble action." Concerning his pessimistic advice, he argued that had he withheld it and war had broken out, he might have been accused of concealing vital information from the government. He challenged De Jonge's ability, referring to the ex-minister's "lack of military knowledge and professional insight." He made short work of De Jonge's argument about never having been informed about the situation, writing that only ignorance of military matters could have led De Jonge to think war with Germany would have a favorable outcome.[141]

Concerning De Jonge's specific allegations, Snijders accused him of misstatements and misrepresentations of fact. He responded to each of De Jonge's seven points:

Snijders cited extensive documents to show his work for improving defenses, in particular fortifications.

A second eastern defense line was being studied but had not been begun because of personnel shortages, and the Minister neither favored building defensive lines everywhere nor demanded faster work on this one.

The proposal for a central inundation bureau, although not necessary for the inundations to take place, had in fact been proposed by Snijders himself; the proposal was delayed because the war minister took 15 months to respond.

Road improvements were another proposal first made by Snijders, but extensive discussions had taken place to determine who exactly was responsible for this work, and that had slowed the process down.

Snijders had placed some battalions into larger formations, and had recommended more such steps, but the Minister never responded to a Snijders letter of 13 December 1917 recommending reorganization.

The attaché in London had no instructions because the government forbade advance negotiations with foreign powers. In any event, such planning would require a British officer to come and talk with Snijders – it was not a matter to leave to an attaché.

Snijders had never heard the Minister complain about deployment. As instructions specifically required him to oppose each violation with force, the army had to be deployed the way it was. Withdrawal of the big concentration in Brabant, for example, would mean the frontier could not be defended. The Minister's views, Snijders decided, were not his own,

but from "unknown to me, irresponsible advisors, whose competence I
. . . question." As for paying more attention to defense and less the
international situation, Snijders called that "a political-military heresy."

Snijders concluded that De Jonge was prejudiced toward him as well
the other professional soldiers, and sought support "among lesser
lights, who behind the scenes, not burdened by any responsibility, can
let their critical spirit have free reign, although they are not sufficiently
informed, to comprehend the great questions in their entirety."[142]

What can we conclude about the Supreme Commander from this
memorandum? Undoubtedly Snijders was right about some of the
criticisms, and had the documents to back up his position. On the point
regarding instructions for the attaché in London, he overlooks or avoids
the fact that De Jonge criticized the absence of instruction *in case of
war*: Snijders treats it as in issue of *negotiations in advance of war*,
which it was not. But that Snijders devoted so much time, effort and
fury to refuting De Jonge's allegations indicates an emotional state
suggesting exhaustion, at the very least. Some of his contemporaries
were critical. Heldring, who was always critical, wrote years later that:

> Fortunately the cloud drifted past and we muddled through to the end
> with our army and its commander, without getting in the war.[143]

Even the naval minister, in many respects friendly toward the general,
complained that Snijders had "undermined the ground for a firm
position by the government." A 1974 study concluded that "Snijders
must suffered a . . . breakdown in those months" (April and after).[144]
Most modern commentary has been sympathetic toward Snijders.

> That Snijders after four years of mobilization was realistic enough to tell
> his government that a German army could wipe out the Dutch forces in
> a very short time should have been appreciated by the government, which
> instead tried to label the man a defeatist. Snijders had attempted to row
> with the oars he had.[145]

Fortunately, as Heldring wrote, the affair did not affect the country's
ultimate fate. Both of the major participants would be affected for
many years, however. Snijders' sudden departure in November was
hastened by the new government having a somewhat jaundiced view of
him from the beginning. The affair would remain one of the best
remembered aspects of his forty years of service. De Jonge would be
the only member of his cabinet who did not receive a decoration for his
wartime service, reflecting the Queen's anger. De Jonge wrote in his

diary that this was all to the good, because otherwise he and the general would have gotten one at the same time, which he did not see as a good thing. De Jonge, a capable, incisive and not very pleasant man, went on to a successful career in business and in 1931 was appointed to the most prestigious post there was, outside of Minister President – Governor General of the Indies. But before he got the job, he was quizzed extensively about his role in the conflict with General Snijders.[146] Given that a large part of the problem lay in the difficult structural relationship between commander and minister, it is all the more remarkable that that was not resolved in time for World War II.

A new government

There was little chance that the issue would be resolved quickly. The military situation was becoming very fluid as the German armies began their withdrawal and the battlefront once again approached Dutch borders. Invasion from Germany now seemed liked a much remoter possibility. The army had received new weapons from Britain and reported far greater readiness to oppose Germany anyway.[147] In addition, the political establishment was busy with the complex politics of establishing the first Roman Catholic government since Spain had been expelled in the seventeenth century.

Wartime is not an ideal moment for a complete change of government, even for a neutral state. The July 1918 elections left no choice, however. The liberals, who had dominated Cort van der Linden's extra-parliamentary cabinet, suffered a huge loss, going from 24 seats (of 100) to 15. All but one of the other parties gained seats, but the big winners were Troelstra's SDAP and the Catholic RKSP. Troelstra was not going to become minister president, although the Queen did have a *pro forma* meeting with him. The RKSP's leaders had not indicated much interest in forming a government, but the election outcome left little alternative. With 30 seats, the Catholic party was twice as large as either of the other parties that might have tried to form a government.[148]

So the organization of a new government should have taken little time, provided the Protestant parties were willing to join an RKSP government. Instead, it took forever, mainly because of the machinations of the Palace. The process of forming a goverment could not begin until the Queen acted. Wilhelmina, however, waited until 8 weeks after the election to act. Under the constitution she was required to name a *formateur*.[xxxv] Superficially her delay was attributable to the difficulty of finding the right candidate. Monsignor Nolens, head of the RKSP, could not put together a coalition and began to suspect that the Queen did not really want him to succeed. Wilhelmina instead suggested the mayor of The Hague, H.A. van Karnebeek, who was considered universally unsuitable. The ARP's Colijn hedged, mainly for financial reasons (he was doing well in business and entering government would have been a costly move). Kuyper, the founder and still patron saint of the ARP, fought the appointment of a priest to the minister presidency. The Queen then agreed to appoint Jhr. Nispen tot Sevenaar, a Catholic nobleman then envoy to the Holy See. After some difficult political maneuvers, however, Nispen tot Sevenaar decided that he had health problems. None of this sounds like the Queen's fault, but she was criticized for her failure to consult advisors about how to handle the situation.[149] Whether the slowdown was due to the Palace or the usual partisan bickering, the result was that for two months amidst the war Holland limped along with a caretaker government.

Finally, on September 9th, the Netherlands had a new government. The RKSP did take the helm, in the person of Jhr. Ch.J.M. Ruys de Beerenbrouck, a Catholic aristocrat.[xxxvi] His coalition contained the three major religious parties – the RKSP, the ARP, and the Christian Historical Union (CHU). For the two Protestant parties this represented a major step. In 1891, Kuyper, had rejected working with the Catholic party, because "of the blood of the martyrs . . . and that clever grey headed man in Rome who pretends to be the representative of Christ on earth." When he became Minister President in 1901, however, Kuyper had accepted 3 Catholic ministers in his cabinet. Perhaps this explains why his 1918 he would grouse that "above the roof of this cabinet flies the Papal pennant" did not stop the Protestant parties from joining the government.[150]

A better explanation is that religious differences were hardly the main issues in September 1918. The political establishment was in the

---

[xxxv] The *formateur* is normally a party leader who, if successful in establishing an arrangement between several parties, usually becomes Minister President.

[xxxvi] Ruys de Beerenbrouck later campaigned on the slogan, "a nobleman, working for the people." This led a Social Democrat in Amsterdam to run under the slogan, "not a nobleman, but still working for the people."

midst of crisis, especially because the leadership found it had to deal with two war-related matters, the relationship with the army and the relationship with the belligerents. The new war minister, G.A.A. Alting von Geusau, was a former officer with wide familiarity with the military establishment. He found in his office yet another memorandum by De Jonge, this one the normal transition document that an outgoing minister is expected to prepare. De Jonge discussed a possible successor for Snijders, noting that he had talked to the general himself about this. He noted the difficulties resulting from the verbal instructions placing the Supreme Commander under the cabinet, not the war ministers.[xxxvii] De Jonge complained that serious reorganization of the army was not possible so long as Snijders stayed.[151] Alting von Geusau shared De Jonge's views about the military-ministry relationship and believed that the general should report to the military ministers. On 24 October 1918 he eliminated the position of *hoofdofficier,* a person who was under the control of both general and minister and functioned as liaison; the existence of this office suggested an equality between the two positions. In hindsight, this looks like a first step toward easing Snijders out.[152]

Relationships with the belligerents were far more important. Germany was ceasing to be a threat, but the increasingly victorious Allies were potentially a greater problem now. There was even a fear the Entente might use Limburg as a passage. That did not happen, but the government had plenty of problems with the Entente, for two reasons. First, the government as a whole was viewed as pro-German. In a message the week after the election, Townley had identified three political parties as friendly to enemy – the RKSP, the ARP, and the CHU. Two months later, those three formed the government. The government did little to reassure the Entente. Besides giving permission for German troops to withdraw via Limburg (discussed below), there was also a low-level contact with Germany regarding a partial Dutch demobilization.[153]

The second reason for problems with the Entente lay in the choice of foreign minister. Loudon allegedly intrigued to remain at the Foreign Office.[154] His staying might have made some sense, both to provide continuity, and as he was viewed as pro-Entente. The Entente,

---

[xxxvii] De Jonge did not find out until 1926 about the changes made to the instruction on the eve of war.

after all, was clearly on the verge of victory. On the other hand, the British representatives in The Hague did not much like him. Townley, the reader will recall, considered him a liar. Oppenheimer, who thought Loudon was actually happy to leave ("[he is] said to be tired, nervous and anxious to retire") regarded Loudon "the least desirable from an Allied point of view." "Loudon had lost the confidence of the commercial world." He claimed Loudon was responsible for NOT "infringements," had favored the sending of the convoy to the Indies (not true), had cost Britain lives because of his handling of the sand and gravel matter, and had failed to interest himself in negotiations then going on in London.

> While the general public was grateful to Mr. Loudon for having kept Holland out of the war, the Press gave him a bad exit. He had pursued an opportunist policy, had lived from hand to mouth, and was leaving behind an inheritance of trouble as the result of having too readily listened to German demands.[155]

Loudon had the last laugh. At the urging of Van Aalst, Oppenheimer wrote a strong letter to Loudon detailing all his grievances. While Loudon was most conciliatory when he received a copy of the letter, it was apparently brought to the attention of the British Foreign Office, where Sir F.O. was not popular. Oppenheimer was fired.[156] Loudon was well-regarded by the French – envoy Allizé stated that he had had no problems during Loudon's tenure – and he also had experience with the United States. Yet there was no real chance that the new government would ask him to stay on. Instead, Ruys called city hall and asked Van Karnebeek to take the job.[157]

It was a peculiar choice, although Van Karnebeek was talented. Heldring regarded him in as more intelligent and better informed than the outgoing Loudon, and named him as the strongest minister in the new cabinet. That was written, however, very early in Van Karnebeek's tenure; Heldring's opinion would soon change. Two things seem odd. First, Van Karnebeek was not a diplomat. This did not bother a businessman like Heldring, who had a low opinion of his country's diplomats. The most likely envoys were not available. Gevers was not possible, because of his long service in Germany; De Stuers in Paris was too old; the Washington legation had been kept vacant by Wilhelmina; and the most likely possibility, De Marees van Swinderen, did not want to be considered. And Van Karnebeek did have personal experience dealing with diplomats.[158]

A greater oddity is that the government would choose an allegedly pro-German foreign minister on the eve of the Entente victory. The argument that there was no alternative seems inadequate. This was especially true because, as Oppenheimer joked, while Loudon's job had been to keep Holland out of the war, Van Karnebeek (whose name Oppenheimer consistently misspells) was supposed to prevent Holland's exclusion from the peace. How could he do this if the Entente mistrusted him from the beginning? Inevitably, he had a rocky start. His attempt to bring the peace conference to The Hague failed. His proposal to have a general UK-Holland economic agreement negotiated in The Hague was rejected, as London insisted on London. Friction quickly developed between him and all the foreign envoys, less due to his leanings than his personality. Van Karnebeek was stiff, pompous and authoritarian. When Rosen, an admirer of Wilhelmina, referred to her as *"Frau und Königin,"* Van Karnebeek immediately responded; *"sie ist nur Königin."* Allizé went so far as to complain to the new Minister President, who agreed that the foreign minister "relates in a much to stiff and weighty manner with the envoys."[xxxviii] By Christmas, Heldring had decided that Van Karnebeek should be dumped. Van Karnebeek would redeem himself with a brilliant performance at Versailles. In the short run, however, he was not a happy choice.[159]

Revolution!

The greatest crisis in the war's closing days, however, did not come from abroad. It came at home in the form of an army mutiny that threatened to blossom into a revolution. The roots of the mutiny lay mostly in the unpopularity of military service, heightened by four years of boredom. De Jonge focused on this problem in 1917, referring to "a mobilized army, that had had enough."

> Initially people tolerated much, but when the mobilisation dragged on, people become less tolerant. . . [m]ilitary leadership was not always exercised with tact and modesty; . . . If there had been fighting, people

---

[xxxviii] We can only speculate why Van Karnebeek was so pompous. One thing that might have affected his personality is the lifelong teasing he endured because of his part-Indonesian background. His nickname in The Hague was, "the negro." Fasseur, *Wilhelmina*, p. 534.

would have accepted everything, but housing an army of nearly 400,000
men for years in temporary quarters while in a posture of anticipation,
naturally gave rise to all sorts of problems.[160]

The unpopularity of service was universal and weakened the army.
Postwar novels and articles ridiculed the army and military service.
The Dutch "cursed their bad lack when drafted," demonstrated "no
national pride" and the soldiers, especially in peacetime, showed at
best a "surly obedience." The public blamed these conditions on the
officers. A whole fort (Spijkerboor, near Amsterdam) was set aside for
those refusing to serve. Troops were considered unreliable for quelling
civilian riots. "A critical attitude and incessant complaining *(kankeren)*
were very much part of the national heritage but never employed as
freely as when talking about the army." "There was no military
tradition to speak of." The "Dutch army was so eroded through
antimilitaristic propaganda that after four years of mobilization no real
fighting force existed anymore."[161] This was an exaggeration, but the
army's reliability in crisis was uncertain.

This were outbreaks long before the revolutionary crisis of October-
November 1918. In 1915, there were troop riots near Utrecht, leading
Bosboom – without consulting Snijders – to propose a parliamentary
commission to investigate. Snijders refused to participate, and the plan
was stillborn. The odds of the general tolerating parliamentary
involvement in military discipline were minimal anyway. The
following year, there were disturbances among soldiers in Maastricht,
Leiden, and a few other places. On November 6, 1917, soldiers in
Laren threw stones through the windows of the officers' mess while the
meal was in progress. The case load of the high military court rose
steadily, from 3,836 in 1915, to 10,562 in 1918, the vast majority being
disciplinary cases. There were also other ways in which soldiers
expressed their dissatisfaction. Troops increasingly refused to act
against civilians. The dropout rate on marches sometimes reached
50%.[162]

This all paled, however, in comparison to the near-revolution in the
war's closing weeks. The origin, at least of the army's troubles, was
innocent enough. As the defeated German armies withdrew through
Belgium, their northernmost divisions faced the same geographical
conundrum that their far more hopeful predecessors had in 1914: the
shortest path between Belgium and Germany lay through Limburg. The
German formations might go through Limburg, with or without Dutch

permission. This the government, let alone Snijders, could not allow. If fully armed and battle-ready Germans were allowed through, the Entente could legally pursue. Snijders therefore withdrew all leaves on 23 October 1918.[163] Ironically, fear of revolutionary activity played a role as well in the decision.[164]

For the bored and tired troops, losing their leaves was too much. On the night of 25-26 October, the soldiers of the 1st infantry regiment at Harskamp mutinied. Harskamp was the army's largest camp; it was also filled with soldiers from the country's poorest rural area in Drenthe. Barracks were burned, officers were shot at and driven out. For two days, the soldiers ran the camp. At first glance, the incident could be viewed as nothing more than soldiers suffering from excessive boredom. So a modern author has concluded. "It was not from revolutionary zeal that the soldiers acted, but a tired and fed-up anti-militarism which once again sought an outlet. The men had enough of playing soldier for the state of the Netherlands." And so it looked to some contemporaries as well. Two commissions were appointed to investigate, one by Snijders, and one by Alting von Geusau, who, perhaps not coincidentally, appointed B.C. de Jonge to head his. De Jonge concluded that "there was no revolutionary activity responsible for the unrests" and attributed the problems to culture; "our nation is not a military nation." An intelligence officer blamed the problems on weak officers and the leaving of units in the field for much too long without relief.[165]

Yet the situation was serious. The army had to appear ready if the Germans really did want to cross Limburg, or if the Entente wished to do the same. Four years of neutrality could go down the drain if the rebellion spread. There was an even more ominous aspect; in case of political unrest, it would be the army that would have to maintain order. Tsar Nicholas II had discovered the risk of revolt amidst an unreliable army. Would this happen to the Netherlands? Snijders, intent on maintaining military discipline, planned to punish the offending regiment by moving it all the way to the border.[xxxix] Alting von Geusau pressed Snijders to re-issue the leaves on the 26th and 27th, but Snijders held firm. On the 28th, the cabinet (presumably at the war

---

[xxxix] In so doing he showed more sense than the hapless Tsar, who allowed his capital to be garrisoned by troops of unknown reliability, while moving his most trustworthy troops to the front. Snijders at least was doing the opposite.

minister's urging) asked Snijders to do so. Two days later, the general capitulated, and on the 31st issued the appropriate orders, but he specifically refused to issue any leave's for Harskamp.[166]

With the inerrant precision of hindsight, we can now say that the five-day delay in resolving the leaves question was fatal to the Supreme Commander, and very nearly to his government as well. The Social Democrats viewed the riot at Harskamp as a harbinger of things to come. Troelstra thought that the troops "showed a real revolutionary spirit" and that the "ruling classes had now lost their main support." Troelstra's insight was not far removed from reality. The years 1917-1919 were a remarkably revolutionary era in Europe, with major instability in nearly every nation. The "ruling classes" – at least the aristocracy – had been grievously wounded by war in several countries, and the overthrow of the Tsar had encouraged dissidents in many countries. Even in Holland the army uprising would eventually lead to its echo in the navy, which, fearing outbreaks, disabled a number of ships' engines and guns and secretly ordered harbor forts to sink the first ship that raised the red flag.[167] This was prudence, not paranoia. Navies are even more vulnerable than armies to class conflict and revolution. Dutch admirals might not have read Marx, but they had certainly heard of the *Potemkin*.[xl]

So, no doubt, had Troelstra. His initial move, however, was more that of a moderate Social Democrat than of a Lenin-style revolutionary. He demanded the removal of the Supreme Commander. This was not a particularly radical step. Many of Troelstra's fellow parliamentarians were irritated by the taciturn general, who wielded immense power, spent fortunes, and never contemplated discussing any of this with parliament. So when Troelstra rose on November 5 to demand Snijders' departure, he was not speaking to hostile audience:

> I do not know the supreme commander, I have never personally heard anything bad about the man, but say: this man must be removed immediately. Because the system, that has led to this situation, has grown under him, and the way in which he acts after the disturbances, that it is personalized in him.[168]

At this point the government compounded its earlier error and overreacted. The immediate cause of the crisis was resolved on the 5th,

---

[xl] In a celebrated incident immortalized in the Sergei Eisenstein film *The Battleship Potemkin,* sailors in 1905 had revolted on the Russian warship and eventually taken her to Constanza, Romania.

possibly even before Troelstra demanded Snijders' firing. Alting von Geusau told Snijders that the biggest complaint was that the Harskamp punishment was collective, without regard for the actual culpability of the individual. Snijders conceded the pointed under some pressure and lifted the collective punishment.[169] There is not the slightest evidence that he was influenced by the Social Democrats' demands for his head, as he regarded them with an even more jaundiced eye than he did other parties.

What the government did at this point, however, was to go along with Troelstra's demand and dump Snijders. This may seem like a perfectly logical step – head off the opposition by pacifying it, meeting a key demand – but in this case the result was the opposite. Alting von Geusau did not cover himself with glory in the affair. The minister had earlier concealed the fact that he had approved Snijders' original punishment plans. He defended Snijders on the 5th but the following day, perhaps sensing the political winds, he announced that the general was out of touch with the times and had been asked to resign. Informed by Alting von Geusau that the government supported the minister's views[xli] Snijders immediately sent his resignation, which the government accepted on November 9.[170]

As a successor was not named until the 11th, however, Snijders remained in his office – if not technically in office – until that day, so that his career came to a sudden and somewhat ignominious end on the very day that World War I ended. There was a fair amount of indignation about his removal; his biographer wrote of him being "chased away like a stableboy who had been lazy" while an intelligence officer in his diary called it "scandalous," "characterless and weak, " and "a grievous injustice toward the General." Van Terwisga, the Field Army commander, sent in his resignation. Alting von Geusau would be criticized for his handling of the situation even by his predecessor. De Jonge wrote: "The way in which he threw General Snijders to the brutes two months later, was unconscionable." In the long run, however, Snijders would have the best of the situation. He left with dignity, thanking his subordinate commanders and expressing his gratitude to all those, civilian as well as military, who had served under him at headquarters. He would have a significant postwar career, most

---

[xli] It is not entirely clear whether this was so, although the government was certainly relieved at Snijders' departure.

notably as an advocate of aviation. In 1919, he was named Knight in the order of the Golden Lion of Nassau, the last Dutchman to receive the award until 1999. Alting von Geusau, by contrast, resigned in 1919 over a dispute with parliament regarding cost reductions. Snijders successor, acting Supreme Commander Lt. Gen. W.F. Pop, served until the abolition of the position in 1919 and then became war minister, but was toppled in 1921.[171]

Snijders' departure did not mollify the Social Democrats. To them, let alone more radical groups, the general was a symbol of militarism and a tool of the ruling classes, not the cause of the existence of either. Therefore, Snijders' replacement by another general, even a more malleable and friendlier one, could hardly resolve their grievances. In their eyes, the gap between rich and poor grew during World War I. Agricultural day laborers lived "a life of poverty" and 23% of Dutch families lived in 1-room dwellings, while another 31% had two rooms. Furthermore, Holland experienced a poor harvest in 1918. There was also some practical political pressure on Troelstra to keep on the pressure; on his left were the Dutch bolsheviks, led by his personal and political enemy David Wijnkoop, who was ready to take advantage of any signs of excessive moderation by the Social Democrats.[172] In other words, to believe that Troelstra would – or could – settle for Snijders' removal represented the height of optimism.

Then again, it might have represented a familiarity with Troelstra and his followers, who were genuine socialists but behaved like bourgeois parliamentarians and had little in common with the *bolsheviki*. In normal times the SDAP[xlii] was not a revolutionary party. The times, however, were not normal. In 1918 a catastrophic war was drawing to a close amidst rumblings of rebellion in many places. Perhaps it was that environment which swept Troelstra away; perhaps it was his exceptional success on the Snijders matter. Regardless of the cause, Troelstra decided to proclaim the socialist revolution in the Netherlands.

The Social Democrats had first met on October 28th to discuss the army situation, and then again on November 2nd and 3rd. That issue soon became moot, however. The government not only fired Snijders, but began hasty partial demobilization on the 9th and 10th and issued a comprehensive demobilization decree on the 11th. On the 10th, the

---

[xlii] *Sociaal-Democratische Arbijders Partij,* Social Democratic Workers Party.

Social Democrats met again, to hear their military expert, K. ter Laan, explain that the dissident soldiers' clubs were not revolutionary councils. Disappointed, the party nevertheless decided to issue a manifesto of demands, and Troelstra, "carried away" by the moment and his own rhetoric, announced that he would proclaim the revolution in Parliament the following day. This he did, after a fashion. A peace loving man, he denounced violence, but warned the government that it did not have the support of the army or police, and announced that the working class would take over on 18 November.[173]

Much has been made of the comical aspect of the revolution – the decision to let everyone know that a revolution would come a week later. Troelstra, however, expected that the bourgeoisie would voluntarily hand power over to the Socialists. If the army and police had lost cohesion, there was no reason to expect a successful counter-move. Certainly many people believed that the revolution was possible. The liberals thought that it could not be stopped. De Jonge, not the panicking kind, believed all his life that if Troelstra had left the chamber after his speech and gone to city hall, where a large crowd had gathered, a true revolution would have broken out. Colijn was highly pessimistic about the survival of the monarchy. More recently, the fear of the revolution has been described as "not completely unfounded."[174] Certainly the leading figures in the Netherlands thought the threat real enough.

These leading figures did not wait to see how strong the revolutionary movement really was. Instead, they promptly embarked on countermeasures. Two things were particularly useful. First, the Catholic party's leading role in government guaranteed that there was no chance that it would sit on the sidelines. Second, the government had been dabbling in counterrevolutionary activity already, especially through its military intelligence arm and police departments. Both military and civilian security personnel infiltrated the Workers' and Soldiers' Councils, although many of their informants' reports turned out to be too imaginative. Much attention was given to Wijnkoop's SDP,[xliii] the bolshevik faction expelled from the SDAP in 1909. Long before the attempted revolution Wijnkoop was regarded as highly dangerous (many were taken by surprise that the revolutionary

---

[xliii] *Sociaal Democratische Partij*, Social Democratic Party. It was probably not coincidental that Wijnkoop had chosen the same name as the Russian Marxist party.

proclamation came from the moderate Troelstra). Wijnkoop had telegraphed his support for the Bolsheviks, who in turn attempted to send money and advisors to the SDP to spread Bolshevik propaganda. At the very least, intelligence was ready, and the importance of this was acknowledged in the wake of the revolution by combining the intelligence services into the Central Intelligence Service.[175] At the same time, GS-III was divided into foreign and domestic intelligence sections, the latter to hunt for revolutionaries in the ranks (and possibly among civilians as well).[176]

So the government was not caught completely unprepared. Intelligence alone was not enough, however. Even the Russian government had had excellent intelligence before its demise in 1917. The difference was that in Russia, the government and counterrevolutionary forces did not or could not act, while in Holland and elsewhere, they did. Most of the counterplotting came from the political parties, not the cabinet. In fact, the ministers at first were allegedly at their wit's end and Van Karnebeek "shook like a reed." Outside the cabinet doors, the party leaders were more purposeful. The Anti-Revolutionary Party and the Catholics began to plot on 8 November, several days before Troelstra's speech. The Catholic party, the country's largest, was especially effective, both German and British legations giving it the credit for stifling the uprising.[177]

The most practical response to the revolutionary threat was to ensure that the forces of law and order had the means to stop revolutionary violence. The regular army's behavior was uncertain. Pop thought that only cavalry and a few infantry regiments could be counted on, but – and this was a significant point – he did not think that troops would act against the government either. The political parties used their unions to organize 7,000 men into Municipal Guards units, while the government called up the small *Vrijwillige Landstorm,* expanded it into the *Bijzondere* (Special) *Vrijwillige Landstorm* (BVL), and started to deploy it in the major cities. The BVL grew rapidly as demobilized soldiers with counterrevolutionary views rushed to The Hague, Rotterdam, and Amsterdam and were added to its forces. Not everything went smoothly, of course, with Protestant and Catholic Municipal Guard units competing for weapons, but at least they were all doing so for the same purpose. All major government buildings soon had troops and reliable police to guard them. Machine guns were set up on high buildings. Plans were drafted for the security of the royal family. The day after Troelstra's proclamation only a few hundred troops had taken up positions in the major cities, but by the 18th their number had grown to 46,000.[xliv 178]

This effort, supplemented by manifestos, public meetings, and appeals to the nation, received important foreign assistance. Britain decided to use its stranglehold (the blockade remained in effect well after the armistice) to influence events in Holland. On the one hand, the Foreign Office was more than willing to increase food supplies so long as a stable government existed. On the other, the British government made it clear that all food supplies would be cut off if a socialist revolution took place. Apparently there was even some discussion, although no promise, of armed assistance.[179] The British were greatly interested in the links between events in Holland and Germany. In late October Townley had expected a revolution in Germany, but opined that it would be a "sham" uprising soon to be followed by a restoration. When the German revolt came, Townley was quick to notice that the Dutch socialists were elated. Cecil believed that the continental uprisings, including Troelstra's, were engineered by Germany as a means of ensuring better terms. The British exaggerated. Troelstra was influenced by events from Germany, but was not in any way manipulated. There had been contacts between German circles and Dutch leaders about revolution, but in the other direction – namely, how to cooperate in suppressing the Bolsheviks. The Germans rightly feared revolution even more than the Dutch did, and brought the troops home rather than fighting to the bitter end precisely to avoid the fate of Russia.[180]

In the end, the revolution fizzled. Troelstra was not a revolutionary and debated revolution in parliament rather than fomenting it in the streets. Even the radical workers on the Amsterdam docks remained quiescent and did not strike. Wijnkoop's radicals, soon renamed the Communist Party in Holland, did march on the army barracks in Amsterdam in order to liberate the soldiers. "The latter refused to be liberated, fired a few shots, and there was no more trouble." The Queen and the crown princess went out in public on foot, and were cheered everywhere. A wave of patriotism and royalism swept a nation that was normally neither. On the 18th, the Queen came out on the Malieveld in

---

[xliv] It is not clear whether this figure reflects only the BVL, or the combined strength of BVL, Municipal Guards, and regulars. My inclination is toward the latter interpretation.

The Hague in her carriage, at which point a cheering crowd removed the horse traces and pulled the carriage themselves. Allegedly this "spontaneous" incident had been carefully planned, but it could hardly have happened in Petrograd or Berlin.[181]

The revolution collapsed completely. Wijnkoop screamed "traitor" at Troelstra in parliament, who in turn left for a "rest cure" in a sanatorium in Switzerland. Heldring later wrote of the "comical impression" made by the revolution. Understandably the government's reaction has been portrayed as exaggerated. "All these precautions were a little excessive." This understates the nature of the crisis leading up to the revolution, however, not to mention the continental environment of revolutions taking place at the time. Virtually all of Europe east of Holland was in a state of revolution. The government took no chances. The BVL was maintained until 1940, and in 1920 still had some 20,000 men. The Queen was encouraged to become less involved in government. Most of the European continent was demonarchized between 1917 and 1920, and Wilhelmina's behavior was blamed by some politicians for the November crisis. "[W]e regard it as probable that the crisis . . . will henceforth make her more reserved regarding the pursuit of personal leadership."[182] It did not, but there was another effect. During the peak of the crisis, Van Karnebeek had agreed to allow 70,000 disarmed German soldiers to retreat through Limburg.[183]

This incident would color the entire relationship between the Entente and Holland during the negotiations at Versailles, at which the Dutch would face the first overt threat to their territorial integrity of the entire war.

NOTES

1   Van Manen, Nederlandsche Overzee Trustmaatschappij,vol. 4, p. 204; Frey, *Der Erste Weltkrieg*, p. 369; Smit, *Bescheiden ... 1914-1917*, pp. 167-68; Van der Wal, *Herinneringen*, p. 30.

2   De Monchy, "Commerce and Navigation," p. 151; Barnouw, *Holland under Queen Wilhelmina*, p. 136; VII Corps to War Ministry, 8 April 1918, Duitse Ministerie van Buitenlandse Zaken – Stukken betreffende Nederland, ARA-II; Townley, *'Indiscretions,'* p. 262.

3   Smit, *Tien studiën*, pp. 52, 131-35, 137, 140.

4   Heldring, *Herinneringen*, p. 225; Smit, *Tien studiën*, p. 27; Van Terwisga to Snijders and margin note, 1 November 1917, Generale Staf, ARA-II; Rosen, *Aus einem diplomatischen Wanderleben*, vol. 3/4, p. 91.

5   Barnouw, *Holland under Queen Wilhelmina*, pp. 145-46, 154-55; De Monchy, "Commerce and Navigation," pp. 132, 133; Porter, "Dutch Neutrality," pp. 139-40, 148-50; De Valk and Van Faassen, *Dagboeken en aantekeningen*, p. 881.

6   Ibid., pp. 71-76; Oppenheimer, *Stranger Within*, pp. 284-85.

7   Van Manen, *Nederlandsche Overzee Trustmaatschappij*, vol. 3, pp. 59, 68-60.

8   Ibid., pp. 68-69.

9   Smit, *Tien studiën*, p. 77.

10   Smit, *Tien studiën*, pp. 95-97; Porter, "Dutch Neutrality," pp. 132, 145-46.

11   Van Manen, *Nederlandsche Overzee Trustmaatschappij*, vol. 3, pp. 447-48.

12   De Valk and Van Faassen, *Dagboeken en aantekeningen*, p. 860; Confidential agent report, 12 January 1917, Duitse Ministerie van Buitenlandse Zaken – Stukken betreffende Nederland, ARA-II.

13   Townley, *'Indiscretions,'* pp. 256, 263, 265; Smit, *Tien studiën*. p. 32; Rosen, *Aus einem diplomatischen Wanderleben*, vol. 3/4, p. 292; Diary of. H. A. van Karnebeek, 7 February 1919, 911, Smit, *Bescheiden ... 1917-1919*, 921; Oppenheimer, *Stranger Within*, pp. 255-57.

14   Gevers to Loudon, 12 July 1918, 587, Smit, *Bescheiden ... 1917-1919*, pp. 504-505; Smit, *Tien studiën*, pp. 32, 69-70; Rosen, *Aus einem diplomatischen Wanderleben*, vol. 3/4, pp. 63, 91.

15   Rosen, *Aus einem diplomatischen Wanderleben*, vol. 3/4, pp. 63-4, 67, 69, 71-72, 75-76; Townley, *'Indiscretions,'* p. 258; Kühlmann, *Erinnerungen*, pp. 570-71; Confidential German report from Rotterdam, 21 June 1918, enclosed with Rosen to Hertling, 28 June 1918, Duitse Ministerie van Buitenlandse Zaken – Stukken betreffende Nederland, ARA-II.

16   Townley to Loudon, 1 July 1917, 139: Wilhelmina to George V, 7 July 1917, 15 July 1917, and 18 July 1917, 144, 147, 151: George V to Wilhelmina, 10 July 1917 and 17 July 1917, 154, 155: Wilhelmina to Wilhelm II, 17 July 1917, 156: Wilhelm II to Wilhelmina, 19 July 1917, 157: Loudon to De Marees van Swinderen, 18 July 1917 and 13 August 1917, 158, 170: Balfour to De Marees van Swinderen, 13 August 1917, 187: Snijders to Loudon, 2 August 1917, 188, Smit, *Bescheiden ... 1917-1919*, pp. 160-61, 168, 169, 172-75, 184, 202-203; De Valk and Van Faassen, *Dagboeken en aantekeningen*, p. 935; Halpern, *A Naval History*, p. 444.

17   Van der Wal, *Herinneringen*,pp. 48-49; Townley to Loudon, 2 November 1917 and

1 March 1918, 275, 402: Minutes, Ministerraad, 19 June 1918, 551, Smit, *Bescheiden ... 1917-1919,* pp. 297-98, 408, 576; Van Manen, *Nederlandsche Overzee Trustmaatschappij,* vol. 4, pp. 293-94.

[18] Treub, *Herinneringen,* p. 350; Smidt, "De bestrijding van de smokkelhandel," pp. 55-57, 61-62; Van Manen, *Nederlandsche Overzee Trustmaatschappij,* vol. 5, p. 162.

[19] Gevers to Loudon, 23 November 1917: Melvill van Carnbee to Loudon, 23 June 1917, Buitenlandse Zaken – Kabinet en protocol, ARA-II; Heldring, *Herinneringen,* pp. 206-207, 253; Memorandum by Sir Walter Townley, 27 February 1918, 396, Smit, *Bescheiden ... 1917-1919,* pp. 399-400; Oppenheimer, *Stranger Within,* pp. 282-83, 324-25.

[20] Loudon to Gevers, 26 March 1917, 74: Gevers to Loudon, 30 April 1917, 93, Smit, *Bescheiden ... 1917-1919,* pp. 83-84, 104-106.

[21] Gevers to Loudon, 24 October 1916, 649: Von Stumm to Loudon, 28 October 1916, 652: Van Weede to Loudon, 5 January 1917, 725, Smit, *Bescheiden ... 1914-1917,* pp. 657-58, 662-63, 739-40; Porter, "Dutch Neutrality," p. 207; Rosen to Michaelis, 26 July 1917, Duitse Ministerie van Buitenlandse Zaken – Stukken betreffende Nederland, ARA-II; A. Wolting, "Uit het dagboek van kapitein van Woelderen," *Militaire Spectator* 135 (January 1966), p. 33; Frey, *Der Erste Weltkrieg,* p. 365; De Stuers to Loudon, 2 January 1917: Van Weede to Loudon, 5 January 1917, Buitenlandse Zaken – Kabinet en protocol, ARA-II; Gevers to Loudon, 18 Feb. 1917, 21, Smit, *Bescheiden ... 1914-1917,* pp. 36-38.

[22] Renner to Bethmann Hollweg, 29 March 1917: Ludendorff to Foreign Ministry, 26 April 1917 (document is illegible): Grünau to Bethmann Hollweg, 7 April 1917: Bussche to legation, 23 March 1918: Rosen to Von Baden, 5 November 1918, Duitse Ministerie van Buitenlandse Zaken – Stukken betreffende Nederland, ARA-II; Gevers to Loudon, 23 November 1917, Buitenlandse Zaken – Kabinet en protocol, ARA-II.

[23] Lutz, *Fall of the German Empire,* vol. 1, p. 467; Halpern, *A Naval History,* p. 347; Gevers to Loudon, 16 March 1917, 60: Loudon to Gevers, 26 March 1917, 73, Smit, *Bescheiden ... 1917-1919,* pp. 69-71, 82; Renner to Bethmann Hollweg, 29 March 1917, Duitse Ministerie van Buitenlandse Zaken – Stukken betreffende Nederland, ARA-II; Porter, "Dutch Neutrality," pp. 211-12.

[24] Rosen to Hertling, 28 May 1918, with report by Schweinitz, 28 May 1918 and Schweinitz report of 9 June 1918, Duitse Ministerie van Buitenlandse Zaken – Stukken betreffende Nederland, ARA-II.

[25] *Legationsrat* Grünau to Foreign Secretary, 3 June 1918: Foreign Office minute, 4 June 1918: Snijders to Schweinitz, 7 June 1918, Duitse Ministerie van Buitenlandse Zaken – Stukken betreffende Nederland, ARA-II; Schweinitz to Snijders, 6 June and 20 June 1918, 529, 552, Smit, *Bescheiden ... 1917-1919,* pp. 556, 576.

[26] Schweinitz to Rosen, 8 June 1918: Report by Schweinitz, 9 June 1918: Rosen to Hertling, 11 June 1918, Duitse Ministerie van Buitenlandse Zaken – Stukken betreffende Nederland, ARA-II; Snijders to Loudon, 12 July 1918, 586, Smit, *Bescheiden ... 1917-1919,* p. 604.

[27] Ludendorff to Foreign Office, 10 June 1918, 11 June 1918, and 12 June 1918: Grünau to Foreign Office, 15 June 1918: Von Berckheim to Bray and Von Langwerth, 17 June 1918, Duitse Ministerie van Buitenlandse Zaken – Stukken betreffende Nederland, ARA-II.

[28] Rosen to Hertling, 28 June 1918: Grünau to Foreign Office, June 1918 (no further

date available): Rosen to Hertling, 13 July 1918, Duitse Ministerie van Buitenlandse Zaken – Stukken betreffende Nederland, ARA-II.

[29] De Stuers to Loudon, 5 May 1917, 96: Lord Bryce to Loudon, 17 October 1917 and 21 March 1918, 259, 431, Smit, *Bescheiden ... 1917-1919,* pp. 108, 285, 433-35; Bryce to Loudon, 27 September 1917, 240, RGP vol. 116.

[30] *Official German Documents,* p. 1266; Fischer, *Germany's Aims,* pp. 410-11, 624, 631; Ludendorff, *Ludendorff's Own Story,* vol. 2, pp. 335, 354-55, 372, 378.

[31] Smit, *1917-1919,* p. 339; Lutz, *Fall of the German Empire,* vol. 1, pp. 478, 505, 514; Michael Dockrill and David French, eds., *Strategy and Intelligence: British Policy during the First World War* (London and Rio Grande: Hambledon, 1996), pp. 169-70; Rosen, *Aus einem diplomatischen Wanderleben,* pp. 182-83.

[32] Frey, *Der Erste Weltkrieg,* p. 282.

[33] Townley to Balfour, 8 August 1917, 86, Bourne and Watt, *British Documents,* Part II, Series H, vol. 3 (Washington, DC: University Publications of America, 1989), pp. 155-56; Schweinitz report, 9 June 1918, Duitse Ministerie van Buitenlandse Zaken – Stukken betreffende Nederland, ARA-II; "Punten, de defensie betreffende, welke met spoed nadere voorziening behoeven," May 8, 1918, Collectie B. C. de Jonge, nr toegang 2.22.095, inv nr 47, ARA-II; C. M. Schulten, "The Netherlands and its Army (1900-1940)," *Revue Internationale d'Histoire Militaire* 58 (1984), p. 76; Bosboom, *In moeilijke omstandigheden,* p. 145.

[34] Bout, "Dutch Army," p. 103; Snijders, "Nederland's militaire positie," pp. 549-51, 563-66; "Figuratief overzicht van den aanwas en den afvoer van de verschillende roepen van dienstplichtigen van Augustus 1914 tot December 1917," Collectie Bosboom, ARA-II; Berg, *Snijders,* pp. 99-100; Bonebakker, *Twee verdienstelijke officieren,* p. 48; Klinkert, "Verdediging van de zuidgrens," , Part 2, pp. 250-54.

[35] De Valk and Van Faassen, *Dagboeken en aantekeningen,* p. 878; Van der Wal, *Herinneringen,* p. 35; Snijders to fortress commanders, 22 August 1916, AHK Bereden artillerie, ARA-II; Klinkert, "Verdediging van de zuidgrens," Part 1, p. 219; Halpern, *A Naval History,* p. 18; VII Corps to War Ministry, 8 April 1918, Duitse Ministerie van Buitenlandse Zaken – Stukken betreffende Nederland, ARA-II.

[36] Snijders to Loudon, 6 March 1917, 45: Tonnet to Snijders, 26 May 1918, 518, Smit, *Bescheiden ... 1917-1919,* pp. 58-60, 525-34; Porter, "Dutch Neutrality," pp. 206, 228-29.

[37] Porter, "Dutch Neutrality," p. 230; Snijders to Tonnet, 5 June 1918, 528, Smit, *Bescheiden ... 1917-1919,* pp. 552-57; Van der Wal, *Herinneringen,* p. 35; Lutz, *Fall of the German Empire,* vol. 1, p. 683.

[38] OHL GS-III report, n.d. but between 23 March and 1 April 1918: Report, information section, Foreign Office, 25 June 1918: Document addressed to Flemish soldiers, 5 May 1918, Hoover Institution, Germany, OHL Records, 1914-1918; Confidential report, 21 June 1918, enclosed with Rosen to Hertling, 28 June 1918, Duitse Ministerie van Buitenlandse Zaken – Stukken betreffende Nederland, ARA-II; Dockrill and French, *Strategy and Intelligence,* p. 161; Lutz, Fall of the German Empire, vol. 1, pp. 380-81; Smit, *Tien studiën,* p. 139.

[39] Van Manen, *Nederlandsche Overzee Trustmaatschappij,* vol. 5, p. 174.

[40] Snijders to Loudon, 11 January 1917, Buitenlandse Zaken – Kabinet en protocol, ARA-II.

[41] De Jonge to Loudon, 12 Feb. 1918, 373, and reply, 18 Feb. 1918, 383, Smit, *Bescheiden ... 1917-1919,* pp. 385-87, 392.

[42] Engelen, *Geschiedenis,* p. 36.

[43] *Official German Documents,* pp. 1116, 1320.

[44] Ludendorff, *Ludendorff's Own Story,* vol. 1, p. 288.

[45] *Official German Documents,* pp. 857, 1153, 1161, 1162; Frey, *Der Erste Weltkrieg,* pp. 80, 83; Ludendorff, *Ludendorff's Own Story,* vol. 1, pp. 288-89.

[46] Frey, *Der Erste Weltkrieg, pp.* 84-86; *Official German Documents,* pp. 1179, 1263-66; Ludendorff, *Ludendorff's Own Story,* vol. 1, pp. 371, 372.

[47] *Official German Documents,* pp. 874-75, 1116, 1184; Haeussler, *General William Groener,* p. 89; Fischer, *Germany's Aims,* p. 307.

[48] *Official German Documents,* pp. 1320, 1321; Ludendorff, *Ludendorff's Own Story,* vol. 1, pp. 377-78; Dockrill and French, *Strategy and Intelligence,* p. 82; Bout, "Dutch Army," p. 220n23; Oldham, *Pill Boxes,* pp. 92-94.

[49] *German Official Documents,* p. 1321; Frey, *Der Erste Weltkrieg,* pp. 90, 93-94; Memorandum of conversation between Kriege and Cort van der Linden, 4 February 1917, Duitse Ministerie van Buitenlandse Zaken – Stukken betreffende Nederland, ARA-II.

[50] Gevers to Loudon, 18 February 1917: Muller Massis report, 17 February 1917, Buitenlandse Zaken – Kabinet en protocol, ARA-II; Renner to Bethmann Hollweg, 29 March 1917, Duitse Ministerie van Buitenlandse Zaken – Stukken betreffende Nederland, ARA-II; Lutz, Fall of the German Empire, vol. 1, p. 357; Frey, *Der Erste Weltkrieg,* p. 87.

[51] De Valk and Van Faassen, *Dagboeken en aantekeningen,* p. 859; Porter, "Dutch Neutrality," pp. 203-204.

[52] Heldring, *Herinneringen,* p. 199; Rosen, *Aus einem diplomatischen Wanderleben,* vol. 3/4, pp. 88-90; De Monchy, "Commerce and Navigation," p. 127; Van Manen, *Nederlandsche Overzee Trustmaatschappij,* vol. 5, pp. 156-57.

[53] Treub, *Herinneringen,* p. 345; Porter, "Dutch Neutrality," pp. 143-44, 198; Zaalberg, "The Manufacturing Industry," pp. 8-12; Van Manen, *Nederlandsche Overzee Trustmaatschappij,* vol. 4, pp. 19-20; Barnouw, *Holland under Queen Wilhelmina,* p. 127; Smit, *1917-1919,* pp. 24-26; Oppenheimer, *Stranger Within,* p. 271.

[54] Snijders to Cort van der Linden, 20 February 1917, 23: Loudon to Gevers, 7 March 1917, 47: Loudon to Wilhelmina, 8 March 1917, 48, Smit, *Bescheiden ... 1917-1919,* pp. 39, 60-61.

[55] Gevers to Loudon, 26 February 1917, 31: Loudon to Gevers, 27 February 1917, 32: Pleyte to Loudon, 27 February 1917, 33: Loudon to Wilhelmina, 28 February 1917, 35, Smit, *Bescheiden ... 1917-1919,* pp. 47-48, 51-52.

[56] Gevers to Loudon, 28 Feb. 1917, 1 March 1917, 15 March 1917, and 16 March 1917, 37, 38, 58, 59: Loudon to Wilhelmina, 14 March 1917, 60, Smit, *Bescheiden ... 1917-1919,* pp. 52-54, 69-71.

[57] Barnouw, *Holland under Queen Wilhelmina,* p. 135; De Monchy, "Commerce and Navigation," p. 150; Snijders to Cort van der Linden, 5 February 1917, 5, Smit, *Bescheiden ... 1917-1919,* pp. 6-8; Smit, *Tien studiën,* pp. 109-13.

[58] Balfour to De Marees van Swinderen, 17 February 1917, 20: Loudon to Minister for Colonies Pleyte, 29 June 1917, 137, Smit, *Bescheiden ... 1917-1919,* pp. 36, 160; De Monchy, "Commerce and Navigation," p. 151; Edgar Turlington, *Neutrality: Its History, Economics, and Law,* vol. 3, *The World War Period* (New York: Octagon, 1976 (1936)), pp. 95-96.

[59] Smit, *Tien studiën,* pp. 113-14; Garrett to Lansing, 9 October 1917, *Foreign*

Relations of the United States, 1917 supp. 2 vol. 1 (Washington, DC: Government Printing Office, 1932); Rappard to Loudon, 7 October and 4 November 1917, 248, 277: De Marees van Swinderen to Loudon, 5 and 7 March (2 messages) 1918, 408, 409, 411: Cabinet minutes, 16 March 1918 , 424, Smit, *Bescheiden ... 1917-1919*, pp. 277-78, 299, 413-15, 428.

[60] Smit, *Tien studiën*, pp. 114-15; Townley to Loudon, 17 March 1918, 427, Smit, *Bescheiden ... 1917-1919*, pp. 430-31; Treub, *Herinneringen*, p. 367.

[61] Turlington, *Neutrality*, p. 96; Porter, "Dutch Neutrality," p. 154.

[62] Turlington, *Neutrality*, p. 97.

[63] Turlington, *Neutrality*, p. 96; Van Manen, *Nederlandsche Overzee Trustmaatschappij*, vol. 4, pp. 247-49.

[64] Treub, *Herinneringen*, p. 367; *Black's Law Dictionary*, 4th ed. (St. Paul: West, 1968), pp. 112-13.

[65] Turlington, *Neutrality*, p. 95; Inbar and Sheffer, *National Security of Small States*, p. 1.

[66] Oppenheimer, *Stranger Within*, p. 310.

[67] Barnouw, *Holland under Queen Wilhelmina*, pp. 138-39; Van Manen, *Nederlandsche Overzee Trustmaatschappij*, vol. 5, p. 208.

[68] Smit, *Tien studiën, pp.* 116-17; Van Manen, *Nederlandsche Overzee Trustmaatschappij*, vol. 4, p. 38; Bout, "Dutch Army," p. 138; Treub, *Herinneringen*, p. 367; Confidential report from Rotterdam, 21 June 1918, enclosed with Rosen to Hertling, 28 1918, Duitse Ministerie van Buitenlandse Zaken – Stukken betreffende Nederland, ARA-II; Bob de Graaff, "Bogey or Saviour? The Image of the United States in the Netherlands during the Interwar Period," pp. 51-69 in R. Kroes and M. van Rossem, eds., *Anti-Americanism in Europe* (Amsterdam, 1986), passim.

[69] Smit, *Tien studiën, pp.* 142-44; Treub, *Herinneringen*, pp. 367-68; Turlington, *Neutrality*, p. 96; Reuters report attached to De Marees van Swinderen to Loudon, 25 April 1918, 462, Smit, *Bescheiden ... 1917-1919*, pp. 473-74.

[70] Cabinet minutes, 25 March 1918 and 5 April 1918, 433, 436, Smit, *Bescheiden ... 1917-1919*, pp. 435, 438-39; De Monchy, "Commerce and Navigation," p. 153.

[71] Treub, *Herinneringen*, p. 368.

[72] Frey, *Der Erste Weltkrieg*, pp. 274-78; Rosen, *Aus einem diplomatischen Wanderleben*, pp. 154-57; De Monchy, "Commerce and Navigation," p. 153; Turlington, *Neutrality*,pp. 97-98; Gevers to Loudon, 23 May 1918, 514, Smit, *Bescheiden ... 1917-1919*, pp. 519-21.

[73] Turlington, *Neutrality*, pp. 97-98.

[74] Smit, *Tien studiën*, pp. 107-109, 145-52.

[75] Ibid., pp. 116-22; Loudon to De Marees van Swinderen, 5 April 1918, 437: Cabinet minutes, 12 April 1918, 442, Smit, *Bescheiden ... 1917-1919*, pp. 439-40, 444; Frey, *Der Erste Weltkrieg*, pp. 273, 367.

[76] Smit, *1917-1919*, p. 86; Barnouw, *Holland under Queen Wilhelmina*, p. 133.

[77] Frey, *Der Erste Weltkrieg*, pp. 274-78; Porter, "Dutch Neutrality," pp. 219-20, 227; De Beaufort, *Vijftig jaren*, part 2, p. 261; Smit, *1917-1919*, pp. 78-79.

[78] Porter, "Dutch Neutrality," p. 220; De Leeuw, *Nederland in de wereldpolitiek*, p. 182; Smit, *Diplomatieke geschiedenis*, p. 315.

[79] Rosen, *Aus einem diplomatischen Wanderleben*, vol. 3/4, p. 158; Frey, *Der Erste Weltkrieg*, p. 366; Smit, *Tien studiën*, p. 22; Smit, *1917-1919*, p. 79; Van der Wal, *Herinneringen*, p. 39.

80 Frey, *Der Erste Weltkrieg,* pp. 255-56; Snijders to Loudon, 12 Nov. 1915, 464: Loudon to Gevers, 23 December 1915 and 28 September 1916, 485, 635, Smit, *Bescheiden ... 1914-1917,* pp. 476-78, 501, 641-42; Oldham, *Pill Boxes,* p. 14.

81 Porter, "Dutch Neutrality," pp. 217-18; Frey, *Der Erste Weltkrieg,* pp. 255-56.

82 Heldring, *Herinneringen,* pp. 219-20.

83 Oppenheimer, *Stranger Within,* pp. 294, 309.

84 Oldham, *Pill Boxes,* pp. 14-18.

85 Smit, *Bescheiden ... 1917-1919,*pp. 13, 14, 15; Frey, *Der Erste Weltkrieg,* pp. 278-79.

86 H. Copijn to Loudon, 19 October 1917, 260: Van Vollenhoven to Loudon, 20 October 1917, 261: Loudon to De Marees van Swinderen, 27 October 1917 and reply, 29 October 1917, 269, 272, Smit, *Bescheiden ... 1917-1919,* pp. 285-86, 291-92, 295.

87 Rosen to Michaelis, 30 October 1917, Duitse Ministerie van Buitenlandse Zaken – Stukken betreffende Nederland, ARA-II; Porter, "Dutch Neutrality," p. 219; Loudon to De Marees van Swinderen, 11 January 1918, 340: Report of the Militär-Generaldirection der Eisenbahnen, Brussels, 7 January 1918 (attachment to 345): De Marees van Swinderen to Loudon, 18 January 1918, 346: Memorandum of 1st Section chief Van Heeckeren, n.d. but between 1 January and 14 February 1918, 352, Smit, *Bescheiden ... 1917-1919,* pp. 346-47, 354-57, 361.

88 Loudon to De Marees van Swinderen, 1 March 1918, 401: De Marees van Swinderen to Balfour, 7 March 1918, 412: De Marees van Swinderen to Loudon, 15 March 1918, 423: Townley note verbale, 20 March 1918, 430, Smit, *Bescheiden ... 1917-1919,* pp. 405-409, 415-417, 423, 427-28.

89 Smit, *1917-1919,* pp. 77; Ludendorff to Foreign Ministry, 20 March 1918, 2 April 1918, and 3 April 1918: Chief of Naval Staff to Foreign Ministry, 3 April 1918: VII Corps to war ministry, 8 April 1918, Duitse Ministerie van Buitenlandse Zaken – Stukken betreffende Nederland, ARA-II; Rosen, *Aus einem diplomatischen Wanderleben,* vol. 3/4, pp. 154-55.

90 Foreign ministry to legation, 4 April 1918, Duitse Ministerie van Buitenlandse Zaken – Stukken betreffende Nederland, ARA-II; Note from German legation, 9 April 1918, 440, Smit, *Bescheiden ... 1917-1919,* pp. 441-42.

91 Balfour to De Marees van Swinderen, 11 April 1918, 441, Smit, *Bescheiden ... 1917-1919,* pp. 442-44.

92 Rosen to Foreign Ministry, Duitse Ministerie van Buitenlandse Zaken – Stukken betreffende Nederland, ARA-II; Townley note verbale, 17 April 1918, 444, Smit, *Bescheiden ... 1917-1919,* p. 456.

93 Colijn to A. F. de Savornin Lohman, 17 April 1918, 445, Smit, *Bescheiden ... 1917-1919,* pp. 456-57.

94 Ludendorff to Foreign Office, 18 April 1918, Duitse Ministerie van Buitenlandse Zaken – Stukken betreffende Nederland, ARA-II; Memorandum of meeting with Baron von Maltzan by C. F. Gerretson, 18 April 1918, 446: Colijn to Loudon, 19 April 1918, 447, Smit, *Bescheiden ... 1917-1919,* pp. 457-61.

95 Legation to Foreign Office, 20 April 1918: Ludendorff to Foreign Office, 20 April 1918 (3 messages), Duitse Ministerie van Buitenlandse Zaken – Stukken betreffende Nederland, ARA-II; Porter, "Dutch Neutrality," p. 221.

96 Grünau to Foreign Ministry, 23 April 1918: Wilhelm II to Wilhelmina, 23 April 1918: Chief of Naval Staff to Foreign Ministry, 23 April 1918: Foreign Office to Rosen, 23 April 1918, Duitse Ministerie van Buitenlandse Zaken – Stukken

betreffende Nederland, ARA-II; Snijders to various commands, 23 April 1918, 453, Smit, *Bescheiden ... 1917-1919*, pp. 466-67; A. Wolting, "Uit het dagboek van Kapitein van Woelderen," *Militaire Spectator* 135 (January 1966), pp. 33-34.

[97] Rosen, *Aus einem diplomatischen Wanderleben*, vol. 3/4, pp. 158-61.

[98] Rosen to Foreign Office, 23/24 April 1918: Foreign Office to Rosen, 24 April 1918, Duitse Ministerie van Buitenlandse Zaken – Stukken betreffende Nederland, ARA-II; Rosen memorandums to Foreign Ministry, 24 and 5 April 1918, 457, 459, Smit, *Bescheiden ... 1917-1919*, pp. 469, 471-73.

[99] Bonebakker, *Twee verdienstelijke officieren*, pp. 55-56; Notulen Ministerraad, 25 April 1918, 460, Smit, *Bescheiden ... 1917-1919*, pp. 472-73; Smit, *Diplomatieke geschiedenis*, pp. 317-18; Rosen to Foreign Office, 25 April 1918: Ludendorff to naval staff, 25 April 1918: OHL to Foreign Office, 25 April 1918: Wilhelm II to Grünau, 25 April 1918, Duitse Ministerie van Buitenlandse Zaken – Stukken betreffende Nederland, ARA-II.

[100] Bonebakker, *Twee verdienstelijke officieren*, p. 56; parliamentary minutes, 26 April 1918, 463, Smit, *Bescheiden ... 1917-1919*, pp. 474-482.

[101] Rosen to Foreign Ministry, 27 April 1918, Duitse Ministerie van Buitenlandse Zaken – Stukken betreffende Nederland, ARA-II; parliamentary minutes, 26 April 1918, 463: Cabinet minutes, 26 April 1918, 464, Smit, *Bescheiden ... 1917-1919*, pp. 474-483; Rosen, *Aus einem diplomatischen Wanderleben*, vol. 3/4, pp. 162, 168-69, 170.

[102] OHL to Foreign Office, 26 April 1918: Rosen to Foreign Office, 26 and 27 April 1918: Grünau to Foreign Office, 27 April 1918, Duitse Ministerie van Buitenlandse Zaken – Stukken betreffende Nederland, ARA-II; Van Weede to Loudon, 27 April 1918, Buitenlandse Zaken – Kabinet en Protocol, ARA-II.

[103] Gevers to Loudon, 29 April 1918, 476, Smit, *Bescheiden ... 1917-1919*, pp. 489-90; Rosen to Hertling, 29 April 1918, Duitse Ministerie van Buitenlandse Zaken – Stukken betreffende Nederland, ARA-II.

[104] Schweinitz reports, 28 May and 9 June 1918: Ludendorff to Foreign Office, 3 June 1918, Duitse Ministerie van Buitenlandse Zaken – Stukken betreffende Nederland, ARA-II; Frey, *Der Erste Weltkrieg*, p. 280; Rosen, *Aus einem diplomatischen Wanderleben*, vol. 3/4, p. 163.

[105] Townley memorandum, 28 April 1918, 471: Townley and Allizé memorandum, 29 April 1918, 473: Loudon *aide-mémoire*, 29 April-1 May 1918, 477, Smit, *Bescheiden ... 1917-1919*, pp. 487-88, 490-91.

[106] Porter, "Dutch Neutrality," pp. 224-25; Frey, *Der Erste Weltkrieg*, pp. 278-79; Smit, *1917-1919*, pp. 80-81; Dockrill and French, *Strategy and Intelligence*, p. 166; Townley to Balfour, 19 April 1918, 131: Harold Nicolson, "Appreciations of the Present Situation in Holland from the Diplomatic Point of View," 24 April 1918, 132, Bourne and Watt, *British Documents*, vol. 8, pp. 305-307.

[107] Rosen to Hertling, 25 June 1918, Duitse Ministerie van Buitenlandse Zaken – Stukken betreffende Nederland, ARA-II.

[108] Townley to Loudon, 17 July 1918 or just before, 591, Smit, *Bescheiden ... 1917-1919*, p. 608.

[109] Loudon to De Marees van Swinderen, 17 July 1918, 592: Loudon to Townley, 24 July 1918, 597: De Marees van Swinderen to Loudon, 30 July 1918, 600: Robertson to Van Karnebeek, 23 September and 4 October 1918, 638, 648, Smit, *Bescheiden ... 1917-1919*, pp. 609, 613-14, 615-16, 655, 677-78.

[110] De Leeuw, *Nederland in de wereldpolitiek*, p. 184 (claiming only 2-4 days

ammunition on hand; this is probably an underestimate, but the situation was not good); Smit, *1917-1919*, pp. 17-21.

[111] J. Kooiman, *De Nederlandsche strijdmacht en hare mobilisatie in het jaar negentien honderd en veertien* (Purmerend: J. Muuses en Herman de Ruiter, 1922), p. 7.

[112] Klinkert, "Verdediging van de zuidgrens" (Part Two), pp. 254-56; GS II interrogation, 29 September 1916, Hoofdkwartier Veldleger, ARA-II.

[113] Bout, "Dutch Army," pp. 143, 144; Robin Higham, "Reflections on Intercultural Command," pp. 217-33 in James Bradford, ed., *The Military and Conflict between Cultures: Soldiers at the Interface* (College Station, TX: Texas A&M University Press, 1997), pp. 228-31; John J. Bout, "The Nature and Extent of Antimilitarism in the Netherlands from 1918 to 1940 and the Degree to which they Contributed to the Quick Defeat in 1940" (Ph. D. Dissertation: University of British Columbia, 1975), p. 246; Klinkert, "Verdediging van de zuidgrens" (Part Two), p. 255; Wolting, "Uit het dagboek," p. 34; Report by General van Terwisga, July 1917, Hoofdkwartier Veldleger, nr toegang 2.13.16, inv nr 942, ARA-II.

[114] Smit, *1917-1919*, pp. 11-12, 15; Berg, *Snijders*, p. 104; Snijders to Cort van der Linden, 30 January and 5 February 1917, 1, 5, Smit, *Bescheiden ... 1917-1919*, pp. 1-4, 6-8; Fasseur, *Wilhelmina*, p. 512.

[115] Cort van der Linden to Snijders, 9 February 1917, 10, Smit, *Bescheiden ... 1917-1919*, pp. 14-21.

[116] Cort van der Linden to Snijders, 9 February 1917, 10: Snijders to Cort van der Linden, 14 Feb. 1917, 15: Bosboom to Snijders, 17 February 1917, 18, Smit, *Bescheiden ... 1917-1919*, pp. 14-21, 24-30, 34-35; Gevers to Loudon, 18 February 1917, Buitenlandse Zaken – Kabinet en Protocol, ARA-II.

[117] De Valk and Van Faassen, *Dagboeken en aantekeningen*, p. 945; Memorandum by N. Bosboom, 27 Feb. 1917, Collectie Bosboom, ARA-II.

[118] Snijders to Loudon, 6 March 1917, 45, Smit, *Bescheiden ... 1917-1919*, pp. 58-60; Bout, "Dutch Army," p. 136.

[119] Porter, "Dutch Neutrality," p. 226; Van der Wal, *Herinneringen*, p. 27; Confidential agent report to Foreign Office on the Netherlands' participation in the war, 16/18 May, 1917, Duitse Ministerie van Buitenlandse Zaken – Stukken betreffende Nederland, ARA-II; De Valk and Van Faassen, *Dagboeken en aantekeningen*, p. 937.

[120] Berg, *Snijders*, p. 94; Bonebakker, *Twee verdienstelijke officieren*, pp. 54-55; Van der Wal, *Herinneringen*, pp. 10, 12, 18, 28, 29, 32, 48; Heldring, *Herinneringen*, p. 923.

[121] Van der Wal, *Herinneringen*, pp. 29n, 30-31; Smit, *1917-1919*, pp. 22-23.

[122] Snijders memorandum, 18 March 1918, 429, Smit, *Bescheiden ... 1917-1919*, pp. 431-32; Klinkert, "Verdediging van de zuidgrens " (Part One), p. 219; Memorandum, "Summary of events in the military leadership April-June 1918," Collectie B.C. de Jonge, ARA-II.

[123] Report of conference between De Jonge and Snijders, 26 April 1918, Collectie B.C. de Jonge, ARA-II.

[124] Report of conference between De Jonge and Snijders, 26 April 1918, Collectie B.C. de Jonge, ARA-II; Berg, *Snijders*, p. 95.

[125] Report of conference between De Jonge and Snijders, 26 April 1918, Collectie B.C. de Jonge, ARA-II; Van der Wal, *Herinneringen*, pp. 40-41; Bonebakker, *Twee verdienstelijke officieren*, pp. 56-57.

[126] Van der Wal, *Herinneringen*, p. 42; B.C. de Jonge, File Memo, 29 April 1918,

Collectie B.C. de Jonge, ARA-II.

[127] Memoranda De Jonge's conversations with Pop and Burger, 27 April 1918, Van der Voort Maarschalk, 4 May 1918, and Col. Fabius, 4 May 1918, Collectie B.C. de Jonge, ARA-II.

[128] De Jonge, memorandum of conversation with Maj.-Gen. Van Terwisga, 8 May 1918, Collectie B.C. de Jonge, ARA-II.

[129] "Is realistic defense of the Netherlands against a German attack possible under the current circumstances?" 29 April 1918: Insinger to De Jonge, 30 April 1918, Collectie B.C. de Jonge, ARA-II.

[130] De Jonge to ministers, 8 May 1918 and 8 June 1918, 499, 531, Smit, *Bescheiden ... 1917-1919,* pp. 503-506, 558-60; Berg, *Snijders,* p. 95; De Jonge to Cort van der Linden, n.d., Collectie B.C. de Jonge, ARA-II; Bonebakker, *Twee verdienstelijke officieren,* pp. 56-57; Bout, "Dutch Army," p. 142.

[131] Van der Wal, *Herinneringen,* pp. 42-44; Bonebakker, *Twee verdienstelijke officieren,* pp. 57-58.

[132] Van der Wal, *Herinneringen,* p. 47; Bonebakker, *Twee verdienstelijke officieren,* pp. 57-58; Cabinet minutes, 8 June 1918, 532, Smit, *Bescheiden ... 1917-1919,* p. 560; Berg, *Snijders,* p. 96.

[133] Snijders to ministers, 29 May 1918, 523, Smit, *Bescheiden ... 1917-1919,* pp. 534-46.

[134] Ibid.

[135] Ibid.

[136] Ibid.

[137] Bonebakker, *Twee verdienstelijke officieren,* p. 58.

[138] Smit, *Tien studiën,* pp. 145-48.

[139] Memorandum of Minister de Jonge concerning crisis in defense leadership, 11 July 1918, Generale Staf, nr toegang .13.70, inv nrs 1, 4, 352, ARA-II.

[140] Memorandum, "Relationship, Supreme Commander – Minister," Snijders, 26 September 1918, Generale Staf, nr toegang .13.70, inv nrs 1, 4, 352, ARA-II.

[141] Memorandum by Snijders in response to Jhr. De Jonge's memorandum of 11 July 1918, 3 October 1918, Generale Staf, nr toegang .13.70, inv nrs 1, 4, 352, ARA-II.

[142] Memorandum by Snijders in response to Jhr. De Jonge's memorandum of 11 July 1918, 3 October 1918, Generale Staf, nr toegang .13.70, inv nrs 1, 4, 352, ARA-II.

[143] Heldring, *Herinneringen,* pp. 682-83.

[144] Memorandum by J.J. Rambonnet regarding the Snijders memorandum of 29 May 1918, 31 May 1918, Collectie B.C. de Jonge, ARA-II; Bonebakker, *Twee verdienstelijke officieren,* pp. 57-58.

[145] Bout, "Dutch Army," p. 147.

[146] Van der Wal, *Herinneringen,* pp. 49, 75.

[147] Frey, *Der Erste Weltkrieg,* pp. 280-82.

[148] Townley to Balfour, 21 June 1918, 236, Bourne and Watt, *British Documents,* Part II, Series H, vol. 3, pp. 393-94; Townley to Balfour, 10 July 1918, 4, Idem, vol. 4, pp. 4-6.

[149] Townley to Balfour, 6 August 1918 and 4 September 1918, 8, 24, Bourne and Watt, *British Documents,* Part II, Series H, vol. 4, pp. 12-14, 45-47; Smit, *Tien studiën,* pp. 152-156.

[150] Townley to Balfour, 4 September 1918, 24, Bourne and Watt, *British Documents,* Part II, Series H, vol. 3, pp. 45-47; Bout, "Dutch Army," pp. 10, 145.

[151] De Jonge, "Memrandum regarding transfer of portfolio," 18 July 1918, Collectie

B.C. de Jonge, ARA-II.

[152] Berg, *Snijders,* p. 97; H.M. Mettes, J.M.M. Cuypers, R. van Velden, and E.A. Heugten, coms., *Inventaris van de Archieven van de Generale Staf, 1914-1940* ('s-Gravenhage: Ministerie van Defensie – Centraal Archievendepot, 1997), pp. 6-7, 21-22.

[153] Townley to Balfour, 10 July 1918, 4, Bourne and Watt, *British Documents,* Part II, Series H, vol. 4, pp. 4-6; Frey, *Der Erste Weltkrieg,* pp. 319-322; Wolting, "Uit het dagboek," p. 34; Smit, *Diplomatieke geschiedenis,* pp. 318-19.

[154] Townley to Balfour, 12 August 1918, 9, Bourne and Watt, *British Documents,* Part II, Series H, vol. 4, pp. 14-16.

[155] Oppenheimer, *Stranger Within,* pp. 326, 328.

[156] Ibid., pp. 328, 330.

[157] Heldring, *Herinneringen,* p. 279; Porter, "Dutch Neutrality," p. 162.

[158] Oppenheimer, *Stranger within,* p. 326; Heldring, *Herinneringen,* pp. 230, 236-37; Heldring diary, 23 September 1918, 637, Smit, *Bescheiden ... 1917-1919,* 654-55; R.L. Schuursma, "Een verdrag in opspraak: Het Belgisch-Nederlandsch Verdrag," *Spiegel Historiael* 13 (No. 1 1978), pp. 34-35.

[159] Oppenheimer, *Stranger within,* p. 332; Frey, *Der Erste Weltkrieg,* pp. 319-322; Memorandum, British Legation, 26 September 1918, 642, Smit, *Bescheiden ... 1917-1919,* p. 658; De Valk and Van Faassen, *Dagboeken en aantekeningen,* p. 394; Rosen, *Aus einem diplomatischen Wanderleben,* vol. 3/4, p. 73; Schuursma, "Een verdrag in opspraak," pp. 34-35; Heldring, *Herinneringen,* p. 279.

[160] Van der Wal, *Herinneringen,* pp. 21, 27.

[161] Bout, "Dutch Army," pp. 92-93, 115, *passim;* A. M. de Jong, *Frank van Wezel's roemrucht jaren – notities van een landstormman* (1958 (1928)), and J. C. van der Does, et al, *Als 't moet* (The Hague: Niigh & van Ditman, 1959); Van der Wal, *Herinneringen,* p. 33; Bout, "Nature and Extent of Antimilitarism," pp. 10, 32, 49.

[162] Bonebakker, *Twee verdienstelijke officieren,* p. 47; Bout, "Dutch Army," p. 115; Idem, "Nature and Extent of Antimilitarism," pp. 51-52.

[163] Berg, *Snijders,* p. 111; De Beaufort, *Vijftig jaren,* part 2, p. 303.

[164] Engelen, *Binnenlandse Veiligheidsdienst,* p. 13.

[165] Porter, "Dutch Neutrality," p. 162; Bout, "Nature and Extent of Antimilitarism," p. 54; Idem, "Dutch Army," p. 149; Wolting, "Uit het dagboek," p. 35; Bonebakker, *Twee verdienstelijke officieren,* p. 59.

[166] Berg, *Snijders,* pp. 111-113.

[167] Bout, "Dutch Army," p. 152; Idem, "Nature and Extent of Antimilitarism," p. 246; Bosscher, "Oorlogsvaart," pp. 338-39.

[168] Bonebakker, *Twee verdienstelijke officieren,* pp. 70-71.

[169] Berg, *Snijders,* pp. 113-14.

[170] Ibid., pp. 114-16; Bout, "Dutch Army," p. 153; Bonebakker, *Twee verdienstelijke officieren,* p. 59.

[171] Berg, *Snijders,* pp. 116-118; Van der Wal, *Herinneringen,* p. 50; Wolting, "Uit het dagboek," p. 35; Snijders to land and sea forces, 11 November 1918, AHK Bereden Artillerie, ARA-II; Mettes, et al, *Inventaris,* p. 23; Heldring, *Herinneringen,* p. 410; Annual report, British Legation, 1919, 110, Bourne and Watt, *British Documents,* Part II, Series I, *The Paris Peace Conference of 1919* (ed. M. Dockrill), vol. 6 (Washington, DC: University Publications of America, 1989), pp. 247-57; *InterNet Krant,* 31 August 1999.

[172] Townley to Balfour, 22 February 1918, 202, Bourne and Watt, *British Documents,*

Part II, Series H, vol. 3, pp. 333-35; Bout, "Dutch Army," p. 6; Heldring diary, 3 October 1918, 646, Smit, *Bescheiden ... 1917-1919*, pp. 662-63.

[173] Engelen, *Binnenlandse Veiligheidsdienst*, p. 13; Bout, "Nature and Extent of Antimilitarism," pp. 41-42, 49; Idem, "Dutch Army," pp. 157-59; Porter, "Dutch Neutrality," p. 164; Townley, *'Indiscretions,'* p. 180; Cabinet minutes, 11 November 1918, 727, Smit, *Bescheiden ... 1917-1919*, p. 729.

[174] Engelen, *Binnenlandse Veiligheidsdienst*, p. 13; Van der Wal, *Herinneringen*, p. 52; Bout, "Dutch Army," pp. 154-56.

[175] Engelen, *Binnenlandse Veiligheidsdienst*, pp. 12-13, 37; Van Diesen, "Nederlandse Inlichtingendiensten," passim.

[176] Mettes, et al, *Inventaris*, p. 9.

[177] Heldring, *Herinneringen*, p. 270; Bout, "Dutch Army," pp. 154-56; Townley, *'Indiscretions,'* pp. 301-302; Annual report of the British legation (1919), 110, Bourne and Watt, *British Documents*, Part II, Series I, vol. 6, pp. 247-57; Rosen, *Aus einem diplomatischen Wanderleben*, vol. 3/4, p. 96.

[178] Porter, "Dutch Neutrality," 1p. 65; Bout, "Nature and Extent of Antimilitarism," p. 236; Townley, *'Indiscretions,'* pp. 301-302; Bout, "Dutch Army," pp. 157-59, 160-62.

[179] Bout, "Nature and Extent of Antimilitarism," pp. 264-65; Porter, "Dutch Neutrality," p. 164; Heldring, *Herinneringen*, pp. 262-63; Heldring diary, 4 December 1918, 790, Smit, *Bescheiden ... 1917-1919*, p. 777.

[180] Townley, *'Indiscretions,'* pp. 300-301; Gevers to Van Karnebeek, 17 October 1918, 666: De Marees van Swinderen to Van Karnebeek, 14 November 1918, 746, Smit *Bescheiden ... 1917-1919*, pp. 686-87, 741-42; Engelen, *Binnenlandse Veiligheidsdienst*, p 13; Wolting, "De eerste jaren," pp. 570-71.

[181] Heldring diary, 789, 3 December 1918, Smit, *Bescheiden ... 1917-1919*, pp. 774-76; Annual report of the British legation (1919), 110, Bourne and Watt, *British Documents*, Part II, Series I, vol. 6, pp. 247-57; Bout, "Dutch Army," pp. 159, 162 (citing H. J. Scheffer, *November 1918: Journaal van een revolutie die niet doorging* (Amsterdam: De Arbeiderspers, 1968)); Townley, *'Indiscretions,'* pp. 301-302.

[182] Heldring, *Herinneringen*, pp. 266-67; Bout, "Dutch Army," p. 162; Idem, "Nature and Extent of Antimilitarism," p. 236; Smit, *Tien studiën*, p. 158.

[183] Van Karnebeek to Loudon, 30 December 1918, 859, Smit, *Bescheiden ... 1917-1919*, pp. 848-49.

CHAPTER SEVEN

THE SPECTRE OF BELGIAN IMPERIALISM

The end of the war brought no relief. The blockade continued, affecting Holland as well as Germany.[1] Instability in defeated Germany threatened to spill across the border. Holland was now an unwilling host to the German Emperor, who had fled his country in the war's waning hours. Instead of being able to balance the interests of two warring alliances, the Dutch now had to deal with only one – and that one had precious little sympathy for the Netherlands, regarding it, however unfairly, as having functioned as a proxy for Germany in many ways.[2] The Entente had championed the "rights of small nations" and "rights of neutrals" during the war, but not consistently. There was no certainty that it would so now that it had won, and there was certainly no way for Holland to compel it to do so.

For months if not years, the Dutch had expected the war to end in a compromise peace, as exhaustion overtook the opposing alliances. Whether or not this outcome was possible amidst the intensity and hatreds of total war is debatable. Ludendorff, for example, preferred to risk defeat rather than settle for compromise. As a noncombatant nation, the Dutch viewed the war with a detached attitude impossible for the participants. The question became moot once the United States entered the war; either the Central Powers would win before America was fully mobilized, or the Entente would prevail afterwards. To Snijders, the American participation caused the Central Powers' destruction.[3] It became evident in the fall of 1918 that there would be no compromise settlement and that Holland would now deal with a victorious and unfriendly alliance.

This had immediate implications for the maintenance of neutrality, although this was less important in a practical sense than it had been. As the allied armies swung toward Antwerp in late October 1918, the use of the Schelde and other Dutch transport routes became an issue once again. The Foreign Ministry pointed out that as Germany had been granted a favorable transit regime (albeit under great pressure), the same would now have to be done for the Entente. Townley was not slow to make this point. His hand was strengthened by the permitted passage of 70,000 disarmed German soldiers through Limburg, a decision made in the panicky period of threatened revolution when it was not known if there would be an army to stop the Germans if they decided to come anyway. Van Karnebeek attempted to defend his action by pointing out that Britain had agreed that Holland could release all interned soldiers. Townley pointed out that this agreement had come after the passage through Limburg, and used the latter event to explain that Britain assumed – no demand was even thought necessary – that supplies could go by way of the Rhine and Schelde and was making plans accordingly. Van Karnebeek was not as used to Loudon to treatment of this kind but, having bent to the Germans, he had little choice. He informed the British that supplies could be shipped via Dutch waterways and railways, as this constituted normal commercial traffic.[4] That decidedly stretched definition of neutrality, as the supplies were for the maintenance of Rhineland occupation troops and peace had not been formally signed yet. Nevertheless, it did allow the foreign minister to retain what little was left of his dignity at this point and let Britain have its way without officially abandoning neutrality.

Concessions to the allies did no harm to the relationship with Germany, which was cordial, perhaps too much so. Given the Entente's suspicions about Holland it was not the best of times to appear too sympathetic to Germany. Rosen praised the tact and sympathy shown by the Netherlands toward Germany after the defeat. The Dutch government allowed German ships and submarines to return home through territorial (but not internal) waters. This caused a stir at the Quay d'Orsay, the French foreign ministry being even more anti-Dutch during this period than the British. As a result, some of the German ships were sent back to Antwerp by the Dutch in December. This reversal does not seem to have caused any trouble with Berlin, however, where more serious matters were occurring. The Foreign Ministry did return to the Eems dispute, as this was one area where strict neutrality had not been maintained. The trouble was, that if the river was treated as a border, then neutrality should have been maintained; if it belonged to Germany, some Dutch towns could only be reached through German waters.[i] Gevers advised against arbitration, as he thought the Dutch case rather weak. He reported, however, that

---

[i] The issue depended, among other things, on whether or not an enfeoffment from 1454 was a forgery.

the new foreign minister, Von Brockdorff-Rantzau, was willing to
negotiate on many issues, although Gevers found him ""somewhat
irritable, as is usually the case with people who drink."[5]

The problems posed by the eternal Eems question paled in comparison to the rumblings from the south, however. The outcome of the
Eems discussions would not affect the Netherlands materially, but
revisions of the border with Belgium would. Belgian annexationism
was not new. Since 1839 a school of thought in Belgium had considered the country's borders to be artificial and inadequate for national
security, which depended solely on the international guarantee of
neutrality. During the war, however, this view had naturally gained
support. Britain had taken the position in 1916 that Belgium needed a
military alliance and possibly a border revision for its protection. The
1916 declaration only suggested incorporating Luxembourg into
Belgium, but Belgian annexationists soon turned their eyes northwards.
Limburg and the Schelde basin looked inviting, the latter especially
because Belgium could never hope to force the Schelde. At one point
in the 19th century the country had no navy, and built only a coast
defense force afterwards. Even before the war ended, some Dutch
attention was being paid to these (as yet unofficial) demands. Military
intelligence reviewed brochures produced by the Belgians on the
matter and was instructed to start giving the press as much information
as possible "to fight the Belgian intrigues." Much more would be
required, however. The problems between Holland and Belgium were
old and deep, and Belgium now held some powerful trump cards with
which to make a play for a favorable settlement.

The Netherlands and Belgium; the issues

There was an atmosphere of hostility in Belgian circles toward
Holland. Despite occasional expressions of gratitude for Dutch aid and
assistance, Belgium could not but contrast its own fate in wartime to
Holland's. The resulting attitude manifested itself in many ways. For
example, the Belgians informed Britain on October 8, 1918, that they
were opposed to Holland hosting a peace conference. On this point, the
Belgians were kicking in the proverbial open door. There was no
chance that the Dutch would get the peace conference or, for that
matter, the League of Nations, as the Americans reportedly "wanted
nothing to do with Carnegie and his peace palace."[6]

The Belgian view had specific roots. One of these was the attitude of some Flemish activists who had supported Germany and had developed connections with a small coterie of Dutchmen favoring a merger of some type with Flanders. On March 17, 1917, the German government had divided Belgium administratively into Flemish and Walloon provinces. A handful of Flemish soldiers had formed the Front Party and secretly negotiated with the Germans. This was more than enough for the Walloon-dominated Belgian government to become concerned, especially when some prominent Dutch politicians (including De Savornin Lohman) formed the allegedly pro-separatist *Volksopbeuring* committee. Officially, the Belgian government was satisfied with the Dutch response concerning the matter, saying that the Dutch government *"a donné un nouveau et précieux témoinage de sa constante sollicitude pour les populations belges"* ("has given a new and precious witness of its constant concern for the Belgian populations"). This was true enough. When Kühlmann spoke with Cort van der Linden and Kuyper, these worthies carefully avoided even hinting at the slightest interest in Flemish territory.[7]

Yet the affair reminded the Belgians that their state was extraordinarily insecure. This was one factor in their growing interest in the annexation of Limburg. Nine years before the war, one Belgian diplomat had opined that *"[e]n donnant à la Hollande la province de Limbourg, la conférence de Londres a confié une des portes de notre maison."* Then in 1914 a rumor spread that the German armies had, in fact, crossed Dutch Limburg to surround Liège. This allegation, made by the Belgian war minister himself on 10 August 1914, proved to be extraordinarily stubborn and deleterious for relations between Holland and all the Entente nations – so much so, that some Dutchmen living in Belgium in 1914 alleged that the Germans had spread the story. In 1914, the British legation in Brussels twice reported (3 and 5 August) that German troops had invaded Holland. Perhaps this explains the British chargé's 1918 claim that the "inability of the Dutch to defend their frontier was proved in 1914 . . ." The French government, including Clemenceau, was equally convinced that it had happened. The story was very much a problem for the Dutch at Versailles, and even afterwards. In 1922, an American publication would allege that Holland had pulled its troops out of Limburg "early in the late war." French writings still mentioned the claim as late as 1926. The explanation may have been quite innocent. As Treub pointed out, the German march route went right by the Dutch border, and the two armies looked much alike. The Dutch army had converted to a field grey uniform that looked much like the German.[8] Unlike their French counterparts, the Dutch generals had realized that the best way to be seen on a battlefield was not to be seen at all.

Yet the government, under pressure from the threat of revolution, had committed an action in 1918 that had lent credence to the earlier rumor. It granted permission for the German withdrawal through Limburg. The German request was not a surprise. Bosboom had predicted in 1914 (!) that a retreating German army might want to cross Limburg, and that this might be fatal to neutrality. He suggested that if such a demand were made, then Germany should be informed that Holland would not prevent a guarantor power from pursuing the Germans. The situation in 1918 was different, however. The guarantor powers were no longer considered such because all, as well as Belgium, were belligerents. In addition, the fighting stopped before the pursuit. The German legation asked on November 9, 1918, and again on the 11th, to allow ill and wounded soldiers to cross Limburg. The Foreign Ministry agreed on the 12th. The cabinet met the following day, and preoccupied by the threat of revolution, decided to allow the transit. At least 70,000 German troops entered Holland between the 14th and the end of the month, and there surrendered their weapons and were carefully watched by the Dutch army.[9]

The Entente governments were furious. Belgium filed a formal protest on 23 November, the Americans and French followed four days later, and Britain and Italy filed theirs on November 29. In Belgium and Britain, the grant of passage became a public political issue. The British chargé concluded that the "inability of the Dutch to defend their frontier . . . has been still more clearly shown during the last few weeks." Clemenceau felt free during the peace conference to use the incident as a justification to force Entente passage if needed: "Means of pressure would be found." Van Karnebeek compounded the situation by issuing justifications that were not believable or, as it turned out, not true. To American observers, the "explanations of the Dutch were lame." This probably refers to the foreign minister's argument that keeping the Germans in Belgium would have harmed the Belgians. In other words, the passage was permitted to help Belgium. This may have been true, but nobody believed it. Worse, Van Karnebeek claimed that he had conferred with the Entente governments before approving the passage. Whether this claim was the result of a misunderstanding or outright dishonesty is difficult to say, although the former seems more probable. The minister could hardly have expected to get away with an outright lie, especially as he restated the point to the Entente envoys, his own government, and his own diplomats. Regardless, the Entente envoys denied the claim and Van Karnebeek was forced to recant, telling Allizé that the minister's message claiming that the crossing was *"après entente"* was wrong.[10]

The earlier enthusiasm for Van Karnebeek's appointment waned. Treub was critical of the passage and felt serious consequences were avoided only because the allies were exhausted. Heldring, an early fan of Van Karnebeek's, thought the government's action was "inexplicable" and suggested to Van Karnebeek that perhaps the Entente should have been consulted first. Loudon "showed himself little impressed" with the government's handling of the situation. Heldring, who did not like Loudon, pointed out to the former minister that the army was unreliable. However, extra Dutch troops had actually been shipped to Limburg during the passage, undermining that argument somewhat. On the other hand, as both Heldring and Treub suggest, the government was not eager to use a large part of its army for interning 70,000 Germans.[11] This makes sense, as the revolution was scheduled for a few days hence and the government perhaps did not wish to send reliable troops all the way to Limburg. In addition, demobilization had already begun.

None of these arguments made any impression on the Belgians. Agitation for border change, and possibly the annexation of Zeeuwsch-Vlaanderen and Limburg, had been building for some time and was only strengthened by the passage incident. Ignoring governmental opposition in 1916, many Belgians supported annexation. Eugène Baie, the propagandist for alliance before the war, was one of the prime movers. Later, his cause would be joined by the *Comité de Politique Nationale,* which pushed for broad border changes and even a League plebiscite in Limburg. Some Flemish papers were opposed, while socialists were interested in the left bank of the Schelde and Catholic politicians thought the government should move carefully. Those who favored territorial demands were very optimistic at the end of the war. There was some foundation for the their demands.[ii] Their borders were part of the 1839 treaty, which had forced Belgium into permanent

---

[ii] It is nevertheless peculiar that the Walloon-dominated state would seek to add two large Dutch-speaking populations, one of them Flemish.

neutrality; Schlieffen and Moltke had made that portion of the treaty obsolete. In addition, the border issue was not new. The areas that would be fought over by the diplomats (Limburg and the Schelde basin) were the same ones that had led to a boundary crisis in 1784.[12]

But would all this translate into an official demand for territory? And would the Entente nations support the demand (for otherwise, the demand meant nothing)? These questions had been asked with increasing frequency throughout war. In September 1914 Heldring asked Walter Runciman, president of the British Board of Trade, point blank if the allies planned to demand Dutch Flanders for Belgium. Runciman assured him that this would not happen. In the same month, however, De Beaufort began to suspect that Belgium would demand both Flanders and Limburg if they were on the winning side. Loudon had pointed out already in 1914 that Belgium might demand territory from Holland, with compensation to come from Germany. Kühlmann reported on 8 December 1915 about a conversation with the incoming Governor-General of the Indies, who also feared annexations.[iii] The Entente victory made the issue far more relevant. On 23 October 1918, the German Chancellor asked Gevers for information concerning rumors that the Entente would soon demand Holland's territory along the Schelde. Less than two weeks later, Rosen reported conversations that he had held with Van Karnebeek and Kuyper on the same topic.[13] Obviously, there was much concern, no doubt heightened by the awareness that there was nothing that could be done.

The Belgian claim on Limburg was weak. The position regarding the Schelde was stronger, especially as Britain had an interest as well. Belgium's interest in the Schelde basin was far greater than in Limburg. The Schelde was Antwerp's economic lifeline, not just a military corridor. Between 1830 and 1900 more than 700 Belgian publications dealt with the disastrous possibility of the river silting up. The 1839 treaty permitted the Belgians to construct a canal from Antwerp to the Rhine, but this was difficult to do with Dutch opposition – and Dutch seaports had fought the scheme ever since it was first proposed in the 17th century. So the Schelde was the city's only foreign

---

[iii] His concern was not just about Belgian, but also about French ambitions. This was reflected in the southern neighbor as well. By the beginning of 1919, Belgium, while seeking to annex lands to the north, was seeking British aid to stop France from annexing Luxembourg. Villiers to Balfour, 9 January 1919, 40, Bourne and Watt, *British Documents,* Part II, Series I, vol. 6, pp. 126-28.

trade link. In late 1917, Belgian authorities began once more to request information on the condition of the channel, a request greeted with lively suspicion by the Dutch. Loudon explained to Snijders that a failure to cooperate might give the Entente a justification for revising the Schelde situation after the war. Snijders was less solicitous of Belgian feelings, as he felt he was being asked to reveal military secrets (he was) and suggested that the Dutch give Belgium assurances that the navigability of the Schelde would be carefully maintained. Once again, the Belgians were reminded that their most vital river mouth belonged to someone else.[14]

Could this be changed – and how could it be justified to the Entente partners? France would probably support a demand, the USA was less likely to. The British government would probably cast the deciding vote – especially as it had the most great-power interest in Belgium's future. Perhaps a territorial swap could be made acceptable if Holland were somehow "compensated" – at Germany's expense. For Holland this idea was extremely dangerous. Not only would national territory and people be lost, but its "gain" would cost it the undying enmity of its huge neighbor. Sir Francis Villiers, British envoy to Belgium, thought it feasible, however. He suggested on 8 December 1918 that the Netherlands might be compensated with territory from Germany, or in Africa, Timor, or the extension of Dutch Guiana. He did not openly commit himself to this scheme, however.[15] Getting the critical British support would now depend on the skills of the Belgian foreign minister – and the ability of the Dutch to stop him.

The Kaiser

The Belgians began the game with a number of advantages, not the least of which was the presence of the Kaiser in the Netherlands. Wilhelm II had become the focal point for much Entente feelings about the war. This was more a result of the Kaiser's rhetoric and behavior than his actions, but he was publicly viewed as an evil figure who should be punished for the war's great destruction. Whether the Entente leaders really wanted to do this may be doubted, as the legal and political problems of trying a former head of state of were (and are) formidable. But his arrival threatened to reinforce Holland's image as pro-German. Hence the decision to admit the Kaiser was not an easy one. On the other hand, he had intervened several times to restrain his government's behavior toward Holland, and the Dutch government knew this.

The Kaiser's flight to Holland was motivated by fear of his own people, not of the Entente. The outbreak of revolution in Germany convinced conservative elements that the Kaiser's presence would stimulate revolution. While his generals had always been loyal, they had little affection or regard for the man and certainly did not look to him for leadership in suppressing the uprising. The Emperor's brother and eldest son, the natural successors, were also ruled unacceptable. Plotting the Kaiser's flight began no later than November 5th and may have been thought about a couple of weeks earlier. On October 20th, Rosen had been instructed to thank Wilhelmina for Holland's steadfast neutrality. On November 5, General J.B. van Heutsz, military advisor to the Queen and former governor-general of the Indies, arrived at Spa.[iv] Certainly the Queen was involved, and equally certainly the cabinet as a whole was not. Whether she would have sent Van Heutsz without discussing it with Ruys de Beerenbrouck, however, may be doubted. He remained for four days, meeting with the Kaiser on the 8th. The Kaiser was not keen on leaving. He hoped to lead the army back into Germany to crush the rebellion. When that proved impossible, he began to worry about whether Bolshevism would rear its head in Holland as well. On November 9th Hindenburg advised his monarch to go to Holland rather than Switzerland because he expected more sympathy for the emperor there, and, more practically, it was only 60 kilometers away. Baron Werner von Grünau and adjutant Hans von Plessen assured the Kaiser that Bolshevism would not break out in Holland. Asylum among the Dutch it would have to be.[16]

Events moved fast. On 9 November, Oscar von der Lancken informed the Dutch envoy in Brussels that the Kaiser was leaving that night and asked him to warn the Queen. Van Vollenhoven did so, sending a message by car to Van Karnebeek (Van Vollenhoven had been denied the official cipher book and could not send a coded telegram). In addition, he sent another car to Eysden to warn the border

---

[iv] It has been pointed out that Van Heutsz's trip to Spa was long planned, and his arrival was a coincidence. Fasseur, *Wilhelmina,* pp. 552-54. This does not explain, however, why he went ahead and made the trip at such a complex and critical time during the war. More importantly, can we assume that the Kaiser's future was not mentioned during the entire visit (November 5-9) especially when the message to Von der Lancken (see text below) could not have been sent any later than the 9th?

guards.[v] The Kaiser had a long delay at the border, the local army sergeant refusing him and his entourage admission.[vi] After some hours, the Emperor was allowed to come just inside the border, to the Eysden railway depot, which in fact sits astride the Belgian-Dutch line. The wait was not pleasant. Hecklers appeared. When the Kaiser asked the station master whether he could go in that worthy's private office, the bureaucrat merely pointed to the sign above his office door, *"Voor onbevoegden verboden"* (no admission for unauthorized persons). Eventually, the secretary of the foreign ministry (Doude van Troostwijk), the provincial governor, and Rosen showed up, to inform the Kaiser that the cabinet, after an emergency session, had agreed to let the emperor in. Part of the delay had been caused by trying to find a suitable spot. The place chosen was G.J.G.Ch. graaf (count) van Aldenburg Bentinck's estate at Amerongen was chosen, but Bentinck was reluctant. Only a second request caused him to agree. The estate was close to the center of the country and was surrounded by two moats. The Kaiser could enter, but he would certainly not be free.[17]

He could not be free, because his presence placed Holland squarely in the middle of a storm of controversy. In the eyes of most of the country, he was an uninvited guest. The Socialists in particular wanted him to leave. For once, their view was completely shared by the government. On December 6, 1918, the government decided to ask him to leave. Rosen was asked to tell the Kaiser that the Dutch government wanted him to go home, but he refused to carry the message. Rosen was a staunch monarchist and never really recovered from the collapse of the house of Hohenzollern. In addition, he was under no obligation to carry the message. The Dutch government had decided to treat the emperor as a private citizen, so Rosen did not have to act as gobetween. Instead, the governor of Utrecht, count F.A.C. van Lynden van

---

[v] Marc Frey has suggested that this courier came from somewhere else as Van Vollenhoven did not have the authority to send the man to the border. Frey, *Erste Weltkrieg,* pp. 333-35. As shown by his earlier cross-border show and tell trip with the German envoy, Van Vollenhoven did not worry too much about his authority (or lack thereof).

[vi] Lamar Cecil, in his otherwise magisterial biography of Wilhelm, claims that the convoy got across the border at Eysden by telling the guard that the cars contained only a general and his entourage. Lamar Cecil, *Wilhelm II,* vol. 2, *Emperor and Exile* (Chapel Hill: University of North Carolina Press, 1996), pp. 293-94. I can only attribute this *faux pas* to Cecil's failure to use Dutch documents.

Sandenburg went to ask (but not pressure) the emperor to leave.
Heldring suggested to his friends in government that the Kaiser should
be shipped to Argentina, if the Entente would permit it. Bentinck also
tired of his unwanted guest. Wilhelm's presence caused trouble from
the moment of his arrival; Bentinck's cook had initially refused to
prepare a meal for the former monarch.[18]

There was never any question of the Kaiser being forced to leave,
however. The law prohibited handing over of aliens who sought refuge
for political reasons. Holland had survived partly through its legalistic
attitude and was not about to abandon it now. Nor was the Kaiser going
to leave of his own accord. There was nowhere for him to go. He
certainly could not return to Germany and had no intention of
submitting to Entente imprisonment. His advisors were also opposed,
pointing out that leaving Holland would look like a second flight;
hoping for a restoration, they could not afford to make their leader look
like a coward. Therefore the Kaiser stayed in Holland until his death
in 1941. Initially he expressed himself warmly toward Holland and
spoke of his ties to the Orange family. The Dutch were less sentimen-
tal. Wilhelmina did not receive him once during his almost 23 years in
the Netherlands. All the Kaiser's mail and messages were carefully
monitored. His asylum in Holland was good for him, and it was good
for Germany, which perhaps explains why Rosen also expressed his
gratitude for Holland's position.[19] But it was not a relationship desired
by either Wilhelm or Holland.

Having decided to accept the Kaiser, and keep him if he chose to
stay, the government now turned its attention to explaining the course
of events to the Entente. The public position of the Entente governments was vociferous. Lloyd George had enthusiastically proclaimed,
"Damn the Junkers, Hang the Kaiser!" but the great Welshman was not
noted for being extravagant with the truth. His true feelings were
probably closer to those of Balfour, whose comment on the Emperor's
flight was: "Poor Dutch." Even so, demands for his extradition had to
be made. Lloyd George and Clemenceau publicly supported a trial,
although Wilson and, interestingly enough, King Albert of the
Belgians, were opposed. The French were furious about the Emperor's
asylum, and their envoy made more of an issue about that than about
the German troop transit. Townley also raised the issue, immediately
demanding that the Kaiser be interned. There was even fear in the
Netherlands that the Entente might go ahead and occupy Dutch
Flanders and Limburg in retaliation.[20]

The actual allied actions on the Kaiser were measured. King George V declined to visit Holland, writing that such a trip would "open to very serious misconstruction" (referring to the presence of the Kaiser). Even he was opposed, however, to treating Wilhelm as a war criminal. The allies did make a formal request for Holland to surrender the Kaiser, but it was not made until 16 January 1920, long after the other issues affecting Holland had been settled. Van Karnebeek easily deflected the demand, pointing out that it grew out of the Versailles treaty, to which Holland was not a party and hence could not be bound by it.[21] The Dutch government even realized a small gain on the affair; Townley disappeared from the scene. This happened because his somewhat eccentric wife Susan decided to go and watch the Kaiser's arrival at Amerongen, and was recognized. This cost her husband any chance of promotion, and he and his wife retired to breed pigs, which they found considerably more remunerative.[22] As happy as the Dutch were to see him go, they would much have preferred to keep Townley and lose the Kaiser. At the beginning of 1919, his presence further poisoned the Holland-Entente relationship. Holland's image as an extension of Germany substantially raised the odds that Belgium's demands would be met. On the other hand, it would require skillful maneuvering by the Belgian foreign minister to connect Belgian demands and the Kaiser's asylum in the minds of the Entente representatives.

Hymans' demands

The Belgian foreign minister, Paul Hymans, was a populist politician who felt keenly his country's devastation during the war, and was determined to prevent it from reoccurring. His strong emotions on the subject lent fire to his public rhetoric but occasionally interfered with his diplomacy, which may explain why "brave little Belgium" walked away from Versailles with nearly empty hands. Hymans had to play a double role at Versailles. He represented his government, but he was also part of an internal debate over annexationism. By no means was Belgium united on the question. While the government was committed to annexation on the eve of the peace conference, some ministers were unenthusiastic. Exactly where they stood is not easy to determine, as they sometimes told the Dutch that they were anti-annexation, knowing Hymans was preparing his case for territory. Prime minister L.

Delacroix told Van Vollenhoven that he favored direct negotiations, but only said so very late in the game; he certainly did not attempt to restrain Hymans. During the war, the Belgian government downplayed any official annexationist tendencies and even fired baron Guillaume from his diplomatic post (ambassador to France) when he proposed seizure of Flanders and Limburg.[23] Victory changed things. Anti-Dutch rhetoric filled the Belgian parliament. The King proved supportive. The Walloon politicians and businessmen who formed the *Comité de Politique Nationale* provided stirring rhetoric to justify demanding Luxembourg, Limburg, and the Schelde. Luxembourg, it was argued, had submitted too easily. Limburg was an access route into Belgium, and had been used by the Germans for the great retreat. The Schelde basin had proven necessary because "neutral Holland had prevented the arrival of British reinforcements in 1914."[24]

The annexationist campaign at Versailles had force and enthusiasm, but little tact or diplomacy. This can be attributed mostly to Hymans. He presented his allies with lengthy statements about Belgium's territorial problems, without suggesting specific solutions. Exactly why he did this has never been resolved. His efforts were undermined by his Socialist delegate, Emile Vandervelde, a man whose "actions so rarely coincided with his words." Vandervelde supported Hymans' claims but blamed all of Belgium's unpopular positions on Hymans and claimed credit for any Belgian restraint.

> Yet Hymans could not blame his failures on Vandervelde. Although the Belgian foreign minister was "suave, intelligent, idealistic, realistic," he lacked experience and was "neither tactful nor agreeable." He irritated, offended or enraged many other delegates. The Belgian "was prickly and a trifle chilly . . . [and] lacked both imagination and humor . . . he certainly had no capacity at all to see matters from the viewpoint of any other nation. In himself, he summed up Belgium's insulated, parochial diplomatic history, and though he had many talents, they were not those most needed for effective competition in the tumultuous Paris scene.[25]

He was also "extraordinarily sensitive to any slight" and protested "sharply" and "explosively." He became "widely disliked" by the key delegations because he bored them with his "excessively long, overly detailed speeches." His naivete put him a disadvantage competing with the Dutch, who were "infinitely more experienced in dealing with the great powers." His campaign for Brussels as the seat for the League of Nations "irritated and bored almost everybody" and undermined his other goals. So focused was he on eloquently stating grandiose principles that he failed to even cultivate the commission assigned to investigate the Belgian claims. Van Karnebeek strove to take advantage of Hymans' blundering to arrange things "so that the odium, if any, falls to Hymans." The best justification for the Belgian's performance – if not a persuasive one – is that he merely adopted "the semblance of annexationism, asking for much in hopes of gaining little."[26] More probably, he did want territory, but just went about it in the wrong way.

Careful reading of the documents demonstrates that there were two foundations for the Belgian demands, which frequently overlapped. First, the general attitude of Belgians (especially Walloons) toward Holland was negative even before the war started, and deteriorated thereafter. The false rumor about a Dutch-permitted German passage in 1914 was easily believed. The Belgian demands were not just the result of the long and barbaric occupation while Holland escaped more or less unscathed. The wartime Dutch envoys to the Belgians reported "mixed feelings" among the population, noting that newspapers frequently discussed the need for border rectification. The Belgian foreign ministry fanned the flames after the war, pressing its newspapers to publish only stories on the Schelde and Limburg that were hostile toward the Netherlands. Hymans could not get along with Van Karnebeek, becoming so nervous during a conversation that he broke a letter opener. If Hymans' language can be taken at face value, he did suffer from a streak of paranoia. During his speech to the peace conference of 11 February 1919, at which he made his territorial demands, he claimed that his country's enforced neutrality under the 1839 agreement was actually a form of Dutch revenge on the Belgians for revolting.[27] In the long run, exaggerated statements like this did Hymans no good at the conference.

Underlying his rhetoric, however, was a more rational foundation of the Belgian demands: security. Belgium was the only western European combatant to be overrun during the war. It had faithfully adhered to its obligations as a neutral. Yet it had been overrun, and aid had come too late. The demands were motivated much more by fear of Germany than hostility toward Holland. From the Belgian perspective, both the Schelde and Limburg posed security problems. The Belgian King wanted to prevent a new invasion. Hymans felt that the whole Meuse line had to be Belgian, or Belgian defenses could be turned easily. He offered the conference a lengthy speech, in which he confused and misstated he history of the Maastricht appendix, and demanded the annexation of Limburg (or at least *"un régime"* there that would guarantee security). In hindsight, this was a peculiar argument. Dutch Limburg shortened the Belgian border, but Belgium still had lacked the strength to even slow down the German assault: How would it withstand an attack across an even longer border? Ironically, his "peculiar argument" would turn out to have some foundation. The German army easily captured the Limburg bridges in 1940 and used them as an invasion route.[vii] [28]

There is plenty of evidence that he came close to success, and could have succeeded in having some of his demands met. Fortunately for the Dutch, Hymans was more suited for the campaign trail than the conference hall. He demanded much, even when his allies were indicating feelings of reservations, and as a result he would wind up creating feelings of irritation, even among the French, his most reliable supporters. Hence he was careful, particularly in conversations with the British, to focus on non-territorial issues. He nevertheless pursued his claims to both the Schelde and Limburg, as well as abrogation of neutrality and absorption of the remainder of Luxembourg.[viii] He was not alone in believing that some of these lands should have been added to Belgium in 1839. He could not make too much of this point, however, because the allies showed little favor toward irredentism. The Belgians presented their demands to the conference on 11 February 1919, coyly telling the Dutch only that demands had been made (without sharing the contents). This mattered little. De Stuers had good sources in the French government who fed him most of Hymans speech, although not the part about Limburg. That did not matter either, because Hymans' views on that province had been leaked to the aging but able envoy the month before.[29]

The Belgian demands were formulated strangely. Hymans discussed the problems of the Belgian borders, but did not demand a territorial transfer. He hoped that the conference would draw the natural conclusion from his exposition and modify the borders. This indirect strategy had a political foundation. At best the country was moderately united for annexation, and the government did not wish to risk that fragile support with a public demand. Even during the war, public calls

---

[vii] This suggests that the Dutch were less prepared to secure and blow these bridges in 1940 than in 1914 – even though they had much more time to prepare.

[viii] About two thirds had been annexed in 1839.

for annexations were repudiated by the government. Cardinal Mercier, the Belgian primate, opposed annexation because of his "profound contempt" for the Flemish. So Hymans tried to obtain his goal indirectly, but the day after the speech an inaccurate Havas telegram reported that Belgium has made territorial claims. This hurt the Belgian position; the source of the telegram has never been traced. Hymans' tactic backfired and resulted in "the worst of both worlds," infuriating the Dutch, alienating the allies and gaining nothing.[30]

The conferees understood perfectly well that Hymans wanted territory, even if he was attacking the issue obliquely. Territorial claims on a peaceful neutral state presented political problems. Compensating Holland at Germany's expense was proposed. Allegedly "a senior Dutch diplomatist in London had indicated that the Netherlands might be willing to cede Limburg and Flemish Zeeland in return for German territory" in 1914. If true, this sounds like it came from De Marees van Swinderen, who tended to think out loud a bit too much. The French suggested such a swap to the Dutch shortly before the end of the war. De Stuers correctly labeled this *"un ballon d'essai"* ("a trial balloon"). Hymans attempted to have a clause put in the Versailles treaty committing Germany to compensating Holland for territory ceded to Belgium, but did not specify which German territories should be transferred, as he "blithely expected the great powers to arrange matters . . ."[31] But would the allies accept such an arrangement, which smacked of the kind of land swaps made more than a century earlier?

Hymans was not insensitive to these problems and attempted to deal with them in two ways. First, he had more reasonable fallback positions, which included a review of the 1839 "imposed" treaty (such a review would allow him to reopen the border question at a later date, of course) a demand for freedom of the Schelde, and a canal through Limburg. Second, to avoid being accused of Metternichean machinations, he decided to claim that public opinion in the affected lands favored his proposal. This was particularly aimed at Wilson and his delegation. While he conceded that he did not have much support for annexation in Flanders, he argued that the inhabitants of Luxembourg and Dutch Limburg did indeed wish to become Belgian. With Hymans' connivance, the Belgian government even sent secret agents into Limburg to try to influence public opinion.[32]

This was not at all a bad strategy, handicapped by an obvious incongruity; he could claim support in Limburg, but his strategic and legal claim was stronger in Flanders. He would somehow have to resolve this problem to the satisfaction of the British and the Americans, as France alone would not push through the changes he wanted. France needed a secure Anglo-American alliance after the war and could not afford to jeopardize that just for the sake of Belgian security. On the American side of the equation, the Belgians did have one advantage; many US delegates and experts were favorable toward Belgium, supporting the acquisition of Flanders (although not Belgium) and arguing that "Holland had violated the 1839 treaty by allowing the German army to retreat through Limburg . . ." This was a vital point. Belgium claimed, with considerable justification, that it should be able to renegotiate the treaty with those powers that had not violated it. If Holland were named as a violator, then it would strengthen the Belgian argument – made throughout – that the decisions should be taken between Belgium and her allies, without Dutch participation. The British were circumspect on that point, hoping that the two low countries could resolve the issue unaided. Several leading figures, however, strongly supported Belgium's need for greater security. These included Eyre Crowe, who approved of the annexation of Luxembourg, and Field Marshal William Robertson, who had already suggested a Belgian-Dutch-German land swap in 1916. Others in the Foreign Office were less complimentary, describing the Belgians as "on the make," but still supportive at the outset of the demand for changing the sovereignty rules concerning the Schelde.[33] In other words, when the peace conference began the Dutch faced either losing a great deal or losing only moderately, but there seemed no chance of emerging unscathed.

A fractured delegation

The gravity of the situation called for an extraordinary diplomatic effort. Van Karnebeek began planning counteroffensive with several advantages. His government had no intention of ceding anything to Belgium, instead using every method it had to oppose the Belgian claims. There was no way that the ruling RKSP was going to relinquish its electoral base in Limburg. A public works program had been launched in the province during the war to reduce public support for the Belgian annexationism. When the Dutch press published an inaccurate version of a Hymans letter, the government responded to a Belgian protest by deciding that it "had no responsibility to publish an accurate text." Claims that Belgium was planning cross-border raids were circulated. The Queen made an official visit to Limburg to help the counter-propaganda effort. By the time that the Versailles conference was in full swing, public opinion in the province was clearly swinging against a transfer to Belgium.[34]

An even greater advantage was the failure of the Belgian delegation to anticipate the Dutch reaction. The Belgians noticed the presence of senior Dutch diplomats but did not ponder why they were in Paris. Hymans did not realize that the Dutch could influence the allies, and that they would act "with immense skill, which seemed to be bred into their bones by centuries of experience in European statecraft." As a result, the Belgians "remained serenely unaware of the this multifaceted and high-powered Dutch counter-campaign." Unlike Hymans, Dutch diplomats proceeded with delicacy and geniality, "appreciating that harried statesmen are often best dealt with briefly or left alone, a fact that Hymans, who tended to pester, did not recognize."[35]

The "high-powered campaign" was a child of necessity. At some point, protocol would require Van Karnebeek to come to Paris himself to plead his country's case, assuming the conference would even allow it. But he could hardly remain in Paris permanently. Aside from the work that had to be done at the ministry, he did not enjoy an image or a rapport that would make his ongoing presence useful. Leaving the matter in the hands of the legation in Paris also was out of the question. There was too much to be done and De Stuers there was showing his age. Accordingly, Van Karnebeek reached out to various individuals to join the effort in Paris. Somewhat chastened by his first weeks in office, he even approached Loudon, whose experience with the Americans was thought useful.[ix]

The diplomats tasked with saving Holland from the victorious Entente were characterized by a high degree of talent, a good record of success, and absolutely no regard for each other. The amount of infighting and backbiting was remarkable, even 80 years after the fact. Some of the infighting was personal, other more class related. Holland had two aristocracies, the hereditary nobles, and the business elite who had made their money on the Amsterdam docks and through imperial

---

[ix] Loudon's willingness to go was linked to his desire to become envoy to France, a position he occupied from 1919 to 1940. Paul Hymans, *Memoires* (Brussels: Institut de sociologie Solvay, 1958), p. 1033.

trade. The separation of these two groups was not absolute.ˣ By the late
nineteenth century the aristocracy of money clearly held greater
influence than hereditary landowners.³⁶ The foreign ministry, however,
was still a traditional aristocratic preserve, known for its modest
interest in commercial affairs, and, protestations notwithstanding, was
not that interested in recruiting from the commercial sector. Young
recruits from business families found the atmosphere little to their
liking and tended to leave. This would play a role because the Dutch
effort in Paris would include representatives from the business world,
such as Ernst Heldring and Joost van Vollenhoven, as well as gentlemen with hereditary titles.

At the apex of the Dutch effort was the foreign minister himself, his
reputation already somewhat sullied. His personality was also a
problem. Heldring's recollections are particularly biting. These might
be dismissed – Heldring's recollections about almost everyone are
biting – except that he often merely reported others' opinions about the
foreign minister, and also because Heldring had welcomed Van
Karnebeek's appointment so enthusiastically. Those feelings had
evaporated. Even amidst an officialdom insistent on dignity and
decorum, Van Karnebeek's behavior stood out. Later in life he
appeared in uniform on every possible occasion. Heldring described
him as "an incorrigible *Wichtichthuer* [pompous ass] and Miss
Vanity," a view shared by the Minister President. Ruys de Beerenbrouck thought his foreign minister was much too stiff necked and
formal when meeting the foreign envoys (who disliked him to a man),
although agreeing with Heldring that the minister was capable and
hardworking, and had brought order to the ministry.³⁷

Ruys de Beerenbrouck hoped that the problems with the envoys
would make Van Karnebeek a little more flexible. It did – if only to the
extent of inviting his predecessor to help him, something that would
have been inconceivable when he took office – but his true personality
could hardly change. He continued to keep a diary in which he referred
to himself with, "His Excellency the Foreign Minister . . ." throughout.
This was not all bad. When Van Karnebeek had to present Holland's
case to the assembled great powers, he would do so without flinching,
hesitation, or fear, an man so fulfilled of his own importance that he

---

ˣ The author's ancestors, for example, were part of the former group, but made a
fortune investing in the Indies. (They also lost that fortune there.)

simply could not be intimidated. At that one moment, no one could have done it better, and he was impressive. But as a diplomat, his frequently unpleasant personality was hardly a plus. The same holds true of his *deutschfreundlich* outlook.[38]

This latter problem led to much mistrust of Van Karnebeek among the Entente, and also in Holland itself. The NOT's Van Aalst felt that Van Karnebeek was regarded as a liar, and should be removed. Heldring was reluctant to go that far but conceded that Van Karnebeek's explanation of the Limburg passage was "not very convincing." Allizé complained that while relations with Cort van der Linden's government had been good, the situation had changed radically within a few weeks. In an unusual action for an envoy, he revealed to Heldring that he wanted the minister replaced. The Dutch businessman discovered similar feelings at the British legation, and found that they were directed at the foreign minister more than his country. Heldring received a very friendly reception, but quickly discovered that Van Karnebeek was *persona non grata*.[39]

Some of this was undoubtedly Van Karnebeek's doing. His own secretary-general faulted him for not trying to cooperate with Britain, even though this was the agreed-upon strategy. His management of the Paris situation left something to be desired; a critical three week period went by in March 1919 without a single communication from the ministry (at least that Heldring was aware of). De Marees van Swinderen and De Stuers both were dissatisfied with Van Karnebeek's handling of the relationship with the Entente, the London envoy arguing that his minister quibbled too much. His diplomatic efforts to influence the location of the League of Nations, its agencies, and the commission that would investigate the border question lacked tact, to say the least. For example, he proposed making Holland's entry into the League conditional on the World Court being seated at The Hague; the Minister President talked this over with Loudon, who pointed out that it was not a good time for Holland to be placing conditions on anything. The idea was quickly dropped.[xi] This kind of attitude may explain why Van Karnebeek's cabinet colleagues initially tried to discourage him from going to Paris.[40]

He certainly could not go there for the duration. The ministry had

---

[xi] To be fair to Van Karnebeek, the idea had come to him from a member of the American delegation.

to be run, questions had to be answered in Parliament, and a permanent presence in Paris might signal that Holland was panicking. On the other hand, he was not predisposed to leave matters in the hands of the legation in Paris. The issues were to great to leave in the hands of a single envoy. De Stuers had taken his post in 1885. A hard worker, the circles in which he moved were now somewhat limited. His energy level was not what it had been 35 years before, and he died on May 4, 1919, before the end of the conference. His legation disappointed Van Karnebeek, who complained in November 1918 that he was not receiving enough information. This may have reflected problems – the relationship between De Stuers and his chargé, Schmolk, was very bad – or the envoy's usual practices. Heldring groused that the aged diplomat knew little but revealed nothing – "the usual secrecy of our insignificant diplomats."[41]

Eventually De Stuers and Heldring made peace, the envoy expressing his satisfaction and Heldring conceding that "De Stuers is not the wash-out that the Dutch press makes him out to be" and "in his own way in still very active." But it took time for a tolerable relationship to develop, and then only barely. De Stuers received Heldring very cordially on 31 December 1918, although he gave the Amsterdam businessman the impression of not being fully informed. Three days later, however, Heldring received a rude letter from De Stuers demanding information about a meeting with Col. House, President Wilson's aide. The letter was written "in a tone of a superior to a subordinate," precisely the relationship Heldring had refused to have. He was willing to go to Paris, but not under one of the diplomats, whose knowledge about economic affairs he considered hopelessly lacking. This was a major irritation because Heldring's official role was economic advisor. Ultimately he would become so frustrated that he would resign and leave Paris.[42]

De Stuers, on the other hand, cannot have been happy about the prospect of independent representatives running around what he regarded as his own domain. In a huff, he first declined participation in the official delegation that would present the Dutch case, although he quickly changed his mind. His feelings were about more than the usual bureaucratic territoriality. To use every diplomat's favorite phrase, the situation was delicate. Plenty of damage had already been done. A commission organized to coordinate Dutch aid for northern France, headed by Joost van Vollenhoven, had nearly seen its efforts collapse because of internal bickering. The publicity had been awful and could not have come at a worse time. In at least that case, De Stuers' worries about amateurs blundering into the diplomatic minefields were justified.[43]

In Heldring's case, De Stuers' feelings were less justified. Heldring's contact with House had been productive, as the colonel revealed that the Limburg passage issue was essentially closed. His negative feelings were more understandable about the appointment of Jhr. J.J. Rochussen, an unusual diplomat in that he had left the service and entered the business world. He and Heldring got along well (at first). Including Loudon, there were now four important Dutch figures in Paris (De Marees van Swinderen would only come later for actual conference sessions). Van Karnebeek did not trust De Stuers; Loudon was De Stuers' nephew; Loudon and De Stuers suspected Rochussen of being a spy for the foreign minister.[44] A two-way split of the delegation was almost inevitable.

Loudon's and De Stuers' skepticism about Rochussen turned out to be justified. He did not have the tact or manners expected from a diplomat. Even Heldring was forced to conclude that Rochussen was "an exceptional worker, but he has no manners," was too nervous and "under his wife's thumb," and was "not tactful, and somewhat clownish, not very reliable." These were not casual opinions, but the result of observing Rochussen at close hand. As soon as the new "minister-resident" arrived in Paris, he immediately headed for the Quai d'Orsay to explain Holland's side of the Limburg passage story. The French received him coldly on 19 December 1918, refused to allow him to go into details, and claimed that the Dutch had allowed weapons to pass through (not true, but undoubtedly believed by the French). A week and half later, he and Heldring dined with Jean Herbette, editor of *Le Temps* and a relative of Allizé. During the conversation Rochussen said that Belgian expansionism would lead to a new war, a statement which caused the Frenchman literally to jump out of his seat, seeing as this sounded like a threat of war. Herbette was eventually calmed down, but the episode left Heldring somewhat shaken; the effect it would have had on Ruys de Beerenbrouck, Loudon, or Van Karnebeek can well be imagined. Rochussen did later mend some fences with the French, obtaining assurances from Georges Mandel, Clemenceau's *chef de cabinet,* that France would not support Belgium's demands.[45]

These assurances, however, turned out to be inaccurate, and Rochussen's career never recovered from his earlier problems. To add

fuel to the fire burning under the hapless diplomat, De Stuers helpfully
notified Van Karnebeek that the French government had taken note of
the fact that Rochussen had been an official under the allegedly pro-
German Kuyper. De Stuers explained that Rochussen was actually
helping the Belgians by making some issues look more important than
they really were. He further pointed out that Rochussen had had no
more success visiting France's military cabinet – another of the
minister-resident's solo voyages – than at the Quai d'Orsay. After
several appeals, Rochussen was recalled on March 31, 1919.[46] He was
a man of unquestionable energy when what was called for was less
energy but more tact and charm.

That exactly matched the description of Loudon. Comfortable in
Paris and in French culture, well-situated with his uncle at the legation,
his reputation rising somewhat because of his successor's problems,
and more realistic and less worried about Belgium's demands than his
contemporaries, he was perfectly situated to function quietly, making
occasional contacts with important Entente figures and functioning
behind the scenes. This was certainly what Van Karnebeek intended
for him to do. Loudon's expenses were to be paid, especially if he had
to use the "services of others." His activities were not to be completely
shared with De Stuers. His work would, at least initially, be considered
unofficial. Communication between Loudon and Van Karnebeek
would be by a private courier service. One of the things being
considered was that old standby, placing friendly articles in prominent
newspapers (with a little bribery if necessary). The French government
blocked this, however, first forbidding newspapers from printing pro-
Dutch articles, and then banning press campaigns on behalf of any
country. But Loudon still had plenty to do.[47]

Of all the Entente powers, the United States attracted the most
attention. The USA was the strongest power at Versailles, and its
President advocated a principled foreign policy (although the Dutch
had some reason to be wary of this) and seemed in a good position to
veto annexationist proposals. Van Karnebeek was one of a number of
Dutch diplomats who felt that contact had to be established with
Wilson. Many felt that "our only protection lies with Wilson." The
envoy to Belgium, who was busily working on the Belgian press to
deflate annexationism, anxiously cabled on 21 December 1918 that "a
highly placed Dutchman" should speak with Wilson, unaware that that
was already in the works. Even Heldring, who did know and was not
a great fan of Loudon's, agreed that the appointment "could do no

harm." Recognizing that Loudon had good American contacts, Heldring "recommend[ed] Loudon because of his tact and integrity, and popularity with the Americans," finishing the thought in typical style; "even though I acknowledge, that in most situations he does not have an own opinion."[48]

The way to Wilson was through his advisors. Loudon had good relations with the Americans, and De Marees van Swinderen was good friends with Robert Lansing, the American Secretary of State. Lansing proved especially helpful, proposing that the Netherlands would not have any "internatonal servitude" placed upon it. No one knew exactly what he meant by this phrase, but it appeared to block proposals for modifying control of the Schelde or giving Belgium *"un regime"* in Limburg to safeguard Belgian security. The influential Colonel House was pro-Belgian, but the Belgians once again failed to properly cultivate the American delegation, completely ignoring Prof. Charles Homer Haskins, who served on the commission charged with resolving issues related to Belgium. Nor did they adequately address Lansing's complaint that Belgium was taking an inconsistent position. Belgium could claim to either be a violated neutral or a full member of the Entente alliance, but it chose neither route, demanding to be relieved of the burden of neutrality, but demanding compensation for the violation of neutrality.[49] Undoubtedly Loudon took full advantage of Lansing's concerns.

This did not cause Heldring to change his evaluation. He referred to Loudon as "the not gifted with an own opinion Minister of Foreign Affairs," quoted another diplomat who saw him as "decent and not uninformed, but weak," and suggested that Loudon was not hard working enough. He commended a later foreign minister, describing him as "more competent than at that time Loudon, who understood little, forgot much and made much good by being a perfect gentleman."[xii] The claim of weakness may be doubted. Regarding the Belgian demands, Loudon had a very definite opinion. "Belgium deserves to be handled firmly by us." It is likely that Loudon's deliberate vagueness and slowness grated on Heldring, who had no truck with the professional diplomats. "Our diplomats are after all not people of distinction, and among them Loudon is still one of the best."

[xii] Since the later foreign minister in question misinterpreted Hitler's designs, Heldring's analysis should not be accepted uncritically.

When the Washington legation became vacant, for example, Heldring wrote that "[f]ortunately none of the diplomats are under consideration."[50]

Loudon had neither the time nor the inclination to worry about Heldring's strictures. He had a bigger problem; how to get in to see the President. His earliest queries, shortly after his mission began, went nowhere, Wilson claiming not to have time. This could very well have been true, although, according to Joost van Vollenhoven, the Americans were not entirely happy with Loudon. Some felt that Loudon's delays had forced them to seize the Dutch merchant ships.[xiii] Heldring's assurances from House were not adequate, for the colonel blithely assumed that the territorial demands would not even be made.[51] Loudon knew better. Eventually, however, he did see Wilson, and utilized his personal charm effectively. According to Townley, who reported on 20 February 1919 that it was "generally believed" that Loudon was on a "semi-official mission,"

> M. Loudon is commonly reported here to have rendered his country very eminent services in this capacity, President Wilson and M. Bourgeois[xiv] having, it is said, shown themselves especially susceptible to his charming manners and engaging conversation.[52]

The mention of the French official reminds us that Loudon had a lot to do, and as the delegation weakened due to De Stuers' declining health, Rochussen's firing, and Heldring's departure, the burden became greater. He was supposed to deal with the Americans on many issues, even taking up Van Karnebeek's favorite issue of getting the League of Nations Court to The Hague. Here, he fared no better than his successor. He was also asked (January 1919) to tackle relations with the British delegation, as all the leading foreign policy figures agreed that a diplomatic conjunction with Britain was the best policy. Van Karnebeek apparently was sensitive to the building burden, sending another diplomat to work with Loudon on League of Nations matters. The death of his uncle in May changed his status entirely, however, as he was named minister to France. He had openly lobbied for the

---

[xiii] This was not too far from the truth. What does not seem to have been understood was that Loudon and his government preferred a ship seizure over conceding the use of the ships, as a concession would clearly have been a neutrality violation entitling the Germans to compensation, at the very least.

[xiv] Léon Bourgois, statesman and former foreign minister.

position, telling Van Karnebeek "Paris or nothing," although making it clear that he would never replace his uncle if the latter were removed (as Ruys de Beerenbrouck indeed wanted to do). Loudon was very highly thought of in French circles. At a diplomatic dinner in March, French Foreign Minister S.J.M. Pichon's comments bordered on adulation, while De Stuers and Van Karnebeek were barely mentioned.[53]

It took Loudon about three weeks after his appointment to get in to see Clemenceau, but the meeting was highly cordial. *Le Tigre* even forgave Holland for letting German troops through in 1914, and was surprised to learn this event had never taken place. He labeled Hymans as tactless and small minded *("un homme de petite envergure")*. He liked Lloyd George, "although he sometimes forgets in the evening what he had said in the morning." Wilson he also professed to like, although the Frenchman was taken aback by the American's lack of knowledge about Europe.[54] That Clemenceau had never been set straight about the false rumor of a 1914 passage must have surprised Loudon. More importantly, the prime minister's obvious friendliness suggests that Belgium no longer could count on much French support. Certainly the French government's attitude toward Belgium cooled at about the time that Clemenceau discovered the falsity of the 1914 passage story. Perhaps the Belgians had been feedingthe French the tale. In any event, Loudon had succeeded in neutralizing it.

This was an important event because France was the great power the most likely to support Belgium. Yet while Holland was rebuilding its relationship with France, albeit clumsily Rochussen's case, Belgium failed to maintain its ties. France desired either to annex Luxembourg, or let Belgium do so provided Belgium became a French satellite. Belgium opposed the former and had no intention of accepting the latter. Belgium also fought a French plan to occupy Limburg in retaliation for the German troop passage. So Hymans wound up opposing France at a series of critical junctures, annoying his most important ally. It was not all Hymans' fault, however. Britain tried to deflect Belgium away from Holland toward Luxembourg, while France tried to do exactly the opposite. Trapped between the two great powers, Hymans tried to pursue both territorial objectives – and annoyed both his allies in the process. Whether he could have done better is speculative; he clearly could have done no worse. The Dutch counter-campaign was doing well. The Netherlands offered France a huge loan, conditional on abandonment of support of the Belgian territorial claims (they were, and the loan came through within days).[55] Loudon's relationship with the French was easily better than Hymans'.

Whether De Marees van Swinderen would have related to the French as well as Loudon did may be doubted. His chance for the position was a real one, though. He was himself a former foreign minister, had served long in a major diplomatic post, and knew French, if probably not quite as well as Loudon. More importantly, Ruys de Beerenbrouck preferred him to Loudon. One historian even labeled him "the most able of the senior Dutch diplomatists." He had too many detractors, however. In addition, Heldring thought him superficial, lazy and unreliable. His representation of Dutch interests in London was considered inadequate. He was prone to make statements and comments that exceeded his instructions, justifying Heldring's reference to "our much too loose lipped envoy." He did not enjoy a great reputation in the *corps diplomatique* in London and even his chargé told "immodest" stories about him to Heldring.[56]

He was nevertheless asked to join the delegation in Paris to make it more "anglophile" (he was unquestionably pro-British), arriving in February 1919. Leaving London presented no practical difficulties with so much of the British leadership in Paris. De Marees van Swinderen was also assigned "help" for his relations with the British. One of those appointed to help was Colijn, another non-professional who might have been expected to impress Heldring for that reason if no other. It was not to be. Heldring thought Colijn's English inadequate for the task and his vanity too great to allow the professional diplomats to do the job (the only diplomat who Heldring actually admired, Jhr. Snouck Hurgronje, who was also accredited to the British). Colijn's "opinion is always immediately formed, even about things, about which he has little understanding." This bothered De Marees van Swinderen little, as his activities and Colijn's did not intersect much. On the other hand, his career, in contrast to Loudon's, received no boost from the conference. The only major open legation was Brussels, and he was reluctant to consider it while France was a possibility.[57] This may have been a miscalculation, although he could hardly have predicted De Stuers' sudden death.

His work to influence the British benefitted from the declining sympathy that the British felt toward Belgium. Lloyd George liked neither Hymans nor Orts, considered the former a French lackey, and felt that Belgium had not done her share during the war. Crowe was more sympathetic toward the Belgians, but his influence was declining and his superior, Lord Hardinge, found the Belgian foreign minister "exasperating." Many Foreign Office officials were "more grateful for Dutch neutrality than for Belgian resistance and thankful that the Scheldt had remained closed as a result of that neutrality."[58] De Marees van Swinderen and the others knew perfectly well, however, that such attitudes would not automatically result in a defeat for the Belgians. The British could easily trade away part of Holland to the Belgian-French axis (if it materialized). The delegation had hard days ahead.

Unfortunately, the Netherlands did not have a delegation in Paris, but a collection of representatives. Somehow they would have to find a coordinated way to present their position to the allies in public, and separate those allies from the Belgians in private. No one was optimistic.

The Dutch position: No.

Pessimism pervaded the Dutch outlook. Even Loudon, the calmest and least worried, at one point thought Dutch Flanders was lost.[59] No one was prepared to concede anything, however. The Belgian land grab attempt, and the Belgians' refusal to provide specific information regarding their demands,[60] stirred deep indignation. The situation

> caused the Dutch negotiators to maintain an intransigent attitude throughout the discussions; no Belgian diplomat ever succeeded in drawing from them any statement which might remotely have resembled recognition of his country's claims.[61]

This position was tactical as well as emotional, because the slightest concession could be viewed as a tacit admission that the Belgian claims had some foundation.

This Belgian foundation was attacked by the Dutch on many levels, official and unofficial. The strongest argument that Belgium had was that its security was compromised by the shape of boundaries. This claim could not be left unchallenged. The security of Belgium had depended on the 1839 treaty. The security of France, and to an extent Britain, depended on Belgium's safety. Now that the mandatory neutrality of the 1839 treaty had been proved useless, Belgium's future security was therefore a legitimate issue at Versailles on both legal and practical military grounds. Regarding the Schelde, the Dutch had little room to maneuver. If the British decided that the river had to be open, that would be that. Limburg was a different matter. Here, the Dutch set out to prove that any problems the Belgians had had in slowing down the German juggernaut in 1914 were more of their own making than due to the shape of the border.

The Dutch position had a common sense basis. If Belgium could not defend its 1914 borders, how could it have defended an even longer one? The Belgian military argument was that Liège was vulnerable because it could easily be outflanked by an attack through or from Limburg. This argument might have fared better had it been made to a panel of soldiers, as it did contain a grain of truth. However, the Dutch argued, Belgium's problems had stemmed mostly from its own actions in 1914. The Belgian mobilization began on 29 July, some three days after Holland's. The Belgian Foreign Ministry, ahead of the army, prepared instructions asking for guarantees of neutrality on 24 July. In a critical communication breakdown, however, the Belgian foreign ministry failed to inform the army of Holland's official decision to defend its neutrality. According to one Belgian general, this was one of the things that led the Belgian army to abandon Liège and the Meuse river line.[62]

At the time the Belgian army began mobilizing, however, the Dutch mobilization was known. Dutch writers also hammered on the point that the Belgian army was not prepared to defend the Meuse line. This was the product of three things – the country's commitment to neutrality, its strategic expectations, and its military planning. The Belgian Chief of Staff, General Selliers de Moranville, had been appointed only in April. On June 2, 1914, Selliers de Moranville issued instructions stopping work on a plan to deploy the whole Belgian army immediately in the east, writing that the work would be continued in October. Snijders later argued that, had the plan been developed and executed, then Liège could have been held against the initial German offensive. This is possible, as Moltke's *coup de main* against Liège was conducted with a force considerably smaller than the Belgian army.[63]

Of course Belgium might have deployed further to the east if it had been blessed with clairvoyance. No one knew of Moltke's plan for the capture of Liège,[xv] understandably assuming that the fortress would be

---

[xv]   British general Henry Wilson had foreseen the possibility in 1911, however. Thomas, "Holland and Belgium," p. 461.

reduced by a conventional siege (an operation the German general correctly saw as dangerously time-consuming). "About the German plans they seem to have remained almost completely in the dark." Ironically, had Belgium deployed its entire army close to the Meuse, the German plan would indeed have collapsed immediately. This view was expressed by none other than Alexander von Kluck, commander of the German 1st Army, who noted that the advance would have been in real trouble had Belgium energetically defended at Liège, Namur, and Huy.[64]

Instead, the Belgian army concentrated behind the Gette river, 40 miles as the crow flies from Liège and the Meuse. There was nothing radical about this decision. Using fortresses to "mask" concentration and mobilization is an ancient military strategy. It contained risks, however. In 1862, for example, Confederate general Albert Sydney Johnston placed his army in southern Kentucky while leaving two forts in the northwest to halt the Union advance. A Union general, Ulysses S. Grant, was able to capture the confederate forts and their large garrisons without interference from Johnston. And so it went with Liège. Instead of combining their limited military strength with their powerful fortifications, the Belgians initially left the Meuse line undefended. As a result, the main Meuse bridge at Liège was not blown, the railroad tunnel was left intact, the Meuse was yielded after only 12 casualties, and the bridge at Maeseyk, just west of Limburg, was defended only by some Belgian civilians with rifles.[65] The claim by P. Orts, the secretary-general of the foreign ministry, that without Dutch cooperation Belgium would again be forced to abandon the line of the Meuse,[66] completely contradicted what actually happened.

Belgian military planning was further complicated by the country's commitment to neutrality. The deployment of July 1914 was exceedingly neutral, with a division facing Germany, another on the coast, and two more on the French frontier. This neutral deployment was unrealistic. Germany had repeatedly refused to issue a new guarantee of Belgian neutrality, arguing that this would place Germany at a disadvantage vis-a-vis the other great powers. Invasion nullified neutrality and Belgium effectively, if not legally, became a member of the Entente. The Dutch would use this to justify the closing the Schelde. Bosboom, it may be recalled, argued (1917) that Belgium could have avoided this by withdrawing to Antwerp without offering further battle. This was not entirely realistic, and the Belgians were careful to maintain some aspects of their neutrality even in the midst of war. They did not sign the Pact of London (September 1914) which prohibited the signatories from negotiating a separate peace with Germany. More accurately, Bosboom predicted that Belgium would gain little from its association with the Entente. Would the allies, Bosboom wondered, fight for Belgium's demands even if military victory were achieved?[67]

This, of course, was the crux of the matter. Just as Belgium could not defend the Meuse line alone, it could not grab the northern Meuse from the Netherlands alone either. Belgium was a weak country with strong neighbors, something with which the Dutch could empathize. Even they conceded that the Belgian withdrawal to Antwerp demonstrated "wise leadership."[68] Yet the Dutch had a strong argument in that Belgium could not defend a longer Meuse line, having failed to defend a shorter one. It might have had a better chance were its forces united with those of its northern neighbor, but that was the result of its own decisions taken 80+ years before.

> Belgium, provoking the division in 1830, has thereby caused that once again the historical Northern Netherlands would exist with its own particular concerns. We know these and do not offer them to Belgium.[69]

These arguments had to be made with some care. Any suggestion that the conquest of Belgium was the fault of Belgium would infuriate the Belgians, possibly irritate the Entente powers, and make the Dutch sound suspiciously like the Germans, who would indeed later argue that the conquest of Belgium was the fault of Belgium. Too many Entente figures already saw Holland as an extension of Germany.[xvi] Fortunately, there were less offensive ways for arguing against the annexation of Limburg. The current border configuration, it was argued, actually benefitted Belgium's security. A direct German advance through Limburg, as would have happened if the province had been Belgian, would have saved the German troops a considerable amount of time, perhaps three days in the case of the northernmost

---

[xvi] This attitude has not disappeared completely. On October 15, 1998, the former French Minister for European Affairs, Alain Lamoussoure, spoke at Georgia Tech University. The author asked the Minister why his government had so vigorously championed a Frenchman for the headship of the new European Central Bank, while all the other governments had favored a Dutchman, Wim Duisenberg. The Minister explained that an agreement existed that, as the Central Bank would be in Germany (at Frankfurt), its first head should not be German. And, the Minister concluded: "Seen from Paris, a Dutchman is a German."

corps. This was a clever argument, because it used one of Hymans' points against him. The Belgian Foreign Minister had eloquently argued that Maastricht was the "vital gate" into Belgium, basing this on a long (and inaccurate) exposition on the town's history. If true, it had been guarded by Dutch neutrality, more effectively than Belgium could have done. Belgium could only have raised an additional 4,500 soldiers from Limburg, far fewer than Holland positioned to defend the province. German forces could have gone straight to Antwerp, blocking the Belgian withdrawal there. One Dutch author concluded that the Belgian demand for Limburg was "thoughtless dilettantism."[70]

This was less offensive than the implied challenge to Belgium's patriotic myth about Liège, that its courageous defense had delayed the German armies. The Dutch argument was that the shape of Limburg had slowed the Germans, but Liège had not. No doubt remains about the this. The Belgian General Staff concluded that despite the "valiant but fruitless resistance of the Liège forts" the German timetable did not suffer "the slightest loss of time." But Belgian strategy had contributed to the debacle. Not only did the Belgian army concentrate far west of the forts, but General Leman, the forts' commander, was forbidden as late as the 31st of July 1914 to construct fieldworks between the forts. This was done to avoid annoying the Germans. The overall level of Belgian military preparation was also called into question. Strategically, Belgium was less prepared than the Netherlands for war in 1914.[71]

The debate over the Schelde did not contain as much emotional baggage, despite the age of the controversy. Here the Dutch were privately more flexible than in public, although they certainly had no intention of abandoning their slice of Flanders. At first Van Karnebeek dabbled with giving up some rights over the Schelde in return for some compensation, but backed away from this quickly. He also planned to promise new canal routes and a deepening of the Schelde, matters of interest to powerful Belgian economic interests (if irrelevant to security). More importantly, an idea began to emerge (it is impossible to say with whom it originated) that the resolution of the Schelde should be part of an international discussion on access to inland harbors. Colijn suggested this to Tyrrell in December 1918. The Dutch then proposed that the matterbe taken up by the League of Nations.[72]

This was a masterstroke. First, the argument over Schelde sovereignty was now expanded into an issue of international law which could affect virtually every nation. While a small state cannot threaten, in the traditional sense, it can say things that have threatening implications – and this certainly did. None of the Versailles powers would wish to place the sovereignty of their own rivermouths on the table. Second, the reference to the League of Nations was a calculated appeal to the Americans, as Wilson would be well predisposed toward referring issues in that direction. Reference of the matter to the League could involve a lengthy delay, the Dutch calculating – correctly – that the longer the issue festered, the better. It was only the Versailles meeting itself that was truly dangerous. Holland was the subject of its deliberations, but had no formal role or rights in those deliberations. In the League, the situation would be completely different.

Participation at Versailles raised a complicated problem. Holland needed to get in the door at Versailles, but it also needed to take the issue away from Versailles. A formal, on the record presentation was absolutely essential. Even a great power would not want to be excluded from a conference relevant to its own interests. It could, however, refuse to honor a demand made by that conference as it was not a party to the negotiations. Technically Holland could do that, but as a small power that was simply not practical. The strategy would have to be to get in the door, present the case, and encourage the matter to be left to the low countries themselves. The issues could be discussed directly with the Belgians, and if Holland were too small to deal effectively with Britain, Germany, or France, it could certainly handle Belgium.

Eventually, Holland did receive an invitation to present its views. De Stuers argued with House about the relatively short deadline for the conference. This was an odd argument, as the invitation was issued in March with the relevant meeting to take place in May (1919). Apparently De Stuers, like his fellow delegates, was attempting to stretch the matter out as long as possible. On this point, he had no chance. Wilson and House were in a hurry because of the political situation in Germany and Russia. Therefore, Holland issued an acceptance of the invitation on April 4. Van Karnebeek recognized quite well that Holland's presence inside the hall was a double-edged sword. Participation might be read as conceding the Entente Supreme Council's power to make decisions concerning Dutch sovereignty. He therefore made clear that the Dutch were coming only to provide information, and that negotiations would be conducted not at the peace conference, but by the powers concerned (The Netherlands and Belgium).[73]

Hymans was not happy about this, but he could hardly demand

publicly that the great powers not hear the Dutch at all. Still hoping for a conference-imposed decision, he consented to the arrangement. In the meantime, the Dutch continued their push for direct negotiations. De Marees van Swinderen endlessly pursued the British on this point, enjoying some success although he could not secure an outright commitment. Colijn told the Belgian upper house on 18 March 1919 that the government's actions had made it difficult for Holland to negotiate directly. This was not at odds with the strategy of securing direct negotiations. Colijn was warning the Belgian legislators that if they allowed their government to continue on its annexationist road, future arrangements with Holland would be difficult – and, Colijn did not need to tell his audience, the Entente would not always be around to help Belgium.[74]

Van Karnebeek decided to suggest to the conference that Belgium be freed from its neutrality, a point that everyone agreed to anyway. Beyond that, he planned to defend the status quo and argue in favor of direct bilateral negotiations. He would categorically refuse to discuss territorial concessions, but was willing to submit solutions emerging from direct negotiations to the League of Nations. He did not intend to alienate the Germans. Under no circumstances would Holland take territory from Germany as part of a "compensation" scheme. This would earn Germany's gratitude[xvii] and Rosen in particular was grateful that Holland would refuse to participate in the *"Länderraub."*[xviii] [75]

Action continued in the public sphere to make those arguments that could not be made officially. Everyone's statements were coordinated. M.W.R. van Vollenhoven, regarded as something of a loose cannon anyway, was chastised for speaking out against radical Flemish activists. It was not the time to alienate any Belgian political movement that might be pro-Dutch. Efforts continued to get pro-Dutch pieces into newspapers, although this proved difficult. Loudon reported that he was unable to do much due to unfavorable attitudes and, he believed, the French government's opposition to pro-Dutch publicity in local newspapers. Rochussen more prosaically explained, that more money

---

[xvii] Until 1940.

[xviii] Not all Dutch diplomats were pure at heart concerning territorial adjustments. De Marees van Swinderen suggested that Holland support Belgium's demand to annex Luxembourg, hoping that this would cause Belgium to forego its other claims. The Dutchman was not being anti-Luxembourgeois. He merely felt that as Holland's view did not matter, it would harm no one to take such a position.

was needed. Newspapers, he reported, would respond to article suggestions with the stock phrase *"pas interessant"* ("not interesting"), meaning that the article would have to be accompanied by cash.[76]

Domestic politics played a role as well, The government had to sell its policy to parliament and public, and the loyalty of the people in the endangered provinces had to be assured. There was no need to say much about the Belgians. Anger ran deep, especially because of all the aid given to refugees during the war. The head of the NOT openly expressed his bitterness about the Belgians to Townley and told him that Holland was ready to fight. Ruys de Beerenbrouck told the British envoy that Belgium's claims were "preposterous." Townley reported that the "hidden feeling here is very bitter indeed" and that there was "great resentment." The Queen was very active. Abroad, she issued invitations for visits; at home, she traveled to Flanders and Limburg, which Townley called "ill-timed" as it "might flan the flame of Dutch resentment" [toward Belgium]. This was exactly what Wilhelmina wished. The visits were perfectly timed, as it solidified the country in an extremely dangerous time, and interfered with the work of the Belgian agents in Limburg. The wave of post-Troelstra patriotism and anger about Belgian behavior did not change the national attitude toward things military, however. When Alting von Geusau tried to used the annexationist threat to get a better army budget, the lower house voted him down 43–35. Whatever the diplomats in Paris could do, they would have to do it without threatening force (Rochussen notwithstanding).[77]

Belgium defeated

Such a threat would have been meaningless. The great powers would have the last word. If they did not back the Belgian claims, Holland was safe. If Belgium presented its case with tact and skill, Holland was doomed. Fortunately, it would do neither, but this does not completely explain Belgium's defeat. The Belgians suffered from handicaps which they might not have been able to overcome under any circumstances. Forcing a neutral state to give up territory was a dubious undertaking. Holland would only lose if it were no longer perceived as having been a neutral state. In addition, Belgium's claims were also handicapped by the conference's decision to weaken the German military threat. European security would be guaranteed by demilitarizing the Rhineland, limiting the size of Germany's forces and denying her certain weapons. If this were successful, territorial adjustments in the west were not necessary. As a result, a peculiar map came out of Versailles. France reclaimed Alsace-Lorraine, which was a foregone conclusion. Belgium was given the tiny Eupen-Malmédy district. But the western powers did not strip Germany of territory for themselves. Her only big territorial losses were in the east, primarily to Poland, in a region where firm historical boundaries did not exist.

Belgium had good reason to be dubious whether treaty restrictions would stop the next German aggression; the treaty of 1839 had not worked, and neither would the treaty of 1919. The Belgians had to convince the great powers that other means were necessary to protect Belgian security, while the Dutch had to persuade the conference that Holland's land was not the means for doing so. It is interesting in hindsight that Belgium did not demand an Entente military alliance and a permanent British military presence. Instead, the Belgians sought relief from the restrictions of mandatory neutrality, decided nevertheless to remain neutral, while essentially attacking its northern neighbor. It was a strange combination, especially because the Entente had demanded as precondition for negotiations during the war that there would be no annexation *of* Belgium. Would the conference now accept annexations *by* Belgium?

Belgium was in an unfortunate position at Versailles. It had "nothing to give and much to seek. . . The Netherlands, on the other hand, had much to give and nothing whatever to seek." The situation called for skill and care. But instead of relying on their most skilled diplomats, the Belgians left vital negotiations to political leaders (perhaps emulating the great powers) while Holland was sending people like Loudon. Nor did Belgium have experience to fall back upon. They were "novices in the harsh world of major-power rivalries." Their failure to gain foreign commitments was blamed on "their acute inexperience in international politics." Like Wilson, "they were novices in international diplomacy."

> Their performance soon indicated that war and exile had not fully erased the effects of the historical fact that although Belgium had long been considered the crossroads of Europe, the Belgians themselves had been primarily bystanders there, watching the traffic.[78]

So Hymans did not have an easy task to achieve, nor was he the right man to achieve. Even Clemenceau, once his most important ally, became annoyed. A story circulated after the conference that the Frenchman became irritated with the length of one of the Belgian's speeches. When Hymans ended by asking if there was any further service he could render his country, Clemenceau answered, "yes." When Hymans asked what, the supposed response was, "go and drown yourself." The story may be apocryphal, but it reflected what was thought of Hymans – and about the French perception of him. The latter was vital, because his international support was weak. Without the French, he was nowhere. His domestic support was uncertain. Some Flemings were opposed to annexation and many Walloons feared that the new territories would strengthen Flemish influence. Vandervelde opposed any forced transfer in public, and claimed the British would not support such an act either – and he told all this to the Dutch envoy![79]

Van Vollenhoven must have passed this tidbit on to Van Karnebeek, who, unlike Hymans, continued to enjoy a solid domestic base. "The country owes Troelstra a debt of gratitude," he wrote Loudon, because the Social Democrat had unintentionally made it more patriotic. Colijn and De Marees van Swinderen reported that Britain's attitude was moderating. Insistence on the Kaiser's deportation was declining. The Limburg transit was increasingly regarded as a "technical error." Allied support for Belgian expansionism was declining.[80]

The allies were not really listening to, or accepting, the Dutch viewpoint, but they were divided. The Americans were least supportive of the Belgian claims, the French the most. Italy supported the claims but not aggressively, while Japan declined to vote. The Belgian foreign ministry was so convinced of the rectitude of its claims that it did not really take the lack of solid commitment into account. The French outlook was related to the poor opinion the French had of Dutch behavior. Heldring reported that Rochussen was not even been allowed to present the Dutch position at the French foreign ministry – an ominous sign, given the Dutch desire to get into the Versailles conference hall. French feelings toward Belgium, however, was not entirely warm either. Heldring wrote of one French official who claimed that after the first few days of the war, the Belgians were "little courageous or useful."[81]

On the other hand, the British and Americans could not be relied upon to block all Belgian demands. This was particularly the case with the Schelde situation. The Americans were willing to support internationalization of the rivermouth, but this was something the Belgians were unwilling to accept. Even Vandervelde told Van Vollenhoven on 18 January 1919 that this proposal ran contrary to the Belgian view.[82] The Belgians wanted complete sovereignty, or at least joint sovereignty, if all else failed. This the Belgians could probably have obtained, had they concentrated on it without burdening themselves with the additional territorial demands. Free access *to* Antwerp, even in wartime, was a far more reasonable demand than the annexation of Dutch Flanders, Limburg or Luxembourg.[xix]

But for Hymans, Belgium might have limited itself to such a demand. The Belgian government had not discussed territorial demands during the war, and had accepted a July 1916 Allied declaration opposing Dutch-Belgian border changes. When Hymans became foreign minister in January 1918, however, Belgian foreign policy changed. His appointment represented a victory for those who wanted to abrogate neutrality. By the end of the war, they could count on overwhelming support. Once the decision was made, "the temptation to seek the revision of other unpopular articles, such as boundaries and water rights, was too great to resist." This was a big step, but he never solidified his foreign support. Balfour already indicated on January 2, 1919, that he would not support the demands. Loudon's February 3rd meeting with Cecil led the Dutch to conclude that the Belgian demands were making a bad impression. Loudon also reported that the British supported conference consultations with the Dutch, although direct participation in the negotiations was not possible.[83] This was music to Van Karnebeek's ears, as he only wanted to go to Paris to present information. Until he could do so, Hymans had the field to himself. If he did well, and the French backed him solidly, the British and Americans might negotiate away Dutch rights and territory as part of a compromise.

Hymans did not do well. Failing in his efforts to secure firm support from the individual delegations, he insisted on presenting his views to the Council of Ten, the plenary Entente group. On February 11 he did so, asking for control of the Schelde, annexation of Limburg, and for

---

[xix] Demanding too much was a constant theme in the negotiations. Hymans would ultimately ask for sovereignty over not one, but *three* waterways – Antwerp to the Sea, Gent to Terneuzen, and a canal to be built through Limburg to the Rhine. A bewildered Woodrow Wilson commented that he did not see how the Dutch could be asked to accept all this. H.T. Colenbrander, *Nederland en België* (Den Haag: W.P. van Stockum, 1933), p. 7.

a sliver of Germany. Initially, there was some queasiness in Holland as the demands leaked out. Would the British and Americans block the demands or let them through, while concentrating on issues that were more important (to them)? Were Loudon's conversations with the Americans having any impact? Wilson's letter to Wilhelmina of February 20th was not reassuring, as it only mentioned Loudon in regards to his having brought the Queen's letter.[84]

Loudon was doing better than that that indicated, however; by this time his relationshipwith Lansing was bearing fruit. as he had managed to ally himself with Lansing. This became clear on 26 February, when Lansing as well as Balfour spoke against using compulsion against Holland. De Stuers reported at the end of the month that the great powers rejected Belgium's demands for territory. Heldring was optimistic, thinking this would "calm the mood somewhat in the fatherland, where the Minister of War is already rattling the sabre." His elation was premature. The British position was, as always, fluid. The Foreign Office at this point in time was not unanimous, as Crowe clung to his pro-Belgian position. British diplomats were not favorable toward the Dutch. Gratitude for neutrality had its limits, and they rejected proposals for placing the League of Nations in The Hague. In addition, the Entente powers did approve the creation of a commission on Belgian Affairs(also known as the Commission of 14), whose conclusions might sway the great powers and yet lead to disaster.[85]

The idea for a commission had come from Balfour and was reluctantly accepted by Lansing. Hymans made the best of the situation and strove for acceptance of all his major points. He was hampered by the fact that the Schelde issue had been sent to the Commission on Ports, Waterways and Railways, meaning that the Belgian Affairs group technically was not considering Belgium's strongest argument. An even bigger problem was that the big four had not given the commission the power to deal directly with the issue of territorial transfers from Holland. Nevertheless, Hymans did a good job persuading the commission on almost every issue. On March 6, it issued a secret report noting that Holland had not protested the violation of the 1839 treaty by Germany,[xx] summarized the charges regarding neutrality

---

[xx] This accusation did not take into account that Holland was not a guarantor of Belgian neutrality. The commission could have solidified its argument, however, by noting that the Dutch *were* guarantors of Luxembourg's neutrality – but no appeal had

violations by Holland in 1918, and reminded the powers that Belgium had asked for the Schelde and Limburg in 1831, and had received neither – being forced to settle for a now voided guarantee of neutrality. This was clearly supportive of Hymans' demands. In addition, the commission agreed that Belgium was permanently endangered because Antwerp could not be relieved, the Meuse could not be defended due to the border shape, and Luxembourg could and had been used by Germany as a base of operations. The Belgian foreign minister had won a major diplomatic victory.[86]

There were three flies in the ointment, however. First, the Dutch found out. The report might be secret (Hymans wished to keep the Dutch in the dark), but De Stuers had not been in Paris for 34 years for nothing. He had information[xxi] in hand by March 8, writing only that it had reached him "via a detour." Second, the commission called for Dutch participation in the process. The Belgian understandably wanted to present The Hague with a great power *fiat*. Finally, while Hymans had convinced a forum, he had not yet convinced the one that mattered; the Council of Four. Pro-Belgian French delegates such as Pichon and André Tardieu might keep the French delegation in his corner, but British and American opinion remained negative.[xxii] Without a clear consensus, the Allied Supreme Council decided only that the 1839 treaty would have to be revised, and that Belgium should be freed of the limits placed on her sovereignty. De Stuers was informed on March 13th that the Netherlands could participate at the conference and should name representatives. He was clearly told, however, that the great powers would be involved in the decisions concerning the treaty revisions that affected the low countries.[87]

This could mean two different things. Either the great powers would

---

been lodged in The Hague from that direction (or from Brussels, for that matter). The commission's point, no doubt, was to show a pattern of Dutch behavior contradicting neutrality – listing the failure to protest, the sand and gravel shipments, and the passage of German troops as a collective body of evidence against Holland. If Holland were found not to have been neutral, then the Belgian demands would become much more credible.

[xxi] It is not certain that he actually received a verbatim copy of the report, but he was definitely familiar with its major conclusions.

[xxii] The Vatican also opposed Belgium's annexationism, despite the fact that Belgium and France were both Catholic countries. Smit, *1917-1919,* p. 141. It is interesting to speculate whether the Vatican's view would have been the same had Holland not just established its first Catholic government.

formally sign off on changes that were negotiated, or the door was left open for imposing a settlement on the two low countries. The British, to Hymans' fury, were solidifying their opposition to an imposed solution. When De Marees van Swinderen told Balfour (14 March) that the Paris Conference should not compel neutrals to give up territory, Balfour agreed unequivocally, leaving open the door for resolving issues related to the Schelde. Hymans remonstrated with Balfour, pointing out that this assurance would make the Dutch more obstructionist. The two "parted coldly." On March 31, Hymans spoke to the Council of Four, "bitterly complaining at the lack of attention to Belgian views." The British were not favorably impressed. "Lloyd George reprimanded him sternly, threatening not to allow Hymans to appear again before the Council."[88] Britain might have entered the war on behalf of a small power, but it was not prepared to be chastised by one. More seriously, there is no evidence that the French attempted to intervene on the Belgian's behalf.

Hymans' chances of obtaining Limburg were declining. He still had a good chance of making progress on the Schelde, as Balfour had not yet foreclosed that route. Yet giving Belgium sovereign rights over the Schelde would mean diminishing or eliminating Holland's sovereignty. This was brought into focus, as Loudon pointed out on 5 April, by the debate over whether League of Nations members could cross member states' territories to assist other members.[89] This was somewhat akin to allowing a guarantor to cross the Dutch Schelde area to help Belgium. The allies were divided over the issue, but it threatened to overshadow Belgium's specific situation and further undermine the Belgian position. Alarmed, Hymans appealed to his monarch, who made an unscheduled – and surprise – visit to Paris on April 8.

The King was the only monarch to attend the peace conference and the first to arrive by air. He first spoke with the British (not even Lloyd George could refuse to see him), who were politely noncommittal. He then twice met with the Council of Four, accompanied by his foreign minister, to plead Belgium's case. His style made a better impression than Hymans;' the door was open. During the discussions on April 11, 1919, however, the Belgians committed a catastrophic error, one that deprived them of the best chance of the entire Versailles conference to take the river away from the Dutch. Things began normally enough, with the King expressing his surprise that the British admiralty wanted the Schelde regime to remain unchanged, which he knew "due to an indiscretion on the part of some member of the naval section" of the

British delegation."[90][xxiii] Lloyd George explained that the Admiralty was "reasoning as it did in 1793," seeing Antwerp as a potential threat. But he went further, agreeing that the Schelde regime in force in 1914 was "absurd." Some British ships in Antwerp had to be blown up.

> It is true that Grey . . . was particularly scrupulous. I do not know if I would have been as much. It is an absurd situation. Belgium must have free access to the sea by way of the Scheldt without having to ask Holland's consent.[91]

Clemenceau jumped in immediately: "There is no difficulty in that." Lloyd George responded: "No, the territorial question is another matter."[92]

In other words, the British had just openly accepted an 80-year old Belgian demand for unfettered access to and from their "national redoubt" and main port, making it clear that they regarded this as a separate question from boundary adjustments. The window of opportunity was, for once, wide open. The Belgians snatched defeat from the jaws of victory. The King shifted his attention to Limburg, merely stating: "Concerning Limburg, the important thing is to know if Holland can defend it." Lloyd George, referring the November 1918 passage, stated that "[i]t is certain that she has not done so." He once again, however, made clear that he wished to keep the Schelde and Limburg issues separate. Hymans, unbelievably, insisted on keeping the issues together, and went even further. He denounced suggestions to make the Schelde an international waterway, instead demanding that Belgium be given complete sovereignty over the river. This demand was for a territorial transfer and clearly contradicted what Lloyd George had just said. The British Prime Minister responded rather subtly that he "would approve of everything which would give Belgium free use of the Scheldt" and – significantly – changed the subject and moved the discussion to unrelated matters.[93] The window of opportunity had slammed shut, and Hymans' fingerprints were on the glass.

There was here a logical problem that was not of Hymans' making. What Hymans was attempting to do, with his various proposed

---

[xxiii] A clerk at the Admiralty had misaddressed the report to the Belgian *Legation* instead of the Belgian *Commission*. Sally Marks, *Innocent Abroad: Belgium at the Paris Peace Conference of 1919* (Chapel Hill: University of North Carolina Press, 1981), p. 261.

territorial transfer, was to return to the land-swapping of traditional diplomacy. Yet his country was the result of a revolt against the such methods, which in 1815 had created the unified Netherlands. At Versailles, one power (the United States) openly denounced traditional secret machinations and the others demonstrated little interest in returning to it. Hymans wanted military security through a larger Belgium (adding Luxembourg, Limburg and Dutch Flanders), to deter or stop the ambitions of his larger neighbors. However, that was exactly why diplomats had created the united Netherlands in 1815. In other words, from 1815-1830 there had been a medium-sized country in northwestern Europe to stop aggression, between 1831 and 1839 this had been broken up by the Belgians, and now Belgium was attempting a partial recreation by absorbing chunks of the other low countries. This may have contributed to the outcome at Versailles: the Dutch came across as internationalistic, Hymans seemed to restating old positions.[94]

Clearly the chance for territorial gains by Belgium had diminished by early April. This was not yet clear to the Dutch, whose information flow out of the peace conference was spotty. Even the League of Nations discussions, to which they attached great importance, were not open to neutrals. By the middle of the month, however, an important decision was made by the big four. On April 16, 1919, they decided that there would be no territorial transfers. Hymans and Tardieu went to the Council to try to save the Commission of 14, which had proved a friendlier venue, but to no avail. The decisions concerning Holland and Belgium were to be finalized *after the peace treaty had been signed.* This was a terrible blow for Hymans, because the international pressure for a settlement between Holland and Belgium would decline once the overall settlement took shape. Whether he would get anything would depend on his presentation, but maybe even more importantly, Van Karnebeek's.[95]

The Dutch foreign minister was under even more pressure than Hymans. Hymans' worst case scenario was not to get anything: Van Karnebeek's was to lose everything – Limburg, Flanders, the Schelde. The decision of April 16th was not a law or treaty, and it could change. His image and previous behavior all counted against him. Nor did he have much time. On May 10, the Dutch legation was informed that the first session would be on May 19. On May 19, Van Karnebeek expressed his willingness to negotiate directly with the Belgians and firmly rejected any possibility of yielding any territory whatsoever.

Hymans again got into a tussle with his own allies during his presentation, and was accused by Lansing of using sophisms in his argument. A consensus developed to set up an international commission, but Van Karnebeek in the best Dutch diplomatic tradition asked for more time to study the situation. Van Karnebeek made clear that, regarding the Schelde, he would not concede sovereignty but gave assurances that Belgium would not go home empty-handed.[96]

The polite Dutch obduracy, and the emphasis on negotiation directly with Belgium, placed the Entente foreign ministers in a quandary. Holland had presented no solutions. To do so would have effectively given the Entente powers the legal right to make a decision. At the same time, the Entente foreign ministers generally backed the Dutch call for direct negotiations. But Holland's refusal to "consent under any circumstances" to yield "a single square yard of territory" (in the words of an American delegate) now meant that the Entente powers saw themselves as having to reconcile the differences between the two low countries. This was not necessarily bad for the Netherlands, but it was disastrous for Belgium, because it meant that its partners in war would now function more as intermediaries than as its allies. Van Karnebeek sensed this, writing on May 21 that "the powers do not know what to do with Belgium."[97]

Van Karnebeek drove home his advantages. At the meeting of June 3rd, he immediately rejected territorial changes, indicated that he was willing to discuss changes to the Schelde regime within the framework of Dutch sovereignty, and expressed his disappointment concerning Belgium's attitude. Hymans could only describe his *"profonde déception"* and mentioned a Belgian town that had been destroyed 6 times in war between 1819 and 1919.[xxiv] Tardieu attempted to save the situation by obtaining agreement that the great powers would "participate" in the final settlement. This was a only a shadow of the original threat. It was only a moderate exaggeration for Van Karnebeek to tell his parliament that "the threat, which came up out of the neighboring country, has been placed aside." The result of the three days discussions (May 19 and 20 and June 3) has been described as a "lasting diplomatic success" for the Netherlands. It was quite an achievement considering his earlier problems, and spoke well for De Marees van

---

[xxiv] A Dutch author investigating this claim could find no such town; Hymans never named it.

Swinderen, who had urged Van Karnebeek to come and present the Dutch case over the objections of the cabinet.[98]

Some of Hymans' disappointment was directed at Van Karnebeek's unwillingness to be more forthcoming concerning a Schelde arrangement, or – in response to another Hymans proposal – about a "regime" in Limburg.[xxv] The Dutch foreign minister was convinced that any concessions on those topics would sooner or later lead to the loss of Flanders, Limburg, and possibly, he even feared, the whole province of Zeeland.[xxvi] He had no objection to the great powers establishing a study commission so long as conference decisions were binding on Belgium but not on Holland. Amazingly Pichon accepted this (June 7), reflecting a major change in the French position. In Holland, indignation was now followed by jubilation. According to the outgoing Townley, however, "a genuine effort appears to have been made not to rub it in to Belgium."[xxvii] The foreign minister he described as "modestly triumphant" and appreciative of the great power attitudes. Van Karnebeek confessed to feeling "somewhat diffident and intimidated" at the outset of the conference, reflecting a sensitivity for which he is rarely credited.[99]

With the signing of the Versailles treaty days away (June 28) it was too late for Hymans to retrieve the situation. He filed a protest against the resolution establishing the study commission, as it gave him nothing:[xxviii] it called for proposals *"n'impliquant ni un transfert de*

[xxv] He was not mollified by Van Karnebeek's suggestion to change the language concerning Schelde governance from "joint supervision" to "joint management." Colenbrander, *Nederland en België,* pp. 68-69.

[xxvi] This latter concern was apparently a vague, long-term view rather than the result of any immediate threats or information. The Entente powers were not contemplating the seizure of the province. At various times in Dutch history, however, the Flemings had attempted to move northwards, and this centuries-old tendency apparently influenced Van Karnebeek's thinking. He may be forgiven this perhaps excessively historical approach to foreign policy. The battle for control of the Schelde was, after all, centuries old.

[xxvii] When Salomon Frederik van Oss interviewed Wilson on June 7th, for example, he never raised the border issue, solely questioning the President on League of Nations matters. Interview published in *Haagsche Post* by S. F. van Oss, June 7, 1919, Link, *Papers of Woodrow Wilson,* vol. 60, pp. 250-55.

[xxviii] American observers called "the terms of reference" of the commission "a triumph for the Dutch." Haskins and Lloyd, *Some Problems of the Peace Conference,* p. 69.

souveraineté territoriale, ni la création de servitudes internationales" ("implying neither a transfer of territorial sovereignty, nor the creation of international servitude"). The Dutch were more welcoming, noting that the commission was acceptable so long as its proposals required both Belgian and Dutch agreement. Pichon assured Van Karnebeek that the intent of the resolution was a unanimous agreement. Pichon had completely abandoned his earlier support of the Belgian position.[100]

The low countries' relationship with the allies had reversed. The Belgians now complained to the British about their lack of support, while the Dutch had cordial conversations with the London government. De Marees van Swinderen visited Curzon on July 17, made conciliatory noises about the relationship with Belgium, and assured him that the Vlissingen fort would not be built and that access to the Schelde would be possible via a League of Nations arrangement. Limburg was not negotiable, but the British were not concerned. "The area in question was masked by the Dutch Army, whose positions on the north-west side rendered it sufficiently secure."[xxix] The British even denounced Belgian denunciations of the Dutch. When Hymans called De Marees van Swinderen's speech to the conference "curt, uncompromising, and uncourteous," the British envoy in The Hague labeled the Belgian's comments "unfair" (4 September 1919). The British appeared to be happy with Holland's assurances that it would adhere to the League, regard a violation of its territory as a *casus belli,* and defend Limburg in case of war (2 of these 3 assurances had been given numerous times, of course).[101]

Hymans continued to batter the British with complaints. He warned that negotiations with the Dutch were close to collapse (4 October 1919). On October 8th, he complained about his lack of support from the British, or the rest of the Entente, for that matter. The commission was now effectively limited to getting Holland into the League. The British government, to Hymans' anger, increasingly accepted the Admiralty view that closing the Schelde in wartime, as Holland had done in 1914, was the best solution. He also griped about Holland giving more visas to Flemings than Walloons, Dutch propaganda

---

[xxix] This was actually an important rejection of Belgian thinking on the issue. The Dutch could defend Limburg indirectly, as Curzon indicates, whereas the Belgians wanted a large troop concentration on the Meuse line itself.

among Flemings, and Dutch press ridicule about a projected Belgian raid on Limburg.[102] One can only speculate that Hymans was overborne by the emotions caused by Belgium's great wartime suffering.[xxx]

The Netherlands' escape from Versailles was narrow. It is tempting to suggest that Belgium never had a chance to prevail. Although Belgium could not have achieved all its goals, it could have made major gains had it planned its diplomatic strategy better. A united Entente could have imposed whatever it wished. Not only was Germany defeated, but it was forced to agree (Article 31 of the Versailles treaty) to accept all new conventions regarding the status of Belgium and the Netherlands. So there was no countervailing power. More importantly, the Versailles treaty contains language in Article 361 showing that the cession of southern Limburg, at least, was regarded as a *fait accompli* (this language was left in the final draft by accident). Small wonder that the Dutch were so worried; small wonder that, as late as September 1919, the danger of war with Belgium was still being discussed.[103]

The Aftermath

The Versailles settlement left countless problems in its wake. This was true even for Holland although, uniquely, the Dutch left Paris with exactly what they wanted. The relationship with Belgium remained unresolved, however. The quarrel dragged on into the 1930s and had small echoes even much later. The Versailles conference required Holland to negotiate with the Belgians as part of a larger conference, and this did take place. It meant little. The conference could not impose a decision. The Belgians were (understandably) in a bad frame of mind. The Dutch were not eager to reward the Belgians for having attempted to seize Dutch territory. The odds were that the negotiations would fail. They did.

The negotiations began in July 1919 and dragged on for nine months. The Belgian government appointed Orts and Paul Segers, minister of state, as Belgian delegates. They sought complete Belgian

---

[xxx] The Dutch were just as angry with Hymans, however. The Belgian foreign minister had publicly claimed (May 19) that he had no territorial objectives, while he was still secretly pursuing them. Colenbrander, *Nederland en België,* pp. 39-43.

freedom on the Schelde and an agreement for joint defense of Limburg. The latter the Dutch rejected, the former no other power favored. Understandably, the Belgians then sought some guarantee of armed support. The Dutch suggested a League guarantee. This, as it turned out, required some type of Anglo-French provisional guarantee. The British, however, were only willing to do this if Belgium returned to its pre-1914 neutrality status, which was not acceptable to the Belgians.[104]

The Belgians were in trouble early in these negotiations for several reasons. First, their relations with Britain had not improved since the fracas with Lloyd George. The British counseled the Belgians to be patient regarding military conventions about Limburg, but Orts insisted on pushing for it immediately. Exactly how he expected Holland to accept a military convention considering the relations between the two countries at this point is inexplicable. Nor could the British have been favorably impressed by their erstwhile ally rejecting its advice — especially as Orts understood where Belgium had gone wrong at Versailles.

> He felt that the Belgians had perhaps made a mistake in not urging their case in personal interviews with the Allied representatives at Paris and at home, as the Dutch had done.[105]

Yet Orts ignored the British view. Contrary to his ally's view, he insisted that an economic agreement "must follow and not precede a political one." This followed naturally from his own extreme support of annexationism. The British, hardly champions of Van Karnebeek, were also annoyed that Orts appeared to be misrepresenting Van Karnebeek's stance: Crowe took "strong exception," writing Curzon that

> I shall of course be quite ready to see M. Orts when he returns to Paris, if he asks me to fix an interview, but previous experience of these conversations does not make me very hopeful that any satisfactory result will be obtained unless a change comes over the whole attitude of the Belgian delegates.[106]

To be fair, one Belgian had; but his effort made relations with Holland even less civil. A M. Pisart had made conciliatory proposals in The Hague. It turned out, however, that he had exceeded his authority, and the Belgian government refused to follow up Pisart's proposals. That created considerable annoyance in The Hague, although by this time it could hardly make matters much worse. The delegations did not get

along. Dutch delegate A.A.H. Struycken[xxxi] particularly disliked Orts'
and Segers' attitude. The publication of documents showing Belgium's
intent to propagandize in Limburg just as the conference was beginning
had not helped the Dutch outlook either. In addition, the Belgian
demand for a military convention regarding Limburg was absurd.
Holland had survived the war partly through rigid adherence to
neutrality and now Belgium was asking – nay, demanding – that this
be abandoned. The Belgian proposal did have some military merit, but
the circumstances of its proposal were so bad that it seems almost as
if Orts and Segers wanted the negotiations to fail. Van Karnebeek had
even tried to signal via the British that a military alliance was out of
the question, but with no effect on the Belgians.[107]

Paradoxically, it was the Belgians who suspected that the Dutch
were trying to create an incident or excuse to back out of the negotiations. The Belgians complained to the British regarding the stopping
of barges on the Schelde, the refusal to admit an Italian training ship,
denial of visas to some officers, and some other miscellaneous matters.
The best evidence that the Belgians had, however, was the Dutch
decision to bring up a claim to the "Wielingen" passage, the southern-
most connection between the Schelde and the North Sea. For the Dutch
to bring this up was peculiar. Most of it ran through Belgian territorial
waters. German submarines had used the Wielingen during the war.
The Netherlands had never claimed more than a right of passage. It had
not been mined. The capture of a Belgian fishing boat there was not
considered a neutrality violation. In June 1917, the Wielingen had been
described in a Dutch note as *"sans aucun doute en eaux territoriales
belges."* Its cession to Holland would have partially cut off
Zeebrugge.[108] Small wonder that the Belgians thought Dutch motives
here suspect.[xxxii] The Dutch brought it up several times, De Marees van
Swinderen raising the issue for the last time at the last session of the
Belgian-Dutch conference.[109]

On March 23, 1920, the conference on Belgian affairs came to an
end. No resolution was reached. The Belgian cabinet rejected an
agreement on the use of waterways because Holland refused to promise

---

[xxxi] Struycken was professor of law at the University of Amsterdam and member
of the *Raad van State* (Council of State).
[xxxii] Dutch sources claim, however, that it was Belgium that pushed the Wielingen
issue forward. Colenbrander, *Nederland en België,* p. 69.

military conversations. An attempt to arrange a bilateral meeting that fall failed. As Belgium refused to continue discussions, the whole status of Belgium in international law remained unsettled. Everyone had agreed that Belgium's status should be changed, but no one had found a universally acceptable formula. This did not bother the Dutch, who very much felt that Belgium had received her just deserts and were relieved that the annexationist drive had failed. Fortunately for Holland, this had never had a clear majority among Belgians. Belgian anger was directed at the small compensation received from Germany, not the failure to annex Dutch Flanders and Limburg. The extreme nationalists who were committed to annexation turned out to be few in number. In November of 1919, they received on 1.05% of the vote.[110]

The outstanding issues were too important to leave unresolved forever. Some sort of regime on the Schelde was necessary, particularly for the Belgians. In 1925-26, Van Karnebeek and Hymans,[xxxiii] who had overcome their earlier animosity and become quite friendly, negotiated new terms on control of the river channel. On April 3, 1925, the two signed the treaty. The Belgians received some concessions regarding management of the Schelde and the construction of new canals, while the Wielingen issue was "reserved." The French and British promptly accepted the treaty. The Belgians were surprised that Van Karnebeek had been so generous.[111]

His countrymen were even more surprised. Extreme nationalists like A. Mussert, later infamous as leader of the neo-Nazi NSB, opposed the treaty. There were more reasonable voices as well in the opposition, however. Opponents formed the *Nationale Comité van Actie* (National Action Committee) and raised several issues. The treaty called for a commission, but did not clarify whether it had jurisdiction over the Wielingen passage (Van Karnebeek had offered to trade his claim for a "servitude" for Dutch warships, but this had been rejected). Holland would have to spend enormous sums that would solely benefit Belgium. Belgian warships might be able to use the river in wartime.[112] One critic concluded that

> This agreement, known and understood from its history, threatens the Netherlands' future and lowers its image. It does not deserve to be ratified.[113]

[xxxiii] Hymans occupied the Foreign Ministry in several different cabinets in the years 1918-20, 1924-25, and 1927-1935.

The arguments against the treaty convinced many[xxxiv] and the political battle became bitter. Van Karnebeek had to fight hard for his treaty but once again he succeeded, achieving a 50-47 vote victory in the lower house of parliament on 11 November 1926. Shortly after the new year, however, the upper house defeated the treaty 33-17. For Van Karnebeek it was the end. He built his reputation beating up on the Belgians, and lost it doing the opposite. He nearly suffered the indignity of being succeeded by his predecessor. There was support for bringing Loudon back after Van Karnebeek's fall.[114] This did not happen, and Loudon remained quietly in Paris for another thirteen years.

From there he watched several more false starts take place. The new foreign minister, Jhr.F. Beelaerts van Blokland, tried to reopen negotiations in 1928-29, but failed. In 1930 he sought Colijn to take a direct role, and made yet another unsuccessful attempt in 1931-32. Some people were apparently working actively to sabotage his efforts. In 1929 a "document" circulated that claimed that in the next war Britain and Belgium would force Holland to participate. The foreign ministry did not believe that the document was authentic, but other prominent Dutchman – like Snijders – did. Whomever was playing games to sabotage the negotiations, however, was gilding the lily. Beelaerts van Blokland could not find any mutually acceptable arrangement. Friction continued; in 1937 the Dutch petitioned the Permanent Court of International Justice to reduce the amount of water entering Belgium's Albert Canal. This failed, but if there was any goodwill left in the southern neighbor, that certainly caused it to evaporate. When the Germans came again in 1940, agreement still had not been reached. The land grab attempt "so embittered Belgo-Dutch relations as to preclude any serious consideration of a Benelux system until after World War II. A new treaty on the Schelde was not signed until 1963. The latest treaty on the Schelde (1994) leaves it firmly under Dutch control, with all 19 members of its governance board Dutch, although there are Belgians on the subcommittees.[115] Holland may have lost its empire in the meantime, but it kept the Schelde.[xxxv]

[xxxiv] Support among Belgians was not unanimous either. The mayor of Antwerp, Van Cauwelaert, claimed that the Netherlands was trying to push Antwerp back into the "Münster era," referring to the time when Antwerp was forbidden from trading via the sea. Colenbrander, *Nederland en België,* p. 84.

[xxxv] Belgium may yet gain revenge. Shortly after World War I, Belgium dumped 35,000 tons of explosive, chlorine gas and mustard gas shells three miles from the coast

The jitters caused by the Belgian land grab attempt hardly created favorable attitudes toward the other Entente members. This was reinforced by the Versailles settlement, which received unfavorable press in Holland. The treaty was viewed as too severe toward Germany. Van Karnebeek was particularly surprised that Poland had gained so much at Germany's expense, a view he perhaps should have kept to himself as it reinforced the Entente's view of him as pro-German. He was only reflecting the opinions of his countrymen, however, even those not particularly favorably disposed toward Germany. Few saw Germany as entirely responsible for the war, and the violation of Belgium had been forgotten because of Belgium's own expansionist policies.[116]

The Entente nations in their turn were slow to warm toward Holland. The stations and cables of the Deutsch-Niederlaendische Telegraphengesellschaft were confiscated at Versailles despite Dutch protests.[117] The League did not go to The Hague, where the court was seen as pro-German by the Entente nations.[xxxvi] While Heldring blamed Van Karnebeek for not trying harder, there was little the foreign minister could have done. The French would not allow their claims against Germany to be subordinated to German commitments to neutrals, including Holland. The French offered the Dutch a positive solution on Wielingen so long as the Netherlands joined Belgium and France in a military accord, and the rejection of this suggestion did little for Franco-Dutch relations. Considering that most of Holland's wartime Entente friction had been with Britain, it is surprising how long negative echoes resonated in Paris. In 1924, for example, the Dutch role in the war was denounced in the *Journal des Débats*.[118]

The Entente attitude was influenced by the fact that the most visible surviving symbol of German aggression remained safely ensconced in the Netherlands. From the very beginning the Kaiser and his eldest son were uninvited guests, but the Dutch had no intention of forcing them to leave, or handing them over to the Entente. Since the Kaiser could not and would not leave, placing the issue was squarely back in the government's hands. Van Karnebeek's counsel was not the most

---

at Knokke-Heist. The fear now exists that the shells will leak and poison the Dutch coast. The Belgians have promised to take sea water samples every three years.

[xxxvi] It is not clear how this image developed. The Queen was not pro-German, her consort was an irrelevancy, and the Queen Mother played no role in politics.

helpful. According to Heldring, "Karnebeek . . . just keeps saying, that it is an extremely difficult question. We don't make progress that way." A month after the war's end, however, the cabinet ended speculation by announcing that the Kaiser could stay. Count Bentinck, the unwilling host, was less than ecstatic.[119]

So were the allies. To them Wilhelm II was a symbol of evil, a man ultimately responsible for a war that had ruined a continent and left ten million young men dead. Politicians such as Lloyd George had made "Hang the Kaiser!" a major political slogan. It would have been politically impossible not to demand his handing over for trial. That he was now comfortably housed in a country whose attitude was suspect to the Entente made matters even worse. What to do about it was less clear. The Italian foreign minister, S. Sonnino, who opposed extradition,[xxxvii] wondered what to do if Holland refused to hand Wilhelm over. Clemenceau was doubtful; Lloyd George suggested sanctions. Ruys de Beerenbrouck held an interview with the *Manchester Guardian* in which he pointed out the many problems the Allies would have if they got the Kaiser, and that Holland would not abandon its traditional right of asylum for those being sought for political reasons – which Wilhelm clearly was.[120]

This signal had no effect on the conference. On 28 June 1919, the allies issued a demand for the Kaiser, couched in terms of relieving the Netherlands of its responsibilities in the matter. It took the Dutch government 9 days to issue its formal rejection. The Entente did not stop its pressure. On July 17th, Holland was informed that additional steps would be taken in the future.[121] De Marees van Swinderen was told that Holland had better not rely on its law of extradition. The Dutch envoy's suggestion of sending the Kaiser to a Dutch colony was quickly vetoed. Finally, the now visibly anxious Dutch diplomat was told:

> Not by any narrow interpretation of words could the Dutch Government, therefore, in all probability be able to escape the important decision which would lie before them.[122]

This all sounded very ominous but reflected less certainty and solidity

---

[xxxvii] This could be related to the fact that the Vatican was vigorously opposed to extradition. J. Verseput, "De kwestie van de uitlevering van ex-seizer Wilhelm II," *Kleio* 4 (November 1963), pp. 6-7.

than actually existed. The allied diplomats knew that there were many legal and political problems with placing a former head of state on trial. Another demand for extradition did not come until 16 January 1920. This time, the Dutch foreign ministry answered in a record 7 days – and again it was no. Yet another new British envoy, Ronald Graham, was instructed to point out the seriousness of the situation, but to no effect. On 31 January 1920, therefore, a sharper note was handed over. A few days later, on February 6th, Graham came back and raised the 1919 Dutch suggestion of a colonial exile. Van Karnebeek rejected this but promised that the Kaiser would stay in Doorn[xxxviii] (in fact, his movements were sharply circumscribed and the Crown Prince, housed in a parsonage and working as a blacksmith on the island of Wieringen, fared no better[xxxix]). This was not acceptable and an even sharper note was sent. Van Karnebeek was told that the Kaiser could not stay in Europe.[123]

Van Karnebeek made no attempt to hide his irritation, which was shared by the Queen. The repeated demands – three in the space of a month – simply ignored his replies, and the belated conversion to his own year-old proposal to export the former monarch impressed him not at all. He deliberately waited a little longer, finally issuing a rejection on 5 March 1920. The Entente envoys met the foreign minister three days later and, instead of intimidating him, found themselves subjected to his considerable indignation. He certainly had a huge advantage; the Entente simply could not think of anything politically feasible that would cause the Dutch to cough up the Kaiser. All sorts of retaliation was talked about, including even a declaration of war. Yet when the Dutch rejections became reality, neither Italy nor France was willing even to use sanctions. A British memorandum contained the conclusion that "[i]t is difficult to resist the unwelcome conclusion that the allies have in reality no weapons for imposing their will on the Dutch."[124] The conference

> had taken the measure of Holland and had ascertained that no amount of persuasion would force that devoted little country to violate the principles of international law concerning hospitality or its own traditions, and that if force

---

[xxxviii] Purchased in the spring of 1920 and occupied that summer. He earlier had sought a castle in the *Achterhoek,* in Gelderland province, but the Dutch vetoed this as too close to the German border.

[xxxix] He remained there until 1923.

were used, Holland would stand against any amount of force that the Allied governments might care to bring against it.[125]

All that the allies could do was to issue the call to retreat. On March 29, 1920, a note was handed to Van Karnebeek saying that the Dutch government was responsible for its actions in the matter. This was a veiled hint that the Dutch might face consequences if the Kaiser escaped, but substantively it meant nothing. What government is not responsible for its actions? The cabinet decided therefore simply to accept the note as information and not respond. Graham issued a Parthian shot, telling Van Karnebeek on about 2 April that the matter had caused "serious dissatisfaction." This was actually a confession that there would be no sanctions. Another article of the Versailles treaty had been rendered meaningless.[126] At no point did the allies consider using the Belgian issues as a lever to capture the Kaiser – or vice versa. Hymans failed to obtain linkage between these points.

Did the allied governments truly care about the Kaiser? The British had pushed heavily for extradition, but it is doubtful that even they were overly anxious for success. Lloyd George in particular may have been happy when the Kaiser's extradition was refused. After all, he had only promised to demand it, and now that he had done so, he could never be accused of breaking his word – yet he did not have the burden of actually arranging a trial, let alone turning the Kaiser from despised former monarch into German national martyr. Besides, no Entente country had a treaty of extradition with Holland, so that the demand was difficult to justify in purely legal terms – something that might have undermined the succeeding trial.[xl] The first 1920 note used Versailles as a legal foundation, but Van Karnebeek, in a reply described as "not pleasing to the Supreme Council," pointed out that the Netherlands was not a party to the Versailles treaty. The French and Italians were obviously cool toward extradition, concerned more about Wilhelm's escape than exactly where he lived. As for the United States, its interest in the matter was limited and its representatives saw Holland's decision as ultimately benefitting everyone, including the

---

[xl] It is well established in international law that a person who is seized illegally from another country for trial cannot use that fact as a defense. But what if the Dutch government had agreed to surrender Wilhelm, and the former emperor had brought a legal action in Dutch court on the basis of the lack of extradition treaty? What if he had been handed over – or seized – in contravention of a Dutch court decision?

Entente. One American delegate concluded that Holland "had too much honor to think of" extraditing the Kaiser, and that "Holland has made the world its debtor by refusing to surrender the Kaiser."[127]

In sum, then, Belgium had been blocked, and an outright crisis with the Entente had been averted, if only barely. That left the relationship with Germany, so difficult during the latter phase of the war but quite easy afterwards. As a defeated power, Germany was in a weak position vis-a-vis even the small states, as shown by the loss of part of Schleswig-Holstein to Denmark. In the period immediately after the armistice, the Dutch-German relationship reflected German weakness. Germany's long-standing policy of attempting to extend its influence over the Netherlands was gone, possibly abandoned as early as 1916. The Dutch showed understanding for the German situation and even tried to support the German economy, hoping to prevent the spread of political instability into the Netherlands. Renner, who had so much experience in the Netherlands, returned to his post in The Hague with the rank of general, confirming somewhat the importance Germany placed on relations with its small neighbor.[128]

Inevitably, the Eems issue came up again, this time in 1919 and 1920. Rosen proposed postponement, arguing that Germany was losing territory everywhere, and compared the situation to Denmark's taking advantage of Germany's weakness. Van Karnebeek agreed to postpone, but the German government then decided to negotiate anyway. Both countries were in a mood to compromise, and a commission was appointed to investigate the issue.[xli] The Dutch government was in no mood to risk a tussle with Rosen and his government while Belgium was still trying to seize southern territory; that would be the diplomatic equivalent of simultaneous wars against the Entente and the Central Powers.[129]

Of course, this conciliatory period could not last. Germany was after all by far the larger and a great power will sooner or later behave like one again. By 1925 the tone of the relationship had clearly reverted to a normal great power – small state relationship. *"Normalität war eingekehrt."*[130] Seen in context, this was not all bad. It meant that by

---

[xli] The issue has come up since. A treaty was finally signed in 1960 and amended in 1962 and 1975. It agreed to accept the Dutch-Prussian treaties of 1816 and 1824, giving Germany most, but not all, of the Eems valley. Discussions on the Eems continue to this day.

the mid-1920s, the last outstanding issues relating to the war had been resolved, and for Holland, at least, the foreign situation was truly *status quo ante bellum*. The Netherlands had survived World War I.

NOTES

[1] Van Manen, *Nederlandsche Overzee Trustmaatschappij*, vol. 5, pp.222-223.

[2] Frey, *Der Erste Weltkrieg*, pp. 331-32.

[3] C.J. Snijders, foreword to Gudmund Schnitler, *De wereldoorlog (1914-1918)* (The Hague: Zuid-Hollandsche Uitgevers Maatschappij, 1928), p. xiii.

[4] Memorandum from Foreign Ministry 1st Section with annotation by Van Karnebeek, 25 October 1918, 678: British note verbale, 29 November 1918, 781: Townley to Van Karnebeek, 12 December 1918, 811: Van Karnebeek to British chargé, 24 December 1918, 845, Smit, *Bescheiden ... 1917-1919*, pp. 694-96, 768, 794, 827.

[5] Rosen, *Aus einem diplomatischen Wanderleben*, vol. 3/4, pp. 270-71; Foreign Ministry to German legation, 14 November 1918, 742: De Stuers to Van Karnebeek, 30 November 1918, 783: Van Karnebeek diary, 24 December 1918, and 12 April and 24 April 1919, 844, 846, 1023: Memorandum, Foreign Ministry, regarding Lower Eems, 24 December 1918, 1033: Gevers to Van Karnebeek, 25 April 1919, 1034, Smit, *Bescheiden ... 1917-1919*, pp. 739, 769-70, 826, 827-31, 1036-37, 1045-46.

[6] Balfour to F.Villiers, October 8, 1918, 38, Bourne and Watt, *British Documents*, Part II, Series I, vol. 6, p. 124; Heldring diary, 19 April 1919, 1027, Smit, *Bescheiden ... 1917-1919*, 1039-40.

[7] Jane Kathryn Miller, *Belgian Foreign Policy Between Two World Wars 1919-1940* (New York: Bookman Associates, 1951), pp. 25-26; Barnouw, *Holland under Queen Wilhelmina*, pp. 211-13; Fallon to Van Karnebeek, 26 Septembeer 1918, 643, Smit, *Bescheiden ... 1917-1919*, pp. 658-59; Frey, *Der Erste Weltkrieg*, p. 66.

[8] Guillaume to Faverau, 7 November 1905, 391, Smit, *Buitenlandse bronnen 1899-1914*, pp. 553-55; Van Weede to Loudon, 7 August and 29 August 1914, 46, 107, and editor's note, Smit, *Bescheiden ... 1914-1917*, pp. 28-29, 75-76, 81-82; Van Weede to Loudon, 10 August 1914: Loudon to Foreign Ministry, 24 November 1926, Buitenlandse Zaken – Kabinet en Protocol, ARA-II; Report from Consul-General C. Hertslet, 3 August 1914, 523: Grey to Chilton, 5 August 1914, 656, Gooch and Temperley, *British Documents*, vol. 11, pp. 288, 339; Villiers to Balfour, 8 December 1918, 39, Bourne and Watt, *British Documents*, Part II, Series I, vol. 6, pp. 124-26; De Beaufort, *Vijftig jaren*, p. 231; Charles Homer Haskins and Robert Howard Lord, *Some Problems of the Peace Conference* (Cambridge: Harvard University Press, 1922), pp. 61-62; Treub, *Oorlogstijd*, pp. 36-37.

[9] Smit, *Diplomatieke geschiedenis*, pp. 334-35; Cabinet minutes, 3 October 1914, 171, Smit, *Bescheiden ... 1914-1917*, pp. 145-49; Notiz from German Legation, 9 November and 11 November 1918, 724, 730: Foreign Ministry memorandum, 12 November 1918, 738: Aide-mémoire, 23 November 1918, 762, Smit, *Bescheiden ... 1917-1919*, pp. 728, 730-31, 737, 752-54; Smit, *1917-1919*, pp. 135-36. Estimates range as high as 120,000. See Sally Marks, *Innocent Abroad: Belgium at the Paris Peace Conference of 1919* (Chapel Hill: University of North Carolina Press, 1981), pp. 76, 76n.

[10] Trueb, *Herinneringen*, p. 376; Van Karnebeek to De Stuers, 21 November 1918, 756: Van Karnebeek diary, 22 November 1918, 758: Van Vollenhoven to Van Karnebeek, 23 November 1918, 762: Fallon to Van Karnebeek, 23 November 1918,

763: Aide-mémoire by Van Karnebeek, 23 November 1918, 764: Van Karnebeek diary, 26 November 1918, 771: Van Karnebeek to De Stuers, 26 November 1918, 772: De Marees van Swinderen to Van Karnebeek, 29 November 1918, 782, Smit, *Bescheiden ... 1917-1919,* pp. 749-50, 752-754, 755, 760-61, 768-69; Villiers to Balfour, 39, 8 December 1918, Bourne and Watt, *British Documents,* Part II, Series I, vol. 6, pp. 124-26; Hankey's notes of a meeting of the Supreme War Council, 114 February 1919, Arthur S. Link, ed., *The Papers of Woodrow Wilson,* vols. 54-56, 59-60 (Princeton: Princeton University Press, 1986-89), vol. 55, pp. 178-80; Haskins and Lord, *Some Problems,* pp. 61-62; Heldring, *Herinneringen,* p. 267n.

[11] Treub, *Herinneringen,* pp. 373, 378-79; Heldring, *Herinneringen,* pp. 267, 269, 293-95; Bout, "Dutch Army," p. 163.

[12] De Beaufort, *Vijftig jaren,* part 2, p. 232; Barnouw, *Holland under Queen Wilhelmina,* pp. 215, 219; De Stuers to Loudon, 27 December 1915, 488: Aide mémoire from Fallon, 3 January 1916, 494, Smit, *Bescheiden ... 1914-1917,* pp. 504-505, 509; Black, *British Foreign Policy,* p. 424; Thomas, *Guarantee of Belgian Independence,* pp. 551, 554-55.

[13] Heldring, *Herinneringen,* p. 256; De Valk and Van Faassen, *Dagboeken en aantekeningen,* p. 642; Kühlmann to Bethmann Hollweg, 8 December 1915: Rosen to Von Baden, 5 November 1918, Duitse Ministerie van Buitenlandse Zaken – Stukken betreffende Nederland, ARA-II; Gevers to Van Karnebeek, 23 October 1918, 674, Smit, *Bescheiden ... 1917-1919,* p. 692; Porter, Dutch Neutrality," p. 122.

[14] Schelde Informatie Centrum. Http://waterland.net/sic/fr-home.htm; Oppenheimer to Goschen, 12 March 1914, Bourne and Watt, *British Documents,* Part I, Series F, vol. 21; Fallon to Loudon, 22 September 1917, 235: Loudon to Snijders, 29 November 1917, 301: Snijders to Loudon, 13 December 1917, 315, Smit, *Bescheiden ... 1917-1919,* pp. 257-58, 318-19, 328-29.

[15] Villiers to Balfour, 8 December 1918, 139, British Documents, Part II, Series I, vol. 6, pp. 124-26.

[16] Frey, *Der Erste Weltkrieg,* pp. 333-335; Haeussler, *General William Groener,* p. 137; Lutz, *Fall of the German Empire,* vol. 2, pp. 543, 546, 547; Cecil, *Emperor and Exile,* pp. 293-94.

[17] Frey, *Der Erste Weltkrieg,* pp. 333-335; Van Vollenhoven to Van Karnebeek, 9 November 1918, 725, Smit, *Bescheiden ... 1917-1919,* pp. 728-29; Cecil, *Emperor and Exile,* pp. 293-97.

[18] Cabinet minutes, 11 November 1918, 6 and 7 December 1918, 727, 787, 791: Van Karnebeek diary, 3 December 1918, 793: Heldring diary, 9 December 1918, 796, Smit, *Bescheiden ... 1917-1919,* pp. 729, 771-74, 777-78, 782; Heldring, *Herinneringen,* p. 270; Cecil, *Emperor and Exile,* p. 298.

[19] Cecil, *Emperor and Exile,* pp. 298, 315; Rosen, *Aus einem diplomatischen Wanderleben,* vol. 3/4, pp. 62, 277-78; Cabinet minutes, 13 December 1918, 814, Smit, *Bescheiden ... 1917-1919,* p. 796.

[20] Frey, *Der Erste Weltkrieg,* p. 333-335; Cecil, *Emperor and Exile,* p. 299; Townley to Van Karnebeek, 10 and 11 November 1918, 726, 629: Stuers to Van Karnebeek, 20 November 1918, 755, Smit, *Bescheiden ... 1917-1919,* pp. 729, 730, 748-49; Treub, *Herinneringen,* p. 374; Smit, *1917-1919,* p. 134.

[21] George V to Wilhelmina, 26 January 1919, 898, Smit, *Bescheiden ... 1917-1919,* p. 907; Cecil, *Emperor and Exile,* pp. 298, 300.

[22] Townley, *'Indiscretions' of Lady Susan,* pp. 282-89, 307-10.

[23] Van Vollenhoven to Van Karnebeek, 10 December 1918 and 25 May 1919, 803, 1059, Smit, *Bescheiden ... 1917-1919*, pp. 787-88, 1071; De Stuers to Loudon, 15 September 1916, 622, Smit, *Bescheiden ... 1914-1917*, p. 631; Miller, *Belgian Foreign Policy*, p. 72.

[24] Van Vollenhoven to Van Karnebeek, 18 December 1918, Buitenlandse Zaken – Belgisch Gezantschap, ARA-II; Miller, *Belgian Foreign Policy*, pp. 57-58, 72; Villiers to Curzon, 27 March and 4 April 1919, 53, 55, Bourne and Watt, *British Documents*, Part II, Series I, vol. 6, pp. 140-41, 143.

[25] Marks, *Innocent Abroad*, pp. 85, 92-94.

[26] Ibid., pp. 94-96, 109-11, 148, 263, 265.

[27] Van Weede to Van Karnebeek, 26 October 1918, 683: Van Vollenhoven to Van Karnebeek, 12 December 1918, 812: Van Karnebeek to Ruys de Beerenbrouck, 27 May 1919, 1061, Smit, *Bescheiden ... 1917-1919*, pp. 698-701, 794-96, 1071-73; Colenbrander, *Nederland en België*, p. 2.

[28] Schuursma, "Een verdrag in opspraak," p. 35; Loudon to Pichon, 14 June 1919, 1015: Van Nispen tot Sevenaer to Van Karnebeek, 2 April 1919, 1072, Smit, *Bescheiden ... 1917-1919*, pp. 1031-32, 1087-89; Colenbrander, *Nederland en België*, p. 6.

[29] Smit, *Diplomatieke geschiedenis*, p. 335; Smit, *1917-1919*, p. 35n2; Miller, *Belgian Foreign Policy*, pp. 70, 73, 77; Villiers to Balfour, 8 December 1918, 39, Bourne and Watt, *British Documents*, Part II, Series I, vol. 6, pp. 124-26; De Stuers to Van Karnebeek, 14 January and 12 February 1919, 880, 921: Van Vollenhoven to Van Karnebeek, 23 February 1919, 959: map of CPN claims, Smit, *Bescheiden ... 1917-1919*, pp. 885, 929, 959-60, after 973.

[30] Marks, *Innocent Abroad*, pp. 43, 82, 86, 89, 144, 147, 148.

[31] Ibid., pp. 19, 64, 153, 262-63; Stuers to Van Karnebeek, 22 October 1918, 673, Smit, *Bescheiden ... 1917-1919*, pp. 691-92.

[32] Van Vollenhoven to Van Karnebeek, 14 December 1918 (2 messages) and 21 January 1919, 818, 819, 892, Smit, *Bescheiden ... 1917-1919*, pp. 799-800, 898-99; Miller, *Belgian Foreign Policy*, pp. 73, 74, 76; Colenbrander, *Nederland en België*, p. 38.

[33] Miller, *Belgian Foreign Policy*, pp. 60, 74-75; De Leeuw, *Nederland in de wereldpolitiek*, pp. 195-96 (quoting from David Lloyd George's memoirs); De Marees van Swinderen to Van Karnebeek, 18 December 1918, 826, Smit, *Bescheiden ... 1917-1919*, p. 808.

[34] Marks, *Innocent Abroad*, pp. 138, 139, 142, 276-77, 278-80.

[35] Ibid., pp. 78, 82, 83, 259, 276.

[36] Heldring, *Herinneringen*, pp. 6-7.

[37] Heldring, *Herinneringen*, pp. 304-305, 752; Heldring, diary, 13 December 1918, 815, Smit, *Bescheiden ... 1917-1919*, pp. 796-97.

[38] Heldring, *Herinneringen*, p. 278-79.

[39] Heldring diary, 8, 13 and 14 December 1918: 30 and 31 January 1919, 815-16, 902-903, Smit, *Bescheiden ... 1917-1919*, pp. 780-82, 796-98 910-13; Heldring, *Herinneringen*, p. 277.

[40] Heldring, *Herinneringen*, pp. 316, 320; Van Karnebeek to Patijn, 22 May 1919, 1044: Van Karnebeek to De Marees van Swinderen, 13 May and 6 June 1919, 1046, 1051: De Marees van Swinderen to Van Karnebeek, 14 May 1919, 1055: De Marees van Swinderen to A. P. C. van Karnebeek, 20 May 1919, 1068: De Marees van Swinderen to Loudon, 9 June 1919, 1070, Smit, *Bescheiden ... 1917-1919*, pp.

1054-56, 1062-63, 1085-86.

[41] Smit, *Tien studiën*, pp. 45-46; Van Karnebeek to Loudon, 23 November 1918, 765, Smit, *Bescheiden ... 1917-1919*, pp. 755-57; Heldring, *Herinneringen*, p. 316.

[42] Heldring, *Herinneringen*, pp. 277, 287, 290-91, 292-93, 300, 319; Van Karnebeek to Wilhelmina, 11 December 1918 809: Heldring Diary, 15 March 1919, 993, Smit, *Bescheiden ... 1917-1919*, pp. 793, 995-996.

[43] De Marees van Swinderen to Doude van Troostwijk, 21 March 1919, 1003, Smit, *Bescheiden ... 1917-1919*, pp. 1017-18; Heldring, *Herinneringen*, pp. 311-13.

[44] Heldring, *Herinneringen*, pp. 277, 287, 292-93.

[45] Heldring diary, 31 December 1918, 9 January and 9 March 1919, 821, 861, 888: Rochussen to Van Karnebeek, 19 December 1918, 989, Smit, *Bescheiden ... 1917-1919*, pp. 810-11, 850-51, 891, 993-94; Heldring, *Herinneringen*, pp. 289, 311-13, 320.

[46] De Stuers to Van Karnebeek, 8 January 1919, 872, Smit, *Bescheiden ... 1917-1919*, pp. 873-74.

[47] Van Karnebeek to Loudon, 23 November 1919, 765: Heldring diary, 15 March 1919, 993, Smit, *Bescheiden ... 1917-1919*, pp. 755-57, 995-96.

[48] Van Vollenhoven to Van Karnebeek, 21 December 1918, Buitenlandse Zaken – Belgisch Gezantschap, ARA-II; Heldring, *Herinneringen*, p. 277; Van Karnebeek to Loudon, 23 November and 11 December 1918, 765, 808: Heldring diary, 24 January 1919, 894, Smit, *Bescheiden ... 1917-1919*, pp. 755-57, 792.

[49] Marks, *Innocent Abroad*, pp. 97, 264, 267, 268; Thomas, *Guarantee of Belgian Independence*, pp. 569-69.

[50] Heldring, *Herinneringen*, pp. 199, 220, 241, 300, 311-13, 1408; Loudon to Van Karnebeek, 1 March 1919, 974, Smit, *Bescheiden ... 1917-1919*, pp. 972-73.

[51] Heldring, *Herinneringen*, pp. 287, 319; Heldring diary, 31 December 1918, 861, Smit, *Bescheiden ... 1917-1919*, pp. 850-51.

[52] Townley to Curzon, 20 February 1919, 42, Bourne and Watt, *British Documents*, Part II, Series I, vol. 6, pp. 128-29.

[53] Van Karnebeek to Loudon, 22 January 1919, 893: Loudon to Van Karnebeek, 1 March 1919, 974: Van Karnebeek to De Stuers, 15 March 1919, 994: Heldring diary, 23, 25, and 28 March 1919, 1004, 1005, 1011: Loudon to Wilson, 22 April 1919, 1030: Pichon to Roosmale Nepveu, 20 May 1919, 1052, Smit, *Bescheiden ... 1917-1919*, pp. 899-90, 972-73, 996-97, 1018-19, 1027, 1042-43, 1063; Heldring, *Herinneringen*, p. 300.

[54] Loudon to Van Karnebeek, 13 June 1919, 1071, Smit, *Bescheiden ... 1917-1919*, pp. 1086-87.

[55] Marks, *Innocent Abroad*, pp. 34, 77, 81, 99-100, 149.

[56] Ibid., p. 301; Heldring diary, 13 December 1918 and 23-28 March 1919, 815, 1003-1005, 1011, Smit, *Bescheiden ... 1917-1919*, pp. 796-97, 1017-19, 1027; Heldring, *Herinneringen*, pp. 205, 313-14, 335; Smit, *Tien studiën*, pp. 43-44; Müller to Bethmann Hollweg, 15 July 1913, 114, Smit, *Buitenlandse bronnen 1899-1914*, pp. 162-63.

[57] Heldring diary, 14 November 1918, 745: De Marees van Swinderen to Doude van Troostwijk, 21 March 1919, 1003: De Marees van Swinderen to Van Karnebeek, 25 March 1919, 1006, Smit, *Bescheiden ... 1917-1919*, pp. 740-41, 1017-19; Heldring, *Herinneringen*, p. 258.

[58] Thomas, *Guarantee of Belgian Independence*, p. 561; Marks, *Innocent Abroad*, pp. 70, 79, 97-98, 112-13, 121, 260.

[59] Smit, *1917-1919*, pp. 137-38.

[60] Colenbrander, *Nederland en België*, p. 8.

[61] Miller, *Belgian Foreign Policy*, p. 75.

[62] Davignon to various embassies, 24 and 29 July 1914, *België betrokken in den oorlog*, pp. 11, 20; Van Voorst tot Voorst, *Over Roermond*, pp. 55-58.

[63] Stevenson, *Armaments*, p. 395; Snijders and Dufour, *De mobilisatiën*, p. 261.

[64] Von Moltke, *Herinnerungen*, p. 431; Stengers, "Belgium," p. 153; Van Voorst tot Voorst, *Over Roermond*, p. 30. See also article in the *Telegraaf,* 24 May 1935.

[65] Van Voorst tot Voorst, *Over Roermond*, pp. 33, 54-55; "Ronduit," *De manoeuvre om Limburg*, p. 12.

[66] Marks, *Innocent Abroad*, p. 271.

[67] John Gooch, *The Plans of War: The General Staff and British Military Strategy c. 1900-1916* (New York: John Wiley & Sons, 1974), p. 293; Miller, *Belgian Foreign Policy*, p. 26; "Memorandum to Council of Ministers from War Minister N. Bosboom," 27 February 1917, Collectie N. Bosboom, ARA-II.

[68] Van Voorst tot Voorst, *Over Roermond*, p. 50.

[69] Colenbrander, *Nederland en België*, p. 140.

[70] "Ronduit," *De manoeuvre om Limburg*, pp. 1, 3, 7, 13-14, 15-19, 22-23.

[71] Thomas, "Holland and Belgium," pp. 322, 327-28.

[72] Schuursma, "Een verdrag in opspraak," p. 36; Heldring diary, 30 December 1918, 858: Rochussen to Van Karnebeek. 12 January and 8 March 1919, 877, 909: Van Karnebeek to Loudon, 15 February 1919, 961: De Marees van Swinderen to Van Karnebeek, 25 February 1919, 986, Smit, *Bescheiden ... 1917-1919*, pp. 847-48, 880-81, 919-20, 980-82, 990-91.

[73] De Stuers to Van Karnebeek and reply, 17/18 March and 2 April 1919, 998, 1014, Smit, *Bescheiden ... 1917-1919*, pp. 1010-12, 1030-31; Colenbrander, *Nederland en België*, pp. 10-11; Miller, *Belgian Foreign Policy*, p. 79.

[74] Miller, *Belgian Foreign Policy*, p. 79; De Stuers to Van Karnebeek, 29 March 1919, 1012, Smit, *Bescheiden ... 1917-1919*, p. 1027; Heldring, *Herinneringen*, p. 318.

[75] De Marees van Swinderen to Van Karnebeek, 12 January 1919, 878, Smit, *Bescheiden ... 1917-1919*, pp. 881-84; Rosen, *Aus einem diplomatischen Wanderleben*, vol. 3/4, pp. 277-78; Miller, *Belgian Foreign Policy*, pp. 79-81.

[76] Van Vollenhoven, *Memoires*, pp. 125-27; Loudon to Van Karnebeek, 14 December 1918, 820: Rochussen to Van Karnebeek, 9 February 1919, 916, Smit, *Bescheiden ... 1917-1919*, pp. 800-801, 924-27.

[77] Van den Heuvel-Strasser, "Vluchtelingenzorg," p. 204; Smit, *Tien studiën*, pp. 157-58; Townley to Curzon, 20 February, 3 and 4 March 1919, 42, 45-48, Bourne and Watt, *British Documents*, Part II, Series I, vol. 6, pp. 128-29, 135-37; Porter, "Dutch Neutrality," p. 250.

[78] Marks, *Innocent Abroad*, pp. 18, 55, 63, 79-80.

[79] Charles L. Mee, Jr., *The End of Order: Versailles, 1919* (New York: E.P. Dutton, 1980), pp. 197-98; Schuursma, "Een verdrag in opspraak," p. 36; Frey, *Der Erste Weltkrieg*, pp. 339-40; Van Vollenhoven, *Memoires*, p. 131.

[80] Van Karnebeek to Loudon, 23 November 1918, 765, Smit, *Bescheiden ... 1917-1919*, pp. 755-57; Frey, *Der Erste Weltkrieg*, pp. 337-38; Heldring, *Herinneringen*, pp. 282-83, 291.

[81] Heldring, *Herinneringen*, pp. 290-91; Marks, *Innocent Abroad*, pp. 60, 100.

[82] Van Vollenhoven to Van Karnebeek, 18 January 1919, 886, Smit, *Bescheiden ... 1917-1919*, p. 896.

[83] Frey, *Der Erste Weltkrieg,* pp. 335-37; Robert Cecil diary, 3 February 1919, Link, *Papers of Woodrow Wilson,* vol. 54, p. 460; Heldring, *Herinneringen,* p. 308; Loudon to Van Karnebeek, 5 February 1919, 910, Smit, *Bescheiden ... 1917-1919,* p. 920; Thomas, *Guarantee of Belgian Independence,* pp. 540-46, 549-50.

[84] Miller, *Belgian Foreign Policy,* p. 77; Duitse Ministerie van Buitenlandse Zaken – Stukken Betreffende Nederland, ARA-II; Seth P. Tillman, *Anglo-American Relations at the Paris Peace Conference of 1919* (Princeton, NJ: Princeton University Press, 1961), pp. 193-94; Wilson to Wilhelmina, Link, *Papers of Woodrow Wilson,* vol. 55, pp. 219-20.

[85] Hymans, *Memoires,* p. 485; Heldring, *Herinneringen,* p. 314; De Marees van Swinderen to Van Karnebeek, 5 March 1919, 980, Smit, *Bescheiden ... 1917-1919,* pp. 977-81.

[86] Committee on Belgian Affairs, 6 March 1919, 43, Bourne and Watt, *British Documents,* Part II, Series I, vol. 6, pp. 129-133; Miller, *Belgian Foreign Policy,* pp. 77, 78, 81-83; Tillman, *Anglo-American Relations,* pp. 194-95.

[87] Colenbrander, *Nederland en België,* pp. 9, 37; De Stuers to Van Karnebeek, 8 and 13 March (2 messages) 1919, 985, 991, 992, Smit, *Bescheiden ... 1917-1919,* pp. 986-90, 994-95; Smit, *1917-1919,* p. 140; Tillman, *Anglo-American Relations,* pp. 194-95.

[88] Balfour to Curzon (2 messages), 14 March 1919, 50, 51, Bourne and Watt, *British Documents,* Part II, Series I, vol. 6, pp. 138-39; Tillman, *Anglo-American Relations,* pp. 193-94.

[89] Loudon to Van Karnebeek, 5 April 1919, 1016, Smit, *Bescheiden ... 1917-1919,* pp. 1032-33.

[90] Villiers to Curzon, 8 April 1919, and Balfour to Curzon, 12 April 1919, 58-59, Bourne and Watt, *British Documents,* Part II, Series I, vol. 6, p. 146.

[91] Mantoux's Notes of Two Meetings of the Council of Four, April 11 1919, Link, *Papers of Woodrow Wilson,* vol. 56, pp. 592-93; Marks, *Innocent Abroad,* pp. 69-70, 119-20, 260.

[92] Ibid., p. 593.

[93] Ibid., p. 593.

[94] Frey, *Der Erste Weltkrieg,* pp. 339-40.

[95] Loudon to Van Karnebeek, 12 April 1919, 1025, Smit, *Bescheiden ... 1917-1919,* pp. 1037-38; Miller, *Belgian Foreign Policy,* pp. 78-79; Political Intelligence Department, "Memorandum on Belgian Affairs," 2 May 1919, 63, Bourne and Watt, *British Documents,* Part II, Series I, vol. 6, pp. 148-51.

[96] Roosmale Nepveu to Van Karnebeek, 11 May 1919, 1043: Van Karnebeek to Ruys de Beerenbrouck, 20, 21, 23 and 24 May 1919, 1051, 1057, 1058, 1070, Smit, *Bescheiden ... 1917-1919,* pp. 1054, 1063-67, 1069-70; Grayson diary, May 20, 1919, Link, *Papers of Woodrow Wilson,* vol. 59, pp. 288-89.

[97] Van Karnebeek to Ruys de Beerenbrouck, 21 May 1919, 1051, Smit, *Bescheiden ... 1917-1919,* pp. 1063-67; Grayson diary, May 20, 1919, Link, *Papers of Woodrow Wilson,* vol. 59, pp. 288-89.

[98] Colenbrander, *Nederland en België,* pp. 51-53, 57-58; Heldring, *Herinneringen,* pp. 337-38; Frey, *Der Erste Weltkrieg,* p. 340.

[99] Pichon to Van Karnebeek, 4 June 1919, 1066: Van Karnebeek to Prof. Struycken, 7 June 1919, 1067, Smit, *Bescheiden ... 1917-1919,* pp. 1082-83, 1084-85; Townley to Curzon, 9 June 1919, 64, Bourne and Watt, *British Documents,* Part II, Series I, vol. 6, pp. 151-52.

[100] Van Karnebeek to Loudon, 24 June 1919, 1078: Pichon to Van Karnebeek, 26 June 1919, 1080, Smit, *Bescheiden ... 1917-1919*, pp. 1094-95, 1096; Heldring, *Herinneringen*, p. 340.

[101] Curzon to Villiers, 9 Juy 1919, 65: Curzon to Robertson, 17 July 1919, 66: Robertson to Curzon, 4 September 1919, 68: Crowe to Curzon, 3 October 1919, 78, Bourne and Watt, *British Documents*, Part II, Series I, vol. 6, pp. 152-56, 157-58, 168.

[102] Gurney to Curzon, 4 and 8 October 1919, 81, 84, Bourne and Watt, *British Documents*, Part II, Series I, vol. 6, pp. 170, 172.

[103] Robertson to Curzon, 4 September 1919, 68, Bourne and Watt, *British Documents*, Part II, Series I, vol. 6, pp. 157-58; Versailles treaty, 1081, Smit, *Bescheiden ... 1917-1919*, pp. 1096-97; Smit, *1917-1919*, p. 148.

[104] Pichon to Van Karnebeek, 26 June 1919, 1080, Smit, *Bescheiden ... 1917-1919*, p. 1096; Miller, *Belgian Foreign Policy*, p. 83.

[105] Gurney to Curzon, 13 October 1919, 87, Bourne and Watt, *British Documents*, Part II, Series I, vol. 6, pp. 175-77.

[106] Marks, *Innocent Abroad*, p. 44; Gurney to Curzon, 13 October 1919, 87, and Crowe to Curzon, 21 October 1919, 90, Bourne and Watt, *British Documents*, Part II, Series I, vol. 6, pp. 175-77, 179-80.

[107] Villiers to Curzon, 18 October 1919, 88: Legation report on Holland, 1919, 110: Graham to Curzon, 11 (2 messages) and 19 November 1919, 94, 95, 97, Bourne and Watt, *British Documents*, Part II, Series I, vol. 6, pp. 177-78, 182-83, 184-85, 247-57; Colenbrander, *Nederland en België*, p. 58.

[108] Gurney to Curzon, 10 September 1919, 70, Bourne and Watt, *British Documents*, Part II, Series I, vol. 6, pp. 159-61; Miller, *Belgian Foreign Policy*, pp. 83-84.

[109] Marks, *Innocent Abroad*, pp. 297-304.

[110] Miller, *Belgian Foreign Policy*, pp. 84-85, 86, 103, 161; Colenbrander, *Nederland en België*, p. 58.

[111] Heldring, *Herinneringen*, p. 604; Schuursma, "Een verdrag in opspraak," pp. 36, 38; Miller, *Belgian Foreign Policy*, p. 105.

[112] Marks, *Innocent Abroad*, pp. 297-304; Schuursma, "Een verdrag in opspraak," p. 38; Colenbrander, *Nederland en België*, pp. 71-77, 107, 114.

[113] Colenbrander, *Nederland en België*, p. 61.

[114] Schuursma, "Een verdrag in opspraak," p. 40; Heldring, *Herinneringen*, p. 688; Colenbrander, *Nederland en België*, p. 59.

[115] De Graaff, "Colijn," p. 33; Heldring, *Herinneringen*, pp. 792-93; Miller, *Belgian Foreign Policy*, pp. 106-110, 255; Schuursma, "Een verdrag in opspraak," p. 40; Schelde InformatieCentrum; Marks, *Innocent Abroad*, p. 256.

[116] Townley to Curzon, May 12 and 16, 1919, 105, 106: Robertson to Curzon, 3 July 1919, 107, Bourne and Watt, *British Documents*, Part II, Series I, vol. 6, pp. 241-42, 243-44.

[117] M.W.M.M. Gruythuysen, S.U. Sabaroedin, and A.M. Tempelaars, *Inventaris van de archieven van Regeringscommissarissen van het Ministerie van Kolonien 1904-1952* (Den Haag: Algemeen Rijksarchief, 1991), pp. 19, 20; "Memorie van de Regeringscommissaris bij de Deutsch-Niederlaendische Telegraphengesellschaft Viehoff inzake het belang dezer maatschappij bij de vredesvoorwaarden" (7 Januarv 1919), 870, *Bescheiden betreffende de buitenlandse politiek van Nederland* (D. Haag: Rijks Geschiedkundige Publikatien, grote serie, Derde Periode 1899-1919) [herinafter RGP] vol. 117.

[118] Heldring, *Herinneringen,* pp. 329-30; Colenbrander, *Nederland en België,* p. 70; Loudon to Van Karnebeek, 5 November 1924, Buitenlandse Zaken – Kabinet en Protocol, ARA-II.

[119] Heldring, *Herinneringen,* pp. 261, 274, 275; J. Verseput, "De kwestie van de uitlevering van ex-keizer Wilhelm II," *Kleio* 4 (November 1963), p. 5.

[120] Verseput, "De kwestie," p. 6.

[121] Verseput, "De kwestie," p. 7.

[122] Curzon to Robertson, 17 July 1919, 66, Bourne and Watt, *British Documents,* Part II, Series I, vol. 6, pp. 153-56.

[123] Verseput, "De kwestie," pp. 7-9.

[124] Ibid., pp. 8-10.

[125] James Brown Scott, "The Trial of the Kaiser," pp. 231-258 and answers to questions in appendix, in Edward M. House and Charles Seymour, eds., *What Really Happened at Paris: The Story of the Peace Conference, 1918-1919* (New York: Charles Scribner's Sons, 1921), p. 475.

[126] Verseput, "De kwestie," p. 10.

[127] Scott, "The Trial," pp. 240, 241, 246.

[128] Frey, *Der Erste Weltkrieg,* pp. 349-350, 370.

[129] Ibid., 351; Rosen, *Aus einem diplomatischen Wanderleben,* vol. 3/4, pp. 276.

[130] Frey, *Der Erste Weltkrieg,* p. 352.

CHAPTER EIGHT

CONCLUSION

The study of the role of the Netherlands in World War I leaves as many
questions unanswered as it resolves. Many critical documents were
destroyed during the Second World War, including large parts of the
archives of the Dutch and German armies, and the secret archive of the
Queen. Snijders, Bosboom, Loudon, and Cort van der Linden, to name
but a few, left few papers or none at all. Hence their actions, views,
and (especially) interrelationships are often shadowy. This has led to
all sorts of misstatements and errors. For example, Loudon's policy has
been described as one of "fearful neutrality."[1] This gross misdescrip-
tion of strict neutrality ignores the minister's endless and creative
delaying tactics. Nor can his refusal to budge when faced with threats
of war in 1918 be described as "fearful". Allegations of pro-German
attitudes overlook the practical foundations for such a feeling. *"[D]er
aussenpolitische und aussenwirtschaftliche Bezugspunkt war in Krieg
und Frieden Deutschland."* ("Germany was the foreign political and
economic policy datum point in war and in peace.")[2]

There has been a lack of study of the World War I-era Dutch leaders
for several reasons. The machinations of the leaders of a small country,
and a neutral at that, are of limited interest to the rest of the world.
Wmall states sometimes exercise an influence on events all out of
proportion to their size, they usually do not. One can easily disregard
the military and diplomatic activities of a small state, and assume that
it is merely the object and subject of the international actions of great
powers.[3] The small state is seen as the football, not a player. Great
powers can and do act without taking the small power's views into
account. On the other hand, such decisions can have devastating
consequences. The Central Powers began World War I by invading two
small countries, and not in the remotest sense did they benefit from
doing so. In neither case had the attacking great powers considered the
capacity or intentions of the victim. But it is understandable that
students of war residing in the great powers have had little interest in
Holland's avoidance of World War I.

What is less explicable is the relatively small interest given the
subject in Holland itself. Maybe the historic Dutch attitude explains the

dearth of scholarship on the generals of the time, but the absence of a scholarly biography of Cort van der Linden is odd, to say the least. Perhaps the Dutch outlook on the war era itself plays a role here. Holland had neither heroism nor tragedy to memorialize. There was deprivation and tension, to be sure. Years of waiting and wondering about the future were worsened by the fact that some of the war's great battles, starting with Liège, were audible in a large part of the country. Even the prospect of war's end, while certainly desired, did not make people all that hopeful. De Beaufort, for example, believed that if Germany won, Holland's independence would be over. If the Entente won, he expected another war in 10-12 years.[4] So the war was a pessimistic period, comprised of economic deprivation, tension, and boredom for hundreds of thousands of conscripts. Not something that stood out in the national memory, not even negative enough to recall as tragedy. The greatest success – the avoidance of the war – was neither celebrated nor studied as it should have been.

The result was a rather myopic, narrow approach to understanding this avoidance. Holland's neutrality was not the function of any single event, decision, or trend. Both economic and military factors have to be taken into consideration.[5] Yet this is precisely what was not done. A myth developed that idealistic neutralism had done the job.[6] The fact that Holland had declared itself neutral and had strictly adhered to that declaration was taken as, by itself, the reason for its having remained neutral. In other words, neutrality was attributed to neutrality.

> Four years of bitter war in Europe did not change the Dutch mentality. Rather than realize the frailty of their peaceful existence, they became all the more convinced that they were destined to remain outside any war as long as they desired to remain out of it. With such a mentality it became natural to pay only lip service to the problems of national defence, something which was made all the easier by the apathetic and indolent nature of the Dutch insofar as national interest was concerned.[7]

Diplomacy and military preparations were viewed as unimportant in retrospect. Wartime military problems were not addressed.[i] In a perverse way, this made sense. If scrupulous evenhandedness was all

---

[i] De Jonge suggested in 1917 that the country needed to decide to have "a good army or no army." The budget, he argued, would have to double. Van der Wal, *Herinneringen,* p. 36. De Jonge must have known what the response would be; De Beaufort was particularly appalled.

that was necessary to avoid war, why spend money on an expensive army? Hence the army became an even greater target for spending reductions than before and many professionals left in disgust. One prominent Dutch politician justified his optimism regarding war avoidance in 1940 by arguing that rumors during World War I that Holland would be invaded were "groundless."[8] The situation was not considered especially dangerous by either the Minister President or the Supreme Commander until the very last moment[9] – a telling comparison with the attitude in 1914. The grousing of former soldiers like W.G.F. Snijders that World War I had not reduced the danger of war were ignored.[10] By 1936 Colijn, then Minister President, confessed that "we have no army."[ii] The conclusion that strict neutrality was enough "led to a deplorable amount of apathy . . . regarding problems of foreign policy and . . . military defence" and "the country [became] dangerously detached from international realities . . ."[11] "Trust in neutrality [was] based on readings or misreadings of the 1914 circumstances . . ."[12]

The events of 1940 swept away any naivete about the maintenance of neutrality. This did not lead to a reappraisal of World War I in the country's history, however, and the lacunas in understanding of the war remained. Some of these can never be filled. There are areas where clear conclusions are possible, while in others only speculation is possible. Among the former is the effect that World War had on the Netherlands.

[ii] It was the army that would have to bear the brunt of this decision-making, or lack thereof, in 1940. Its brief but stubborn resistance ended with its surrender (the Dutch surrendered only the army, not the country – an option the French specifically rejected as surrender "à la Hollandaise."). The army did not always strengthen its own case in the post-world War I era. Disagreements between generals after the war meant that the army did not speak with one voice and thereby reduced its own influence. One retired general, H.A.F.G. van Ermel Scherer, did argue publicly that the strengthened Dutch army caused Germany to change its plans, but weakened his argument significantly by claiming that reforms in 1904 had caused Germany to change its plans in 1906 – whereas Schlieffen did not write his famed plan until 1905. Kecksmeti, *Strategic Surrender,* pp. 42-43; Van Campen, "How and Why," p. 175; De Leeuw, *Nederland in de wereldpolitiek,* pp. 156-57.

What the war did to the Netherlands

The Netherlands emerged from the war with a changed relationship between state and nation. The role of the government in 1914-1918 had no precedent. Extensive regulations permeated every aspect of the economy. Taxes and borrowing increased substantially to keep pace with the rapidly growing national budget. In 1913, the Dutch government spent some 239 million guilders; in 1918 the figure zoomed to more than a billion guilders. A cumulative deficit of 1.23 billion guilders had been run during the war, of which 1.1 billion was directly attributable to the war. Total "crisis expenditures" for 1914-1918 equaled 1.14 billion guilders, or five times the entire prewar budget.[13]

Most of this spending can be attributed to costs of the defense budget. Military expenditures exceeded a billion guilders for the war. Some of this was for relief for families whose breadwinner had been mobilized, but most went directly to the army. One estimate places real military costs, including all sorts of "indirect" expenditures, closer to 2 billion guilders, which would amount to about 10-15% of national income.[14] In either case, it was a gargantuan amount of money which necessitated a great deal of borrowing, as much per year as the prewar annual budget.

The country lost even more money on the Bolshevik revolution than it spent on the army, however. Estimates of the total amount lost when the Bolsheviks repudiated Russia's debts reached 1.25-1.5 billion guilders. Although Dutch losses were smaller than those of France and Britain, the damage was proportionately greater – and avoidable. To the diplomats, the revolutionary crisis did not come as a surprise. In July 1916, the Dutch envoy had commented on the unprecedented discontent when the Russian government attempted to call up more men. The government had to back down. Was this information relayed to Dutch business interests, encouraging them to sell out if possible? On the whole it is unlikely. Oudendijk did his best to protect the Dutch banks in Petrograd, but there was only so much he could do.[15]

The most public losses suffered by the Dutch were in regards to their merchant fleet. One hundred and forty seven ships were sunk, while about as many were damaged and disabled.[iii] Sixteen percent of the fleet, more than 200,000 tons of shipping space, was put out of

---

[iii] This includes fishing vessels.

action. The losses do not appear catastrophic. Only 377 sailors and 648 fishermen lost their lives. The merchant fleet grew in size and tonnage during the war. The 1918 fleet counted 907 ships of all types, 120 more than in 1915. Tonnage had also risen, from 770,000 to 801,000. This led some foreign writers to suggest that Holland's claims of a wartime shipping crisis were fraudulent, pointing to the rising dividends paid by shipping companies. The twelve largest companies paid 11% dividends in 1913, 28% in 1915, and almost 20% in 1917.[16]

Using these numbers to minimize Holland's wartime difficulties shows a misconception of the role of seaborne trade in the Dutch economy. The issue was not the profitability of the shipping companies, but rather the ability of Dutch *and foreign* ships to bring in what the country needed. Domestic shippers were reluctant to take to the water at all. The government finally entered the insurance business itself, insuring 90% of any commercial vessel and collecting premiums accordingly. This was a success in two ways. Shippers could now send out their precious vessels again, and the government made money, collecting 18 million guilders in premiums while paying out only 12 million in claims. This resolved part of the shipping problem, but only a small part. In 1913, a total of 16,996 vessels had arrived in Dutch ports. In 1918 only 1,779 did, a drop of 89.5%. Dutch vessels did not do much better than the average. Entries into port fell 82% during the war.[17]

This had two results. The less obvious one is that the country's ties with its Indies colony became quite tenuous, as the government had feared they would. Economic connections deteriorated. In 1913, 215 vessels had sailed from the Indies to Holland. By 1917 the number had fallen to 21, and in 1918 not a single vessel plied the route. It took a major diplomatic tussle before Britain permitted Dutch ships to sail to the colonies. The colonial relationship was considerably weakened by the war.[18]

> The Netherlands East Indies had long striven for independence; they desired to possess their own industrial enterprises, and they wished to be less dependent commercially upon the mother country. The years of war largely contributed to accelerate these changes, . . . [19]

The other – and much more obvious – result was to impose considerable deprivation on Dutch citizens as food supplies and heating fuel ran low. Superficially, the Dutch were not impoverished. Industrial employment remained steady and output grew. Until the postwar recession, high government spending maintained the artificial level of welfare so often common in wartime economies. Foreign trade, however, was devastated. In 1918 the total values of exports and imports were only 13% and 16% respectively of their prewar levels. For a commerce-based economy this was catastrophic. Bread rationing was imposed in the war's last year. Fuel was unobtainable and even the royal palace was cold and dark in wintertime. Deaths from illnesses that would have been survivable in peacetime increased. "The war was also responsible for the weakening of the power of resistance of a great many persons in consequence of insufficient food or clothing, . . ." The allied blockade was viewed with as little favor as the German invasion of Belgium.[20]

Behind the physical, quantifiable effects of the war on the Dutch people lay more subtle results. The psychological effect of the endless waiting for a possible invasion must have been painful. True, there were periods when people and cabinet alike thought the risk of war remote, and attempted to demobilize (blocked, of course, by the uncooperative Snijders). This ceased with the increasingly public threats of war in 1917-1918. As mentioned earlier, the war was clearly audible. Always during the great offensives on the Western Front there was " . . . that eternal rumble of artillery so plainly heard at The Hague."[21]

Side by side with this was another result that cannot be expressed in numbers: the increasingly dominant and intrusive role of the state. Government became "the omnipotent motive power of the national life."[22] This may well have laid the groundwork for the country's shift to social democracy at midcentury. De Beaufort worried about the socializing impact of a war in which rationing and other regulations leveled the difference between social classes.[23] Certainly the relationship between government and business would never be quite the same. In the words of a prominent businessman,

> All these regulations interfered drastically with the ideas of liberty prevailing in the commercial and shipping circles of the Netherlands, . . . This liberty, however, was restricted by the way in which the Great War developed. The struggle was no longer between armies, it was a conflict between nation and nation, and the consequences of the war were designedly brought home to the citizens themselves. Under such circumstances there was no more room for the old and tired principles of liberty, and neutral were faced with difficulties unknown in previous wars.

He concluded optimistically:

> The Kingdom of the Netherlands, however, was blessed with a Government which knew how to take the altered viewpoints into account and to frame such measures as were calculated to meet the situation.[24]

He was referring to the government's domestic policies, not its foreign and security policies, which were generally assumed to have had no effect on either the country's own future or the situation in Europe generally. As to the former point, this assumption was clearly wrong; more surprisingly, it was wrong on the latter issue as well.

What the Netherlands did to the war

Inadvertently and unintentionally, the Netherlands had an enormous impact on World War I.

Beginning students of the war are always puzzled by its extraordinarily rapid spread. Why, they wonder, does a dispute in the Balkans lead a continent to plunge itself into ruin? The new students do see a certain logic to the events in eastern Europe. After Austria declares war on Serbia, it was only logical that Russia would honor its alliance with Serbia, and it was also logical for Germany to threaten Russia with war if it did not demobilize. The Russians refuse, and the Germans declare war. This sequence makes sense, although it still leaves questions unanswered for the more percipient students. One can argue about whether the Russian mobilization triggered Germany's march to war, or whether Germany's overt threat to Russia (the demand to demobilize) was the more significant event. There is also the question of the precise meaning of the "blank check" that Germany gave Austria, allowing (or encouraging?) Austria to do whatever it chose, confident of complete German support.

Yet then the war suddenly jumps west; in a matter of days Belgium, Luxembourg, France, and Britain are all embroiled in the conflict. There are two ways of looking at this. The first is simply to attribute this to the plan made by Schlieffen, which called for Germany to make most of her effort in the west. That decision was cast in stone. The German army had even ceased working on the alternative, which would be to face east and defend in the west. Yet stopping the analysis of the rapid spread of the war with a reference to Schlieffen is unsatisfactory.

It does not take into account the speed with which the war spread, nor the importance of that speed.

To analyze this issue, we have to consider: how did Germany's leading statesmen feel about the war? Basically, they were willing to fight and their foreign policy behavior was aggressive, but they did not particularly desire an all-out war. They had planned for it; they were ready for it; but they did so out of a pessimistic view of Germany's strategic position. The Russian Revolution has obscured the fact that Russia was in many ways a growing power. Its industrial might would at some point translate into greater military force. More importantly, the Germans were absolutely convinced that their two larger neighbors, France and Russia, were waiting for the right moment to invade and destroy Germany. The German decision to go to war therefore had a preemptive character.

But the German leaders did not necessarily want war at once with all their neighbors. What they were hoping for in 1914 was ideally for Austria to destroy Serbia without outside interference. If this failed, a rapid war without British interference seemed to be the best possible solution. Pessimism, fear and paranoia, not a grandiose plan of conquest, underlay the German mindset. Remember Moltke's view: "If there is war – good: no war, better." Recall Bethmann Hollweg's comment a few years before the war, when he was planting trees at his estate and wondering if it was worth the trouble, since the Russians would probably have his property in a few years anyway. Consider his attempt to resign in 1914 when instead of a local conflict, his government now faced a European-wide war. Think about the Kaiser's answer, refusing the resignation: "You cooked this soup, now you must eat it." Remember Schlieffen's prediction, written shortly before his death, when he predicted that at a certain moment, the enemy's gates would open, the drawbridges would come down, and the French and Slavic hordes would pour into Germany. Finally, there is the Emperor's margin comment when he heard that Britain had entered the war: "Now we bleed to death." These are not the sentiments of leaders filled with positive excitement about the war.

Then why did they do it? Again, the Schlieffen plan is usually blamed. But the Schlieffen plan does not explain the speed of the spread of the war. The army needed *two weeks* from the beginning of mobilization before it could begin its westward march. Two weeks is a long time in diplomacy. Many political and diplomatic solutions might have been advanced. More importantly, the more days that went by before the invasion of Belgium began, the clearer it would be that Britain would not stand idly by.

This was a core concern for the Germans. Their hope that Britain would stay out might seem like folly today. Britain, however, had not sent an army to the continent since the Crimean War. Enormous energies went into keeping the British out. Jagow kept up a constant campaign of deception aimed at Grey so as to lull the British into a false sense of security about Belgium. The idea was obviously to present Britain with a *fait accompli,* and get the job done before Albion arrived. No one in Germany wanted war with Britain at this moment. Some feared a British attack, but that is a completely separate issue. Even the navy, the service constructed to threaten Britain, considered its job just that. It would be *two years* before the High Seas Fleet emerged from its bases to face the entire British navy – and it never did it again.

How strong the hope of British non-involvement was can be seen from Jagow's last, desperate attempt to keep the British out. He went so far as to write Grey that German sincerity was proved by the fact that Germany was honoring its promise not to invade Holland, only going through Belgium. This was a bizarre telegram, essentially trying to convince the British of Germany's good intentions by openly stating that the German government was only ignoring international law in regards to one low country, not both. Presumably he thought it might work.

He may have believed this because the speed of the crisis prevented Britain's position from becoming clearer; had it, the Germans might have had second thoughts about the invasion of Belgium. The Kaiser's feelings about war with Britain certainly raise this as a possibility. Grey is often blamed for not making Britain's position clearer. Yet his failure to restate Britain's commitment to Belgium was hardly culpable negligence. For one thing, he never even hinted that Britain would fail to live up its treaty regarding Belgium. Additionally, Britain had never accepted hostile control of the channel coast. Finally, he had little chance. During the first weeks after Sarajevo, Germany pretended that nothing was happening. Then, Jagow acted as if Germany were merely an onlooker, causing Grey to suggest mediation – unaware of the extent to which Germany was backing Austria. Even when the picture began to clear, a confrontational, unambiguous statement from Grey would have two problems. First, it would deprive Germany of any face-saving way out of the crisis. Second, Grey could be accused in Cabinet and

Parliament of taking unilateral action. He could only threaten war once the political establishment had solidified behind him. The crisis was much too rapid for political and public opinion to have gelled completely. Given a few more days, Grey might have sorted out his political problems and the diplomatic picture and clarified Britain's posture to the Germans.[iv]

He did not get a few more days. Neither did anyone else. And we know why: Moltke's *coup de main* against Liège. Moltke was no fanatical warmonger, but he had to capture the Belgian fortress immediately or his entire war plan collapsed. This was, of course, a breathtaking risk, to gamble the whole future of his country on the successful attack on single point on the map. Small wonder that he demanded to be allowed to go ahead. Therefore he had to resist the Kaiser's last minute attempt to cancel the *entire westward invasion*. The Emperor (and his Chancellor, for that matter) were perfectly willing to fight a war only in the East. But he simply had to have Liège. If he had not, he could easily have suggested that the mobilization would have to continue until around August 15th anyway, so the decision could be postponed. Every power would have had more time to clarify its position, to communicate. No diplomat could have known about Moltke's urgency; small wonder that they could not react quickly enough. Contrary to much that has been written, Europe's diplomats were not too slow, and their nations' fates were not ruined by their mobilization timetables. They were ruined because of Moltke's timetable for the attack on Liège.

> It is particularly tragic that by refusing to violate Dutch neutrality and making provision for the *coup de main* on Liège instead, the younger Moltke should have aggravated the political situation even further. If his *coup de main* was to succeed at all, it had to be set in motion immedi-

---

[iv] More speculatively, other things could have happened during a longer mobilization. The evaluation of Russia's posture might have changed. A realization that Russia was advancing more quickly than anticipated might have led to the transfer of troops eastwards; an evaluation that Russia overall was weaker than expected, would paradoxically have made a quick victory over France less urgent. Austria might have requested more direct assistance. Belgium would have fully mobilized and perhaps advanced to the Meuse – hardly a threat to the Germans, but certainly evidence that Belgium was definitely going to fight (another thing that the Germans thought might not happen). All these guesses are just examples of the possible effect a bit more time on the crisis.

ately after the declaration of a state of war. . . . [T]he presence of time on the statesmen . . . was much increased. . . . [Therefore] all efforts at a political settlement . . . came too late."[25]

The catastrophically rapid spread of World War I was due to Moltke's decision to avoid the Netherlands. Part of this can attributed to passive factors over which the Netherlands had no control. Its geography was what forced Moltke to put so much emphasis on Liège. If Limburg had belonged to Belgium, he could have by passed Liège, as Schlieffen had intended, without having to invade Holland. The other "passive" factor was Holland's economic value to Germany, the "windpipe" concept.

Yet the emphasis on the "windpipe" role of the Netherlands in German thinking has been exaggerated. First, Holland was not the only coastal neutral on which Germany bordered. Germany could import through Denmark also. Denmark could be blockaded by the British, but then so could Holland. Second, the Schlieffen plan called for a short war. If Belgium, Luxembourg, and France were conquered, and the war was essentially over, imports would no longer be nearly as crucial.[v] Defeating the Russian armies was not expected to be difficult, and a Russia bereft of all its allies save Britain could not wage offensive war (she might remain unconquered, but no longer a threat).

Moltke's decision to avoid Holland in 1908-1909 and his firm commitment to the attack on Liège over the ensuing 5 years can only be explained by reference to military concerns. What were these concerns? The presence of British troops in Holland was one, but this was not the primary issue. Britain's army was small. If it would come to defend Holland, it would certainly come to defend Belgium. Exactly where it showed up was not at the forefront of Moltke's thinking. True, it would complicate the grand Schlieffen sweep enormously if the BEF sat on the German right flank, *but it could accomplish that in Belgium.* In other words, the flanking problem would occur even if the British only went to Antwerp, and this might be even worse than if they went to Holland. Antwerp with its sea access would be an excellent position for the British, even better than the Dutch *waterlinie* because the latter was further away from the German flank.

---

[v] Germany was dependent on Chile for nitrates, necessary for the making of explosives, but it is inconceivable that even the most optimistic German expected Britain to allow militarily useful materials to cross the Atlantic unmolested.

If not the BEF, the only other concern that Moltke could have would be the Dutch army. The Dutch army was not a particularly good one, but the Dutch did have an organized Field Army, a defensive position recognized by the Germans as the most powerful in Europe, and talented senior officers. While the Dutch army had come in for a lot of derogatory comments in German reports over the years, references to generals to whom the German military observers spoke were often quite positive – and this was particularly so, interestingly enough, regarding both Snijders brothers, C.J. and W.G.F. In addition, Holland mobilized an army equivalent to about 10% of its German counterpart. The Germans were expecting even more, closer to 15%. Neither Schlieffen nor Moltke had a man to spare in their grand design, so the presence of such a force on the German right flank was potentially fatal – too many German troops might have to be detached as a covering force.[vi]

The only way that the Dutch army could be disregarded and masked with a small force (Schlieffen set aside 2 divisions, 5% of his invasion force) was if the Dutch military was so weak and disorganized that it could be almost disregarded. Schlieffen did so; Moltke did not. Why? Because the Dutch army improved in number, equipment, and organization in the decade before World War I. This was no secret to the Germans. Even public sources on military affairs in Berlin reported the Dutch army's growing strength. Had the Dutch army remained – to take an extreme case – the complete disaster that it was in 1870, Moltke would have had no reason to avoid Holland. The Dutch army's growth was not the only reason that he left Holland unmolested, but without that growth and improvement, there is little chance that the Dutch would have escaped the war.

In other words, the Dutch decision to rearm probably preserved Holland from war. Inadvertently and unintentionally, this Dutch activity led Germany to plan on the huge gamble that Liège could be captured quickly. This in turn slashed the time that diplomats and

---

[vi] Moltke apparently never doubted that the Dutch would fight. Yet he had hopes that the Belgians might not. Was this because of Holland's preparations? Or was it a subtle racial/cultural distinction between the Belgians and Dutch? Belgium is, after all, half French. Yet Holland was hardly known for her martial ardor or battlefield achievements. His differing expectations regarding the two low countries defy easy explanation.

leaders had to make decisions by 10-12 days and triggered the unstoppable descent of western Europe into the abyss.[vii]

A balancing act

Macro-calculations of this type were far from the Dutch government's collective mind in 1914. Even in peacetime, few Dutch politicians had much interest in international balance of power politics. Now that the country was threatened with war, the government's only interest was in preserving the country's neutrality. None of the country's major leaders were so naive, however, to believe that Holland would stay out of war simply by adhering to legalistic neutrality. Many were advocates of a new and peaceful international order, pleased to have hosted the prewar international peace conferences and the construction of the Peace Palace.[viii] The ideas there espoused were now without meaning. Instead of *relying* on legalistic neutrality, the government had to *use* legalistic neutrality as a tool for balancing itself in a fine edge between the Entente and the Central Powers, or more precisely, Britain and Germany.

In other words, what mattered most about Dutch actions is whether they looked neutral to the warring powers, not whether they actually were by some mythical objective standard. Diplomacy and the balancing of strategic resources and liabilities were the only ways to survive. Fortunately, there was a rich resource of experience in both areas. "The Dutch are past masters at both."[26] The government could not sit back and expect the balance of power to keep the country

---

[vii] Germany would diplomatically and politically have been better off not using the Moltke plan. Would Schlieffen's original plan have worked better? It bought Germany an additional albeit small opponent, at least 200,000 opposing troops who probably would have received military supplies from Britain, and who could retreat behind their inundations at any time and then launch new counterattacks. Neither plan considered the moral effect of invading small neutrals. The outrage provoked by events in Belgium was an unquantifiable but powerful boost to the Entente's struggle; this would only have been strengthened if two low countries had been invaded. I am obviously not addressing the eternal debate over the proper strength proportions of the right and left wings in the German army.

[viii] A French writer passing the building during the war wrote: "On a envie d'accrocher à la grille, en passant, un écriteau: *Huis te huur* . . ." ("One wished to hang on the fence, while passing, a sign: house for rent . . .") Pierard, *La Hollande,* p. 56.

secure. A balance of power by itself will not do so. In World War II, for example, three small states were destroyed in areas where there was a balance of power, while three survived in areas where there was no balance.[27] Holland's survival depended on the execution of a careful balancing act. Neutrality would survive only so long as each great power's interest in permitting that neutrality remained greater than the benefit of occupying Holland.[28] To see Holland's neutrality as inevitable is a serious mistake. The alternative was perfectly plausible.[29]

So how was the "balancing act achieved? What actions, decisions, and factors enabled the government to steer between Scylla and Charybdis? The first thing we have to look at is the role of the rapid mobilization in 1914 and the intelligence that it was based upon. The possession of the knowledge gained from Le Roy's telegram was only one half of the equation. There are plenty of examples where intelligence information was misinterpreted or ignored. Among the best known cases are the World War II German threat to the Netherlands (1939-1940), the invasion of the Soviet Union (1941), Pearl Harbor (1941), and the Yom Kippur war (1973).[30] In a sense, the reliance on Le Roy's telegram was a cost free gamble, as no country could possibly take offence at Holland's mobilization. What is notable, however, is the willingness to rely on a single piece of intelligence information, and the pessimism that underlay it. In 1914, the army and to an extent the government were fairly certain that Germany would cross the border, and took no chances.

The resulting was a mobilized army of 200,000 soldiers that, by 1917, could be expanded to 450,000 with a few days' notice. Evaluations of the importance of the army in maintaining neutrality vary. There are several ways of looking at this issue. There was no neutrality policy that could exclude having a ready army. Holland was clearly a buffer state, and buffer states do not have neutrality alone as a viable option.[31] Without the unsheathed sword, the buffer state would look to either belligerent as a tempting target; far worse, it would look to either belligerent like a good target for the enemy great power. The possession of an army may not be enough; it has to be good enough to be capable of meaningful deterrence. An obviously weak army would be a liability.

> It serves no purpose to establish a protection force and then to vitiate it to the point where it can no longer protect. Indeed, an inadequate

military institution may be worse than none at all. It could be a paper tiger inviting outside aggression; strong enough in appearance to threaten powerful enemies, but not strong enough in fact to defend against their predations. Alternatively, it could lull leaders into a false confidence, lead them to rash behavior, and then fail in the ultimate military contest.[32]

Holland's army was not a threat, nor did it lull Dutch leaders into any false confidence. Was it strong enough, however, to act as deterrent force? Several authors have suggested it was. Michael Handel concluded that "Holland's ability to mobilize an army of up to 450,000 soldiers may have helped it to maintain its neutrality during the First World War." C.J.E. Harlow decided that Holland "succeeded in maintaining a policy of strict neutrality in the First World War, partly by the mobilization of a large army of 450,000 men, but also because it suited the interests of the belligerents."[33]

Inevitably, the role of the army was strongly emphasized by Holland's soldiers. This was partly pride, partly in response to the advocates of disarmament between the world wars. Neutrality was attributed to the "timely and completely calm mobilization." De Jonge concluded that the mobilized soldiers "kept us out of the war." W. G. F. Snijders thought the Dutch army was a major reason for Moltke's decision to avoid the Netherlands. Another Dutch officer and future general studied the war and noted that Holland's army was qualitatively competitive during the war and that without it a strong army the country would have become part of the conflict[34] The army-disarmament debate is made clear in his analysis:

> Clearly the influence of our forces and defenses must be determined in contradiction to the claim of the apostles of disarmament, of anti- and a-militarists and from unthinking types, that our army neither in 1914 nor during the continuing war nor now and nor in the future has served, nor can serve as a means of protection against a war.[35]

Of course, this could be written off as the inevitable conclusion of career soldiers, especially while fighting for decent budgets after the war. There are two reasons why their views matter, however. First, they found support among some civilians – including Treub, not known as an advocate for military spending.

> But if the Netherlands had not made the impression, that with taking away its neutrality the result would have been an enemy that, although

not of great importance by itself, nevertheless in a struggle between
powers that were for so long equal, might have tipped the scales toward
the opponent [of the invader], then our country would not remained
outside the tremendous struggle.[36]

Treub's somewhat laborious analysis brings us to the other reason that
the views of the Dutch generals cannot be disregarded. They had
studied the German viewpoint, and in particular Moltke's diary, and
arrived at a conclusion that has already been mentioned in this book:
Germany's weakness and Holland's strength lay in the bare adequacy
(if that) of Germany's army. The Central Powers were outnumbered at
war's outbreak.[37] From 1910 on, Moltke emphasized Germany's
numerical difficulty in relation to her neighbors. The German war
minister, General Josias von Heeringen, demanded more troops in 1911
because of the likelihood that Belgium and Holland would defend their
neutrality had increased. Schlieffen set aside 4 reserve and 1 active
corps and a cavalry division to mask a belligerent Holland – an
impossible drain on the German army. Critically, German sources
noted the improvements in the Dutch army, and its field army's
effective doubling between 1905 and 1911.[38] In 1915 the information
section at German army headquarters concluded concerning the
Netherlands and its army:

*Selbst England oder Deutschland würden einen beachtenswerten
Gegner an ihnen finden.*[39]
(Even Britain or Germany would find in them a noteworthy opponent.)

The mention of Britain in this quotation – as much as the implied
respect for the Netherlands – should for once and for all end the debate
over whether Holland's mobilization mattered. Respect for Holland
might cause Germany to think carefully about *whether* to invade; but
Holland's ability to be a respectable opponent of Britain (in Germany's
eyes) would take away a major reason *for* invading. Surely Germany
would have moved in in a flash had (a) Holland been disarmed, and (b)
Britain appeared ready to invade Holland, or (c) the Germans were
sufficiently paranoid to think Britain was about to do so. Paranoia was
not unknown among German decision makers. Yet there is evidence
that Germany became more satisfied with Holland's ability. Early in
the war, the German units near Holland could enter the country in case
of a British invasion without waiting for orders from army headquarters; at some point during the war, this was changed. A hair-trigger
response was no longer thought necessary.[40] At the same time, the fear

of British landings *plus* some respect for Dutch military capacity made a difference in the opposite sense as well. The Germans knew that the Dutch could keep them from reaching the coast before British troops arrived to help. This has been labeled a major factor in Holland's neutrality in World War I.[41]

This military balancing act was very important in regard to the two most vulnerable outlying areas, Zeeland and Limburg. Both sides in the war benefitted from a strongly defended Zeeland.[42] Snijders paid a lot of attention to Zeeland, placing a large force on its eastern boundary to make it impossible for an enemy landing there to advance inland. He also strengthened the defenses of the province's islands and peninsulas, especially trying to deal with aerial (British) and naval (German) incursions. In the case of Limburg, besides the obvious difficulties that the Germans would have had with an enemy army in the rear, the Dutch railroaded a division to the south before the German march even began. This turned out to be unimportant in 1914 – Moltke had no intention of violating Holland at that point – but it certainly signaled the intention to defend the southern outlying areas of the country. Three of the army's four field divisions were posted close to Limburg, together numerically equal to two German corps.[43] The most interesting comment perhaps came from Kühlmann, writing in his memoirs. After the war, Colijn asked him why Germany had avoided Limburg. Kühlmann did not write exactly how he answered the question, but he did note that had Germany done this, the Netherlands would have considered itself at war with Germany. Hence, he explained, the haste with which the Dutch were working at night to prepare the explosives at the Limburg bridges.[44] In other words, the Germans knew very well that there would be no free passage, that the Dutch army would contest an invasion everywhere. Even in Limburg.

Most authors have discounted the military dimension in explaining Holland's neutrality. Some have continued to explain it in terms of the balance of power. One historian wrote that Holland's war avoidance was due to the balance of power, plus "an opportune timidity" and "considerable good fortune." A prominent Dutch politician wrote that "it was not Dutch virtues but the balance of power" which Holland's policy possible. He also suggested that there was a de facto alliance between Britain and the Netherlands.[45] As explained earlier, the balance of power argument is inadequate. A balance of power may preserve peace, but there is no consensus that it protects the independence of small states *unless the military factor is considered*, which unfortunately is often not the case. In a true balance, the strength of a small state can make a difference, and that might deter an invasion.

A more realistic approach is to attribute Dutch neutrality to its being in line with the interests of both Britain and Germany. This is a view first outlined before the war by Eyre Crowe, who concluded in 1911 that Dutch neutrality would be in both British and German interests.[46] His view was echoed after the war in many different quarters. Treub pointed out that had Germany not counted the advantage of going through Limburg less than the benefit of Holland's harbors (for trade[ix]), then the Dutch would have suffered the same fate as the Belgians. The harbors did not benefit the Germans, however.[47] Yet a recent dissertation attributed the maintenance of neutrality in 1914-1918 solely to "deliberate actions by the Germans."[48]

The most prolific Dutch author on the World War I era, C. Smit, also did not give military factors a very large role. Smit suggests that neutrality succeeded do to "special circumstances," including that neither great neighbor wanted to invade, and that the colonies were not part of the war. Germany wanted to use Holland for trade access, while Britain did not want to risk Germany obtaining more submarine bases. Both countries were interested in a neutral Holland for espionage purposes. Major Von Schweinitz even concluded that this was the most important reason for leaving Holland unmolested. Wully Robertson, Chief of the Imperial General Staff, wrote that a hostile Holland meant the end of the British Secret Service "as it is through [Holland] that almost all our best information is received." In addition, Holland handled diplomatic interests for both Britain and Germany in countries where the belligerents could not have diplomats. Smit concludes by attributing Britain's tolerance of Dutch neutrality to the role of the N.O.T., the submarine base concern, the role of the secret service, and Holland's handling of issues regarding British prisoners. Germany's forbearance, Smit believed, was due to economic considerations, postwar concerns, the cover Holland gave to the German right flank, the

---

[ix] It is interesting that the Dutch "balancing act" extended even to such matters as the granting of credits. When the war was over, the credits issued to foreign countries were almost equal between Germany (197 million guilders) and the Entente (191 million). The addition of Austria gave the Central Powers a clear edge, but this was not important because the Entente nations hardly developed the hatred for Austria that they had for Germany. Vissering and Holstein, "Effect of the War upon Banking and Currency," p. 29.

continued (if narrow) supremacy of German civil authorities over the military, the influence of individual Germans such as Kriege and Rosen, the use of Holland for intelligence, and Holland's representation of German diplomatic interests.[49] This gave precious little credit to the Dutch "balancing act," especially the military side of it.

Smit does note that the belligerents were very interested in public opinion in the Netherlands and tried to influence it.[50] Here, however, there was little "balance." National opinion was overwhelmingly anti-German, although not pro-British. The only great power for which there was much affinity was France. The Germans began with one huge disadvantage: in the eyes of most Dutchmen, they had started the war (in the West, they had) and they had invaded neutral Belgium and caused great devastation. Nor were the legalistically-minded Dutch much impressed with Bethmann Hollweg's infamous explanation that necessity knows no law and that therefore Germany was justified in breaking it.[51] Although a concerned government tried from time to time to temper the anti-German tide of public opinion, there was no chance that public opinion would force a major change in policy. The Dutch mistrusted all great powers[x] and backed their government's neutrality policy without dissent. Distaste for Germany did not mean going to war with Britain. Bosboom reflected the feelings of many people when he wrote after the war:

> German injustice strikes as an unexpectedly delivered blow, under the motto, necessity of war: British injustice creeps closer via detours, dressed in the mantel of justice.[52]

In other words, no one could be trusted. This meant that Holland could not and should not ally with either side, but neither could it depend on goodwill in Berlin and London to avoid the war. It could depend only on itself.

Issues and answers

Yet how was that possible? The Netherlands' resources were limited. There was no large land mass into which to withdraw or maneuver, no huge population from which to conscript, no powerful army with which

---

[x] As shown in the Dutch proverb, very loosely translated, "it's dangerous to dine with powerful men." Barnouw, *Holland under Queen Wilhelmina*, p. 101.

to intimidate. Somehow, Holland was spared. While many individual crises can be studied, and have been in the preceding pages, the overall result leaves many unanswered questions – some of which cannot be answered with the state of the documentation.

What enabled the Netherlands to remain neutral?

The Netherlands survived World War I intact because it was able to utilize its scarce resources in an efficient way. Whether by design or by accident, the policies of the government, foreign ministry and army created a relationship with the major foreign powers that did not collapse until April 1918. Until then, there was always an area in between the most extreme demands of Germany and Britain. Only in April 1918 did the situation reach a point where Holland was forced to make concessions to each side which the other side found unacceptable. Even then, the country was able to make the best of the situation and escape disaster. Economic policies prevented the country from becoming so dependent on one alliance or the other that it would be forced to surrender its neutrality.

What were the arrangements for the API API telegram?

Le Roy's telegram could only have been issued on the basis of a telegraphic intercept, a personal observation, or the receipt of confidential information. No other explanation is credible. But what could Le Roy and Forbes Wels have agreed upon in advance that would have been so unambiguous that the army began the mobilization process? We will never know. The date of the arrangement is not known either. My guess is that Le Roy agreed to send the telegram if he observed certain *specific* events in Cologne which indicated imminent marching by the German orders. For that to be true, some segment of the German army would have to have been ahead of the official mobilization timetable. As individual states were instructed by the general staff not to send written reports to the war ministries, the steps taken by German military authorities before the official mobilization in July 1914 cannot be determined.

Why was Snijders recalled so late?

The general was on vacation at a most peculiar time. He was not recalled as the Serbian crisis reached its peak, nor when the Austrians mobilized. He was not recalled when the pre-mobilization began; he was recalled after those steps had been taken. It seems an odd summer for the government to allow its chief of staff and putative supreme commander to be relaxing in Scandinavia.

Why did Moltke think that Holland would fight, while Belgium might not?

Nothing in Moltke's diary or surviving documents suggests that he saw chance that Holland might not fight. The assumption that the Dutch would resist can be found everywhere. This was not true, incidentally, of Schlieffen. Yet Moltke hoped that Belgium might only protest, and even hoped that the Belgians would stop fighting after Liège. It was a fatal error, of course, for Belgium's resistance galvanized her allies (particularly the British). But why such different assumptions about the low countries? The difference may have been occasioned by racial/cultural or historical factors. Holland had been an independent state in some form since the sixteenth century and was fairly homogeneous. Belgium had no existence as a state before 1830, and there was no "Belgian race." At the beginning of the 20th century, these things mattered, and Moltke did see the Dutch as a related race.

Were there any secret contacts between Britain and Holland concerning the Indies?

Holland was a colonial empire at Britain's sufferance. The war exposed the Indies to several perils, the most importance of which was the growing threat of Japan. Britain was far happier to see this enormous empire in the hands of a small country than a legitimate competitor for imperial power – especially as the Indies would constitute a good jumping-off point towards Malaya, Burma, or India. From the perspective of the Dutch, the Indies were economically valuable and the richest companies in the country were involved in the exploitation of the region. Colijn was in London frequently in his role as oil company director. Confidential conversations about the security of the colony were probably held. If Holland were forced to surrender in case of a German invasion, there was no chance that Britain would allow Germany to occupy the colony. What would happen to the interests of Dutch businesses? Is it likely that Colijn and others similarly situated left this to chance?

Did the government ever contemplate doing something about the poor relationship between Snijders and the political establishment?

Politicians and generals regarded each other with jaundiced eyes in many countries (and often still do). In Snijders' case, this was a particularly unhealthy and potentially damaging situation. The general had astounding powers and his constitutional position was hazy. The government mostly took the short-term politically expedient approach of doing nothing. True, Bosboom, who could not govern the general, was let go; but that was nearly three years into the war. Nor was the appointment of De Jonge the cleverest choice to resolve the problem – admittedly he knew the war ministry very well, but the ministry was not the problem.

How much understanding was there for the plight of the warring powers?

I have often referred to the behavior of the great powers and their misinterpretations of Dutch attitudes. Were the Dutch – from the Queen down – more understanding of the belligerents, and the emotions resulting from a struggle without peer and unbelievable human losses? In general, I would say no. The Dutch simply lacked a frame of reference and many showed little understanding. A better understanding of what Germany and Britain were experiencing would have been useful during the 1918 crises.

What was the relationship between the Foreign Ministry and the military?

The military and diplomatic establishments had the country's future in their collective hands. They certainly did communicate. There are plenty of documents that show interchange of information. But did their officials ever meet, exchange strategic ideas, tips on what the Germans were up to, and so on? There was not much friction, the issue of whether to have military attachés being one of the few exceptions. In addition, Loudon and Snijders had certain things in common. Most notably, they were both highly pragmatic individuals. On the other hand, it is difficult to imagine them developing a close Schlieffen-Holstein type relationship.

What was the role of the Queen?

Despite Cees Fasseur's recent research, there is still a great deal we do not know about the Queen's role. The destruction of much documentation may render it impossible to decide definitively on many points. On how many occasions did the palace intervene in war-related matters, or attempt to do so? Did she make pre-war attempts to strengthen Holland's position through personal ties with her German and English relations? If not, why not? Did she really blame Loudon for what she saw as a weak foreign policy? Did she consider going to Paris in emulation of Albert? What was her personal reaction to Prince Hendrik's visit to German officers in Limburg? Wilhelmina is the only major Dutch figure of the era for whom we have a modern academic biography, and even in her case, the lacunas persist.

What did Van Heutsz talk about at Spa?

General Van Heutsz, former governor general of the Indies and chief military officer at the palace, was at Spa, November 5-9. The collapse of Germany was imminent. There is no documentary evidence that he discussed exile with the Emperor. Did Wilhelm not even think to mention the possibility? Taciturnity was not the Emperor's outstanding characteristic. Was Wilhelm still so convinced that he could stay in office that he did not even mention the alternative? Did no else at headquarters, where the Emperor's departure was definitely being plotted, mention it to Van Heutsz? If it was hinted at, did the general not believe it sufficiently to report it – or were he and the Queen still thinking things over when the Emperor arrived at the border?

What motivated Belgium's demand for territory at Versailles?

This question is beyond the scope of this book, as only the Dutch reaction to the demands has been of interest. Nevertheless, the issue affected Dutch-Belgian relations for so long that it can not be ignored completely. The Belgians could have been motivated by domestic politics, strategic needs, or perhaps simple revenge – not only for past Dutch sins, but for Holland's escaping the war entirely.

To what extent did the war change the Netherlands?

This is undoubtedly the area in which the most research remains to be done, as of this writing. Here we have a period which saw unprecedented government involvement in society and economy, the introduction of extended voting rights and an entirely new electoral system, and an attempted revolution. Eventually Holland would go down the path of social democracy, but considerably later. Was there a connection? Did the war change Dutch society in other ways? What were the social effects of the lengthy mobilization, for example?

What was the role of politics in the maintenance of neutrality?

The political system experience no dissent worthy of the name. It is true that the political truce of August, 1914 broke down in the ensuing months, but not to the point of undermining the government's policies. No party particularly desired an early election. No party wanted to be held responsible for creating an increased risk of war through political instability. No one broadly questioned the government's approach to neutrality because there was no obvious alternative. On an issue such as demobilization, support and opposition for this crossed party and ideological lines, so there was no clear break here either. Debates might be vigorous, ministers might occasionally fall (such as with Treub and Bosboom), newspaper criticism might be strong to border-line vicious, but the Cort van der Linden cabinet's position was never seriously threatened. The biggest result of this was that Loudon could pursue his work with little interference; Snijders was less affected, as he did not tolerate parliamentary interference anyway, but his autonomy was definitely enhanced by cabinet stability.

What was the role of diplomacy in the maintenance of neutrality?
    Loudon gets surprisingly little credit for Holland's peaceful escape from World War I. Here was the one Dutchman, after all, who dealt directly and regularly with both armed camps. A lot of negative opinions about him surfaced in the last year of the war. The Queen allegedly thought he was weak and cowardly, the Germans felt he was pro-Entente, and the British envoy called him a liar. Most of this surfaced after he had been foreign minister for quite some time and had had to deal with the increasing demands of the neighboring powers. A close examination of the record reveals an entirely different story. Loudon was much cleverer than anyone gave him credit for. He was a master of delaying tactics. He balanced not only British and German demands, but also his commitment to strict neutrality and the pragmatic needs of the moment. He was no coward. He held firm against German demands in 1918, forced to yield only by Rosen's end run to the government. He was perfectly willing to issue protests. Finally, criticism of Loudon fails to consider the mess that his successor wound up in after only a few weeks on the job. Loudon may not have been the perfect foreign minister, but he may well have been the perfect foreign minister for the World War I era.

What was the role of the army in the maintenance of neutrality?
    Snijders and his army have received a little more attention than

Loudon, but not much. How the army came to be nearly written out of the history of a war era is peculiar. From the moment of mobilization, its presence was absolutely essential. The army might deter an immediate German invasion. Its absence might encourage Germany to move through the southern Netherlands even if that was <u>not</u> part of the original plan. Either Britain or Germany might view a lack of defensive effort as a reason to occupy Holland to keep it out of the hands of the enemy. A failure to mobilize immediately would signal to the public that the crisis was not viewed as particularly serious, which would make it extremely difficult politically to mobilize later if invasion became more likely. Such a later mobilization would have to occur when all belligerents had fully mobilized and could invade quickly. The whole defense of the country depended on slowing down an invader just enough to prepare the vaunted *waterlinie* – the flooded areas which would protect the western heartland. Strict neutrality demanded retaliation against neutrality violations in every corner of the country, and the regular peacetime army was much too small to accomplish this. An undefended frontier would look like an inviting place for a defeated neighbor to cross while continuing to fight. A belated mobilization would be an easy and tempting target for interruption by a neighboring state. Policing the border to deal with smuggling (and possibly espionage) required troops as well.

Without a reasonably strong army, the Netherlands' neutrality would have come to an end sometime during the war. The Netherlands had such an army. Its shortcomings were legion. Yet it had the capacity to fight, to challenge neutrality violations, to slow down an invasion until the inundations were ready. Could it have held out long enough, either for the inundations or the arrival of allied troops? The inundations required two weeks; for allied assistance I would estimate a week for the British, less for the less likely scenario, German assistance against a British invasion. In 1940, the Dutch army was at a far greater disadvantage than in 1914, yet remained in the field for five days; Germany resorted to terror bombing in 1940 to bring resistance to an end. A German invasion force of a few divisions could not possibly have ended all Dutch resistance in less than two weeks in 1914. What is less clear is whether a German advance toward the *Waterlinie* could have been stopped long enough to prevent penetration of that zone before the water reached the required levels. A possible scenario might involve a German force perhaps penetrating the inundated zone, but then counterattacked by arriving British troops. World War I com-

manders were *very* sensitive about their flanks, etc. and this would tend
to slow an advance unless the Germans sent so many troops that they
could maintain a continuous front along the whole battle zone.

The bottom line is that Holland had an army adequate for its
strategic purpose, and this was a major factor in keeping the country
out of the war. The pre-war work of people like Snijders and Colijn
had not been wasted. Snijders summarized the situation well when, in
1930, he spoke at a ceremony granting Colijn an honorary doctorate:

> You never hesitate, where it is necessary, to stand up for your convic-
> tion, that in the current world situation, for a small country, located in a
> strategically vulnerable position at an intersection of international
> entanglements and possible conflicts, a proper defensive capability is the
> only achievable guarantee for the maintenance of its right of self-
> determination to ensure its neutrality.[53]

NOTES

[1] Fasseur, *Wilhelmina*, p. 525. Fasseur may be describing the Queen's views, but seems to be citing them with approval.

[2] Frey, *Der Erste Weltkrieg*, p. 370.

[3] Ibid., p. 11.

[4] Fasseur, pp. *Wilhelmina*, 497, 510.

[5] Frey, *Der Erste Weltkrieg*, p. 87.

[6] Porter, "Dutch Neutrality," p. vii.

[7] Bout, "Dutch Army," p. 196.

[8] Ibid., pp. 64, 165, 167-70, 188.

[9] Pearson, *Weak State*, p. 43.

[10] Snijders, *Der wereldoorlog*, p. 343.

[11] Roitero and Hoff, "Militaire misstappen," pp. 171-72; S.I.P. van Campen, "How and Why The Netherlands Joined the Atlantic Alliance – Part 1," *NATO Review* (August 1982), p. 9.

[12] Pearson, *Weak State*, p. 43.

[13] Bordewyk, "War Finances," p. 170; M.J. van der Flier, "War Finances," pp. 34-35, 94.

[14] Van der Flier, "War Finances," p. 36; Bout, "Nature and Extent of Antimilitarism," p. 233; Bout, "Dutch Army," p. 184.

[15] Bordewyk, "War Finances," p. 211; Bout, "Dutch Army," p. 184; Oudendijk to Loudon, 18/31 January 1918, 362, Smit, *Bescheiden ... 1917-1919*, pp. 374-77; Sweerts de Landas Wyborgh to Loudon, 10/23 July 1916, 588, Smit, *Bescheiden ... 1914-1917*, pp. 583-86.

[16] De Monchy, "Commerce and Navigation," p. 154; Flier, "War Finances," p. 55; Bosscher, "Oorlogsvaart," p. 337; Philip C. Jessup, *Neutrality: Its History, Economics and Law*, vol. 4, *Today and Tomorrow* (New York: Octagon, 1976 (1936)), p. 33.

[17] De Monchy, "Commerce and Navigation," pp. 126, 143, 144.

[18] Ibid., pp. 143, 144; Zaalberg, "The Manufacturing Industry," 7; J.H. Carpentier Alting and W. de Cock Bunning, *The Netherlands and the World War: Studies in the War History of a Neutral*, vol. 4 (New Haven: Yale University Press, 1928), p. 104.

[19] De Monchy, "Commerce and Navigation," p. 124.

[20] Bordewyk, "War Finances," p. 216; Zaalberg, "The Manufacturing Industry," pp. 15-25; Rullman *Colijn*, pp. 82-83; Tucker,*The European Powers*, p. 503; Van der Flier, "War Finances," pp. 34-35; Treub, *Herinneringen en overpeinzingen*, pp. 344-45; Vissering and Holstijn, "Effect of the War upon Banking and Currency," pp. 20, 22, 34.

[21] Porter, "Dutch Neutrality," p. 167; Townley, *'Indiscretions,'* p. 280.

[22] Barnouw, *Holland under Queen Wilhelmina*, p. 152.

[23] De Valk and Van Faassen, *Herinneringen*, p. 938.

[24] De Monchy, "Commerce and Navigation," p. 135.

[25] Ritter, *Schlieffen Plan*, p. 90.

[26] Pearson, *Weak State*, p. vii.

[27] Karsh, *Neutrality*, p. 99. The destroyed were Belgium, the Netherlands and Norway, while the survivors were Switzerland, Sweden and Ireland.

[28] See Barston, *Other Powers*, pp. 64-65.

[29] Bout, "Nature and Extent of Antimilitarism," p. 195.

[30] Pearson, *Weak State*, p. 135.

[31] Karsh, *Neutrality*, p. 83.

[32] Peter D. Feaver, "The Civil-Military Problematique: Huntington, Janowitz, and the Question of Civilian Control," *Armed Forces & Society* 23 (Winter 1996), p. 152.

[33] Handel, *Weak States*, p. 3; C.J.E. Harlow, *The European Armaments Base: A Survey* (London: Institute for Strategic Studies, 1967), part 2, p. 51.

[34] Buijs, "De Spoorbrug," p. 412; Alting von Geusau, *Onze weermacht*, p. 3; Snijders, *De wereldoorlog*, p. 341; Van Voorst tot Voorst, *Over Roermond, pp.* 61, 63; Van der Wal, *Herinneringen*, p. 48.

[35] Van Voorst tot Voorst, *Over Roermond*, p. 13.

[36] Treub, *Herinneringen en overpeinzingen*, p. 293.

[37] Count Max von Montgelas, quoted in *Official Documents*, pp. 101 ff.

[38] Van Voorst tot Voorst, pp. 15, 42, 46, 60-61; Stevenson, *Armaments*, p. 202.

[39] *"Die militärpolitische Lage der Niederlande,"* 5 July 1915, Information Section of GHQ (Germany), 10, Smit, *Buitenlandse bronnen 1914-1917*, pp. 15-17.

[40] Report from Lt. Col. W. G. Muller Massis, Netherlands military attaché, 23 February 1917, Buitenlandse Zaken – Kabinet en Protocol, ARA-II.

[41] Barnouw, *Holland*, p. 111.

[42] Klinkert, "Verdediging van de zuidgrens," part 1, p. 218.

[43] "Ronduit," *Manoeuvre om Limburg*, p. 21.

[44] Kühlmann, *Erinnerungen*, p. 389.

[45] Voorhoeve, *Peace, Profits and Principles*, p. 34; Bolkestein, "Netherlands and the Lure of Neutralism," p. 2.

[46] Smit, *Het voorspel*, pp. 180-81.

[47] Treub, *Herinneringen en ovepeinzingen*, p. 293.

[48] Roitero and Hoff, "Militaire misstappen," p. 174.

[49] Smit, *Diplomatieke geschiedenis*, pp. 325-26; Smit, *Tien studiën*, 11, pp. 24-25.

[50] Smit, *1914-1917*, p. 117.

[51] Barnouw, *Holland under Queen Wilhelmina*, p. 167; De Beaufort, *Vijftig jaren*, part 2, p. 229; Beijens to Davignon, 4 August 1914, *België betrokken in den oorlog*, pp. 43-44.

[52] Bosboom, *In moeilijke omstandigheden*, p. 24.

[53] Rullmann, *Colijn*, p. 101.

BIBLIOGRAPHY

Research Note

As mentioned many times in the text, a large quantity of critical archives were destroyed in World War II. There is no remaining documentary archive of Military Intelligence, GS-III; its records were either destroyed in bombing raids in 1945 or were lost. In Germany, many General Staff and War Ministry documents were destroyed in bombardments in 1942 and 1945. The royal house's secret archive was deliberately destroyed to prevent it from falling into Nazi hands. In addition, parts of Moltke's and Bethmann Hollweg's papers were expurgated after World War I. Finally, a great deal happened that was never committed to paper at all. In the words of Captain H.A.C. Fabius, the early chief of GS-III, the people who had a significant role in the 1914 crisis in Holland "made few notes – many in the highest places none at all – so that of all these historical and important happenings, the how and why, along with causes and results, in the long run will be lost."

Primary sources

Archival materials

Collections and materials at the General State Archive *(Algemeen Rijksarchief)*, The Hague:
    Collections of papers and documents of the following individuals:
        Bosboom
        Van Heutsz
        De Jonge
        Röell
        Loudon
    Documentary collections pertaining to the military establishment:
        AHK Bereden Artillerie
        Generale Staf
        Koninklijke Landmacht - Archief van het Veldleger
        Koninklijke Landmacht: Algemeen Hoofdkwartier
        Koninklijke Landmacht - Hoofdkwartier Veldleger
        Ministerie van Oorlog
    Other government document collections:
        Ministerie van Kolonien
        Ministerie van Buitenlandse Zaken
            Kabinet en Protocol
            Belgisch Gezantschap
            Registers van ingekomen stukken
        Ministerraad
    Other resources of the *Algemeen Rijksarchief*:
        ARA Stamboeken

Duitse Ministerie van Buitenlandse Zaken – Stukken betreffende Nederland
Hoover Institution. Records of the Oberste Heeresleitung, 1914-1918
Koninklijke Bibliotheek – Afdeling Documentatie, The Hague
Sectie Militaire Geschiedenis, The Hague

Published Documents

België betrokken in den oorlog: Verzameling van diplomatieke stukken. 's-Gravenhage: Martinus Nijhoff, 1914.
Bethmann Hollweg, Theobald von. "The September Programme (1914)." Published in Immanuel Geiss, *German Foreign Policy, 1871-1914.* London: Routledge & Kegan Paul, 1976, 217-18.
Bourne, Kenneth, and D. Cameron Watt, eds. *British Documents on Foreign Affairs: Reports and Papers from the Foreign Office Confidential Print.* Part I: *From the Mid-Nineteenth Century to the First World War War.* Series F: *Europe, 1848-1914* (ed. David Stevenson). Vol. 21. Washington, DC: University Publications of America, 1990.
——, eds. *British Documents on Foreign Affairs: Reports and Papers from the Foreign Office Confidential Print.* Part II: *From the First to the Second World War.* Series H: *The First World War, 1914-1918* (ed. David Stevenson). Vols. 1, 3, 4, 5, 7, 8. Washington, DC: University Publications of America, 1989.
——, eds. *British Documents on Foreign Affairs: Reports and Papers from the Foreign Office Confidential Print.* Part II: *From the First to the Second World War.* Series I: *The Paris Peace Conference of 1919* (ed. M. Dockril). Vol. 6. Washington, DC: University Publications of America, 1989.
Crowe, Eyre. "Crowe Memorandum, 1907." Published in Geis, *German Foreign Policy,* 194-200.
Dugdale, E.T.S, ed. *German Diplomatic Documents, 1871-1914,* vol 3: *The Growing Antagonism, 1898-1910.* New York: Barnes & Noble, 1969 (1930).
——, ed. *German Diplomatic Documents, 1871-1914,* vol IV: *The Descent into the Abyss, 1911-1914.* London: Harper & Brothers, 1931.
Engeland in oorlog voor de gewaarborgde rechten van kleine naties. 's-Gravenhage: Martinus Nijhoff, 1914.
Foreign Relations of the United States 1917, Supp. 2, vol. 1. Washington, DC: Government Printing Office, 1932.
"German Secret War Documents." *International Conciliation* (May 1920).
Germany. Army General Staff. *Der Handstreich gegen Lüttich vom 3. bis 7. August 1914.* Berlin: Mittler & Sohn, 1939.
Germany. Foreign Office.[Auswaertiges Amt]. *European Politics During the Decade Before the War as Described by Belgian Diplomatists: Reports of the Belgian Representatives in Berlin, London, and Paris to the Minister of Foreign Affairs in Brussels, 1905-1914.* N.p., 1915.
G.P. Gooch and Harold Temperley, eds. *British Documents on the Origins of the War, 1898-1914,* vols. 3, 11. London: His Majesty's Stationery Office, 1926-1928.
Goschen to Grey, Berlin, 29 July 1914. Published in Geiss, *German Foreign Policy,* 216-17.
Link, Arthur S., ed. *The Papers of Woodrow Wilson,* vols. 54-56, 59-60. Princeton, NJ: Princeton University Press, 1986-89.
Krämer, F.J.L., ed. *Gedenkschriften van Gijsbert Jan van Hardenbroek.* Amsterdam:

Johannes Müller, 1918.

Moltke, H. von. Memorandum of H. von Moltke, 1911(?) In Gerhard Ritter, *The Schlieffen Plan: Critique of a Myth*. Foreword by B. H. Liddell Hart. New York: Praeger, 1958 [Munich: R. Oldenbourg, 1956], 165-67.

Nederland en Duitschland: Een keur van Documenten bijeenverzameld door een Nederlander. Den Haag: N. V. Expl. Mij. Van Dagbladen, n.d.

Montgelas, Max, and Walther Schuecking, eds. *Outbreak of the World War: German Documents Collected by Karl Kautsky*. Tr. Carnegie Endowment for International Peace. New York: Oxford University Press, 1924.

Official German Documents Relation to the World War, vol. I. Tr. Carnegie Endowment for International Peace. New York: Oxford University Press, 1923.

Schlieffen, Alfred von. Memoranda by Count Alfred von Schlieffen, December, 1905 ("War against France"), February 1906, 1911 (comments on General Windheim's plans), and December 28, 1912. Published in Ritter, *Schlieffen Plan*, 134-164, 169-186.

Schröder, Ludwig von, "Memorandum: An Operation Against Antwerp (Berlin, November, 1897), in Jonathan Steinberg, "A German Plan for the Invasion of Holland and Belgium, 1897." *The Historical Journal* 6 (No. 1 1963): 107-119

Smit, C., ed. *Bescheiden betreffende de buitenlandse politiek van Nederland 1848-1919, Derde Periode 1899-1919*. 's-Gravenhage: Martinus Nijhoff, 1957-1974.

United Kingdom. *Collected Diplomatic Documents Relating to the Outbreak of the European War*. London: His Majesty's Stationery Office, 1915.

United States. War Department. *Histories of Two Hundred and Fifty-One Divisions of the German Army which participated in the war (1914-1918)*. Washington: Government Printing Office, 1920.

Valk, J.P. de, and M. van Faassen, eds. *Dagboeken en aantekeningen van Willem Hendrik de Beaufort 1874-1918*. 's-Gravenhage: Instituut voor Nederlandse Geschiedenis, 1993.

Wank, Solomon, ed. *Aus dem Nachlass Aehrenthal: Briefe und Dokumente zur Oesterreichischungarischen Innen- und Aussenpolitik, 1885-1912*, 2 vols. Graz: Wolfgang Neugebauer Verlag, 1994.

Woltring, J., ed. *Bescheiden Betreffende de Buitenlandse Politiek van Nederland, 1848-1919. Tweede Periode, 1871-1898*. 's-Gravenhage: Martinus Nijhoff, 1962-1968.

Memoirs and diaries

Bosboom, N. *In moeilijke omstandigheden: Augustus 1914 - Mei 1917*. Gorinchem: J. Noorduyn & Zoon, 1933.

Bülow, Prince Bernhard Heinrich von, *Memoirs of Prince von Bülow*, vol. I: *From Secretary of State to Imperial Chancellor, 1897-1903*. Translation by F. A. Voight. Boston: Little, Brown, 1932.

Colenbrander, H. T. *Nederland en België: Adviezen en opstellen uit de jaren 1919 en 1925-27*. 's-Gravenhage: Martinus Nijhoff, 1927.

Fabius, H.A.C. "De Inlichtingen dienst van den Generalen Staf," 196-212 in *Bijdragen voor vaderlandsche geschiedenis en oudheidkunde* (Den Haag: Martinus Nijhoff, n.d.).

Groener, Wilhelm. *Das Testament des Grafen Schlieffen: Operativen Studien über den Weltkrieg*. Berlin: Mittler, 1929 [1927].

Heldring, Ernst. *Herinneringen en dagboek van Ernst Heldring (1871-1954)*. Ed. by Johann de Vries. Groningen: Wolters-Noordhoff, 1970.

House, Edward M., and Charles Seymour, eds. *What Really Happened at Paris: The Story of the Peace Conference, 1918-1919*. New York: Charles Scribner's Sons, 1921.

Hymans. Paul. *Memoires*. Brussels: Institut de sociologie Solvay, 1958.

Kluck, A. von. *Der Marsch auf Paris und die Marneschlacht 1914*. Berlin: Mittler, 1920.

Kühlmann, Richard von. *Erinnerungen*. Heidelberg: Lambert Schneider, 1948.

Lichnowsky,Karl Max. *My Mission to London 1912-1914*. Toronto: Cassell, 1918.

Ludendorff, Erich von. *Ludendorff's Own Story, August 1914 - November 1918*. 2 vols. Freeport, NY: Books for Libraries Press, 1971 (1920).

Moltke, Helmuth von. *Erinnerungen Briefe Dokumente, 1877-1916*. Foreword and edited by Eliza von Moltke. Stuttgart: Der Kommende Tag, 1922.

Oppenheimer, Francis. *Stranger Within*. London: Faber and Faber, 1960.

Oudendyk, William J. *Ways and By-Ways in Diplomacy*. London: Peter Davies, 1939.

Repington, Charles à Court. *Vestigia: Reminiscences of Peace and War*. Boston: Houghton Mifflin, 1919.

Rosen, Friedrich. *Aus einem Diplomatischen Wanderleben,* 4 vols., vol. 1. Ed. by Herbert Müller-Werth. Berlin: Transmare, 1931.

———. *Aus einem Diplomatischen Wanderleben,* 4 vols., vol. 3/4. Ed. by Herbert Müller-Werth. Wiesbaden: Limes, 1959.

Snijders, C.J. "Nederland's militaire positie gedurende den wereldoorlog." *Militaire Spectator* 92 (September 1923): 536-66.

Townley, Susan. *'Indiscretions' of Lady Susan*. London: Thornton Butterworth, 1922.

Troelstra, Jelle. *Mijn vader Pieter Jelles*. Amsterdam: Arbeiderspers, 1955.

Treub, M.W.F. *Herinneringen en overpeinzingen*. Haarlem: Tjeenk Willink, 1931.

———. *Oorlogstijd. Herinneringen en Indrukken*. Haarlem: Tjeenk Willink, 1916.

Unter Emmich vor Lüttich: Unter Kluck vor Paris. 3rd ed. Schwerin: Friedrich Bah, 1915.

Vollenhoven, M. W. R van. *Memoires*. Amsterdam: Elsevier, 1948.

Wal, S. L. van der, ed. *Herinneringen van Jhr. Mr. B. C. de Jonge: Met brieven uit zijn nalatenschap*. Utrecht: Historisch Genootschap, 1968 (Groningen: Wolters-Noordhoff, 1968).

H.R.H. Wilhelmina, Princess of the Netherlands. *Lonely But Not Alone*. Tr. John Peereboom. New York: McGraw-Hill, 1960.

Secondary sources

Books

Alapuro, Rista, Matti Alestalo, Elina Haavio-Mannila, and Raimo Väyrynen, eds. *Small States in Comparative Perspective: Essays for Erik Allardt*. Norway: Norwegian University Press, 1985.

Alting von Geusau, G. A. A. *Onze weermacht te land*. Amsterdam: Ipenbuur & van Seldam, 1914 (1913).

Baetens, R., Ph.M. Bosscher, and H. Reuchlin, eds. *Maritieme Geschiedenis der Nederlanden*, vol. IV: *Tweede helft negentiende eeuw en twintigste eeuw, van*

1850-1870 tot ca. 1970. Bussum: De Boer Maritiem, 1978.

Banse, Ewald. *Raum und Volk im Weltkriege.* Oldenburg: Gerhard Stelling, 1932.

Barnouw, A.J. *Holland under Queen Wilhelmina.* New York: Scribner's, 1923.

Barston, R.P., ed. *The Other Powers: Studies in the Foreign Policies of Small States.* New York: Harper & Row, 1973.

Beaufort, J.A.A.H de. *Vijftig jaren uit onze geschiedenis, 1868-1918,* II. Amsterdam: P.N. van Kampen & Zoon, 1928.

Berg, D. van den. *Cornelis Jacobus Snijders (1852-1939): een leven in dienst van zijn Land en zijn Volk.* Den Haag: Reverdeem, 1949.

Bircher, Eugen, and Bode, Walter. *Schlieffen: Mann und Idee.* Zurich: Albert Nauck, 1937.

Black, Jeremy. *British Foreign Policy in an Age of Revolutions.* Cambridge, UK: Cambridge University Press, 1994.

Bonebakker, J.W. *Twee verdienstelijke officieren.* Nieuwkoop: Heuff, 1974.

Bradford, James C. *The Military and Conflict between Cultures: Soldiers at the Interface.* College Station, TX: Texas A&M University Press, 1997.

Bucholz, Arden. *Moltke, Schlieffen, and Prussian War Planning.* Oxford: Berg, 1991.

Carlson, Andrew R. *German Foreign Policy, 1890-1914: A Handbook and Annotated Bibliography.* Metuchen, NJ: Scarecrow Press, 1970.

Carroll, E. Malcolm. *German and the Great Powers 1866-1914: A Study in Public Opinion and Foreign Policy.* Hamden, CT: Archon Books, 1966 [Prentice-Hall, 1938].

Cecil, Lamar. *Wilhelm II,* vol. 1: *Prince and Emperor, 1859-1900.* Chapel Hill: University of North Carolina Press, 1989.

———. *Wilhelm II,* vol. 2: *Emperor and Exile, 1900-1941.* Chapel Hill: University of North Carolina Press, 1996.

Coetzee, Marilyn Shevin. *The German Army League: Popular Nationalism in Wilhelmine Germany.* New York: Oxford University Press, 1990.

Colenbrander, H.T. *Nederland en België: Proeve tot beter waardering.* Den Haag: W. P. van Stockum, 1933.

Dockrill, Michael and David French, eds. *Strategy and Intelligence: British Policy during the First World War.* London and Rio Grande: The Hambledon Press, 1996.

Dunk, Hermann von der. *Die Niederlande im Kräftespiel zwischen Kaiserreich und Entente.* Wiesbaden: Franz Steiner, 1980.

Engelen, D. *Geschiedenis van de Binnenlandse Veiligheidsdienst.* 's-Gravenhage: Koninginnegracht, 1995.

Fabius, G.C.A. *De verhouding tussen volk en weermacht.* Amsterdam: van Holkema & Warendorf, 1916.

Fasseur, Cees. *Wilhelmina: De jonge koningin.* Meppel: Balans, 1998.

Fischer,Fritz. *Germany's Aims in the First World War.* New York: W W Norton, 1967. (*Griff nach der Weltmacht* (Düsseldorf: Droste Verlag, 1961.)

———. *War of Illusions: German Policies from 1911 to 1914.* New York: Norton, 1975 (1969).

———. *World Power or Decline: The Controversy Over Germany's Aims in the First World War.* New York: Norton, 1974 (*Weltmacht oder Niedergang.* Frankfurt am Main: Europäische Verlagsanstalt, 1965.)

Forbes Wels, P. *De Nederlandse Cavalerie.* Bussum: C. A. J. van Dishoek, 1963.

Fox, Annette Baker. *The Power of Small States: Diplomacy in World War II.* Chicago:

University of Chicago Press, 1959.

French, David. *British Strategy and War Aims, 1914-1916*. London: Allen & Unwin, 1986

Frey, Marc. *Der Erste Weltkrieg und die Niederlande: Ein neutrales Land im politischen und wirtschaftlichen Kalkül der Kriegsgegener*. Berlin: Akademie Verlag, 1998.

Georg, Wilhelm. *Unser Emmich: Ein Lebensbild*. Berlin: A. Scherl, 1915 .

Geiss, Imanuel. *German Foreign Policy, 1871-1914*. London: Routledge & Kegan Paul, 1976.

——, ed. *Julikrise und Kriegsausbruch 1914*. Hannover: Verlag für Literatur und Zeitgeschehen, 1963.

Goerlitz, Walter. *History of the German General Staff 1657-1945*. New York: Praeger, 1959.

Gooch, G.P. and J.H.B. Masterman. *A Century of British Foreign Policy*. Port Washington, NY and London: Kennikat Press, 1971 (1917).

Gooch, John. *The Plans of War: The General Staff and British Military Strategy c. 1900-1916*. New York: John Wiley & Sons, 1974.

Greven, H.B., ed. *The Netherlands and the World War: Studies in the War History of a Neutral*. Vol 1 by M.J. van der Flier. New Haven: Yale, 1928.

——, ed. *The Netherlands and the World War: Studies in the War History of a Neutral*. Vol. 2 by C.J.P. Zaalberg, E.P. de Monchy, A.J. Romeyn, F.E. Posthuma, & H. W. Methorst. New Haven: Yale, 1928.

——, ed. *The Netherlands and the World War: Studies in the War History of a Neutral*. Vol. 3 by J.H. Carpentier Alting and W. de Cock Bunning. New Haven: Yale, 1928.

——, ed. *The Netherlands and the World War: Studies in the War History of a Neutral*. Vol. 4 by G. Vissering, J. Westerman Holstijn, and H.W.C. Bordewyk. New Haven: Yale, 1928.

Haeussler, Helmut. *General William Groener and the Imperial German Army*. Madison: State Historical Society of Wisconsin, 1962.

Halpern, Paul G. *A Naval History of World War I*. Annapolis: Naval Institute Press, 1994.

Hamel, J.A. van. *Nederland tusschen de mogenheden: De hoofdtrekken van het buitenlansch beleid en de diplomatieke geschiedenis van ons vaderland sinds deszelfs onafhankelijk volksbestaan onderzocht*. Amsterdam: Van Holkema & Warendorf, 1918.

Hampe, Karl. *Belgien und Holland vor dem Weltkriege*. Gotha: Friedrich Andreas Perthes, 1918.

Handel, Michael. *Weak States in the International System*. Totowa, NJ: Frank Cass, 1981.

Harlow, C.J.E. *The European Armaments Base: A Survey*. London: Institute for Strategic Studies, 1967.

Haskins, Charles Homer, and Robert Howard Lord. *Some Problems of the Peace Conference*. Cambridge: Harvard University Press, 1922.

Headrick, Daniel R. *The Tools of Empire: Technology and European Imperialism in the Nineteenth Century*. New York: Oxford University Press, 1981.

Herwig, Holger H. *The First World War: Germany and Austria-Hungary, 1914-1918*. London: Arnold, 1998.

Hildebrand, Hans H., and Ernest Henriot. *Deutschlands Admirale 1849-1945:*

militärischen Werdegänge der See-, Ingenieur, Sanitäts-, Waffen- und Verwaltungsoffiziere im Admiralsrang, vol. 3. Osnabrück: Biblio Verlag, 1990.

Hildebrand, Klaus. *German Foreign Policy from Bismarck to Adenauer: The Limits of Statecraft.* Translation by Louise Willmot. London: Unwin Hyman, 1989.

Höll, Otmar, ed. *Small States in Europe and Dependence.* Boulder, CO: Westview, 1983 (Laxenburg: Austrian Institute for International Affairs, 1983).

Inbar, Efraim, and Gabriel Sheffer, eds. *The National Security of Small States in a Changing World.* London and Portland, OR: Frank Cass, 1997.

Iongh, Jane de, and M. Kohnstamm. *Wilhelmina: Een levensgeschiedenis in foto's.* Amsterdam: De Bezige Bij, 1948.

Jessup, Philip C. Neutrality: Its History, Economics and Law. Vol. 4, *Today and Tomorrow.* New York: Octagon, 1976 (1936).

Kabisch, Ernst. *Lüttich: Deutschlands Schicksalsschritt in dem Weltkrieg.* Berlin: Otto Schlegel, 1936.

Karsh, Efraim. *Neutrality and Small States.* London and New York: Routledge, 1988.

Kecskemeti, Paul. *Strategic Surrender: The Politics of Victory and Defeat.* Stanford, CA: Stanford University Press, 1958.

Klinkert, W. *Het Vaderland Verdedigd: Plannen en opvattingen over de verdediging van Nederland 1871-1914.* Den Haag: Sectie Militaire Geschiedenis, 1992.

Kluiters, F.A.C. *De Nederlandse inlichtingen-en veiligheidsdiensten.* 's-Gravenhage: Koninginnegracht, 1993.

——. *De Nederlandse inlichtingen-en veiligheidsdiensten. Supplement: Crypto en trafficanalyse.* 's-Gravenhage: Koninginnegracht, 1995.

Kooiman, J. *De Nederlandsche stijdmacht en hare mobilisatie in het jaar negentien honderd en veertien.* Purmerend: J. Muuses en Herman de Ruiter, 1922.

Lademacher, Horst. *Zwei Ungleiche Nachbarn: Wege und Wandlungen der Deutsch-Niederländischen Beziehungen im 19. und 20. Jahrhundert.* Darmstadt: Wissenschaftliche Buchgesellschaft, 1989.

Lamborn, Alan C. *The Price of Power: Risk and Foreign Policy in Britain, France, and Germany.* Boston: Unwin Hyman, 1991.

Leeuw, A.S. de. *Nederland in de wereldpolitiek van 1900 tot heden,* 2nd ed. Amsterdam: Pegasus, 1939 (1936).

Longstreet, Stephen. *The Canvas Falcons: The Men and the Planes of World War I.* New York: Barnes & Noble, 1970.

Lutz, Ralph Haswell, ed. *Fall of the German Empire, 1914-1918.* 2 vols. Stanford: Stanford University Press, 1932.

Manen, Charlotte A. van. *De Nederlandsche Overzee Trustmaatschappy. Middelpunt van het verkeer van onzydig Nederland met het buitenland tydens den wereldoorlog 1914-1919.* 's-Gravenhage: Martinus Nijhoff, 1935.

Marks, Sally. *Innocent Abroad: Belgium at the Paris Peace Conference of 1919.* Chapel Hill: University of North Carolina Press, 1981.

Marshall, S.L.A. *World War I.* New York: American Heritage Press, 1985.

Maurer, John H. *The Outbreak of the First World War: Strategic Planning, Crisis Decision Making, and Deterrence Failure.* Westport, CT: Praeger, 1995.

Mee, Charles L. Jr. *The End of Order: Versailles, 1919.* New York: E.P. Dutton, 1980.

Le Mensonge du 3 Aout 1914. Paris: Librairie Payot & Cie, 1917.

Miller, Jane Kathryn. *Belgian Foreign Policy Between Two World Wars 1919-1940.* New York: Bookman Associates, 1951.

Steven Miller, Sean M. Lynn-Jones, and Stephen Van Evera, eds. *Military Strategy and the Origins of the First World War.* Princeton: Princeton University Press, 1991.

Oldham, Peter. *Pill Boxes on the Western Front: A Guide to the Design, Construction and Use of Concrete Pill Boxes 1914-1918.* London: Leo Cooper, 1995.

Pearson, Frederic S. *The Weak State in International Crisis: The Case of the Netherlands in the German Invasion Crisis of 1939-40.* Washington, DC: University Press of America, 1981.

Pierard, Louis. *La Hollande et la Guerre.* Paris and Nancy: Librarie Militaire Berger-Levrault, 1917.

Rapaport, Jacques, Ernest Muteba and Joseph J. Therattil. *Small States & Territories: Status and Problems.* New York: Arno Press, 1971.

Repington, Charles à Court. *Essays and Criticisms.* London: Constable, 1911.

Rich, Norman. *Friedrich von Holstein: Politics and Diplomacy in the Era of Bismarck and Wilhelm II.* 2 vols. London: Cambridge University Press, 1965.

Ringoir, H. *Nederlandse generaals van 1568 tot 1940.* 's-Gravenhage: Sectie Militaire Geschiedenis, 1981.

Ritter, Gerhard. *The Schlieffen Plan: Critique of a Myth.* Foreword by B. H. Liddell Hart. New York: Praeger, 1958 [Munich: R. Oldenbourg, 1956].

Ritter, P.H. *De Donkere Poort.* 's-Gravenhage: Daamen's, 1931.

"Ronduit," Captain. *De manoeuvre om Limburg: Eene studie over de strategische positie van Limburg.* Utrecht: Bruna, 1919.

Roon, Ger van. *Small States in Years of Depression: The Oslo Alliance, 1930-1940.* Assen and Maastricht: Van Gorcum, 1989.

Rullmann, J.C. *Dr. H. Colijn: Een levensschets.* Leiden: Sijthoff, 1933.

Ryan, W. Michael. *Lieutenant-Colonel Charles à Court Repington: A Study in the Interaction of Personality, the Press, and Power.* New York: Garland, 1987.

Scheffer, H.J. *November 1918: Journaal van een revolutie die niet doorging.* Amsterdam: Arbeiderspers, 1968.

Schou, August, and Arne Olav Brundtland, eds. *Small States in International Relations.* Stockholm: Almqvist & Wiksell, 1971.

Smit, C. *Diplomatieke geschiedenis van Nederland inzonderheid sedert de vesting van het koninkrijk.* s'Gravenhage: Martinus Nijhoff, 1950.

Smit, C. *Nederland in de Eerste Wereldoorlog (1899-1919).* Vol 1, *Het Voorspel (1899-1914).* Groningen: Wolters-Noordhoff, 1971.

——. *Nederland in de Eerste Wereldoorlog (1899-1919).* Vol 2, *1914-1917.* Groningen: Wolters-Noordhoff, 1972.

——. *Nederland in de Eerste Wereldoorlog (1899-1919).* Vol 3, *1917-1919.* Groningen: Wolters-Noordhoff, 1973.

——. *Tien studiën betreffende Nederland in de Eerste Wereldoorlog.* Groningen: H. D. Tjeenk Willink, 1975.

Snijders, C.J. Foreword to Gudmund Schnitler, *De wereldoorlog (1914-1918).* Den Haag: Zuid-Hollandsche Uitgevers Maatschappij, 1928.

——, and R. Dufour. *De mobilisatiën bij de groote mogendheden in 1914 en de invloed van de generale staven op het uitbreken van den wereldoorlog.* Leiden: Sijthoff, 1927.

Snijders, W.G.F. *De Wereldoorlog op het Duitsche Westfront.* Amsterdam: Maatschappij voor Goede en Goedkope Lectuur, 1922.

Stevenson, David. *Armaments and the Coming of War: Europe 1904-1914.* New York: Oxford, 1996.

Thomas, D.H. *The Guarantee of Belgian Independence and Neutrality in European Diplomacy, 1830's–1930's.* Kingston, RI: D. H. Thomas Publishing, 1983.

Tillman, Seth P. *Anglo-American Relations at the Paris Peace Conference of 1919.* Princeton, NJ: Princeton University Press, 1961.

Turlington, Edgar. *Neutrality: Its History, Economics and Law.* Vol 3, *The World War Period.* New York: Octagon, 1976 (1936).

Vandenbosch, Amry. *Dutch Foreign Policy since 1815: A Study in Small Power Politics.* The Hague: Martinus Nijhoff, 1959.

Voorhoeve, J.J.C. *Peace, Profits and Principles: A Study of Dutch Foreign Policy.* The Hague: Martinus Nijhoff, 1979.

Voorst tot Voorst, J.J.G. baron van. *Over Roermond! Een strategische studie.* 's-Gravenhage: H. P. de Swart & Zoon, 1923.

Wallach, Jehuda. *The Dogma of the Battle of Annihilation: The Theories of Clausewitz and Schlieffen, and Their Impact on the German Conduct of Two World Wars.* Westport, CT: Greenwood, 1986.

Wedel, Oswald Henry. *Austro-German Diplomatic Relations 1908-1914.* Stanford, CA: Stanford University Press, 1932.

Weinberg, Gerhard L. *A World at Arms: A Global History of World War II.* New York: Cambridge University Press, 1994.

Weingartner, Steve, ed. *A Weekend with the Great War: Proceedings of the Fourth Annual Great War Interconference Seminar.* Shippensburg, PA: White Mane, 1994.

Wilson, Keith, ed. *Decision for War 1914.* New York: St. Martin's, 1995.

——, ed. *Forging the Collective Memory: Government and International Historians Through Two World Wars.* Providence: Berghahn Books, 1996

Articles and chapters

Bertil, H., and Petersson, A. "Das Oesterreichisch-ungarische Memorandum an Deutschland vom 5. Juli 1914." *Scandia* (No. 1 1964): 138-190.

Bolkestein, F. "The Netherlands and the Lure of Neutralism." *NATO Review* (October 1981): 1-6.

Brugmans, H. Book review. *Telegraaf.* 24 March 1935.

Buijs, J. "De spoorbrug bij Roermond: Oorzaak van Nederlandse neutraliteit in 1914?" *Militaire Spectator* 161 (September 1992): 411-415.

Campen, S.I.P. van. "How and Why the Netherlands joined the Atlantic Alliance - Part 1." *NATO Review* (August 1982): 8-12.

Dijk, Anthonie van. "The Drawingboard Battleships for the Royal Netherlands Navy, Part III." *Warship International* 26 (No 4 1989): 395-403.

Frey, Marc. "Deutsche Finanzinteressen an der Vereinigten Staaten und den Nederlanden im Ersten Weltkrieg." *Militärgeschichtliche Mitteilungen* 53 (1994): 327-353.

Feaver, Peter D. "The Civil-Military Problematique: Huntington, Janowitz, and the Question of Civilian Control." *Armed Forces & Society* 23 (Winter 1996): 149-178.

Gallhofer, I.N., and W.E. Saris. "The decision of the Dutch Council of Ministers and the military Commander-in-Chief relating to the reduction of armed forces in autumn 1916." *Acta Politica* 14 (No 1 1979): 95-105.

Graaff, Bob de. "Bogey or Saviour? The Image of the United States in the Netherlands during the Interwar Period," 51-69 in R. Kroes and M. van Rossem, eds.,*Anti-Americanism in Europe.* Amsterdam, 1986.

———. "De 'Intelligence Revolution' van de 20e eeuw en haar geschiedschrijving: Een historiografisch artikel." *De nieuwste tijd* 6 (6 June 1996): 5-16.

Hardenberg, H.K. "Opperbevelhebber en Algemeen Hoofkwartier." *Militaire Spectator* 90 (1921): 388-396.

Herre, Paul. "Die kleinen Staaten und die Entsehung des Weltkrieges." *Berliner Monatshefte* (July 1933): 662-678.

Heuvel-Strasser, E.A van den. "Vluchtelingenzorg of vreemdelingenbeleid: De Nederlandse overheid en de Belgische vluchtelingen, 1914-1915." *Tijdschrift voor geschiedenis* 99 (No 2 1986), 184-204.

Le Journal (21 Jan. 1911).

Kennedy, P. "Imperial cable communications and strategy, 1870-1914." *English Historical Review* 86 (October 1971): 728-752.

Keohane, Robert O. "Lilliputians' Dilemma: Small States in International Politics." *International Organizations* 23 (Spring 1969): 291-310.

Klinkert, W. "De Nederlandse Mobilisatie van 1914," pp. 24-33 in W. Klinkert, J.W. M. Schulten, en Luc de Vos, eds., *Mobilisatie in Nederland en Belgie:1870-1914-1939.* Amsterdam: De Bataafsche Leeuw, 1991.

———."Oorlog in de Betuwe: De grote manoeuvres van September 1911." *Mededelingen van de Sectie Militaire Geschiedenis* 13 (1990): 43-65.

———. "Verdediging van de zuidgrens 1914-1918" (Part One). *Militaire Spectator* 156 (May 1987): 213-219.

———. "Verdediging van de zuidgrens 1914-1918" (Part Two). *Militaire Spectator* 156 (June 1987): 250-257.

"One World." *The Economist* (October 18, 1997): 79-80.

Sauerwein, Jules. "Neue Tatsachen ueber die Vorgeschichte des Weltkrieges." *Dreigliederung des Sozialen Organismus* 3 (12 October 1921), in W.G.F. Snijders, *De Wereldoorlog op het Duitsche Westfront.* Amsterdam: Maatschappij voor Goede en Goedkope Lectuur, 1922, 383-390.

Schulten, C.M. "The Netherlands and its Army (1900-1940)." *Revue Internationale d'Histoire Militaire* 58 (1984): 73-95.

Schuursma, R.L. "Een verdrag in opspraak: Het Belgisch-Nederlandsch Verdrag." *Spiegel historiael* 13 (No 1 1978): 34-40.

Smidt, H.A.R. "De bestrijding van de smokkelhandel door het leger tijdens de Eerste Wereldoorlog." *Mededelingen van de Sectie Militaire Geschiedenis* 15 (1993): 43-72.

Steinberg, Jonathan. "A German Plan for the Invasion of Holland and Belgium, 1897." *The Historical Journal* 6 (No. 1 1963): 107-119

Thomas, T.H. "Holland and Belgium in the German War Plan." *Foreign Affairs* 6 (January 1928): 315-328.

Trumpener, Ulrich. "War Premeditated? German Intelligence Operations in July 1914." *Central European History* 9 (March 1976): 58-85.

Verseput, J. "De kwestie van de uitlevering van ex-keizer Wilhelm II." *Kleio* 4 (Nov. 1963): 5-11.

De Volkskrant. 16 April 1998.

The Windmill Herald. 7 May, 8 June, and September 1998.

Wolting, A. "De eerste jaren van de Militaire inlichtingendienst (GS III, 1914-1917)." *Militaire Spectator* 134 (December 1965): 566-571.

———. "Uit het dagboek van Kapitein van Woelderen, GS III." *Militaire Spectator* 135 (January 1966): 32-35.

Miscellaneous sources

American Historical Association Committee for the Study of War Documents. *A Catalogue of Files and Microfilms of the German Foreign Ministry Archives 1867-1920.* New York: Kraus Reprint Company, 1970 (1959).

Beening, André. "Onder de vleugels van de adelaar: De Duitse buitenlandse politiek ten aanzien van Nederland in de periode 1890-1914." Ph.D. Dissertation: University of Amsterdam, 1994.

Black's Law Dictionary, 4th ed. St. Paul: West, 1968.

Bout, John J. "The Dutch Army in World War I." M.A. Thesis: University of British Columbia, 1972.

———. "The Nature and Extent of Antimilitarism and Pacifism in the Netherlands from 1918 to 1940 and the Degree to which the Contributed to the Quick Defeat in May 1940." Ph.D. Dissertation: University of British Columbia, 1975.

van Diesen, P.J. "Nederlandse Inlichtingendiesten Tussen 1914 en 1940." Unpublished paper. Den Haag: Sectie Militaire Geschiedenis, n.d. Held by ARA library.

Graaf, Bob, de. "Accessibility of secret service archives in the Netherlands." Unpublished paper, n.d.

Grolleman, J., and J.C. Ruiter, "Interne en externe invloeden op de legerforming in Nederland van 1870 tot 1920." Unpublished paper. Koninklijke Militaire Academie, May 1981. Held by Sectie Militaire Geschiedenis.

Gruythuysen, M.W.M.M., S.U. Sabaroedin, and A.M. Tempelaars. *Inventaris van de archieven van Regeringscommissarissen van het Ministerie van Kolonien 1904-1952.* Den Haag: Algemeen Rijksarchief, 1991.

Koomans, N. "Geschiedkundig overzicht van het radiobedrijf van den rijksdienst der posterijen en telegrafie." http://home.luna.nl/~arjan-muil/radio/ptt.htm. Overgenomen uit het "Gedenkboek ter herinnering aan het tienjarig bestaan van de Nederlandsche vereeniging voor radiotelegrafie 1916-1926."

Lamassoure, Alain. Speech, Georgia Tech University, October 1, 1998.

Meier, M de. "Geheime Dienst in Nederland 1912-1947." Unpublished, classified internal history. Leidschendam: Binnenlandse Veilighijds Dienst [B.V.D.] (Internal Security Service), n.d. Quoted with permission of the Ministry of the Interior of the Netherlands.

Mettes, H.M., J.M.M. Cuypers, R. van Velden, and E.A. Heugten, compilers. *Inventaris van de Archieven van de Generale Staf, 1914-40.* 'S-Gravenhage: Ministerie van Defensie - Centraal Archievendepot, 1997.

Porter, James John. "Dutch Neutrality in Two World Wars." Ph.D. Dissertation: Boston University, 1980.

Roitero, Domenico L., and Maarten C. Hoff. "Militaire misstappen van de Nederlandse leeuw." Ph.D. dissertation: Rijksuniversiteit Groningen, 1995.

Schelde InformatieCentrum. http://waterland.net/sic/fr-home.htm.

Tuyll van Serooskerken, H.O.R. van. Information supplied by prof. dr. H.O.R. baron van Tuyll van Serooskerken.

Vinke, A.J. "De Nederlandse Militaire Attache 1907-1923." Unpublished paper: Koninklijke Militaire Academie, 1984. Held by ARA library.

INDEX

Aachen 27, 41, 66, 129
Aalst, C.J.K. van viii, 140-42, 182, 244, 285
Aboukir 151
Aceh 10, 111, 111n
Africa 273
Albania 49
Albert Canal 316
Albert, King of the Belgians 129, 276, 279, 306-307, 353
Alcor 138
Aldenburg Bentinck, G.J.G.Ch. graaf van 275, 276, 318
Allizé, H. 224, 244, 245, 271, 285, 287
Alsace-Lorraine 301
Alting von Geusau, jhr. G.A.A. xv, 243, 247ff, 300
"Altman Jansen, E. " 47
Amerongen 275
Amsterdam 6, 165, 168, 179, 200, 230, 231, 232, 233, 242n, 246, 252, 253, 286
angary, right of 205-207
animal feed 9, 179
Anti-Revolutionaire Partij (ARP) 242, 243, 252
Antwerp 2, 4, 28, 33, 58, 91, 95, 97, 100, 105n, 108, 136, 151, 154, 155, 157, 162, 229n, 266, 267, 272, 295, 296, 297, 303, 305, 307, 316
Api Api 40n, 59ff, 350
Apple Electric Company 47
archives 332, 359
Arnhem 43, 107
Asquith, Herbert 53, 162
Australia 64n
Austria 4,
Austria-Hungary 16, 17, 45n, 51-53, 55, 57, 59, 68, 69, 178, 337, 339, 340n, 348n
    Foreign Ministry 54, 57

Baarle-Hertog 163, 196
Baerle-Nassau 196

Baie, Eugène 16
Bailey, Thomas 210
Balbi, M. de 4n
Balfour, A.J. 192, 193, 204, 205, 213, 216, 217, 276, 303, 304, 306
Balkan wars 15
Bank voor Russischen Handel 180
Banque Russo-Hollandaise 180
Barnardiston, N.W. xv, 33
Batavian Petroleum Company 138
Beaufort, W.H. de 16, 73, 109, 162, 168, 201, 230, 272, 332, 332n, 336
Beaverbrook, W.M.A. baron 196
Beelaerts van Blokland, jhr. F. 316
Beer Poortugael, jhr. J.C.C. den 95
Belgium 3, 4, 7, 17, 45, 58, 90, 101, 154, 155, 165, 188, 189, 193, 195, 204, 214, 223, 266ff, 337, 339, 340n, 341, 351, 358n27
    and Britain 6, 280, 306, 307, 311, 313
    and France 280, 291
    and the war 97, 107, 128, 129, 131, 132, 156, 210, 212, 229n, 236, 279
    annexationism 268-73, 277-82, 293, 300-12, 315, 353
    Catholics 271
    Flemish 155-56, 196, 269, 281, 299, 302, 310n, 311, 312
    military strategy 28, 91, 94, 294-97, 311n
    relationship with the Netherlands 5, 25, 33, 57, 108, 184, 268, 312-17
    socialists 271
    Versailles strategy 272n, 273, 277-82, 300-12
    Walloons 156, 170, 269, 279, 302, 312
Belgrade 59, 69
Berchtold, L. graf 52, 54-56, 67
Bergen op Zoom 136
Berlin 51, 56, 89, 145, 146, 160, 166, 184, 195, 220, 222, 254, 267
Bern 165
Bernhardi, Friedrich von 17

HISTORY
OF WARFARE

History of Warfare *presents the latest research on all aspects of military history. Publications in the series will examine technology, strategy, logistics, and economic and social developments related to warfare in Europe, Asia, and the Middle East from ancient times until the early nineteenth century. The series will accept monographs, collections of essays, conference proceedings, and translation of military texts.*